Goin' Viral

THE NEW BLACK STUDIES SERIES

Edited by Darlene Clark Hine and Dwight A. McBride

For a list of books in the series,
please see our website at www.press.uillinois.edu.

Goin' Viral

Uncontrollable Black Performance

GABRIEL A. PEOPLES

An earlier version of Chapter 2 appeared in *Frontiers: A Journal of Women Studies.*

An earlier version of Chapter 3 appeared in *Women & Performance: A Journal of Feminist Theory.*

1 2 3 4 5 C P 5 4 3 2 1
♾ This book is printed on acid-free paper.

Cataloging data available from the Library of Congress
ISBN 9780252046643 (hardcover)
ISBN 9780252088742 (paperback)
ISBN 9780252047954 (ebook)

Contents

Acknowledgments

A book does not begin as such but becomes one, requiring a team on Earth and beyond to help birth it.

Let me start with my mom, though. Thanks to you, Mom, for always encouraging me to spread my wings, never giving me the answer, and kindly telling me to look something up if I didn't know what it meant. The many times I tagged along while you went to review microfilm at the Kresge Library and I played computer games were my first encounters with the conventional archive. I think my intellectual curiosity began with you. I have gained a strong ancestor in you, Yvonne.

Thanks, Dad, for reminding me to stay attuned to my voice amid the many that would influence me. I appreciate the unconventional advice (between cisgender straight men), too, like there being nothing wrong with crying or complimenting another man. Rockin' Rufus P., you echo through me, especially regarding performance. It's no wonder you also wanted to pursue DJing, albeit as a radio personality.

Thank you to the rest of my family for all your support through the years. Yes, I've been writing this when I said I was doing research.

Thanks to Detroit, MI, for its Black-centered repertoire. Whose sounds motivated me from Mason in the morning playing Sammy Davis's 1984 "Hello Detroit" to afternoon renditions of The Spinners while my dad reminisced about a Black city before deindustrialization and a Black business corridor razed by the construction of I-375. In what some would consider ruins, I felt like I occupied sound that was intact, whether Motown, Soul, or Ghettotech, or the Black Pneuma of Bishop Bonner while my grandmother gave me peppermints, they all cradled my daily experience where Blackness was the majority, centered, and generative.

No one challenged me more during my early years as a young scholar than Nesha Z. Haniff. Nesha, you are a scholar where activism, interpreted broadly, is a requirement because there would be no Black Study or Gender Studies without it. Feminism did not begin in books for me but in reflecting on myself and engaging in communities of people (whether in Michigan, Jamaica, or South Africa). Your pedagogy of action continues.

I am especially grateful to two mentors from the Midwest who would become family both intellectually and personally.

I came to the American Studies PhD program to work with you, Jeffrey Q. McCune Jr., and that's what I did and continue to do, even after achieving a PhD. With your guidance, I developed this book, which was not the idea I started with, reminding me that flexibility in thinking and concepts can be a fruitful exercise as a scholar. Significantly, I realize how your heuristic, what you now call "disobedience," was present as you pushed me to question how I know what I know and to allow for other ways performance can operate beyond the obvious. Thanks for taking the time to walk with me along my journey. I can only hope to have sharpened you as much as you have sharpened me.

Marlon M. Bailey, thanks for providing guidance that helped me through my everyday life, tenure, and promotion. Even though Indiana was a very different Midwest than the Detroit we both grew up in, you helped it to feel more like home. You model how there is a false division between fictive kin and kin. Indeed, there is only kin, which requires labor, being an accomplice, and withnessing to maintain.

I'm so grateful to everyone from the University of Maryland, College Park. You all guided me through earlier iterations of this work and ensuring that the foundation of the book was solid: Faedra C. Carpenter, Psyche Williams-Forson, John Caughey, and Jason Farman.

To my cohort from College Park, Maryland, Aaron Allen, Maria Vargas, Maria Velazquez, Michele Prince, Cristina Perez, Bettina Judd, Tiffany Lethabo King, Ana Perez, Renina Jarmon, Jessica Walker, Doug Ishii, Terrance Wooten, T'sey-Haye Preaster, and Darius Bost rock on.

Much of this book was discussed and reimagined (sometimes in one breath) with my Black Performance Theory family; thank you. I'm forever grateful for the many side conversations with Mark Broomfield, Lisa B. Thompson, Thomas DeFrantz, Stephanie Batiste, Javon Johnson, and Xavier Livermon over the years. As well as those whose effect on me continues to reverberate though they have changed terrestrial form: Tayo Jolasho and Marcus White, may you each mature in your spiritual forms.

Many programs aided me through the writing and research of this book. These included the Indiana University Faculty Writing Groups, Inaugural Bloomington Symposia on Contagion, Indiana University's Institute for

Advanced Study, and Indiana University's Faculty Assistance in Data Science Grant. The Ford Foundation (which lives on in other forms) was also critical in the becoming of this book, and it came right on time. It is bittersweet because I only got to experience a brief moment of the spirit of the "Fordies" that I would always hear about, and then the funding was discontinued. Programs such as this are crucial to maintain and grow for the benefit of future scholars, and I can only hope that it shapeshifts into something grander. The postdoctoral fellowship allowed me to care for my dad during a tumultuous time. I especially want to thank Koritha Mitchell, who reminded me then that I had already done so much, and that was enough.

Thanks to the Department of African and African American Studies at Washington University in St. Louis for hosting me during my fellowship year. Rafia Zafar's sage advice, Raven Maragh-Lloyd, and our writing sessions to get these books out of our hands, and Marlon M. Bailey for mentoring me during that year. Also, thanks to Joe Lowenstein and Ken Keller of the Digital Humanities workshop for our conversations on digital considerations within the book. I also want to thank every participant of the Live and Mediated Performance roundtable, which helped me to stay in thought and conversation with discourses in Performance Studies while I was on fellowship.

My colleagues in Gender Studies saw my promise early on and awarded me the Department of Gender Studies Postdoctoral Fellowship, which helped to fund my research activities for this book. I especially want to thank Brenda Weber for the many moments of advice, whether on pedagogy or research. I appreciate your reminders to reward myself for successes and failures (because the attempt is also worth something). Maria Bucur, for the mentoring, many side chats, and emails that helped me tremendously with professionalization, and our hangouts that took us beyond the classroom for a spell. Thank you, Solimar Otero, for your generous spirit and for always being frank and insightful about performance both without and within academia. I'm grateful to have had you join the Department of Gender Studies when you did. May our paths continue to generate and cross!

Thank you to Miriam Petty, Miriam Felton-Dansky, Marlon M. Bailey, and Jeffrey Q. McCune Jr. for offering me rich feedback and valuable insights for my book manuscript workshop.

For my many colleagues who have written or otherwise collaborated with me, perused my materials, or just given me an orange pen for final edits or a listening ear for spring boarding. Thank you! Robeson Taj Frazier, Freda Fair, Shane Voguel, Faye R. Gleisser, Ciara Miller, Bill Barnett (of WordcraftIthaca.com), Jhani Randhawa (of jkrandhawa.com), Dominique "Dom" Moore, Dana Johnson (of yourwordsonlybetter.com), Jennifer Argo, Brian Peoples, Meredith Lee, Judy Rodriguez, Olga Rodriguez-Ulloa, Rose Afriyie, Eric Meyer-Garcia, Shane Greene, Micol Siegel, Rasul Mowatt, Chaz Mottinger, and Cale at Back Door, David at Blockhouse, the sound crew of Mike and Jarred, Dan at the Bishop, Danny at the Root Cellar, Laura Ochoa, Harlyn Pacheco, Kwame Otu, J.T. Roane, The Bloomington Poetry Slam, Dreams (for always picking up the call), Portugal Posse, Pedagogy of Action, and the Church of Doubt and the many group calls that got us through the pandemic.

To the many libraries, archives, and archivists that helped me focus my research. Kofi Acree of the John Henrik Clarke Africana Library, Ben Ortiz of Cornell's Hip Hop collection, Sarah Horowitz of Haverford College's Quaker and Special Collections, Vera at the British Library, Paul Terry of Rare Books & Music Reference at the British Library, Lisa McQuillan Assistant Head of Library & Archives—Archivist & Records Manager for Quakers in Britain, Robert W. Woodruff Library, Herman B. Wells Library, John M. Olin Library, McKeldin Library, Olin and Uris Library.

Thank you to Darlene Clark Hine and Dwight McBride, the New Black Studies series editors, for their intellectual contributions to Black Study. It is an honor to be a part of an important series that already informs my thinking and writing. Also, thank you to each of the reviewers who took part in the rounds of reviewer feedback that have helped to shape the book. Again, a book becomes.

Thank you, Elena Guzman, for your partnership in every sense of the word. Achieving this kind of milestone is sweeter and richer with you as my companion to share the achievement with. Con mil gracias!

This is an incomplete list, and so many have been foundational in my arrival to where I am today that I will not be able to name-drop everyone. IYKYK. So, I thank you for being a part of the journey in which musings, ideas, and countless conversations came together to become a book.

Goin' Viral

Introduction

On the evening of July 13, 2013, I was a passenger on a Washington, DC, Metrobus as I arrived in Silver Spring, MD. The feeling on the bus shifted in a matter of minutes. I will never forget the look of hopelessness on the faces of others on the bus that night and my feelings that the Department of Justice (quite the misnomer) did not value or protect Black folk. Without having stayed updated on the news, I had a strong sense that the grand jury had declared George Zimmerman not guilty in Trayvon Martin's second-degree murder case.

I relied on a Protoweb to gather information on the bus that day. I used the networked interface of feeling to collect what I needed to know between the heaviness in the air and other people's facial expressions.[1] News spread rapidly without words being spoken or written.[2] In my disappointment, disbelief, and sadness, I rushed home to my apartment near East-West Highway and Sixteenth Street. Against the toxic feeling that no one and nothing but his Blackness was responsible for the fatal shooting of Trayvon that night, I tweeted through my laptop, "We are not expendable, we are not disposable, we are valuable, we are loved."[3]

I was floundering. The fabled Mason-Dixon Line felt like it surrounded the country, not just the northern border of Maryland. The white supremacist logic that influenced the narrative allowed no escape or pause from the injustice, as it deemed whiteness innocent and Blackness guilty. At any point, someone could make my Black livelihood expendable based on comparable reasoning. I wrote and broadcasted with and against those visceral feelings.

My tweet received no likes or retweets, nor did I search for them. Its lack of widespread recognition did not diminish its value or the importance of broadcasting how I felt during a collective moment of mourning another Black life lost that many were aware of. During that time, the opportunity arose for the

US criminal justice system to provide an equivalent level of justice for Black individuals as it did for white individuals. However, a predictable betrayal occurred. That same predictability mingled with the numbness I felt after witnessing yet another anti-Black travesty of justice, a justice uninterested in liberation. The air was heavy with disappointment and disillusionment.

Today's complex #BlackLivesMatter hashtag—an interactive symbol and index used in social media to communicate, categorize, and increase the significance and spread of messages—was created on Twitter (now X but which I refer to as Twitter, as that was its name at the time of my research) soon after my tweet and the Zimmerman verdict.[4] Hashtags serve as viral devices given how easily people share and recall them and how readily others recognize a hashtagged subject in circulation. In this way, hashtags are symbols of performances that survive the events that occasioned them, and they perform through how they travel. The hashtag #BlackLivesMatter captures a certain resilience within that moment of despair and archives a movement that is inclusive of yet goes beyond Trayvon and, later, Michael Brown and his fellow Black people and allies in Ferguson, Missouri. Indeed, the hashtag discursively tethers all such heinous civilian and police violence toward Black people and Black bodies, making a general pattern of anti-Black violence more visible and ubiquitous while insisting on a pro-Black stance.[5]

People used #BlackLivesMatter only forty-eight times a day across Twitter the month before the fatal shooting of the unarmed Brown by Ferguson police officer Darren Wilson. #BlackLivesMatter remained relatively dormant until the wake of Brown's murder, when people tweeted it over 52,000 times that month.[6] As folks made sense of the Ferguson shooting, the moment of death and Brown's position as a young Black man with his hands up assumed a central role in the reactions.

Brown's best friend and witness, Dorian Johnson, said that he last saw his friend with his hands up in a "don't shoot" gesture, yelling, "I don't have a gun, stop shooting," before Wilson killed him.[7] After hearing Johnson's testimony, Missouri civilians thrust their hands up in a gesture of opposition to police brutality and an assertion of vulnerability, chanting in chorus, "Hands up, don't shoot!" Interactors transferred the chant to t-shirts, magazines, and newspaper covers, as well as through word of mouth. It also traveled as online interactors archived it—across Twitter, Facebook, and other media.[8] The communal response of solidarity and compassion for Brown led to a hashtag, #HandsUpDontShoot, to index people's activities, acts of anti-Black violence, or peaceful protests against police brutality.

What began as a rallying cry during the aftermath of Brown's death circulated in many communities where the ongoing mistreatment of armed and unarmed Black people by police officers was a reminder of what had happened in Ferguson. Virtual and real iterations of #HandsUpDontShoot found such widespread circulation and meaning that they reverberated nationwide. Four members of the Congressional Black Caucus used the hands-up-don't-shoot gesture and chant during a speech they delivered on the House floor, "Black in America: What Ferguson Says about Where We Are and Where We Need to Go."[9] Members of the St. Louis Rams performed the gesture as they entered the field to face the Oakland Raiders—a stunning visual symbol of solidarity with protesters and vulnerability as Black people.[10]

While journalistic news sources have disputed some accounts of Brown's surrender,[11] within them is a truth claim—a statement about the world taken as true when other evidence is scarce.[12] Thus, while some accounts become rumors, the descriptions make cultural sense against a contemporary backdrop where anti-Black surveillance, enforcement, and acts of violence carried out by the police and vigilantes are more visible than ever. Given what is heard or read, people can imagine a Michael Brown with his hands up.

Under its section on racial bias, the Department of Justice Civil Rights Division eventually evidenced the very thing that had circulated only as an unsubstantiated rumor: that police were discriminating against Black folk in the United States. The federal investigation into the Ferguson Police Department uncovered that the charge of Manner of Walking in Roadway, which started the official police report of Brown's encounter with Wilson, was cited in stops of African Americans 95 percent of the time.[13] With that alarming enforcement rate for an easily ignorable "offense," who can say that Black folk did not feel vulnerable, as though they had raised their hands in a gunfight?

The viral hashtag #HandsUpDontShoot represents two primary considerations: First, it uses word of mouth to bring visibility to Brown's death and to index how the event allegedly unfolded in the streets of Ferguson, thus serving as a precedent for testimonial and medical evidence in a court of law. Second, many activists and protesters use it as a symbol of their commitment to nonviolence, documenting and highlighting instances where armed police and civilians kill unarmed and armed Black people using only the *fear of their Blackness* as evidence for a defense.

As the rumor and symbol entered the viral archive, people continued using #HandsUpDontShoot to reference Michael Brown and other Black lives who had experienced excessive force in police encounters, with a caveat. Some interactors on Twitter exploited the value and visibility that Brown's death brought to the hashtag to describe what Cecil the lion should have done,[14] to prank someone with airsoft guns,[15] or to wield as a hashtag response. They used #PantsUpDontLoot, which attributes sagging pants and looting to Black people in moments of vulnerability and trauma.[16] Many interactors scripted how other spectators should understand resistive and resistant Black bodies in discourse.[17] Their scripts fixed racism in a representation from which Blackness cannot escape. The act of violence and cultural appropriation in parodying this hashtag undermined the impact it could have in shedding light on the extraordinary vulnerability of Black lives to excessive force at the hands of police and vigilantes.

The far-right parody #PantsUpDontLoot produced discursive violence—not least through its being crowdfunded by a Tennessee man for display on a billboard in the heart of Florissant, Missouri. With the understanding that agency is always limited, the rescripting that countered the hashtag allowed for the potential for liberation from scripts.[18] "Cosby would say pants up don't loot" brings attention to the hypocrites who police the morals of Black people with their conservative politics of respectability.[19] Another white-identified critic flatly refused to affirm #PantsUpDontLoot. Rejecting the righteous premise of the hashtag, he tweeted, "#PantsUpDontLoot IS NOT RIGHT," adding, "I support racial equality and justice."[20]

Other interactors leveraged the visibility of the hashtag to bring attention to fourteen-year-old George Junius Stinney Jr., who was the youngest person in the United States to be executed for murder in the twentieth century (in a case involving two white girls, aged seven and eleven).[21] Critiques of #PantsUpDontLoot grappled with an assumption that underlies the hashtag: that Black people sag their pants, that such sagging links to the fashion choices of looters, and that these references to fashion choice and criminality are inherent to the Black body in discourse. Those who critiqued #PantsUpDontLoot also educated those who trafficked in the hashtag about George Jr. Discursively, #PantsUpDontLoot manifests a wish for proper decorum that includes how people wear their pants and how they express rage in ways that do not involve "theft," otherwise risking any claim to credibility, dignity, or due process. Yet George Jr. haunts the hashtag's discourse with *what happens when the pants are up, when sagging is not a fashion trend, no one loots, and the state still executes* a young Black boy.

During the exponential spread of #HandsUpDontShoot, Twitter users tweeted #BlackLivesMatter roughly 10,000 times on the day and 92,784 times on the following day that the grand jury reached its decision not to indict Wilson for his fatal shooting of Brown.[22] I mention these examples to reveal the complexity of repeating a hashtag as the tag shifts in meaning, use, and significance. The specificity of each hashtag varies on different levels. The visibility of #HandsUpDontShoot and #BlackLivesMatter helps to raise awareness of police and citizen performances of anti-Black violence while also delivering them a blow, so to speak, with demonstrations of activism by circulating activists' discourses in broader communities and enabling the quilting together of activist experiences.

A Theory of Black Virality

This is not a book about hashtags. Yet I start with those symbols to theorize the rapid circulation of Black performance (or performances of Blackness) that becomes commonplace and uncontrollable because of that spread—what I call "Black virality." *Goin' Viral* uses Black vernacular in the title to nod at Black virality while challenging the idea of associating speech with race or blending how a person sounds with how they appear.[23] I argue Black virality creates spreadable "things" that reinscribe generalized beliefs about Blackness while also creating space for alterity, challenging and transgressing essentialist understandings of Blackness.

In *Goin' Viral*, I employ the concept of Black virality to examine how Black discursive bodies are shaped by sensory fields such as the visual and sonic. These fields create a dichotomy between simplified personhood, where individuals or groups are easily understood, and complex personhood, where people and groups exhibit contradictory behavior and collaborate in ways that challenge their understandings by others.[24] In particular, I explore Black virality in images and material objects (Hank Willis Thomas's *B®anded* series), film (Spike Lee's *Do the Right Thing*), viral video (The Gregory Brothers' "Bed Intruder Song!!!"), and viral cell phone video (Derrion Albert's murder) that generate, quickly circulate, and rework misunderstandings and understandings of Black behaviors and imaginaries into commonsense beliefs.

Black virality accounts for the knowledge of Black people that others bring to initial encounters with viral performances. Thus, Black people and their representations experience a dual virality, the one prior to the point of encounter that marks them before they are met and the rapid spread resulting from what is goin' viral. Black virality is also about the "Black ways" that things go viral. Boom boxes were not supposed to be used the way that Black people used them, but that way became cool *because* of how they used them. This resulted in the mass production of boom boxes that were louder, larger, and more portable—and even generated the association of the "ghetto blaster." These Black ways extend to terminologies, phrases, gestures, and dances that go in and out of vogue and uniquely emerge from, or become a part of, the African diaspora and gain popularity.

What I call the "viral afterlife"—a viral performance that continues long after its peak, at times exceeding that climax—hinges on African-diasporic ways of knowing. These ways of knowing encompass the cosmographic knowledge present in ring shouts and other African and African Diasporic ancestral traditions.[25] Thus, with Black virality, there is no death without simultaneous birth, and vice versa. The performances resurface as soon as they seem to have disappeared, changing spiritual or physical form into something else that continues to be shaped by its previous viral livelihood.

I see the latter cosmology as intimately related to Black performance theorist, poet, and playwright Stephanie Batiste's notion of "darkening mirrors," or how many Black performances are recognized through meditating on one—a Black structure of racial performativity.[26] In a house-of-mirrors effect, one performance's prior lives (simultaneous deaths and births) can be witnessed, suggestive of performance, like a fractal, having complex points of origin. *Fractal virality* (which I explore in chapter 1) is conceptually sharpened by witnessing African approaches to clothing, village, and street design, where patterns nest within patterns.[27] While Africanness does not necessarily denote Blackness, for this project, Blackness denotes African Diaspora. Without these African-diasporic understandings of the world, specific concepts, such as the ones named, are impossible.

I begin with my experience on the bus as the ground on which I write this manuscript. I write with a Chicana feminist understanding that the everyday experiences of individuals across groups constitute theory and that "theory in the flesh" underpins the discursive word that is as limiting as it is capacious.[28] Even though my tweet failed to attract widespread attention, I write with a deep sense that we, as flesh and discursive Black bodies, are valued and value one another beyond juridical decisions, spectacularity, and the social and economic capital that results. We matter before and because of our Blackness. In the flesh, we, as people, exist before the scripts, labels, and discourses that we label others with, are labeled with, and identify with.[29]

Nonetheless, something "undoes" the capacity of prediscursive reality once we use words to describe who we are in relationship to other people and systems, even to gain protection or freedom by positioning with or against those people and systems.[30] Black virality is a type of Black performance (or performance of Blackness) grounded in this everyday interpolative and counter-interpolative knowledge—it just spreads quickly enough between people to become rapidly commonplace. I lay out points of conceptual encounter whose interlinked relationships account for the myriad ways I use performance throughout this text. The conceptual network I am theorizing includes performance theory, Black performance theory, and viral performance.

Performance

An average performance becomes viral—involving an act or behavior that persistently appears in the vanguard of our popular consciousness—when producers, performers, and spectators quickly repeat their participation in reproducing it across an extensive population. This travel blurs the duality between the audience and the performer. In this way, performance theory is pivotal to my conception of Black virality. Indeed, fluidity between performer and audience is foundational to performance studies, where marginalized perspectives in theater and anthropology have sought to disintegrate the ideas of performance, act, and play from exclusive reference to the performing arts. Thus, to use performance as an analytic approach and form of activism rejects the boundaries between art and life and accepts the inextricability of our consumption of performance from its production. This posits the audience as a performer, and vice versa. Many in performance studies say the anthropologist Victor Turner and theater scholar Richard Schechner liberated their respective disciplines, developing pathways to examine how performance exists in everyday actions, drama, sports, music, and theater.[31]

Performance theorist Shannon Jackson explains the etymology of *performance* by citing a Greek root meaning "to furnish forth," "to carry forward," and "to bring into being."[32] In these iterations, other people experience performance as it happens. Thus, performance is an action in the present, after which it becomes memory, artifact, and history (or does it?). Performance theorist and feminist scholar Peggy Phelan suggests that performance entails liveness and ontology:

> Performance's only life is in the present. Performance cannot be saved, recorded, documented, or otherwise participate in the circulation of representations *of* representations: once it does so, it becomes something other than performance. To the degree that performance attempts to enter the economy of reproduction it betrays and lessens the promise of its own ontology.[33]

Here, referring to the photograph, Phelan touches on the pulse of cultural theorist Walter Benjamin's contention in "The Work of Art in the Age of Mechanical Reproduction" regarding how mechanical reproduction sacrifices the aura of an original piece of art.[34] Reflecting a merging of the two perspectives, the originary aura of performance becomes something else once reproduced mechanically (or otherwise).

So is there a truly original performance, without appearing as a mere illusion of the ontology it presents? Could the initial this or that, as we perceive it collectively, merely be a slightly distinct duplicate of something that came before it? Could Phelan and Benjamin have faced a reproduction masquerading as an original? Might a performance be a reproduction of a feeling or a knowing, an active projection of an earlier affect? Might an oil painting be a reproduction of an unfolding landscape and the painting of it a reflective gesture that many have done prior?[35]

Gender studies scholar Judith Butler's concept of gender performativity inspires my questions about performance and reflects how a drag queen's gender becomes a captivating presence without any original reference, only repeated stylized actions that have become normalized in society's perception of gender.[36] Schechner claims performance as "twice-behaved behavior," implying there is no original performance or "aura," only repeated acts.[37] Reiterating this point, feminist performance theorist Elin Diamond views performance as "always a doing and a thing done."[38] Performance accounts for the simultaneity of the present and past.

When someone shares a photo, video, or song or reenacts a performance, they make a "thing" performed in the past a "thing" performed in the present, with signal differences. The repeated ideas, discourses, and feelings that emerge after encountering an object transform it into a "thing." American literary theorist Bill Brown suggests that what makes the "thing" is created after the encounter of the subject-object relationship.[39] The simultaneity of the thing and the object means that "*the thing seems to name the object just as it is even as it names some thing else*."[40] Following Brown's theorization, the relationship between a taken-for-granted object and the repeated post-encounter between it, its audience, or its subject makes that object a "thing." Similarly, cultural historian Robin Bernstein suggests that "things" stand out from objects because their performance in a particular moment forces people to be aware of "things" in relation to themselves.[41] In the subject-object relationship involving "things," the unacknowledged is linked to the highly perceived, amplifying the potential for what is relegated to the background to be highlighted through the spectacular.

The spectacularity, liveness, and action of today's performance cannot be identical to yesterday's performance, as replicating every element is a physical impossibility. To achieve Black virality, one must re-create or re-present the liveness of performance to bring forth a new experience; thus, Black viralities are performances that are always reproductions. Repeatedly connecting with a Black performance allows spectators to share it and make it go viral, investing it with new meanings ranging from elation to dismay. Through their interaction, spectators cocreate meaning and invent liveness from the reproduction (be it a rumor, song, meme, video, or other medium).[42]

For some people, encountering Black virality evokes a kind of communal ecstasy, for others, a collective disgust, while some find themselves caught between those two feelings or disinterested altogether. Any interaction exemplifies affective friction, where those vulnerable to the performance invest it with new meaning, which may spur it to be shared. Performance is indeed a "vital act of transfer."[43] Without transferring performance, we lack a language of the body or tongue to communicate. Transferals of performances take place through vulnerability to spreadable material. A spectator's unique vulnerability to a Black performance's content pushes them to commit it to memory, record, share, and mimic it so that others encounter a reproduction of said performance. In this way, a performance transfers by moving back and forth between performer and audience, an affective multidirectional path that is crucial to going viral.

Black Performance

Gender is already a dysphoric experience, and the theory of performativity reveals gender as a social construct. But the theory does little good to stop there, to stop at gender as a social construct, for those who experience Black precarity—or ongoing vulnerability to anti-Black harm—based on racialized gender and sexuality.[44] Black performance, thus, answers the "so what" of performativity, thinking through a racial performativity that already interplays with gender. My use of the word *a* is important here, as I am not thinking of racial performativity for everyone. We must follow what happens after the Black body in discourse comes into being, such as how it continues to travel, refuse, and create. This journey offers insight into the agency of Black people.

As scholars of Black performance establish it, I find the concept of racial performativity helpful for understanding how the interreferentiality of Blackness does not render racial experiences of Blackness any less real.[45] Interreferentiality concerns how race is socially constructed and represents the many events and histories making up the discursive body that everyday people project onto the material body. Performativity recognizes how we compound social meanings across time through evidence and rumor projected onto people, affecting how we understand them.

As a crude example, compounding meanings across the media coverage of Hurricane Katrina, Michael Brown's murder, and Kendrick Lamar's album visuals of *To Pimp a Butterfly* led a Twitter interactor to associate Black Americans with wearing sagging pants and looting stores.[46] Yet the interactor is so myopically focused on disparaging the Black body in discourse that they fail to realize the nuances of the image as an act that survived the performance and continues to perform (as the paper material of the album, as the silicon material in the data center that preserves the memory, or through the interactor's affectual response). As an "active witness," I notice experiences of the sudden victory the image expresses.[47] I see and feel a cross-generational joy between Black masculine adults and children, a joy so overwhelming it might have killed the white judge in its foreground lying on his side with crossed-out eyes. And I see and feel a disregard for what anyone thinks, including me, highlighted by a child flipping off whoever surveils the image. There is also the absent Black presence of then President Barack Obama in the White House behind the group. Says Lamar, he was "just taking a group of homies who haven't seen the world and putting them in these places that they haven't necessarily seen . . . and them being excited about it."[48] His homies do not represent who typically occupies the White House, or even its lawn, yet they unapologetically experience taking up that space. Black performance theory is concerned with the multivalence of that experience.

I intervene in Black performance theory to address how Black bodies that circulate widely and spread rapidly in discourse are invested with social meaning by those vulnerable to their accompanying discourses. Thus, Black virality is the rapid circulation of the Black body in discourse, the ideas generated as a result, and the myriad ways that the spectators of and interactors with a Black performance play vital roles in its rapid spread into ubiquity. Without the discourses of racialized gender that abound in #HandsUpDontShoot and #BlackLivesMatter, I may have missed what was indexed, never been moved to consume it, and never been pushed to circulate reflections on it in written form as I do here. Black virality arises through the interaction between vulnerability to the knowledge of Black bodies in discourse and the rapid circulation that results from that defenselessness.

Black performance is essential for comprehending the phenomenon of goin' viral. Indeed, Black people gain rapid ubiquity through knowledge of their racialized genders and sexualities. When we talk about race, we are already talking about class, gender, and sexuality, because race marks gender, class, and sexuality just as each marks race.[49] The body holds history but also repurposes it.[50] Thus, Black performance theory intervenes in gender performativity by accounting for racialized gender and sexuality in its focus on everyday performance and its liberatory potential in anti-Black realities. When discourse fails to account for materiality, it inadvertently places more importance on the standpoints of individuals who have not been subjected to oppression beyond the singular dimensions of their gender or sexuality.[51]

Black virality, as a rapidly commonplace and stylized repetition of acts, is a technology associated with Butler's notion of gender performativity. Yet to leave the genders and sexualities of Black bodies in discourse unmarked, decontextualized, and deconstructed prevents Black people from embracing their racial experiences and organizing and mobilizing around racial evidence. Black performance accounts for the refusal of performativity to recognize that *racialized* gender is also a social construct that manifests repeatedly in our daily lives.[52] As a result, Black performance can assess how structures of power collectively affect Black people, how Black people materially and discursively organize and mobilize against those structures, and how Black people imagine and manifest new worlds despite and regarding the power leveraged against them. Therefore, Black performance does not deconstruct white power structures merely for the sake of revealing and critiquing norms of gender and sexuality; it grapples sincerely with race as gender and with race as sexuality.[53]

Black virality requires a Black performance that is rapidly commonplace. For instance, reproduced photographs produce new auras through their circulation by the people who interact with them. Often, a legacy performance generates new auras that evoke liveness for spectators, such as when you encounter the image of the slave ship *Brooks* for the first time. New auras of performances might inspire new circulation and relevance. The liveness available in the reproduction of a Black performance (or performance of Blackness) is the lifeblood of goin' viral. However, that liveness was not present in the initial production, emerging only through mechanical technology's literal decay, making every reproduction and replay unique and alive, done for the first time.

All movement is performance. Cellular and atomic decay, renewal, movement, and transfer complicate how we understand performance. This is because this level of performance is microscopic, occurring at the atomic level, and may not be witnessed as moving until years and decades later. This atomic behavior suggests something dynamic beyond human perception. For example, film, paint, and text decay over time with enough exposure to light and oxygen. This decay gestures toward the possibilities of performance, as a doing and a thing done, existing beyond what is readily perceived.

Additionally, Black and First Nations' ways of animating the inanimate (such as altars and avatars of spirits) deepen what liveness and its relationship to performance mean. Performance studies' dilemma may not be with liveness as it exists in material culture, but with the liveness we value for study. Some performance scholars understand liveness, particularly concerning mediated performance, as not living apart from an interactor's encounter.[54] Performance studies must change their relationship to what they consider live. Doing so will open different modes of inquiry and change our relationship to material, to "things." Yet I agree that what also adds to a mediated performance's liveness is how audiences imbue reproductions and replays with their meaning, energy, and auras.[55] "Haptic images," or performances that demand physical encounters and the labor of imagination, feelings, and sense of being that result—otherwise known as "affective labor"—are essential in constituting the visual culture of Black viralities.[56] These encounters motivate interactors to share these performances, spurring their rapid commonplaceness.

If performance is a "vital act of transfer," then Black performance in viral video, film, photography/images, and material objects transfers through affectual processes.[57] Black performances fall by the wayside of widespread awareness without the desire/repulsion, joy/pleasure, pain/trauma, and imaginaries experienced by coperformers, pushing them as agents to share performance. Once an interactor witnesses a performance, they embody it—but without feeling vulnerable to its contents, the witness might be unmoved to transfer the performance beyond themselves. Black viralities, therefore, are transferred through affect and move between representation, embodiment, and memory. This affectual process can push the witness to react to a pleasurable or unpleasurable friction (between the represented and the embodied) that they pass on through reenactment, word of mouth, and digital circulation whose spread impacts the currency, economic or otherwise, of the act circulated.[58]

As narrated in the hashtag example of this chapter's opening, Black virality is the rapid circulation of Black behaviors, Black bodies in discourse, and the livable and unlivable ideas around them to where those things are commonplace. In contrast to viral Blackness, Black virality allows for recognizing and reorganizing specific occurrences of Black life that quickly and widely circulate, shaping the perception of Black bodies in discourse and Black lives.[59] Thus, Black virality is a testament to the fluidity of Blackness and its liberatory potential; it is also a critique of white supremacy and the fixity of Blackness. Yet Black virality can also rapidly cement the racist hierarchies and discourses established by white supremacy that regard Blackness as highly recognizable.

I pursue three objectives with Black virality in *Goin' Viral*: (1) I convey how the mass production of a "thing" that people accept as a proxy for racialized gender knowledge in American popular culture creates pedagogy; (2) I clarify how viral mechanisms that transfer knowledge (like rumors, word of mouth, mass-produced materials, images, and videos) create the rapid ubiquity of a performance, and in understanding this, it becomes clear how narratives and representations that affect Black people's lives circulate faster now than ever before; and (3) I narrate, through the lens of Black virality, how rapid ubiquity hides the complexity of a "thing" by making it so widely available that interactors take its nuances for granted. Additionally, I show how rapid ubiquity paradoxically reveals the complexity of a "thing" by leaving patterns in its wake that repeatedly bring that "thing" to the vanguard of popular conscience. These patterns reveal a noticeably Black aesthetic, as Black virality also centers on how "things" spread in Black ways.

Viral Performance

As a concept and theory, Black virality draws from and extends what theater and performance scholar Miriam Felton-Dansky has called "viral performance." Felton-Dansky explores deliberate performances by artists that exploit communications technologies, resulting in the contagious spread of information by spectators as viral performance.[60] I use Black virality, however, as a theory to examine Black lives and the rapidly commonplace Black body in discourse. Black viralities prioritize Black racialized gender and address its intersectional encounters, something that viral performance alone does not require. When we interact online and in person, we can participate in the circulation of Black virality. Both negrophilia and negrophobia guide understandings of Blackness, and the currency of Blackness is an incentive for its circulation. But Blackness also encompasses a diasporic richness that is resistive to fetishistic understandings of it and profit-driven incentives.

Media scholar Henry Jenkins's "spread" metaphor helps me think through the mechanisms contributing to viral performances and address how and why sharing is so common. Regarding this metaphor, spreadability makes it easier for some media artifacts (through economic structures, attributes that motivate, and social networks) to be shared more widely by some audiences than by others. Jenkins defines spreadability in relationship to "stickiness," a marketing term used by Malcolm Gladwell. Stickiness relates to how companies corral audiences on websites online, weaken their ability to exit, and tally their visits and visit lengths. Spreadability has less to do with that sort of capture and more with "actively listening to the way media texts are taken up by audiences and circulate through audience interactions" through their social connections. Unlike stickiness, spreadability occurs in "easy-to-share formats," is inviting, and is uncontrollable. Whereas stickiness points toward user awareness of an online space or media artifact, spreadability points toward the active engagement of a user.[61] The form of something also determines its spreadability and whether or how it is widely shared (the size of a short-form video compared to a 16K Ultra HD film, for example).

Culture and experience affect one's vulnerability to Black viralities, and both phenomena motivate people to share performances in specific ways and contribute to their quickly becoming commonplace. For instance, a widely and rapidly circulated statement about the world taken as accurate when other evidence is scarce—what sociologist Gary Alan Fine and American folklorist Patricia Turner call a "truth claim"—can be readily accepted in one culture as a fact while categorically rejected in another as a falsehood.[62] In the Black virality of #HandsUpDontShoot, the importance of facts diminished in the scarcity of some evidence and the predominance of other evidence. The cultural sense and affect of a truth claim become vital in determining how vulnerable certain people are—or are not—to the claim.

Structure also affects vulnerability to Black viralities. Black people experience a higher degree of predisposing conditions, such as insecurity in housing, water, food, and employment, rendering them more susceptible to pandemics, natural disasters, and structural violence. The pervasive presence of structural racism, sexism, and ableism magnifies the impact of insecurities on Black people, as they face interplaying forms of violence and discrimination that heighten their susceptibility to physical ailments. These interactive phenomena lead to the faulty notion that race alone, rather than the violent conditions that structure reality, renders Black people more vulnerable than non-Black people to disease and, for my purposes, spreadable discourses of racialized gender that stigmatize them. But preexisting negrophilic and negrophobic epistemologies that contribute to Black viralities also make people privileged by structures that oppress Black people susceptible to discourses affecting Black lives.

Viral performances can attain iconicity. That is, viral performances can become recognizable enough to represent a collection of "things" of which they are only one instance; they can become synecdoches. In relationship to a viral performance's iconicity and drawing from curator, critic, and cultural theorist Nicole Fleetwood, I use "noniconicity" as a generative lens to assert that, within Black virality, performances generate a multitude of meanings beyond those within easy reach.[63] In concert with Fleetwood, rather than question why Black bodies trouble visual fields (and more), I am interested in the generative potential of Black visual culture, sound, and performance to trouble vision, what is heard, and what is felt. "Things" also perform noniconicity, remaining indecipherable aside from those who are a part of them or who meditate on, research, and question them enough to reveal their meaning beyond the surface.

Acknowledging the noniconicity of Black virality, therefore, becomes a means of identifying and theorizing the rapidly widespread Black performances that challenge generalizations. These performances circulate what is resistant to and excluded from generalization, encompassing notions of complex personhood, alterity, and subjugated knowledge. I amplify the noniconic during discrete moments of refusal, density, and collective livable possibility, usually muted by the loudness of Black virality. Through its noniconicity, Black virality unsettles and refuses the pedestrian, often denigrating, and essentialist ways that people typically understand Black bodies in discourse.

To better comprehend the vulnerability of Black individuals within viral performances and their resistance, or resistiveness, to such vulnerability, it is crucial to shift our focus toward Black virality. This means acknowledging that examining virality or viral performance alone is insufficient. By understanding the dynamics of Black people in relation to viral performances, we can grasp how they are resistive to and actively resist such vulnerability.

As with some hashtags, the outcome of Black viralities is that their frequencies place them at the forefront of the attention economy and the back end of context, history, and critical understanding. Context collapse is a feature of viral phenomena whereby people bring their contexts and conversations to networked performances, causing a collision of awkwardness and misunderstanding.[64] Despite but also because of context collapse, #HandsUpDontShoot gives digitized form to lived Black experiences. When interactors rapidly grapple with that digitized aesthetic in agreement or disagreement, they affect the hashtag's virality and the virality of its indexed performances. In this way, Black virality is an uncontrollable aesthetic that manifests through the need of its interactors to respond to the Black body in discourse to which they are vulnerable. In all its discursive complexity, the hashtag effortlessly travels bidirectionally. When interactors convert its form as affect into electronic data, indexes, or visual culture, bidirectional travel occurs in that it subsequently converts back to affect for the new interactor.

Here, the hashtag's ability to index stereotypes of Blackness or critical critiques of and through Blackness, as well as the ability of interactors to share it through networked media like X, the Meta platform's family of applications, and YouTube, makes it a tool for achieving Black virality.[65] As such, the hashtag can redouble limited notions of Blackness even while expanding them, thus narrating its nuances. The latter multivalence is crucial for understanding the noniconicities of Black virality.

Still, we must recognize that viral performances, including Black viralities, have limitations.[66] Along its timeline of existence, a performance becomes viral in an explosion of figurative and literal visibility and spread. Like a nuclear explosion, the closer one is (in time and geography) to the explosion, the more visible and viral the performance is. As time passes, the intensity of that visibility diminishes almost as rapidly as it first manifested, yet the atmosphere and environment in proximity to the point of explosion are affected for years to come—what I think of here as "viral fallout." Viral fallout sustains the second wind of a viral performance, its viral afterlife. Almost as soon as Black virality dies out, it is rebirthed in another form. Therefore, a Black performance, or its referent, that travels at astonishing speed and scope during its existence is a form of Black virality, whereas, outside of those factors, a Black performance is not viral.

Significantly, something has "gone viral" when it becomes rapidly commonplace—quickly being found in some form everywhere. Black virality infiltrates multiple worlds. Yet Black virality already exists; it has touched phenomena (i.e., MP3s, mundane conversations, cartoons, and video games) within those worlds and, through that touch, transformed them.

The consumption of Black virality creates an affect best witnessed in visceral reactions to viral material, for example, being compelled to say, post, or gesture something in response or to reproduce viral material in some form. Consequently, as a Black performance goes viral, capturing its impact in numbers is challenging. I should qualify a Black virality as epidemiology classifies an epidemic, or the point at which an illness (or *illness*—meaning "the undeniably cool") can affect a susceptible population.[67] Thus, what went viral at the onset of YouTube in 2005 does not require viewership analogous to something that goes viral in 2025.

Intel's Racial Intelligence: Goin' Viral through a Racist Incident

Benjamin Lawless, an employee of an unnamed business, publicly alleged (on a site that has since been redacted) that he was given a Dell catalog in July 2007, as he was the only person in the office who used a personal computer.[68] Lawless found the Intel ad (see figure 1) in the catalog offensive.[69] He rendered the image digitally from the paper catalog and posted it on his *Penciled In* WordPress blog on July 19, 2007, cheekily titling the post "Intel, Racism Inside." A copywriter and gadget critic named copyranter found it online, posted it on Blogspot on July 30, 2007, shared it with Gizmodo on the same day, and reposted it on Gawker on July 31, 2007. This is where the ad found incredible traction, as it could be discovered only on such online blogs because Intel had pulled it from all publications except the Dell catalog.

FIGURE 1 Wily Ferret, *Inquirer*, "White Men Can't Run," August 10, 2011. URL delisted.

Due to this censorship, the ad gained popularity and mass production through outrage marketing—a strategy or tactic where the outrage at something offensive or being outraged at the outrage at something offensive functions to escalate the attention on the "thing" in focus. This "embarrassment" allows the person or company responsible for the offense to benefit from the currency of the attention while taking a moral high ground by retracting the content of the offense they created (willfully or inadvertently). Outrage marketing reinforces the adage "All publicity is good publicity." The suppression of this Intel advertisement led to other viral means of its spreading beyond the catalog, with the ad circulating through online news, gadget blogs, and personal blogs. The blogs and news platforms questioned the offensive creation of tropes of race and sex and, regrettably, critiqued how other people could take offense.

After reposting the ad, initially framed by Lawless's more apt critique, copyranter posted a lazy critique of the ad on Blogspot. There, copyranter's liberal sarcasm belied the anti-Black racism it intended to critique. Even their Blogspot title, "Bow to Your Cotton Khaki-Panted Master," almost reads as copyranter's support of the ad's underlying racist discourse. They end the post with "Fellow Crackers? I am calling for a boycott of all Intel products. Join me, in this noble fight against reverse racism!" This type of liberal sarcasm set the stage for Gizmodo, where Adam Frucci made copyranter's Blogspot post more visible and published a hyperlink on Gizmodo titled "Intel Ad Might be Racist, but Boy Does It Make Me Want a Core 2 Duo." When it reached Gawker, the analysis of the ad was similar, but copyranter had framed the repost with the title "Intel Ad: Stupid? Or Stupid and Racist?," as though stupidity is mutually exclusive from racism. Their liberal sarcasm continues: "Is the ad racist? Yes it is. As a slow white man, it offends me to the core of my whiteness."

Stereotypes regarding white male athleticism aside, my focus remains on Black virality. The mid-2007 Intel advertisement was an early recognition of Black virality in media that got under my skin. Six carbon-copy Black masculine figures are dressed in track uniforms and readied for a race, staring straight down at the floor. Intel and the ad agency McCann Erickson had substituted track lanes with office desks, and turf with tiled floors. Examining the image further, we see that the athletic Black masculine figures are almost bowing in the presence of a white masculine figure in a typical IT uniform. The IT person stands over them, arms folded, smirking, and staring at the viewer. The ad's text further illustrates a visual hierarchy: "Multiply computing performance and maximize the power of your employees." Here, the Black masculine figures are suggestively employees, and the white masculine figure is an employer or, if employee, manager.

The ad unwittingly explains how Black virality works: by visualizing rumor and harnessing the optics of shared commonsense notions of the Black body in discourse. In this depiction, McCann Erickson and Intel represent the white masculine figure as the employer or manager, while they equate the Black masculine figures with computer processors. The ad agency depicts the Black figures as disposable objects capable of working/running fast and whose function activates at the user's discretion. In this performance, historical Black stereotypes and rumors of being devoted servants and superior athletes return.[70] The office space resonates also with ownership over people. The ad suggests that Black masculine figures serve as forced labor behind business performance, whereas the white masculine figure reaps the benefits of this labor at their leisure, arms comfortably folded while others work as processors—multitasking to meet the user's demands. Today's exploitation of the hidden human labor behind content moderation is anticipated by the discursive content of Intel's pulled advertisement.[71]

Further, this image reinforces a hierarchy of racialized gender. The white masculine figure's direct stare at the camera signifies pride, whereas the Black masculine figures look toward the floor and signal shame, abjection, or subservience as their condition. Moreover, the Black masculine figures' identical appearance reinscribes anonymizing mythologies that suggest all Black people "look alike," while the white masculine figure remains unique and distinct.[72]

Intel also brands the discursive bodies presented in the ad. The white-masculine-as-nerd stereotype, unavailable to those who are not white or masculine, does the epistemological work to let audiences know who this is.[73] Powerful corporate groups and individuals have forced Black lives in the United States, however, into a fraught relationship with branding that refers to the confinement and regulation of slavery in the United States.[74] Intel manipulates the Black masculine bodies differently from the white masculine body, who escapes their lot through a specific legacy of racialized gender. The ad agency merges the particularities of Black masculine experiences into one maximizing image, transforming them into runners preparing for a race, influencing unspoken yet visualized notions of *a race*.

Although this seems like a simple Intel ad, branding creates discursive scars. In this advertisement, McCann Erickson and Intel portray Black masculine bodies as naturally superior in athleticism and obligated to serve the needs of others, especially white masculine figures. This branding also works to erase other possibilities of Black masculinity: each of these bodies may possess the skill needed to manage and maintain the Intel technology, but we lose that narrative possibility in the face of the commitment to a linear narrative that calls forth and sustains historical tropes of Black-white masculine relations and hierarchies. This rendering is a signpost for the friction Black virality creates within our society—popular audiences consume Black bodies in discourse as fixed in capacity and status. Even so,

Black bodies in discourse move and break away from static notions of their personhood.

Viral performances of Black masculine tropes produce political responses from those who are vulnerable to such acts even if the people involved are white, as said Blackness frames their whiteness and vice versa. Indeed, absent Black virality, the critique (as it turned sarcastically racist) would otherwise have gone unnoticed. Thus, we must also consider how a viral context may transform meaning.

The title of the first blog post to expose the Intel ad, "Intel, Racism Inside," lacks a thorough tracing of the material culture that the ad summons around the exploitative use of Black lives to create superior technologies. Those same technologies also contribute to the media infrastructure that permits discursive critique. According to Intel's white papers, this ad preceded their first "conflict minerals" supply chain survey in 2009.[75] Intel articulated the difficulty involved in eliminating, without doubt, conflict minerals not limited to coltan, tungsten, and gold extracted from locations such as the Democratic Republic of the Congo, or DRC. This observation suggests that in 2007, Intel needed to educate its smelters regarding the origins of their minerals if it hoped its suppliers would mine only conflict-free minerals, so called because armed factions are financed through their sale. So by producing and purchasing Intel processors (at least before 2014), Intel and I were funding armed conflicts between people in the DRC and its bordering regions, even as I first began exploring the meaning of this image.[76] That does not sit well with me. Yet the image's ability to provoke such a critical thought suggests its capacity to hold more than insult.

Thus, while Black virality may generalize beliefs about Black people and Black bodies in discourse, it also opens paths along which it is possible to challenge those beliefs and transform how Black people are understood.[77] Although an Intel spokesperson noted that Intel and McCann Erickson had collaborated on the ad and later deemed it offensive, the ad's use of Black virality has the potential to subvert racist imagery.[78] The small print states, "Actual performance may vary." This admission suggests that, while these Black masculine figures appear identical, they all perform (race, gender, sexuality, and other interplaying ways of being) differently, intercepting some issues that I have raised regarding anonymity and racialized gender roles. One blog interactor saw the advertisement as comedic and unsuccessful because, given their posture and positioning, the opposing sprinters would collide when the starter gun goes off, suggesting the inefficiency of Intel processors.[79] In a similar train of thought, the image illustrates the unsustainability of the Black labor that powers the technologies the modern world has become so reliant on. The resulting collision would also symbolize failure to manage Black bodies in discourse, indicating their uncontrollability. As media studies scholar Kim Christian Schrøder writes, "We simply cannot take for granted that the meaning intended by the sender is identical to the meaning actualized by the audience."[80] Indeed, Black virality keeps Blackness in motion while concurrently fixing it in place, working multivalently, "symbolically in a number of directions at once."[81]

• • •

The Intel ad on which I have focused here illuminates other ideas and thoughts that will be important throughout *Goin' Viral*. It conveys how rumor is viral (spreading uncontrollably and becoming rapidly commonplace in the popular imagination), is saturated in political motives, and functions in contemporary performances of Black discursive bodies in popular culture. We also see in this Intel ad how viral ideas travel through Black bodies in discourse (i.e., rendering an image that uses preexisting ideas of Black bodies in discourse as fungible, athletic, and strong, then commodifying and distributing them). Nevertheless, despite the way these viralities ensnare Black masculine figures and suggest larger narratives of deviancy and inferiority, it is also through these viralities that Black bodies in discourse can resist and be resistive to such narratives. The Intel ad conveys how the currency of Blackness in popular culture—both the popularity and fiscal value of Blackness—incentivizes its commodification, which influences how Black people "define, locate, and understand [them]selves via identification."[82]

Goin' Viral is a critical engagement on the risks and rewards associated with Black subjects in performances that have rapidly become commonplace. In this book, I consider how visual and sonic cues found in Black viralities are often overly deterministic. So much is ingrained in Black viralities that they require extraordinary labor from the audience to be comprehended—an analysis of that which is there but remains out of easy grasp, visibility, or audibility. The difficulty in understanding uncontrollable Black performances resembles the difficulty of understanding synesthesia. It is within the fluidity of the senses, or the seeing of what one hears and the touching of what one sees. When seeing is haptic, or hearing is visual, rapidly ubiquitous Black performances that are "easily" known demand attention to these complexities. Indeed, *Goin' Viral* acknowledges our familiarity with certain aspects of Black virality while suggesting there will always be unknowns and lingering uncertainties, regardless of its visibility or audibility. Visual technologies with the potential for mass production, such as online viral videos, cinematic film, connected television, and photographs/images, have significantly enhanced Black virality. But visual technologies portray images of Blackness so pervasive and commonplace that those decoding them may take for granted certain social assumptions and metaphors embedded within the portrayals of racialized gender.

In *Goin' Viral,* I decipher four viral performances where Black virality creates or informs a commonsense ideology about Black bodies in discourse. While I focus significant attention on the "original"[83] Black viralities, I also interrogate how other acts that precede them and that they inspire necessitate a critical assessment of their multivalence.

I have limited my examinations of Black virality to online viral videos, film, and photography/images. Despite this focus, we can find viral performances of Blackness in various channels, including stand-up comedy, popular moments with artificial intelligence, sports, stage plays, and everyday acts like "What are those?!"[84] Illustrating many Black viralities and noniconic Black performances across time, in the 2016 single-channel, high-definition digital video montage *Love Is the Message, The Message Is Death,* video artist and cinematographer Arthur Jafa explores the tensions between Black uncontrollability and the people and forces that attempt to control Black life and Black representations. Yet we each explore very different moments of these phenomena, likely due to how innumerable Black virality is. An exemplar of the very phenomena that I am writing about—these popular cultures, places, and mediums where people negotiate Blackness—is hip-hop.

Here, I want to broaden the appeal of my discussion by gesturing toward the subtle ways that I embed hip-hop in my manuscript as a refrain and medium. Even though I did not focus the bulk of my attention on hip-hop, as the entire project reached completion, I realized that hip-hop idioms and aesthetics resonate throughout each chapter, creating a type of hip-hop motif. That motif is unquestionably a result of how I have participated in hip-hop culture as a fan in the audience at concerts, as an artist in its cyphers, and as a DJ for parties that feature music from the African diaspora. Moreover, this hip-hop refrain reflects the aural conditions that shape my writing. I contrapuntally arrange samples of discourse, images, and audio, interpret them, and convey the meanings and feelings that arise in response.[85] Hip-hop is a part of my project, even considering how people appropriate it as the quintessential meaning of Blackness. Yet hip-hop should not dominate the meaning or potential of Blackness, let alone my manuscript. Undoubtedly, I have worked within a specific aesthetic of vision and sound with Black viralities that centrally recur between and reverberate before and after 2007 and 2014.

Between 2007 and 2014, each performance I analyzed went from being objects to "things." While objects can sit in the background, "things" animate us and demand to be engaged; we are viscerally vulnerable to them. As the performances continually became things, I could not ignore them; absolutely, I was vulnerable to various discourses embedded in the performances from my stance as a cisgender heterosexual Black man from Detroit, Michigan, with Black feminist sensibilities. As the performances continually reappeared through visual culture and music, I felt a need to critically address what I saw and heard unfolding.

Each performance speaks to contemporary phenomena linked to the historic performances that precede them. In 2007, Hank Willis Thomas's *B®anded* series showed me, in modern and persuasive ways online, how organizations and individuals used representations of Black people to market products and ideas in the transatlantic slavery past that have a semblance to present-day marketing and design. Five years later, I again encountered Thomas's art in the *30 Americans* exhibition of the now dissolved Corcoran Gallery of Art in Washington, DC.[86] I noticed a phenomenon in the art: that virality offered liberation from traumas while also being a traumatizing force. At that moment, I grappled with what it meant for my ancestors to free themselves from slavery by advertising its abolition through a brand, label, or seal of a stereotypical enslaved African. While the latter branding phenomenon was just one of many freedom strategies, it created a pattern where abolitionists projected the desire for freedom from bondage alongside a Blackness enslaved to a subservient and denigrating representation: a kneeling figure in chains.[87]

Although one cannot escape the pain of losing a child, solace can come from ensuring those responsible are held accountable and from preventing the loss from going unnoticed or repeated. In Chicago, on September 24, 2009, Derrion Albert's peers murdered him. The viral footage, which was brutal and reminiscent of a snuff film, affected many people. Thanks to the crucial role played by the same cell phone video footage that captured his last moments, spectators identified his peers who killed him, police arrested them, and they were later sentenced. The video and its afterlife left me with many unanswered questions about the structural culprits of Albert's murder and how people remembered him in gendered ways after his life.

One year later, my focus on the video "Bed Intruder Song!!!," like the phenomenon I noticed in Hank Willis Thomas's art, was primarily due to the powerful impact of traumatic factors in the liberation from trauma. The video, which was hard to miss in US popular culture in 2010, hearkened back to similar kinds of street testimonials and the value and shame they hold in the communities where they take place. I also needed to understand how a brother who had thwarted his sister's sexual assault could become the focus rather than the sister who had experienced the trauma.

At the tail end of the peak virality of "Bed Intruder Song!!!," police killed Eric Garner by choke hold on Staten Island in 2014. Spike Lee anticipated a similar moment in *Do the Right Thing* through the murder of the character Radio Raheem. The scene reminded me of the many other state-sanctioned police killings of young Black people that the news media had inundated me with, and it made me intensely aware of my vulnerabilities to the state as a cis Black man. In the 1989 film, white or white-passing people imagine Black and Brown lives as life-threatening and loud. Indeed, the police kill Radio Raheem for refusing to mute the same music that Rosie Perez dances to with raw emotion in the film's opening credits. Also, Lee posted an unlisted video on Facebook spliced between Garner and Raheem to gesture toward the many parallels of their murders by choking. For all these reasons, I wanted to wrestle with the contemporary resonance of Raheem amid the many visually and aurally documented Black killings that had immediately preceded and inspired it. Beyond the latter moments that had gripped me, interactors continued to reproduce each performance past the point of when they had been viral phenomena.

For *Goin' Viral* I have chosen to work within a specific set of performances (as Black viralities can exist in many acts) to explore possibilities in greater depth than a broader consideration. As a result, I critically examine performances considering the discourses and the institutional and structural forces that Black viralities shape and are shaped by. I reflect on oppressive forces that deny decent housing, limit economic opportunities, and discriminate based on race and gender, with a focus that would have been more difficult to achieve with a broader consideration of Black virality.

Methods Informing *Goin' Viral*

My overarching approach consists of critical discourse analysis. Critical discourse theorist Norman Fairclough explains that discourse develops along "three dimensions": analysis of texts, how texts are produced and consumed, and the sociocultural context of a text.[88] Fairclough uses *text* linguistically (to include those written and oral) and semiotically (to include photographic images, the visual layout of images and their settings, and their sonic accompaniments).[89] His critical attention to the sociocultural context of a text as its circumstantial context, the structural practices the text is situated in, or the larger society and culture the text is a part of, provides a model for my engagement here.[90] Of greatest importance to my approach is recognizing that newer media practices are shifting toward relaxing the boundaries between entertainment and public affairs.[91] Overall, critical discourse analysis supplies a means of examining forms of knowledge and theory. I focus on social identity and social interactions exhibited in linguistic and semiotic mediums and embodied performances.

While I theorize through Black virality across multiple sites, I couple "lurking" with my overarching critical discourse analysis. This coupling emerges as a position from which I research and write about Black virality in situated spaces online that I extrapolate and use beyond the Web. Media and communications scholar Robert V. Kozinets describes a lurker as an "active observer who learns about a [web]site through initially watching and reading."[92] Even where I do not focus on the Web, every chapter in this book requires lurking—a shallow "hanging out" in public scenes of Black virality, where my continual return to those scenes generates depth of understanding.

More specifically, in the chapter on Hank Willis Thomas's *B®anded* series, I lurk in the visual culture archive, out of which I curate Black virality to clarify how it exists in Thomas's photos/images. By lurking in Radio Raheem's film archive, *Do the Right Thing*, I move lurking into the hip-hop past to anticipate and create links to other fatal encounters involving Black people decades later. I adopt lurking to observe online interactions on video-sharing/aggregation sites where comments are posted about "Bed Intruder Song!!!" or "Tragic: Teens Give a Chicago Student from a Rivarly [*sic*] Hi [*sic*] School a Deadly Beating with Huge Wooden Boards! *Warning* (Very Graphic) (R.I.P. Derrion Albert) (This Has to Stop)."[93] In each instance, I encounter discursive moments that require critical discourse analysis to parse out nuances of meaning against distinct cultural and institutional backdrops.

In each chapter, I engage with sites of cultural production and explore racialized gender and sexuality within exemplary visual and sonic performances of Black virality. In chapter 1, I examine Black viralities of the conceptual artist Hank Willis Thomas's *B®anded* series. Specifically, I interpret articulations of the abolitionist seal and the slave ship *Brooks*. Here, I consider how abolitionists leveraged racialized gender knowledge of Black bodies in discourse to represent abolitionist ideas. While not viral art by itself, Thomas's conceptual images and material objects use viral images and rumor from the archives of transatlantic slavery to consider other nuances of abolitionist propaganda.[94] I end the chapter with a brief consideration of how the visual properties of the abolitionist seal unexpectedly resurface in our present moment and what it suggests about the successes and failures of abolition.

In chapter 2, I use a material culture analysis to understand Black people's use of the boom box from the 1970s to the present. Throughout the chapter, I focus on the often-ignored character Radio Raheem in *Do the Right Thing*. In addition to critical discourse analysis, I use a Black feminist film and performance analysis to interrogate how sonic cues anticipate imaginaries of racialized gender and sexuality through the visual culture of the film. The medium of cinematic film has played a vital role in magnifying the image of Raheem, making him the iconic representation of Black men playing their boom boxes even in the twenty-first century.

In chapter 3, I conduct a critical discourse analysis of the precursor to the most viral grassroots video of 2010 to identify how editorial choices in the news media erased the Black woman at the center of the video's sexual trauma. Furthermore, I consider how erasure might function within a politics of refusal. Importantly, this chapter imagines the Black feminist work of such a move of resistiveness and resistance. The form of vernacular testimony here became the reference point for a new trope I coin in the chapter.[95]

While the previous chapter focuses on Black virality in a viral video for a news channel in 2010, chapter 4 focuses on 2010's most viral video (excluding Vevo music videos). Here, I examine spectatorial viewpoints from situated spaces online, a methodology called "netnography," to explore intersections of racism, classism, sexism, and homophobia in "Bed Intruder Song!!!" I also consider noniconic engagements with the latter intersections to reckon with how the least iconic sometimes carries the most substantive critique of the unlivable. I then follow how the video continued to travel beyond 2010 through other viral videos, memes, and indexes and what that travel has meant for the Black people involved and not.

Lastly, in my coda, I employ critical discourse analysis to approach the cell phone video footage of Derrion Albert's murder in Chicago and emphasize the importance of framing Black virality. I close with a critique of Derrion's resulting heteronormative sainthood that gained the attention of President Obama in 2009 and consider the possibility that such a crime can awaken a liberation from the factors that caused it. I then offer connections between Black virality and the use of visual evidence and propaganda in the civil rights and Black Power movements and the movement for Black lives. Finally, I gesture toward other performances that occurred while writing this book that are worth further consideration as Black viralities.

My understanding of how Black bodies in discourse exist in the shadows of liberation informs my approach, into which I adopt lurking as a performative mode of being. This mode of being is a form of hanging out, with an ethical sensibility and attention to experiences of deep (but also not-so-deep) significance. Performance scholar D. Soyini Madison discusses experiences of deep significance and their inextricability to performance ethnography. She writes, "Experience begins from our uneventful, everyday existence. . . . But then something happens, and we move to moments of experience. . . . We give feeling, reason, and language to what has been lifted from the inconsequential day-to-day."[96] Reflecting on experience within the scope of performance is not to think about just any experience, but the experience that ruptures the ordinary. Madison's approach, however, leaves the inconsequential day-to-day less explored.

In tandem, I am interested in what is not made spectacular—tandem because of the unstable binary between the ordinary and the sensational. In *Feels Right,* gender and performance scholar Kemi Adeyemi encourages thinking with the ordinary for a different attention that does not fetishize the spectacular when performing ethnography, especially of queer folks, as that which is extraordinary becomes the expectation. Adeyemi writes, "Subtle, quieter, less public, often invisible, and entirely ordinary modes of living [B]lack life are devalued as seemingly carrying less political force and have been thus devalued as sites of critical analysis."[97] Lurking is another way for media scholars to critically engage in performance ethnography in a virtual space that refuses to disavow the ordinary, subtle, and that which does not make itself easily known. Lurking is a less public and often invisible mode that requires repeated doing, returning to the performance, and following how it travels. To understand how my experience of a performance is remarkable or pedestrian requires a central element of viral performance: an ongoing and, at times, unwelcome return that distills what goes viral from what gets lost in oblivion.

My critical discourse analysis of the four Black viralities and my production of images (as well as video and data visualization that I use in presentations) to further investigate the acts under study are coproductions of media and racialized gender and sexuality knowledge. My approach further blurs divisions between performer, audience, and scholar. I chose these specific Black viralities also because of how commonplace they once were as performances. These performances have forever affected their social worlds, which reflects their importance in the popular imagination and the material and social effects of perceptions of Black bodies in discourse. The urgency for scholars to critically analyze such reenactments in popular culture and everyday life is heightened by the implications these performances have, as they simultaneously reinforce and challenge the daily material obstacles that Black people experience.

Because this is the first project to examine Black virality closely, I travel analytically across various instantiations (image, film, and online viral video). I also use multiple approaches to Black viralities, drawing from visual and material culture, critical discourse analysis, performance theory, Black feminism, media studies, and netnography. My interdisciplinarity puts distinct approaches to Black virality in conversation while acknowledging that Black virality functions differently depending on the object of analysis. While Black virality serves as the through line of the entire project, it does not work uniformly in each medium I encounter.

People entertain themselves online, particularly by visiting websites that use image- and video-sharing and streaming, consuming artifacts of Blackness in a progressively diverse manner. In addition, mobile applications, and technologies such as TikTok, Snapchat, Meta's family of applications, nonfungible tokens, ChatGPT, artificial intelligence image/video generators, tablets, cell phones, mixed-reality headsets/glasses, and laptops have facilitated the circulation and sharing of images, sounds, and text to unprecedented levels worldwide. All these interfaces allow performances like Hank Willis Thomas's, Radio Raheem's, Kelly Dodson's and Kevin Antoine Dodson's (referred throughout as Antoine Dodson), and Derrion Albert's to forge and infiltrate fresh sites of news, entertainment, and social engagement to reach spectators with fresh eyes. As a result, we will continue to see the influence of Black virality in popular culture and everyday life as access to the Web increases through the development of both mobile and stationary interface technologies, the innovation of generational standards for the Internet, and the evolution of Web3.

The referent that conjures the theory of Black virality for this entire project is the saturation of viral videos that have become a part of the American popular imagination. I follow a trajectory that takes us from the earliest form of Black virality (rumor) to more contemporary forms (viral video) to consider how Black virality has functioned to script and rescript people and things with a legacy that persists into the present. That is, old technology is the new technology. Thus, my analytic of Black virality is inspired by the present and is helpful across time. It identifies and interrogates the products and social impacts of Black bodies in discourse that have become rapidly commonplace and affects the material worlds where Black people live. Yet solely analyzing Black people through the lens of viral content can reduce their experiences to mere trends and spectacles. This can further reinforce harmful stereotypes and neglect the complex realities and diversity within Black communities. Critical discourse analyses, like those in *Goin' Viral*, assure that discussions regarding Black lives and representations are abundant with nuance, sensitivity, and context, and that Black performances are not reduced to mere objects of scrutiny and entertainment but expanded to "things" that matter, whether we notice them or not.

CHAPTER 1

People Hear What They See

Branding Abolition and the Black Virality of Kneeling

> Maybe that was my little taste of what it is like to be black. It helped me understand.
>
> —Nate Boyer

Using a kneeling Black figure as their seal, abolitionist visual propaganda of the eighteenth- and nineteenth-century United States and Western Europe was created to stir the convictions of those with white privilege, like retired Army Green Beret Nate Boyer, quoted in the epigraph above. An actual kneeling Black man has stood for a different abolition that Boyer could ally himself with. In 2016, as Boyer stood next to the kneeling Colin Kaepernick during the national anthem and was booed, Boyer wondered if he himself had experienced a feeling of what it was to be Black and stigmatized by the way one's skin is seen and imagined. To be sure, he did not, but this is part of the affective labor involved in allying one's self in performances of abolition (an accomplice, or "withness," might have knelt with him).[1] At least it helped him understand . . . but what he understood is still a mystery.

As a conceptual artist, Hank Willis Thomas of Philadelphia links contemporary representations of Black bodies in discourse to the most popular iconic and mass-produced images from the archives of transatlantic slavery. He does this without subtracting from the foundation and context behind them.[2] For instance, Thomas crafted the seal of the Society for Effecting the Abolition of the Slave Trade (SEAST) into a gold chain. The seal still stands for improving and abolishing the immoral and inhuman conditions that enslaved Africans endured through the Columbian Exchange, but it now also suggests the less popular fact that the seal was made into a fashion symbol and sold as a commodity to produce a profit. In referencing popular signs of Blackness, Thomas builds on the foundations and contexts of images gleaned from the archives of transatlantic slavery, illustrating and challenging their legacy in today's terms. In the sections of this chapter, I discuss images and material objects from Thomas's *B®anded* series that link present modes of branding with the legacy of the visualization of rumors about Black bodies in eighteenth- and nineteenth-century abolitionist and proslavery marketing.[3]

Thomas crafts a creative visual archive in his uniquely titled series *B®anded*, a gesture toward how advertisers use Black people and Black bodies in discourse to give substantive meaning to mass-produced images and brands. By visualizing rumors of Blackness, abolitionists and proslavery advocates engaged in one of the earliest forms of Black virality. In this way, Thomas illuminates Black virality within visual culture, showing viewers the craft of rapidly ubiquitous representation and its role in creating, sustaining, and distorting Black life.

The *B®anded* series featured in Thomas's book *Pitch Blackness* emerged from the sense of loss that he experienced for his cousin Songha Willis, who was murdered outside of a Philadelphia club by robbers seeking his gold chain. Songha's murder suggests that the thieves valued his life as a Black man less than they did the things he possessed. Repeatedly reducing beings to things devalues human life and inflates the value of things. Thomas places Songha's death in the frames of animations and photographs, moving this moment of loss into illustrations of the Black virality of intracommunal murder and suggesting that such violence has become numbing in the iterative, inundating ways that Black virality can operate.

Rather than making Songha Willis appear a mere statistic, Thomas presents his cousin's life and accomplishments through digitally scanned photographs. The corresponding chapter in *Pitch Blackness*, "Winter in America," is a collaboration with visual artist Kambui Olujimi, featuring stills from their stop-motion animation project that used G.I. Joe action figures to interpret the details of his cousin's last five minutes of life. Thomas and Olujimi pose action figures to imagine how children, especially (tom)boys, are socialized to reenact violent situations and to examine how ordinary violence experienced by Black people is reduced to a child's game.[4] The chapter fades to an ending with a photo of Songha Willis in a morgue. We then see visuals of the family that Songha left behind, bringing us into the next chapter: "Bearing Witness: Murder's Wake."

This chapter gives us a glimpse into the many lives that Thomas's cousin affected beyond his immediate family. As the chapter progresses, more faces appear, and thumb-sized black squares increase. These black spaces illustrate the futility of attempting to find every individual whose life was touched by Songha, standing in for those whom he touched as well as for those who will never know about his death. The preceding chapters in Thomas's book function as a memorial to Songha. Once the *B®anded* chapter begins, the affective labor of the previous chapters has laid the groundwork to enable readers to think about the relationship of Blackness to gun violence, alcohol, loss, and how Black lives function as things less important than the commodities they wear, produce, or represent.

The gold chain involved in the death of Thomas's cousin also summons how Blackness is pitched, convincing consumers to accept its authenticity and cultural value. The excess of imagery designed to signal authenticity and culture creates a pitch B/blackness, a B/blackness devoid of light or escape, a B/blackness that is integral to one's lived encounters, so dark and assumed that it remains unseen. Yet the B/blackness is also so excessive that it prompts the questioning of its existence and how it is pitched; it is so rapidly commonplace and varies to such a degree that one would rather pitch—toss out—the idea of B/blackness altogether. However, if we deny Black identity, we lose the basis for naming our experiences of pleasure and theft. Rather, pitching Blackness here is a post-Black feeling that captures the desire to engage with other aspects of life that do and do not interplay with one's experience of Blackness. Postblackness is much more about the densities of Blackness than its elimination.

Still, people have eliminated and killed Black people for less than a gold chain. Through the last half of 2014 and into the summer of 2020, we witnessed massive protests by people advocating that Black lives matter, from Palestine to Ferguson, Missouri, and from the United Kingdom to Minneapolis, Minnesota. The deaths of Trayvon Martin, Michael Brown, Breonna Taylor, and George Floyd and the climate of police brutality that permeates the United States and resonates in various diasporas that experience related traumas throughout the world catalyzed the latter support. Black men's performances, in life and death, have been central to the iconography and motivation of the #BlackLivesMatter movement and #M4BL (Movement for Black Lives). Even though it is a movement that does not place one form of Blackness above another and whose founders strived to affirm the value of all Black people, it still needs to be said that "#BlackLivesMatter is not #BlackMenMatter."[5] From the abolitionist propaganda of the eighteenth and nineteenth centuries to the popular understanding of the leadership of #BlackLivesMatter, the male privilege in which each campaign traffics emerges where Black men and representations of them are the most recognizable and well-known icons in the popular imaginary. This is a problem.

#BlackLivesMatter feels like #BlackMenMatter through the interactions that people have with publicly indexed information regarding the various forms of theft (of life, of limbs, of loved ones) that Black men experience, which enhances their visibility. Yet, as much as rumors and propaganda can become visual and material via people's rapid mass circulation, people, especially in working-class life, are not cultural dopes.[6] People understand how representations become real but do not need to dominate their lives. Indeed, interactors, via word of mouth, mediated imagery, and digital information, exercise agency in their media literacy to wrestle with what they encounter rather than simply bank all rapidly ubiquitous information as facts.

In this chapter, I explore the interplay between racialized gender, visual propaganda, and commerce in select conceptual art from Thomas's *B®anded* series. This analysis reveals numerous ways that brands transform Black bodies in discourse into "things" that go beyond mere commodities. The brands go beyond by standing out from the mundane as they are used by activists and businesses to sell more than just the products they represent. By visualizing rumors, Thomas rescripts Black viralities—the rapid discursive circulation of Black bodies, their behaviors, and the ideas around them to the point of ubiquity—that have deformed Black bodies in discourse throughout history.

Through rescripting rumor, Thomas remembers stereotypical narratives to suggest alternative truths that better reflect the complexity of Black experiences.[7] Sociologist Gary Alan Fine and folklorist Patricia Turner identify three types of rumors, one of which best fits the images I analyze in this chapter. That type they call the "formula rumor"—the efficacy of which "depends on the knowing and skilled use of stereotypes."[8] My attention to rumor and this reconfiguration of Black "truths" exemplifies a methodological approach that Thomas uses in his work on branding. Here, I interrogate critical rumors, which I read as viral performances of an "other truth," against formulaic rumors circulated by Quakers and proslavery advocates that reverberate from selected images and creations of the Black body in discourse in Thomas's *B®anded* series.

The title of this chapter, "People Hear What They See," suggests that we begin to understand and misunderstand at the nexus of the senses.[9] The underpinning idea suggests that the optic is always already steeped in the aural.[10] Rumors influence a person's visual perception and hearing of Black people. When we encounter Black bodies in discourse within view or earshot, they often support and critique formulaic rumors about them, creating "other truths" that we may remember, whose rumor we may spread, and whose performance we may repeat. The Black bodies within the images and material culture that follow are representations of socially designated scripts, such as superior strength, anonymity, and helplessness. Yet Thomas also renders them "re-scripters"—subjects who do not occupy positions of authority yet create new roles, critiques, and possibilities.[11]

I am interested in how rumor, a viral form of discourse that often derives from the experience of the optic "thing" (directly or indirectly), scripts and functions as the semantic foundation of what we see. Rumor is part of the discursive register, making meaning through the verbal as much as through the visual. We can and must extend discursive analysis to understand the content of rumor, how rumor repeats itself, and the many mediums in which the latter repetitions take form. Thus, I connect the visual image to performance, discourse, and scripting through my interrogations of rumor in images. Rumors raise and dull awareness and carry spreadable content robustly and quickly, generating significant discourses as much as rumors are generated from prior discourse. Rumors harbor secrets, which are central to their power, making it difficult to prove or disprove them. The meanings, implications, and circulation of images in Thomas's *B®anded* series hinge on the suggestive power of rumor.

As one artist of the *30 Americans* exhibit, which "showcases works by many of the most important African American artists of the last three decades," Thomas has achieved revered status within both the academic and artistic worlds.[12] As a conceptual artist, Thomas has documented the lives of Black people and their representations, African Americans in particular, as diasporic subjects. He captures the fate of many Black people by referencing popular signs of Blackness through the medium of the "still image," material objects, and the vernacular language of advertising—an instrument marketers use that employs popular discourse to communicate information about their products. More and more, his images, the brands, Black people, and the Black bodies in discourse he portrays have appeared in public spaces: billboards and public signs display them, museums exhibit them, indoor exhibits present them, and outdoor sculptures reveal them. Thomas is emblematic of an artist who considers the discourses surrounding Black people expressed through brands and branding. His unique position as an African American also makes him a narrator of, and an actor in, the images he creates, facilitating both a critique and the perpetuation of the rumors he materializes through conceptual photos and material objects. I am struck, when considering Thomas's *B®anded* series, by his invocation of formulaic rumor and his production of critical rumor, a Black virality taking place outside of, and within, the frames of his images and material culture.

The *B®anded* series, found in his book *Pitch Blackness* and some of which was curated for the *30 Americans* exhibit, is an ideal location for theorizing Black virality. *B®anded* summons historical and contemporary representations of Blackness, such as the inherently athletic, superhumanly strong, or anonymous Black body, and creates conceptual art ready for mass consumption. Using popular material culture, images, and ideas of Blackness, which are pervasive within US culture, Thomas deploys performances of Blackness that have already gone viral and performs an artistic-cultural critique that challenges the discourses they summon. Thomas's work is also helpful for me in three specific ways: (1) it uses historically mass-produced images of Blackness, revealing early forms of Black virality; (2) it manifests how rumors materialize into visual and material forms, revealing how what is heard or read interplays with what is seen; and (3) it relays the dialogic and historical relationship between Black virality and branding—the deliberate as well as unintentional marketing of ideas through transforming Black bodies in discourse into "things."

B®anded does the cultural work of bringing attention to, questioning, and imagining the rumors and stereotypes that everyday marketing appends to Black bodies in discourse. These marketing appendages weaponize Blackness as a frame to restrict, enclose, and script further iterations of a performance, what African American literary theorist Maurice O. Wallace calls "enframing."[13] The series demands a close analysis of how Thomas brings attention to other ideas concerning the politics of marking, enframing, and scripting Black bodies in discourse. For example, instead of using the letter *r*, Thomas uses ®. By overtly using the registered trademark symbol for its alphabetical value, Thomas's subtle change begins to connect branding to trademarking, recalling the things, marks, words, or bodies that represent a specific product, business, or commodity, thus expanding the meaning of branding. He also reframes images, cutting them off at particular points or enclosing them in new containers and materializing them in new forms, thus expanding the meanings and rumors concerning the subjects of an image, which both agrees with and challenges Wallace's notion that a frame limits an image's range of meaning.[14] Last, as an African American artist, he critiques the troping of the Black body in discourse through reproducing, with "signal difference," those very tropes.[15] Indeed, Thomas disidentifies with designated roles for Blackness by deepening those roles and making them more noticeable, even grotesque, in the present day. While he is responding to the historic illegibility of the Black body in discourse—how Blackness is not easily deciphered—Thomas makes the marketing of Black bodies in discourse highly legible.

In *Camera Lucida*—a foundational text on the criticism and theorization of photography—semiotician Roland Barthes considers the photographed subject as a motionless actor.[16] In contrast to Barthes's viewpoint and in closer alignment with cultural theorist, performance studies scholar, and poet Fred Moten's challenge to the stillness of an image, I see the subject in an image as moving and making sound, as an image in motion like the discourses around its being.[17] Indeed, Barthes's idea of this "motionless made-up face beneath which we see the dead" does not describe the motion of a dead body changing form or the photograph—the object through which the image appears—as constantly changing form. Photography and the human body become parts of other beings as that body is remembered and circulated (through memory, recounting its narrative; through bacteria, causing its fermentation; and through gravity and oxygen, causing its deterioration)—alas, there is no death without birth.[18]

Songha Willis lives on palpably, affectively, and figuratively through, respectively, his deterioration, people's emotional connection to him and the circumstances that ended his life, and his being one of many representations of Black bodies in discourse. The image and photograph are thus these "things" that travel and perform with spectators and consumers and have lives of their own. Throughout this chapter, bodies in images perform, functioning as acts of performance events that survived them and as the visual and sonic staging of people, or representations of people, and their behaviors. I consider how Black people and the Black bodies in discourse framed by Thomas engage with the larger politics of Blackness that go beyond their enframing and enact Black virality. Considering Black virality in *B®anded*, therefore, emphasizes the mutations brought about by the mass-reenactment of performance events, revealing how meanings and material change as acts travel. I am interested in how Thomas intertextually distills Black virality and uses it to teach us something about the production of Black gender in a postmodern moment.

Racist for a Good Cause: From Broadsides to Bottles and Chains

Many Black voices, such as Olaudah Equiano's, Ottobah Cugoano's, and others' in the Black lobby group Sons of Africa, advocated alongside Quakers for improving slavery conditions and abolishing slavery.[19] By the late eighteenth century, the inhumanity of transatlantic slavery was so undeniable that people concerned with its existence brought grievances before Britain's Society of Friends annual Meeting for Sufferings. This kind of sharing was a part of the witnessing practices of Quakers. The slavery of the Columbian Exchange was flagrantly egregious and required immediate action, prompting the formation of a Committee on the Slave Trade in 1783. It was sometime around this meeting that the most well-known ephemera, which advocated abolishing the slave trade, was made.

Broadsides

The cover of the minutes book for the Meeting for Sufferings, as seen in figure 2, was likely sketched circa 1783–92, during the lifespan of the Committee on the Slave Trade. The identity of the sketch's creator remains a mystery. It is unclear whether the sketch inspired Josiah Wedgwood, an English abolitionist and potter, or if it was inspired by him and later created by an unidentified attendee of the meeting after 1787. If Wedgwood did not sketch it, the person who did either failed to remember or willfully excluded the words accompanying many future renderings of the image ("Am I Not a Man and a Brother?"). The omission leads me to believe that the sketch was prototypical of all ephemera that abolitionist printers and engravers followed.

FIGURE 2 LSF STC/M1 Committee on the Slave Trade 1783–1792 (cover only). © 2024 Britain Yearly Meeting of the Religious Society of Friends (Quakers).

But more importantly, it is unknown whether an artist rendered the kneeling figure from a live model who posed for the image.

The figure is a probable example of visualizing a rumor or memory about a Black body in captivity. The visualization quickly and widely circulated, effectively representing the material realities of enslaved Africans. This representation of what we might call Blackness today went viral in the late eighteenth century. Indeed, committee members eventually adopted it as the symbol of the campaign to abolish the slave trade, placed it upon many forms of ephemera and literature, and circulated it as antislavery propaganda.

As "perhaps the most reproduced symbol of the abolitionist movement," the trope of the kneeling African subject was popular.[20] The Committee on the Slave Trade reflects as much on a sculpture of a kneeling African featured in the garden of the St. Clement's Inn, which today is a residential and office space in London, with these remarks (circa 1790):

> The condition of slaves is as little understood in this country, as the duties of the masters. The statue, in St. Clement's Inn, of the kneeling slave holding the sun-dial, rendered celebrated by the sarcastical lines against the profession of the law, gives the only idea of the abject situation of one; whilst the beams of the sun, whose rays he so patiently awaits, gives the idea of the prosperity of the other.[21]

In the described whitewashed sculpture, the sundial becomes a burden, forcing the figure who holds it to kneel under its weight. The figure is burdened by time, which recalls the concept of "black patience"—a tarrying for "the nonevent of emancipation" required of Black people, which functions as an anti-Black form of waiting forced by the violence endured in the little-changing passage of time under white supremacy.[22] The abolitionist sketch, while summoning notions similar to those of other kneeling African figures occasioned by the sculpture, was different in that chained wrists visually represented the burden of the figure. Also, an unidentified artist (or a bored person at the meeting) had loosely filled in the skin's color and the hair's woolliness. Abolitionists used this image as the seal of their committee.

Wedgwood adapted the seal, either from the meeting notes cover or elsewhere, into a medallion and mass-produced it in 1787, leading to its rapid circulation among abolitionists. Importantly, Wedgwood distributed all related ephemera for free, but this did not stop illicit profitmaking through resale and duplication, especially in the United States. As president of the Pennsylvania Abolition Society, Benjamin Franklin received a large package of these ephemera from Wedgwood, which, upon further distribution, spread uncontrollably among US slavery abolitionists. This image featured on the medallion became commonplace through its distribution on covers of literature and banners and its sale on coins, hairpins, and crockery to advertise, fundraise for, and show affiliation with the British, and eventually American, abolitionist agenda.[23]

Wedgwood is the father of modern marketing (think: "buy one, get one free," direct mail, traveling salespeople, money-back guarantees). Thus, modern marketing has, as a starting point, the mass production and distribution of an imaginary enslaved African body that was "sufficient" to represent Africans' struggle and their bodies to the world. For this reason, it is appropriate for Thomas to incorporate the medallion into his *B®anded* series, serving as a reminder of its many uses. Meant to call attention to the unethical and cruel conditions that enslaved Africans were made to endure, the medallion spoke with two tongues. In one tongue, the medallion tried to upgrade the living conditions of enslaved Africans as well as abolish slavery. In the other tongue, the medallion perpetuated notions insinuating the inferiority of Black bodies in discourse and the reduction of Blackness to visual cues.

In this early iteration of the abolitionist seal, I refuse to interpret the sketch as an imagined Black "brother." Instead of using visual cues popularly associated with masculinity to overdetermine the imagined figure in the sketch, I offer the possibility that the discursive body in figure 2 is genderqueer and nonbinary. My interpretation does not suggest that gender is imaginary, but that this imagined body becomes forever appended to future Black viralities of kneeling Black bodies in discourse or Black people in everyday life. This highlights that how Blackness is understood and misunderstood must include the "Trans*-ness" of Blackness as an experience and approach.[24] This understanding maps a viral arc from an imagined Black non-binary body into the more widely and quickly circulated binary configurations of the Black body that later appeared in abolitionist propaganda as man and brother or woman and sister.

The December 1788 broadside of the lower deck of a slave ship captured in an engraving by T. Deeble (see figure 3) for the Plymouth Chapter of the

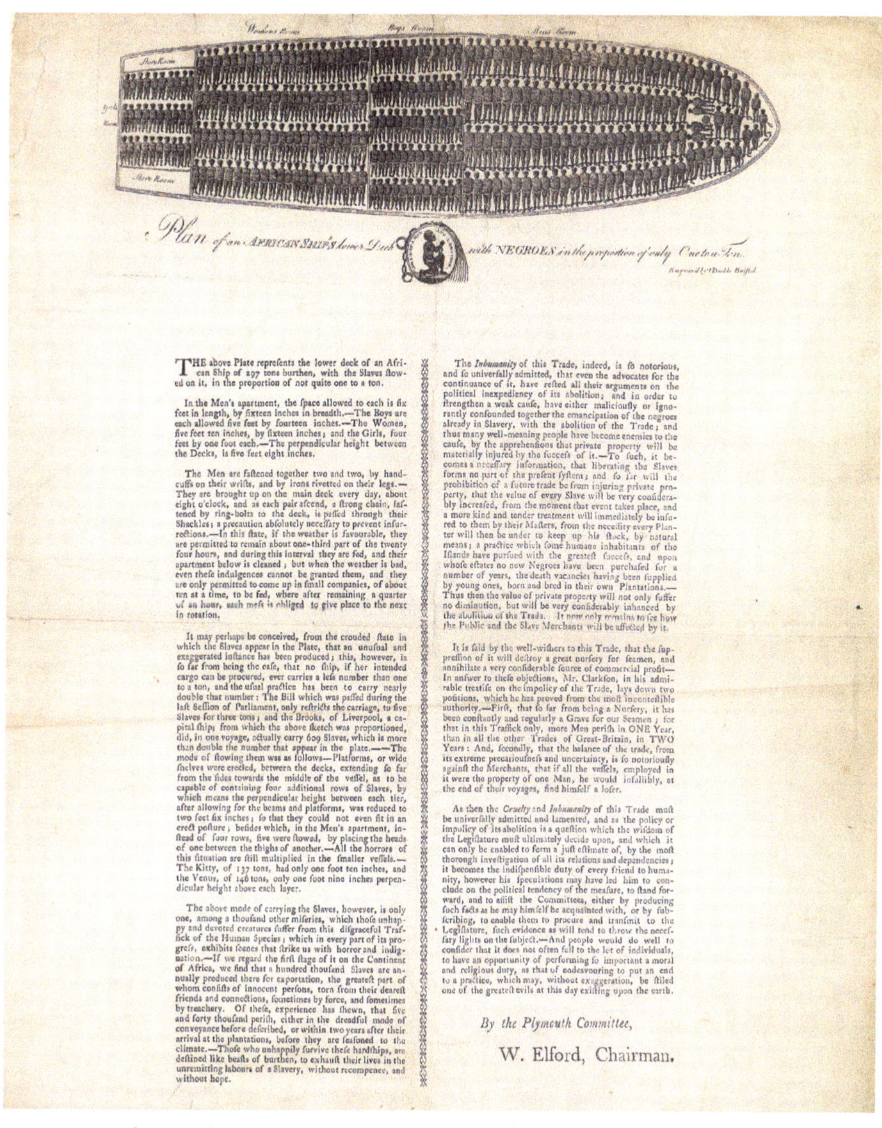

Plan of an AFRICAN SHIP'S *lower Deck with* NEGROES *in the proportion of only One to a Ton.*

THE above Plate repreſents the lower deck of an African Ship of 297 tons burthen, with the Slaves ſtowed on it, in the proportion of not quite one to a ton.

In the Men's apartment, the ſpace allowed to each is ſix feet in length, by ſixteen inches in breadth.—The Boys are each allowed five feet by fourteen inches.—The Women, five feet ten inches, by ſixteen inches; and the Girls, four feet by one foot each.—The perpendicular height between the Decks, is five feet eight inches.

The Men are faſtened together two and two, by handcuffs on their wriſts, and by irons rivetted on their legs.—They are brought up on the main deck every day, about eight o'clock, and as each pair aſcend, a ſtrong chain, faſtened by ring-bolts to the deck, is paſſed through their Shackles; a precaution abſolutely neceſſary to prevent inſurrections.—In this ſtate, if the weather is favourable, they are permitted to remain about one-third part of the twenty four hours, and during this interval they are fed, and their apartment below is cleaned; but when the weather is bad, even theſe indulgences cannot be granted them, and they are only permitted to come up in ſmall companies, of about ten at a time, to be fed, where after remaining a quarter of an hour, each meſs is obliged to give place to the next in rotation.

It may perhaps be conceived, from the crouded ſtate in which the Slaves appear in the Plate, that an unuſual and exaggerated inſtance has been produced; this, however, is ſo far from being the caſe, that no ſhip, if her intended cargo can be procured, ever carries a leſs number than one to a ton, and the uſual practice has been to carry nearly double that number: The Bill which was paſſed during the laſt Seſſion of Parliament, only reſtricts the carriage, to five Slaves for three tons; and the Brooks, of Liverpool, a capital ſhip; from which the above ſketch was proportioned, did, in one voyage, actually carry 609 Slaves, which is more than double the number that appear in the plate.——The mode of ſtowing them was as follows—Platforms, or wide ſhelves were erected, between the decks, extending ſo far from the ſides towards the middle of the veſſel, as to be capable of containing four additional rows of Slaves, by which means the perpendicular height between each tier, after allowing for the beams and platforms, was reduced to two feet ſix inches; ſo that they could not even ſit in an erect poſture; beſides which, in the Men's apartment, inſtead of four rows, five were ſtowed, by placing the heads of one between the thighs of another.—All the horrors of this ſituation are ſtill multiplied in the ſmaller veſſels.—The Kitty, of 137 tons, had only one foot ten inches, and the Venus, of 146 tons, only one foot nine inches perpendicular height above each layer.

The above mode of carrying the Slaves, however, is only one, among a thouſand other miſeries, which thoſe unhappy and devoted creatures ſuffer from this diſgraceful Traffick of the Human Species; which in every part of its progreſs, exhibits ſcenes that ſtrike us with horror and indignation.—If we regard the firſt ſtage of it on the Continent of Africa, we find that a hundred thouſand Slaves are annually produced there for exportation, the greateſt part of whom conſiſts of innocent perſons, torn from their deareſt friends and connections, ſometimes by force, and ſometimes by treachery. Of theſe, experience has ſhewn, that five and forty thouſand periſh, either in the dreadful mode of conveyance before deſcribed, or within two years after their arrival at the plantations, before they are ſeaſoned to the climate.—Thoſe who unhappily ſurvive theſe hardſhips, are deſtined like beaſts of burthen, to exhauſt their lives in the unremitting labours of a Slavery, without recompence, and without hope.

The *Inhumanity* of this Trade, indeed, is ſo notorious, and ſo univerſally admitted, that even the advocates for the continuance of it, have reſted all their arguments on the political inexpediency of its abolition; and in order to ſtrengthen a weak cauſe, have either maliciouſly or ignorantly confounded together the emancipation of the negroes already in Slavery, with the abolition of the Trade; and thus many well-meaning people have become enemies to the cauſe, by the apprehenſions that private property will be materially injured by the ſucceſs of it.—To ſuch, it becomes a neceſſary information, that liberating the Slaves forms no part of the preſent ſyſtem; and ſo far will the prohibition of a future trade be from injuring private property, that the value of every Slave will be very conſiderably increaſed, from the moment that event takes place, and a more kind and tender treatment will immediately be inſured to them by their Maſters, from the neceſſity every Planter will then be under to keep up his ſtock, by natural means; a practice which ſome humane inhabitants of the Iſlands have purſued with the greateſt ſucceſs, and upon whoſe eſtates no new Negroes have been purchaſed for a number of years, the death vacancies having been ſupplied by young ones, born and bred in their own Plantations.—Thus then the value of private property will not only ſuffer no diminution, but will be very conſiderably inhanced by the abolition of the Trade. It now only remains to ſee how the Public and the Slave Merchants will be affected by it.

It is ſaid by the well-wiſhers to this Trade, that the ſuppreſſion of it will deſtroy a great nurſery for ſeamen, and annihilate a very conſiderable ſource of commercial profit—In anſwer to theſe objections, Mr. Clarkſon, in his admirable treatiſe on the impolicy of the Trade, lays down two poſitions, which he has proved from the moſt inconteſtible authority.—Firſt, that ſo far from being a Nurſery, it has been conſtantly and regularly a Grave for our Seamen; for that in this Traffick only, more Men periſh in ONE Year, than in all the other Trades of Great-Britain, in TWO Years: And, ſecondly, that the balance of the trade, from its extreme precariouſneſs and uncertainty, is ſo notoriouſly againſt the Merchants, that if all the veſſels, employed in it were the property of one Man, he would infallibly, at the end of their voyages, find himſelf a loſer.

As then the *Cruelty* and *Inhumanity* of this Trade muſt be univerſally admitted and lamented, and as the policy or impolicy of its abolition is a queſtion which the wiſdom of the Legiſlature muſt ultimately decide upon, and which it can only be enabled to form a juſt eſtimate of, by the moſt thorough inveſtigation of all its relations and dependencies; it becomes the indiſpenſible duty of every friend to humanity, however his ſpeculations may have led him to conclude on the political tendency of the meaſure, to ſtand forward, and to aſſiſt the Committees, either by producing ſuch facts as he may himſelf be acquainted with, or by ſubſcribing, to enable them to procure and tranſmit to the Legiſlature, ſuch evidence as will tend to throw the neceſſary lights on the ſubject.—And people would do well to conſider that it does not often fall to the lot of individuals, to have an opportunity of performing ſo important a moral and religious duty, as that of endeavouring to put an end to a practice, which may, without exaggeration, be ſtiled one of the greateſt evils at this day exiſting upon the earth.

By the Plymouth Committee,

W. Elford, Chairman.

FIGURE 3 Plymouth Abolitionists, Bristol City Council Record Office, "Broadside notice issued by the Plymouth Committee, not opposing slavery but campaigning against the conditions of the slave trade and slaver ships; headed by plan of a slave-ship, lower deck packed with negroes, engraved by T. Deeble, Bristol," 1788–1789, Bristol Archives, document reference number 17562.

SEAST and famously known as the slave ship *Brooks* represents an early form of Black virality involving the mass-produced representation of enslaved African and African-diasporic people that spread rapidly and extensively. Its mass reproduction and circulation makes *Brooks* a slave ship icon. It also symbolizes the extremely cruel experiences at the heart of transatlantic slavery: forced migration, humiliation, traumatic separation, dehumanizing living conditions, loss of control over one's body and home, and restricted access to food and water.[25] A less prototypical iteration of the seal, potentially spawned in a Quaker's imagination circa 1783–92, appears forever beneath the broadside.

People around the world saw this latter image of the slave ship, which depicted 297 bodies representing enslaved Africans separated by gender and age.[26] As a result, it influenced and supported ideas about how the men, women, and children in the image were perceived by a broader public. The broadside was a distributed notice that was part of a more extensive campaign that initially did not oppose slavery but fought against the deplorable conditions that enslaved Africans endured through the slave trade.[27] Abolitionists distributed the broadside alongside other antislavery prints, posters, books, and lectures, which points to another set of bodies in discourse and politics absent from the visuals of the broadside.

Here, "outline" and "shadow" function as metaphors for things that exist (if at all) in the margins of the visible, things that are not central to a performance's frame but may indeed construct the limits of the performance.[28] In an interview, Thomas echoes this idea: "Photographs [and drawings and paintings] lie. What's going on outside of the frame of any camera—even this camera right now—can say so much about what's really going on, perhaps even more about the truth than what you see inside the box [or frame]."[29] Likewise, the absence of white Europeans in the broadside of the *Brooks* reveals a symptom of white supremacy, which makes whiteness so normalized that it is invisible and taken for granted.[30] This visual erasure, as a result, also censors the systemic involvement of people who support white supremacy through their investments in slavery.

The illustrators of the lower deck of the slave ship *Brooks* were white British. However, the white British people who structured the image and its referents are visually absent from the sketch. While Thomas Clarkson, a renowned Quaker abolitionist, is mentioned along with the Plymouth Committee and its chairperson, William Elford, who signed the broadside, art historian Cheryl Finley writes about what else the visual absence of white British bodies means: "The absence of slavers in the plan is a significant omission. What remains completely invisible as well, perhaps too great to be seen at all, are the individual investors in the slave trade, the governments that supported the industry, the African traders who supplied the slaves, and the church that condoned the trade."[31] The absent presence of the illustrators of Black confinement evokes the invisibility of systemic white supremacy, out of sight yet omnipresent—the difference being an intention to abolish said confinement.

The presence of individuals and institutions we cannot see offers insight into the subjectivity of images. The illustrators of the abolitionist seal and the *Brooks* broadside saw and imagined enslaved Africans in particular ways, framed by their distance from the cultures and their proximity to the struggles of enslaved Africans. From a distance, the repetition of bodies and almost identical appearances are stereotypical of what enslaved African bodies in discourse should look like—dark, muscular, captive, and anonymous across time and distance—all stereotypes that haunted both proslavery and antislavery campaigns in Western Europe and the United States.

Bottles

The image of the slave ship *Brooks* is used by Thomas in combination with Absolut Vodka's campaign slogan, which usually places the word *Absolut* in front of a word associated with the image.[32] The artist uses the aesthetics of this campaign that might trigger alcohol consumption to critique alcohol consumption and to imagine how we internalize the racialized gender of Blackness.

Figure 4 shows a work that Thomas calls *Absolut Power*, the word *Power* replacing the word *Vodka*. Instead of placing the usual vodka bottle above the phrase, he re-creates the bottle using the 1788 broadside image of the slave ship *Brooks* created for the SEAST at Plymouth. Thomas manipulates the broadside to fit inside the frame of a vodka bottle. He inserts an additional space in the slave ship in the bottle's neck, adding 11 enslaved Africans, bringing the total to 308 bodies. Looking more closely at the image, we see white bodies or lighter Black African bodies imposed as well. Just below the bottle's neck, Thomas positions the bodies to symbolize the liminal space between liberation from confinement and the oppression of being confined in a bottle. Yet the drink, like slavery itself, is marketed as a Black problem.

Thomas, by imposing white or lighter Black bodies in a historical context of enslaved Africans, also marks accountability and how by enslaving another, one enslaves oneself in markedly different ways. This conceptual rendering encompasses the perpetuation of colorism by lighter-skinned bodies and the privilege they experience while still being contained by the absolute power of anti-Blackness. It highlights the relationship between skin pigment and proximity to freedom. Thomas draws connections for us between the containment, consumption, and commerce of Black bodies, which also operate to hierarchize Blackness.

FIGURE 4 Hank Willis Thomas, *Absolut Power*, 2003, Inkjet print on canvas. © Hank Willis Thomas. Courtesy of the artist and Jack Shainman Gallery, New York.

Masculinity and femininity are both colonial forms of racialized gender supported through mass marketing and socialization, around which alcohol can be a facilitator. The unrestricted consumption of alcohol is a performance of masculinity, whereas its measured consumption is a performance of femininity.[33] The consumption of alcohol is one way that everyday people perform and transgress the popular imaginary of femininity as conservative and masculinity as aggressive. In a song from his critically acclaimed album *good kid, m.A.A.d. city*, rap artist Kendrick Lamar outlines some of the reasons people drink alcohol:

> Some people like the way it feels /
> Some people want to kill their sorrow /
> Some people want to fit in with the popular /
> That was my problem.[34]

Lamar's narrated drinking problem came from the peer pressure of feeling as though he needed to drink to fit in with popular people. That peer pressure is also a result of alcohol marketing, associating the drinking of it with what is fashionable. But regarding *Absolut Power*, I want to focus on Lamar's line about killing sorrow. When we consider Thomas's image, the desire to forget or kill grief or whatever ails brings salience.

The design of the image vividly portrays the diverse techniques and technologies used since the classical period to subjugate and manage bodies: biopower. If biopower depends on life, there is an effort to enhance life without making it more difficult to exert power over it. As philosopher Michel Foucault emphasizes, "It was the taking charge of life, more than the threat of death, that gave power its access even to the body."[35] Indeed, the design of the container and those who fabricated it take charge of the lives of those within it by disallowing their escape into death, which is a type of absolute power. The image's frame in figure 4 encloses the container, which also contains enslaved Africans whose heads, hands, arms, legs, and feet contain them, and white enslavers absent from the visual maintain the scheme of containment, a fractal containment.

Life's containment and incarceration can cause its fermentation, commonly known as dying or what occurs after death, leaving behind a foul odor. The power to contain and keep enslaved Africans in check is a toxic move, reaping the poison that it sows. The proximity of the word *Power* to the poison it creates is a deconstructive move suggested by Thomas's image. Thus, when consuming the drink Absolut Power, even in the desire to forget about other worries, as Lamar suggests, pain and suffering are ingested. It concerns the act of drinking for forgetting and remembering. The poison from the drink kills the memories of sorrow but not without replacing them with more sorrow from the same poison that enslaved African bodies produce in this scene of containment. An alcohol company's modern advertising techniques assembled with the slave ship *Brooks* gesture toward the legacy of historic traumas that Black people continue to experience in the present.

A viewer of this image can only imagine the blood, urine, fecal matter, sweat, semen, menses, and tears that are swallowed from the slave ship galley of this drink. Those outside the bottle enjoy greater freedom and are not subjected to the same level of confinement as those inside the bottle. However, slavery is such a corrupting force that present-day individuals still have a connection to the legacy of those inside the bottle, as survivors, beneficiaries, or both, of the slave trade. Even temperance will not insulate one from the corruptive power of this drink. Multiple bodies represent a swallow of alcohol. The substance is poisonous and can kill, another of Thomas's implicit messages: people are dying or being killed directly and indirectly from consuming this drink, which takes power and control out of their hands, placing it absolutely in another's. Black men who consume alcohol are more likely than Black men who do not to experience fatal consequences, and one can feel the urgency of Thomas's messages through his visual language.[36] The advertising and consumption of alcohol have a powerful influence on human lives, particularly Black lives.

The image is symbolic of Frederick Douglass's discussion of drinking in *Narrative,* where he describes the strategic use of alcohol during holidays on plantations to exert power over and control enslaved Africans: "When the slave asks for virtuous freedom, the cunning slaveholder, knowing his ignorance, cheats him with a dose of vicious dissipation, artfully labeled with the name of liberty."[37] Douglass then describes how enslaved Black people would feel worse after holidays because of alcohol consumption, duped by the "gift" of alcohol from the slaveholder.

The name of the substance in the figure is addictive and misleading, like the gifts of alcohol advertised by the enslaver as liberating, celebratory, and empowering—*Absolut Power*—camouflaging its toxic and disempowering content, symbolic of the slaveholder's perpetuation of power over those enslaved. Rather than highlight the power the drink has over consumers, its marketers promise them that by drinking it, they will attain power. Sometimes, however, the cure lies within the poison.

Alcohol use in Black communities is sometimes ritualized, connecting it to more profound healing and spiritual experiences and acts of rebellion.[38] On a closer look, practices such as Santeria and Obeah reveal a spiritual and religious association between alcohol and the African diaspora that does not suggest its misuse. Here, even libations take on a generative meaning. If Thomas were to pour out Absolut Power, the act would reconnect enslaved and exiled Africans—whom enslavers violently circulated between Europe, the Americas, and the Caribbean.[39] Through this ritual of remembrance, ancestors lost in bodies of water during the violence of the Columbian Exchange or disembodied on foreign lands can be reunited with the kin who recall them.

I share *Absolut Power* as an example of how Thomas reappropriates mass-produced historical artifacts to recall the memory of slavery and consider its legacy in the present. Thomas brings our attention to the shadows of the notice that becomes erased through its iconicity. Nicole Fleetwood, Black feminist scholar of visual culture, concurs: "Black iconicity serves as a site for black audiences and the nation to gather around the seeing of blackness. However, the focus on the singularity of the image effaces the complexity of black lived experience and discourses of race."[40]

While a magnified look at the broadside of *Brooks* reveals detailed bodies in various positions and appearances (with some bodies appearing white or of brighter skin complexion in Thomas's rendition), the bodies appear the same to the naked eye. This sameness further circulates the fungibility of Black bodies in discourse within viral visual cultures: the mistaken assumption that renderers can precisely contain, determine, and identify representations of Blackness by a singular mass-produced image. So even though we see Blackness, at a cursory glance or description, we see and hear its simplicity rather than its complexity. Certainly, the insertion of white or at least brighter-skinned bodies brings our attention not only to their erasure from—and likely involvement in—the advertisement but also to the uncritical ease with which we see Blackness or certain shades of Blackness. One may posit that white bodies do not belong in a representation of the *Brooks*, but who, indeed, belongs on any slave ship?

Thomas forces us to imagine the absurdity and complexity of the lived experience upon the slave ship: the sands of the ocean floor the bodies traversed over, the body of liquid upon which the boat floats, the poisonous fluids awash onboard the vessel, the drowning of Black people, the sealing away of Black people, the governing people who sealed them away, and the internalization of the discursive bodies paramount to the image as fungible (through drinking vodka from a glass bottle).

The country of origin of the Absolut Vodka brand also summons Sweden's relationship with Britain during the slave trade. Sweden was a significant supplier of the iron used to outfit ships meant to confine enslaved Africans.[41] Importantly, *Absolut Power* shows how the consumption of and commerce in Black bodies make many complicit beyond the frames of marketed media. Even if those involved do not drink alcohol, their taxes pay for the government to seal the bottles, which also signals the wide-reaching involvement of the world in the Columbian Exchange—a gesture toward complicity absent in the original broadside and the SEAST seal found beneath it. Western Europe and the United States abolished the consumption and commerce of Black noncriminals only when they had "other deep black resources to extract" and alternative means to extract them, not because of some altruistic mercy from abolitionists worldwide, particularly Abraham Lincoln.[42]

Chains

Thomas represents historical artifacts from transatlantic slavery and uses Black virality to distill, elaborate, and complicate the Black body in discourse, despite its being commonplace. The seal of the SEAST, which accompanies some versions of *Brooks* broadsides, is another iconic image of Blackness that Thomas adapts in his work (see figure 5). Transposing the seal into an alternative form ensures that viewers never forget the commodification of the Black body in discourse and the ideas around its representation that occurred through popularizing the political agenda of the abolitionists. In the central picture of a gold medallion titled *Ode to the CMB: Am I Not a Man and a Brother?*, Thomas transforms the seal into a product that could be readily sold as jewelry today: a gold medallion featuring a cubic zirconia stone. This accessory, the enslaved African coated in gold, immortalizes an image of the

FIGURE 5 Hank Willis Thomas, *Ode to the CMB: Folks Say, "Take That Chain Off Boy Ya Blindin' Me"*; *Ode to the CMB: Am I Not a Man and a Brother?*; *Ode to the CMB: Lucy Is a Slave with Diamonds*, 2006–7, 24 karat gold and cubic zirconia.

man supplicating and in chains, fingers prayerfully intertwined, pleading and surrounded by the words "AM I NOT A MAN AND A BROTHER?"—except, in this image, he is holding a cubic zirconia stone.

In relationship to the diamond, with its cultural symbolism—"A diamond is forever"—the cubic zirconia stone reminds us that just because it looks like a diamond does not mean it is a diamond. Yet, to the naked and untrained eye, a cubic zirconia stone may be sufficient for a diamond. The addition of cubic zirconia on the medallion highlights the image's "optic blackness." Cultural historian and theorist W. T. Lhamon Jr. describes optic blackness as "a function of cultural optics that do not render experiential reality for [B]lacks or any ethnic group but give, instead, a convenient, pliable mediation of the real—a fiction that seems sufficiently real for cultural symbolism."[43] Just because it looks Black does not mean it is Black. Yet the optic object may pass for Black to the naked eye or passive ear. Juxtaposing the cubic zirconia with this enslaved African implies the medallion is a fiction of Blackness, though sufficient to imitate Blackness.

Forged into a medallion by Wedgwood in 1787, the seal of the Quakers and abolitionists was used in Britain and the United States to support the campaign to abolish slavery that exploited the free labor of noncriminals.[44] Wedgwood's visual propaganda was one of many forms of pedagogy, cunning, and protest in Britain, leading to its Slavery Abolition Act of 1833. The act meant the British abolished slavery, except for in its Asian colonies, thirty years ahead of the United States (but twelve years behind Mexico). A lesser-known fact related to this success is that the government forced citizens of the United Kingdom, even those whose ancestors were enslaved Africans, to pay a tax. The tax compensated the government for the money it had used from its treasury to purchase from past slavers the freedom of enslaved Africans in many of the British colonies. Reparations to slavers totaled £20 million before today's inflation and were paid by UK taxpayers until 2015.[45] Those payments show that through abolition, slavers continued to benefit from the UK's approach to abolishing slavery, which maintained the political economy of racial capitalism in the same gesture it eliminated one of its most visible manifestations.

The fight for the "nonevent of emancipation," which abolitionists mobilized around, and the battle for the "recognition of black humanity and citizenship" were inextricably linked for Black people in the United States.[46] Unfortunately, abolitionists were unable to bring about this recognition due to the prevailing racist attitudes, and emancipation was rendered a nonevent due to anti-Black postbellum laws that perpetuated slavery through legislation, prison systems, and sharecropping. The struggles for emancipation and acknowledgment of humanity were closely tied to the recognition of Black manhood, but later struggles for racial equality, couched in the rhetoric of Black manhood, would "call for an acknowledgment of the human rights of both black men *and* women."[47] Yet Black manhood dominated the discourse accompanying the social and political struggle for civil rights, marginalizing Black women's unique obstacles.

The framework constructed by the added phrase "Am I Not a Man and a Brother?" repositioned Black men early on as the embodiment of the perils of slavery, with servitude, muscularity, and infantility as the trademark of the most prominent organization aimed at emancipation. In this way, abolitionists positioned Black men as the embodiment of the perils of slavery, linking their crisis of submission and incarceration to a history where they have always been Black, male, and at the moral mercy of others, a precarious situation.

The seal underscored the dilemma that Black feminists later articulated in response to their involvement in Black nationalism, the civil rights movement, and the Black Power movement, where sexism was an unacknowledged issue: "All the Blacks are men."[48] The caveat from the seal is "All enslaved Africans are men," but quite the contrary was the reality. As Black feminist scholar and literary critic Hortense J. Spillers writes, "It was the rule, however—not the exception—that the African female, in both indigenous African cultures and in what becomes her 'home,' performed tasks of hard physical labor—so much so that the quintessential 'slave,' is *not* a male, but a female."[49] Nonetheless, the seal's propaganda had a viral afterlife in that the framing of the oppressed (enslaved) Black male subject drew attention away from the significant treatment, traumas, and triumphs of Black women in ways that continue to resurface in everyday life today.

To make matters worse, the seal on the Wedgwood medallion was one of the most recognizable images of the Black figure.[50] Abolitionists represented the racialized genders and behaviors of enslaved Africans through one supplicating Black man. Along with eliding Black women in slavery, abolitionists' representation of the kneeling enslaved African flattened the varying ethnicities and personalities that enslaved Africans possessed across the African diaspora into one appearance and behavior to the rest of the Western world.[51]

While the medallion argues (or perhaps begs) for human equality with its rhetorical question, challenging narratives defining who was human, it also contradicts its purpose by circulating a familiar image of a submissive (yet physically powerful), dependent, and enslaved African man. It embodies simplicity. The image supported the rumors and myths in circulation that suggested the unparalleled strength of the body, infantility of the mind, and powerlessness of Africans, which served as evidence justifying their perpetual enslavement.[52] It is as cultural historian Keeanga-Yamahtta Taylor and feminist literary historian and performance theorist Saidiya Hartman write: "Within the liberal framework, even abolitionists were complicit in reinforcing conceptions of abject Blackness while decrying slavery."[53] Rebellion by Maroon communities and smaller acts of resistance to slavery by enslaved Africans in a plethora of European colonies countered these ideas of abjection, proving the medallion's suggestion of abject inferiority, docility, and powerlessness to be unequivocally inaccurate. Nonetheless, true to the two tongues of Black virality—advancing the potential for both general and critical meanings—the image and medallion did function as visual propaganda that helped mobilize support for slavery abolition (for noncriminals in the United States context) even though doing very little restoratively regarding the harm to enslaved Africans and their descendants.[54]

As American historian Eugene D. Genovese states in his critique of American historian Stanley Elkins's Sambo thesis—a popular thesis that essentialized the behavior of enslaved Africans as docile (perhaps the medallion achieved the same effect)—"Neither slavery nor slaves can be treated as pure categories, free of the contradictions, tensions, and potentialities that characterize all human experience."[55] The ways people encounter enslaved Africans must consider their complex personhoods. The central seal of the SEAST simplifies the personhood of enslaved Africans, reducing it to Black and male, strong and subservient, well spoken, and polite. Indeed, the symbol embodies the same racism found in liberal corners today, with people who help fight against the oppression of Black people unable to appreciate that Black people, too, are philanthropic and capable of giving assistance as well as receiving it, thus further infantilizing them as a group.

The initialism "CMB," in Thomas's adaptation of the seal, *Ode to the CMB: Am I Not a Man and a Brother?*, suggests a reference to the Cash Money Brothers from the 1991 film *New Jack City*. Thomas's title juxtaposes this medallion, an iconic moment in late eighteenth-century American popular culture, with scenes from an iconic moment in late twentieth-century African American popular culture. The gold chain, signifying wealth and fashion, is a significant link between the two disparate moments.

The Cash Money Brothers were a narcotics consortium that sold drugs in a fictional New York City out of a building named The Carter. After their initial success in the drug-dealing business, the leader of the CMB, Nino Brown—played by Wesley Snipes—repeatedly chants, "Am I my brother's keeper?!" Later in the movie, when he finds out that his brother Gee Money—played by Allen Payne—has been using the drugs they are selling, Brown holds a gun to his brother's head. Gee Money kneels, as pitiful, powerless, and passive as the enslaved African on the seal, and pleads, "Am I my brother's keeper?!" Responding firmly, "Yes," Nino Brown pulls the trigger.

The tragedy of the scene is that a person cannot expect another's sense of morals or empathy (even of their nuclear family or "skinfolk") to align with their own, especially when that person's life is at stake. Thomas's representation also suggests Wedgwood created the seal and abolitionists made it a commodity to appeal to the morals and fashion sense of other "free" people, inspiring them to mobilize on behalf of enslaved Africans while investing in slavery abolition. Yet *Ode to the CMB: Am I Not a Man and a Brother?* suggests an inevitable disillusionment with white liberal anti-Black racism, questioning the idea that the lives of Black people should be determined by those who benefit most from their disenfranchisement. As American literary scholar Xine Yao states, "To depend upon white feelings as the catalyst for social change reinscribes the world that enables their power."[56] This performance of a white United States and Western European brand of brotherhood and manhood illuminates how the devalued lives of Black men circulate virally as a concept, visually portraying profits, power, and entitlement as products of violence that overshadow Black lives.

To appeal to the morals and sympathy of liberal white Western Europeans and white US citizens of European descent, abolitionists depicted enslaved Africans in objects such as the seal of the SEAST as motionless, oppressed, and dreading the next moment. These visual appeals supported the limited ideas that liberal white people of Western Europe and the United States already held about enslaved Africans. Thus, even "where African American abolitionists were quite vocal within the pages of the antislavery press, [w]hite editors illustrated this rhetoric with the image of a kneeling supplicant who inquired about his or her humanity rather than asserting it as fact."[57] In contrast, wanted posters of Africans who had escaped slavery in the United States, which disrupted the popular narratives promoting their laziness, comfort, and happiness in confinement while still maintaining their anonymous fungibility, portrayed escaped men and women as carefree, fugitive, in motion, and looking forward to the future.[58] But the latter portrayal also meant that these Africans were out of control. Through juxtaposition, Thomas reminds us that the tensions between the two types of mass-produced images—the seal of the SEAST and wanted posters of escaped Black people—were based on ideas that white antislavery and proslavery Western Europeans and US citizens of European ancestry commonly held about captive and free Black people.

Unlike antislavery campaigns, proslavery propaganda, as seen in figure 6 as a manufactured, stereotyped cut "used on handbills offering rewards for runaway slaves,"[59] created alarm as Africans and their descendants who escaped slavery faced many unknowns. The motion of their bodies, free from captivity, signaled impending danger—including the fall of slave societies. Thomas bases a medallion on the infamous etching of a fictional Black person with a knapsack over their shoulder. Thus, one of the, if not the, most popular wanted posters used for recapturing enslaved Africans seeking freedom was nothing more than a mass-produced image of the same etching under various names, with unique descriptions of those who had escaped and monetary

THE

ANTI-SLAVERY RECORD.

VOL. III. No. VII. JULY, 1837. WHOLE No. 31.

This picture of a poor fugitive is from one of the stereotype cuts manufactured in this city for the southern market, and used on handbills offering rewards for runaway slaves.

THE RUNAWAY.

To escape from a powerful enemy, often requires as much courage and generalship as to conquer. One of the most celebrated military exploits on record, is the *retreat* of the ten thousand Greeks under

FIGURE 6 The American Anti-Slavery Society, *The Anti-Slavery Record*, for 1837. Vol 3. (New York: The American Anti-Slavery Society, 1838), 73. https://archive.org/details/antislaveryrecv013n001amer.

rewards attached to each, visibly supporting popular notions of the Black body in discourse as anonymous, carefree, solitary, criminalized, and on foot.[60]

American historian William L. Van Deburg reveals that, between 1830 and 1860, novelists, when choosing between ambiguous, more complex illustrations of enslaved African characters or fictional, simplified types—which we find in visual anti/proslavery campaigns—all too often chose the latter, informing discourses about the fungibility of Black bodies.[61] This informal consensus created a commonsense understanding of Black freedom, which publications had predicated on a singular archetype. Thomas's handling of this image critiques how our access to the image as an archive produces a means of knowing how enslaved Africans performed escapes, when, in fact, such escapes visually varied in style, strategy, and expression.

The titles of Thomas's imitation-Wedgwood medallions, shown in figure 5—*Ode to the CMB: Folks Say, "Take That Chain Off Boy Ya Blindin' Me"* (left) and *Ode to the CMB: Lucy Is a Slave with Diamonds* (right)—illustrate the sentiment that others, particularly proslavery white people in the United States, expressed when they saw or imagined someone else, especially Africans and their descendants, as free and even prosperous. The phrases used beyond the colon, "Folks Say, 'Take That Chain Off Boy Ya Blindin' Me'" and "Lucy Is a Slave with Diamonds," affirm the riches within and among free Africans and their descendants while reflecting the attitudes of enslavers and allies of slavery and their inability to see freedom as a possibility for or a condition embraced by Black people. American filmmaker Barry Jenkins fictionalized this occurrence in *The Underground Railroad* (2021), the television miniseries adapted from Colson Whitehead's Pulitzer Prize–winning novel of the same title. Here, a fictionalized Black community is thriving in their secluded vineyards somewhere in Indiana until white men find its location, upon which they execute as many Black people as they can.[62] Thomas's medallions of interchangeable self-liberated Africans in wanted posters go beyond fiction and summon the raids in Cass County, Michigan, where white enslavers from northern Kentucky—attracted to the fortune of the largest rural Black county in early Michigan—attempted to recapture the escapees.[63]

I decipher Thomas's focus on women in his exploration of marketed Blackness as an expansion of the limits of performances of Blackness that have virally centered men. Thomas also references the Beatles' "Lucy in the Sky with Diamonds"—a song about a woman on the move—from their 1967 album *Sgt. Pepper's Lonely Hearts Club Band.* The interplay of the song's title with wanted posters underscores the Black woman's fixity as much as it does her movement. In the song, the Beatles describe a woman who disappears when she appears.

The specter of Lucy's identity mirrors the simplified personhood of the wanted image. As Black feminist and visual culture scholar Jasmine Nichole Cobb writes, "With the popularity of racist caricature, free women of African descent appeared everywhere, were seen by everyone, but with no thorough attention given to the character of their individual appearances."[64] Yet, like the Intel advertisement in the introduction, this visual omission recedes when considering the diverse and contradictory information conveyed in the descriptions of wanted advertisements, as seen in figure 7. The detailed description from the *Louisiana Courier*, a weekly New Orleans newspaper, unsettles the generalizations of the stereotyped cut that Thomas renames Lucy. The ad reads, "Runaway from the subscriber the day before yesterday, the negress Melitte, aged about 24 years, very tall and thin walks very fast; has lost her front teeth; speaks French and English, and is well known in the city." Tracing how the image of Thomas's medallion circulated in everyday life thus moves beyond reinforcing Lucy's simplified personhood and uses the complexities of gender portrayals in popular culture to nuance perceptions of Blackness in slavery's visual culture. The fungibility of the image of "runaways" was betrayed by the density of Melitte's Blackness, which was described in the wanted ad in such detail.

Lucy does as much work as the imagined supplicating non-binary enslaved African from the cover of the minutes book at the Quaker Meeting of Sufferings. Her image enables us to think through how iconic performances of Blackness bring our attention to the noniconic, which troubles simplified Black personhood. Indeed, using the essentialism (both unplanned and strategic) of Black bodies in discourse provides evidence of the injustice and hope that Black people face and strive to redress as a group.[65] The interplay of injustice and hope allows for organization and mobilization toward

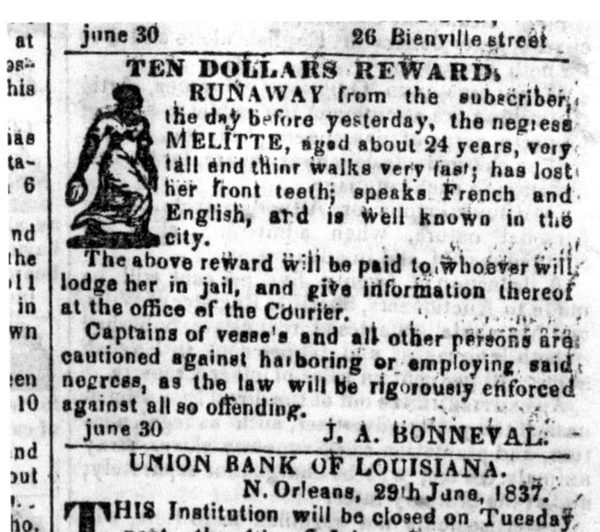
june 30 26 Bienville street

TEN DOLLARS REWARD.

RUNAWAY from the subscriber, the day before yesterday, the negress MELITTE, aged about 24 years, very tall and thinr walks very fast; has lost her front teeth; speaks French and English, and is well known in the city.

The above reward will be paid to whoever will lodge her in jail, and give information thereof at the office of the Courier.

Captains of vessels and all other persons are cautioned against harboring or employing said negress, as the law will be rigorously enforced against all so offending.

june 30 J. A. BONNEVAL.

UNION BANK OF LOUISIANA.

N. Orleans, 29th June, 1837.

THIS Institution will be closed on Tuesday next, the 4th of July

FIGURE 7 J. A. Bonneval, "Ten Dollars Reward," *Le Courrier de la Louisiane*, June 30, 1837, Louisiana State Museum, accessed May 31, 2014.

liberation for Black people, even if it means the evidence that is the focus of the organizing and mobilizing becomes iconic and a commodity.

One such commodity, the abolitionists' seal, was used to decorate bracelets, ceramics, and hairpins, to name a few objects, which, in today's terms, "went viral." We could have a sketch from a Quaker's or evangelical's imaginary that first became a seal and then a shareable and durable object. An everyday symbol of slavery became a fashion symbol that adorned people's necks, embellished people's hair, and decorated people's dishes—a case of Black virality indeed. People first circulated these commodities as things to share or consume while intending to reveal the inhumane conditions of the slave ships and the slave trade; their meaning developed alongside the abolitionists' political agenda to abolish slavery that exploited the free labor of noncriminals in the United States. The sketch, refined and printed on the broadside of the slave ship *Brooks* and impressed on other commodities, was so iconic that it came to represent the institution of slavery to the world.[66]

Thomas's work clarifies how discourses travel in Black virality, such as through rumors and mass-produced images, while also showing how artists shift discourses by manipulating what is viral or branded. In his work lies the opportunity to learn about how the mass-produced representations of Black bodies that circulated throughout the United States and Western European abolitionist culture advertised its political agendas and conveyed how cruel the institution of slavery was. What is more apparent in *B®anded*, however, is how the personhood of Black men and women was simplified and commodified, consumed, and used to advertise the political agendas of abolitionists and proslavery advocates. In processes to essentialize, erasure occurs. Beyond exchanging abolitionist and proslavery agendas, the representations exchanged pejorative notions already held in eighteenth-century discourse, mentioning Black bodies as superhumanly strong, dependent, and in need of taming. We also see how the abolitionists' politics involved agendas that sought to better the conditions of the slave trade and ships and also wanted to abolish slavery altogether. Through Black virality, abolitionists popularized the abolition of the form of slavery that exploited the free labor of noncriminals by translating rumors about Black bodies into visual and material representations, like broadsides, medallions, banners, coins, hairpins, and crockery.

Thomas shows us that this type of abolitionist and proslavery signification by corporate and marketing organizations continues today, with the advertising of brands and ideas on one end and the constant selling of understandings and misunderstandings of Black people on the other. Nike's Air Jordan is one such brand.

Branded Icons: E-rumor, Black Masculinity, and Conceptual Art

And born in New Orleans get killed for Jordans[67]
—Lil Wayne

Broken promises, steal your watch and tell you what time it is / Take your Js and tell you to kick it where a Foot Locker is[68]
—Jay Rock

Death over dishonor / They killing niggas for Js, that's death over designer[69]
—J. Cole

It's best that you stay awake than snooze / They taking lives or they taking shoes[70]
—Elzhi

Never thought project life was promised nothing but to die trife / For steppin' on the next man's Nikes[71]
—Nas

Leave you lyin' in red. . . . Now who will be the next to get they fuckin' shoes took off[72]
—Mia X

These epigraphs convey a chilling phenomenon: the loss of life or assault because of the type of shoes a person wears. I begin with words from Jay Rock (Watts, Los Angeles, California), J. Cole (Fayetteville, North Carolina), Elzhi (Detroit, Michigan), Nas (Queensbridge, Queens, New York), and Mia X (New Orleans, Louisiana) to briefly convey how widespread it is and for how long it has been that people, particularly Black people, have been assaulted or killed for marked-up, limited-quantity shoes. Additionally, I am highlighting the awareness among Black American artists of the pain, fear, and misfortune associated with having Nike Air Jordans (Js) stolen, even at the cost of one's life. They perform reflections or wisdom that is also a form of critical rumor: the viral performance of "other truth" that ties structures of power to their effects in everyday life. Artists' meditations on a common subject, namely the significance of fashion in relation to death (specifically Nikes and Js), serve as a testament to the power of marketing and branding. This influence is so systematic that it affects people in visceral ways regardless of their geographical location within the United States, and sometimes over the course of decades. Modern Black male brand ambassadors like Michael Jordan and

Colin Kaepernick have been pivotal in establishing and perpetuating Nike's past and present relevance and reliance upon tropes of racialized gender. Here, I explore the risks and rewards of tethering spectacular Black people to brands and how Hank Willis Thomas rescripts the trope in conceptual art.

Growing up in 1990s Detroit, I remember the viral trend of people suffering trauma or even death due to their fashion choices, particularly wearing Js. Though Nike's Air Jordan design was superb and culturally attractive, I avoided it along with brands like Triple F.A.T. Goose (who made a then popular goose-down bubble jacket) because my parents and I knew those brands were being stolen from people, or that people were being assaulted or even killed for them—and they simply cost too much for gym shoes. While I have always admired the design of retro Js, I would wear anything else—Nike Air Force 1s, Gary Payton Nikes, and even Joe Dumars Adidas. I both desired and feared Nike's Air Jordans. Like Songha Willis's gold chain, Js were valued more than those who wore them. These recollections align with Thomas's work, which calls attention to the absurdity of these crimes, the work that fashion advertising does to encourage or instigate them, and advertising's branding power to give certain products intrinsic social value.

Often identified as brands, clothing carries associations with specific cash values, style, and, important for this chapter, Black bodies in discourse. Clothes embody racial and gendered associations, like skin, timbre, and physique. The perception of clothes, much like that of the people who wear them, changes as they travel between contexts. The rumor concerning clothing that Thomas captures and that I discuss in this next section exists within an e-rumor as a poem.

The poem, "Clothes," was circulated in the late 1990s to early 2000s via email by an anonymous author posing as the late Maya Angelou. It became so pervasive in US cyberculture that Heather Newman, a writer for the *Detroit Free Press*, wrote an article concerning how anonymity, made possible through posting under a fake or nonidentity online, made it difficult to screen art for legitimacy after it had spread.[73] This deception anticipates technologies like generative artificial intelligence that use existing art as source material to create "original" art. The Web has made linking authors to their original work challenging.

"Clothes" gained popularity as people shared it anonymously on websites and through forwarded emails, and Angelou's alleged endorsement lent credibility to the poem's originator. In this way, even though she did not write it, Angelou functioned as an authenticating device of the information conveyed in the poem, which gave the anti-Black racism it referenced more validity. The combination of the "evidence"—subsumed by rumors about anti-Black conspiracy in the fashion industry—and Angelou's position as truthteller gave the poem enough currency for successful publication as an e-rumor. The poem reads as follows:

> This is a poem by Maya Angelou to blacks and a message for us to think about. Please read carefully and try to interpret as best as you can.
>
> CLOTHES
>
> You are in love with Tommy, Because his last name is Hilfiger, But behind closed doors, Tommy is calling you a nigger, But you could care less, Because you have been taught to dress to impress, If I ask you about your true history, You would have to look on the back of your jeans and Guess, You come up in the club wearing Versace, Clothes made by a homosexual male, So even when you say you are straight, It is very hard to tell, And for footwear, you wear Timberlands, Even under the sun, That some tree that the symbol for them, Could have been the same one your ancestors were hung from, I cannot forget Nautica, When was the last memory you have of ships, Coming to North America in shackles, Being beaten over the back with whips, And to my beautiful black queens, Whose creative womb has become barren, I am confused because your face says Nefertiti, But your sweater reads Donna Karen, When was the last time you saw Liz Claiborne, Conversing with black women, But as soon as her name is printed on a purse, To Macy's you quickly go, running,
>
> Ralph Lauren doesn't even look at black men, Unless they are driving him around town, But as soon as that slave master appears on the back of a horse, You put whatever you have picked up down,
>
> My people, reclaim your status in this world and in your life, FUBU in case you didn't know, stand for (For Us By Us), Buying black will someday suffice, Do you know who owns Timberland fashion? Well, Timberland is owned by the president of the KKK, Surprised? Don't be. Read more books black people, Always hope for the best and prepare for the worst, You may not get what you pay for, But you'll surely pay for what you get.
>
> Maya Angelou[74]

In this poem, which for all we know was a viral marketing ploy carried out by other brand competitors, everything, except for Versace's being gay (which, contrary to the poem's suggestion, determines nothing about the sexuality of someone who wears his clothing) and Timberland's racist suggestions years prior, is false.[75] Nonetheless, the poem manifests the power of Black virality. Although Angelou did not write the poem and none of the brands listed have proven to be racist in the ways described, such rumors have circulated online, playing on fears of same-sex desire and stoking those familiar with North America's concealment of racism and its legacy in material products. With people passing along "Clothes" through email forwards and blog posts, increasing its presence and currency online, the poem itself solidified as a rumor.

The following lines stand out to me—"And for footwear, you wear Timberlands, Even under the sun, That some tree that the symbol for them, Could have been the same one your ancestors were hung from"—for how they tie into a conceptual image that Thomas renders in his *B®anded* series. Even though lynching had occurred in the United States during the antebellum period, it surged postbellum. The latter violence strengthens the correlation between the fear expressed in proslavery propaganda and the anti-Black reactions to both the abolition of slavery and the Confederate casualties that resulted. What ensued was "ninety-five years of what has been called the 'Second Slavery,' namely disenfranchisement, debt peonage, Jim Crow, and legally sanctioned official and private terrorism."[76] The combination of these acts of terrorism, sentiments, and laws manifested white desire to reinforce social, political, and economic dominance over Black people throughout the United States.

If Thomas has focused on anything from the poem "Clothes," it would be a single reference: Timberland's logo depicting an "oak" tree used to lynch by hanging.[77] Shown in figure 8 is Thomas's *Jordan and Johnnie Walker in Timberland Circa 1923*, an image from his *B®anded* series. On the one hand, the work interrogates the visual portrayal of rumors and, on the other, illuminates the relationship between icons used for brands and Black and white masculinity and white femininity. It corroborates and troubles this viral narrative and offers a visual recap and revision of the more prominent cultural myth.

Paul Laurence Dunbar, named "Poet Laureate of the Negro Race" by Booker T. Washington, narrates aspects of the racially motivated mythos surrounding the oak tree in his poem "The Haunted Oak," written in 1900. Dunbar based his poem on a story he had heard from an elderly man who was formerly enslaved and lived on Howard University's grounds. The story involved the hanging of the man's nephew, accused of rape, from an oak tree.[78] The man's story of accusation and rumor is part of a long list of stories with parallel thoughts and reactions: a lynching steeped in fear of racial mixture, the notion of the lustful and criminal Black man, and the need to preserve the inherent racial purity of the white race and protect defenseless white women. While the poem performs a necessary critique of lynching, it may have unintentionally created a rumor regarding the type of tree (or device) used as a standard in the violent process.

As in the "Clothes" poem, people commonly refer to trees as the locations for lynchings by hanging. Yet history has shown that anything will suffice for lynching by hanging, from trees to lampposts—anything sturdy enough from which to hang a body by the neck.[79] Additionally, lynching is not limited to

FIGURE 8 Hank Willis Thomas, *Jordan and Johnnie Walker in Timberland Circa 1923*, 2009, 3/16" polished aluminum. © Hank Willis Thomas. Courtesy of the artist and Jack Shainman Gallery, New York.

hanging someone by the neck, as it refers to any extralegal means of killing someone through a mob or the force of a mob, often involving mutilation. In *Living with Lynching: African American Lynching Plays, Performance, and Citizenship, 1890–1930*, African American literary historian Koritha Mitchell writes of the illogic that sparked the signal increase in lynching: "After the Civil War, when blacks were no longer property, there was no financial reason not to kill them. This is when lynching . . . became ritualized murder."[80] I would add that free Black people also represented the Confederacy's defeat and the fear that the same violence that enslaved Black people had experienced would befall ex-Confederates.

Patricia Turner analyzes the anti-Black conspiracy associated with the Timberland e-rumor through a slightly different rumor. She shares a rumor from an informant about the Ku Klux Klan controlling an athletic wear company intending to exploit his African American generation. This rumor hinges on the reality of Black people's exclusion from and marginalization in the fashion industry.[81] Turner gives insight into the use of the KKK as a narrative device that signals the abuse of Black people, discussing how plausible the rumor is today when one considers the KKK's ability to elude punishment for atrocities that its members and sympathizers committed against Black churches and civil rights workers in the 1950s and 1960s.[82] The Timberland e-rumor focuses on lynching as one of these atrocities. Instead of a poem, Thomas's work uses an image that remarks upon the relationship between the commodification of the Black male athlete, figurative icons and social bodies, and the lynching "oak" tree.

Jordan, Johnnie Walker, and Timberland

In 2012, I unexpectedly encountered an animation of figure 8. I was attending a showing of Thomas's animated short in the *30 Americans* feature at the Corcoran Gallery of Art in Washington, DC. Deep into the exhibition, I entered a room where reproduced images of an identical Black man being lynched were displayed to my left, and a flatscreen behind me displayed digital images of basketball players dunking basketballs into nooses. A display in front of me showed black and white animation; I put on the display's headphones.

The animation begins with the Jumpman approaching the Morton Salt girl. Johnnie Walker appears in the background while empty quote bubbles appear above the Jumpman and the Morton Salt girl. The Jumpman and Morton Salt girl wobble off in opposite directions. The camera zooms in on Johnnie Walker and freezes for a moment, emphasizing his disbelief and surprise regarding what he has witnessed: a Black man speaking to a white girl. He then approaches a large group of Johnnie Walkers, and a quote bubble containing the image of the Jumpman and the Morton Salt girl appears above his head, conveying what he has seen. Many empty quote bubbles appear above the heads of the other Johnnie Walkers in what seems like expressions of outrage. The other Johnnie Walkers move in a sweeping motion to the left of the screen. In the next frame, the Jumpman wobbles along to the right. When the Jumpman sees the mob of Johnnie Walkers coming his way, fearful for his life, he quickly wobbles offscreen to the left. He is too late, however, and the Johnnie Walker mob carries the Jumpman toward the right of the screen. The Johnnie Walkers bring the Jumpman to an oak tree, represented by a Timberland logo with a noose hanging from one of its branches, and toss him into the noose. The animation is likely the source of the image in figure 8, or its extension.[83]

Illustrating one atrocity synonymous with white mobs in the antebellum and postbellum United States, Thomas creates an ad that illustrates how brands conflate with social identities. Whereas the titles *Folks Say, "Take That Chain Off Boy Ya Blindin' Me"* and *Lucy Is a Slave with Diamonds* evoke fear because "black success [whose visual cue is jewelry] *attracts* the mob," figure 8 shows how merely speaking with a white woman will do the same.[84] The illustration depicts a fabricated lynching, highlighting how rumors materially affect people's lives. Thomas also challenges the dangerous way we associate business brands with discursive bodies, constructing the violence through a short animation clip in which figure 8 represents the ending scene.

Figure 8 displays three objects we know as brands: a silhouetted Michael Jordan (the Jumpman) jumping with legs outstretched and holding a basketball with one hand, representing Nike Air Jordan, a basketball shoe. It also displays a white man in midstride wearing a top hat, two-tailed suit jacket, white breeches, and black boots, holding a walking cane, representing Johnnie Walker, a brand of Scotch whiskey. A massive tree silhouette resembling an oak symbolizes Timberland, a clothing and boot company. The Jumpman is hanging from a noose attached to a branch of the Timberland logo while Johnnie Walker is walking away from the crime scene. Objects, however inanimate, reflect politics that move them beyond their objecthood.

More than symbols of clothing and alcohol, the three brands in figure 8 are proxies: The Jumpman for Black American men, Johnnie Walker for white American men, and Timberland for the racist geographies that allow lynching between the two racial groups to take place. Companies racialize and gender brands in ways that simplify the personhood of the bodies they represent. A racialized gender or landscape becomes a sanitized commodity for sale and a "referent for other things, a doubled quality that centers it at the symbolic surround of consumer culture . . . [making it possible] to recall in half-consciously nostalgic tones the older image of the [B]lack body as desirable merchandise."[85] It follows that the white symbol is recalled as the purchaser or owner of said merchandise. The merchandising of bodies in discourse is a flattening process, as portrayed in figure 8 and further revealed in the roots of the silhouette.

The silhouetting of Michael Jordan physically and symbolically united his masculinity with a business brand, making it a highly desirable commodity. Silhouetting is a reductive act rooted in the practices of European geneticists to make race more accurately identifiable. US historian Matthew Pratt Guterl discusses some of the history of the silhouette, almost the epitome of simplified personhood:

> The general and historic point of the silhouette, literally, was to focus on the trace outline of the face or the body, and to force the eye to attend to the edge. And through that concentrated focus to reveal, with an authority derived from our confidence in sight, the objectively revealed inner character of the subject, stripped of emotion and adornment. . . . Racial sight turns to the silhouette to reveal the desired truth to help establish clear identifications where confusion would otherwise reign. Just as that

> trio of craniometricians had desired, the silhouette is understood to be a reliable, honest piece of evidence, easily read and understood. In a set of bumps and ridges, peaks and swells, it reveals the outline of whiteness, or blackness, or brownness, and of race more generally.[86]

The silhouette simplifies perceptions of racialized gender, referencing the outline of such while avoiding the intricacy and nuance within the outline's interior. The color of the Jumpman silhouette on Nike's Air Jordan 3 is so inhumanly red that it appears nonracial. However, the logo's physique remains recognizable as Black because of Michael Jordan's global popularity and the popular associations of Blackness with superior strength and athleticism. As much as silhouetting erases one background, it reveals another.

Not only does Thomas support the rumor that Timberland uses iconography from slavery in the United States, and not only were European geneticists foundational to the creation of the silhouette, but we also witness an illustration of how rumor can viscerally affect Black people. The material effects on Black people include how others perceive and treat them because of this perception. We cannot see the *30 Americans* animation as separate from the image in figure 8 because we reach its frame through what happens in the animation.

For instance, in the short animation, I could see how Johnnie Walker interprets the interaction that he witnesses between the Jumpman and the Morton Salt girl as an assault on the girl and whiteness itself. The combined investment in the myths of the Black brute, white women's inability to consent to any contact with Black men, the purity of the white American race, and the resulting contamination from contact with the Black American race allows Johnnie Walker to hold his misguided belief. Johnnie Walker hears something about Black men, which frames what he saw in the Jumpman–Morton Salt girl interaction.

We see an illustration of how one performance of Black masculinity, the Black brute, gets virally represented and reproduced: One Johnnie Walker tells the other Johnnie Walkers about what he "saw." The word-of-mouth transmittal of a reductive image of Black masculinity incites the Johnnie Walkers, who did not witness the Jumpman's interaction, to react unanimously with violence against something as pedestrian as greeting someone, asking for directions, or flirting. Such racism combined with the defense of white womanhood spurred the Rosewood massacre of 1923, which Thomas summons by dating the image "Circa 1923."[87]

The animation is as referential as it is prophetic, anticipating similar acts of uncritical rumor that would materially affect Black lives from Emmett Till's to Treasure Hilliard's. Using the Nike and Johnnie Walker brands' campaign slogans, "Just Do It" and "Keep Walking," which can be seen on Artnet's auction of the image and in *Pitch Blackness*, is a reminder of how words were mnemonic devices on postcards of lynchings, advertising and documenting their violence.[88] Neglect by civilians, the state, and local authorities have allowed crimes such as lynching to go unpunished, and the words serve as a reminder of this.

Mitchell's *Living With Lynching* uses lynching plays as archives to explore the identity-sustaining ways that African Americans read or acted out scripts about lynching that also challenged popular conceptions of Black men as brutes. These plays also functioned to memorialize the dead, a possibility that popular lynching photographs had all but rendered invisible. Mitchell argues photographers took lynching photographs from positions of privilege and safety during the egregious acts, which affects how we must view the photo as an objective piece of evidence.[89] Instead, we must see the latter performance as a moment a photographer captured through a subjective (read: white) perspective. If someone had requested a Black volunteer to capture photos of a lynched Black person, the resulting photographs would likely resemble those taken by James Presley Ball, a Black daguerreotypist who sensitively photographed lynching victims and memorialized them instead of further dehumanizing and objectifying them. Rather than sensationalize their death, Ball highlighted the person's life before the spectacularity of their lynching, and even during their lynching and at their funeral.[90]

The narrative that brings us to figure 8 calls attention to what else marketers sell that is inseparable from the everyday brands that we consume. For one, marketers sell the idea of the exceptionally athletic Black male who can still palm a basketball even when hanging from a noose. Near this idea is the fear of the Black male brute, such an incredibly strong criminal that even by speaking to white women, he has essentially raped them. We, as consumers of visual culture, are reminded of white men who believed in the myths so profoundly that they would rather kill such a man than allow him to transgress racial segregation or see him as a full citizen entitled to constitutional rights and responsibilities, including the presumption of innocence, the right to plead the Fifth, the right to a fair trial, the right to sue for libel and slander, the right to self-defense, and so on. Murderers left lynched Black bodies in public view both as an expression of disrespect and as a reminder that if anyone else pursued a similarly rumored path, the same would happen to them, a type of collective intimidation through highly visible violent acts.

Thus, advertisers brand and assign meaning to Black men's bodies and script them with narratives that existed before their bodies appeared in ads. The continued focus on the unparalleled strength and athleticism of Black men has connections to the entertainment of larger non-Black audiences during slavery. As Nike replays the "slaveholding emphasis" on the superior strength of Black athletes, they also resurrect its linking to the Black brute "whose strength was matched by his rapacious appetites."[91] Nike ads for Air

Jordans rely on the racial (il)logic that attributes Blackness to strength and athleticism, two attractive qualities to people shaping their Black masculinity, and notions that Nike can communicate through a gym shoe that began in controversy.

Michael Jordan unveiled the Nike Air Jordan 1 on November 17, 1984, during a game against the Philadelphia 76ers. His shoes became available to the public shortly thereafter. Once purchased, the consumer could access the featured hangtag created from a photo shoot, where Michael Jordan dunks a basketball in midflight on a Chicago street court with the city's skyline in the backdrop. His body in that photo was silhouetted, becoming the Jumpman logo. Jordan wore the red and black Air Jordan against the wishes of NBA commissioner David Stern—they defied the Chicago Bulls color scheme with their absence of white. As a result, Stern fined the Bulls $5,000 every time Jordan wore them, with Nike paying the fine. The performance suggested that the shoes gave a competitive advantage that justified the fine. This message appealed to consumers and possibly contributed to the growth of sneaker culture beyond Chuck Taylors.

On October 18, 1985, Stern banned the shoes. Nike spun this controversial dilemma on its head in a commercial called "Banned." The camera panned from Jordan's head to his Air Jordan 1s, censured from the commercial, with the narrator commenting, "Fortunately, the NBA cannot stop you from wearing them."[92] In the advertisement, Nike suggests that by wearing Air Jordans, one could also manifest themself as an outlaw—something that could appeal to a rebellious person, who, like Jordan, could be seen as superior to other players who followed the rules.

Already, Jordan was troubling the vision of the NBA with qualities—those of an athletic outlaw—that echoed popular notions of Black masculinity. Nike's photo shoot for the Jumpman logo occurred in Chicago, where Jordan rose to global fame from a local basketball court. This location further represented an unfounded natural synergy between city life, Black masculinity, and basketball, contributing to reductive ideas of Black authenticity. The Air Jordan 3 was the first gym shoe to feature the Jumpman logo, replacing the previous wings logo of the Air Jordan 1 and 2. It symbolized a merger of Black masculinity with a business brand, manifesting what media commentator and pop culture scholar Todd Boyd called "the individual-as-brand concept."[93]

The popularity of 1988's Air Jordan 3 benefited from Nike's general "Just Do It" campaign and the specific "Mars and Mike" campaign, which took Nike to new financial heights and global recognition. Between 1988 and 1990, Nike's 1988 haul of $1,203,440 in revenue garnered even higher revenue, with basketball footwear as the highest-grossing segment of their entire line of products, including different categories of footwear and apparel.[94] The 3s are the shoes that Spike Lee, in collaboration with Nike and Jordan, first advertised. Lee appeared as the immature, diarrhea-of-the-mouth Mars Blackmon from his 1986 feature-length film debut, *She's Gotta Have It*. In the film, he is a short and skinny bicycle courier and New York Knicks fan sporting a Brooklyn cycling hat, big, black-framed glasses, a Hoyas shirt, shorts, folded white crew socks, a "MARS" chain and belt, and last but not least, the Jordan 3s. In the black-and-white commercial for the Jordan 4 shoes, Blackmon, aka the athlete's hype man, asks Jordan, "What makes you the best player in the universe?" After a barrage of guesses, Blackmon says, "Money, it's gotta be the shoes," a memorialized statement that shifted a trope rumored to be intrinsic to Black bodies in discourse—superior athleticism—to the shoes. The consumption of the Jordan iconography had aligned with a desire to wield the "natural" strength and prowess of Jordan, the Jumpman, a proxy for Black men. However, with Mars's statement, this natural strength was no longer seen as coming from Jordan but from his shoes, emphasizing the Js, not the athlete, as the embodiment of his undeniable talent.

Contrasting narratives surrounded Jordan—one depicted him as an outlaw and a talented athlete, while the other linked his shoes to a series of shootings in Black communities. These shootings started in the late 1980s, coinciding with the release of expensive and highly anticipated Jordan shoes. The discussions about Jordan and the violence surrounding his shoes were unexpected. With the phenomenon reaching a national breaking point, and looking past their involvement in the proliferation of sports fashion ads directed at Black youth, the editors of *Sports Illustrated* felt they had to publish a piece concerning the trend. The title of their May 14, 1990, issue was "Your Sneakers or Your Life." Their cover featured a Black hand holding an Air Jordan 5 in one hand and a black revolver in the other. The news media also played their part, portraying these violent crimes and socializing the public to understand them as Black problems, ignoring the structural and systemic issues involving classism, racism, and sexism that had also informed the acts.[95] Like viral vectors, Black youth were depicted by writers, producers, and editors as carriers of sneaker desire in need of quarantine.

In sports columnist Rick Telander's *Sports Illustrated* article, he begins with a story about Michael Eugene Thomas, who was killed for his Air Jordan shoes on May 15, 1989. His murder showed the material dangers involved in merging corporate brands with social identities. Telander writes,

> Thomas loved Michael Jordan, as well as the shoes Jordan endorses, and he cleaned his own pair each evening. He kept the cardboard shoe box with Jordan's silhouette on it in a place of honor in his room. Inside the box was the sales ticket for the shoes. It showed he paid $115.50, the price of a product touched by deity.
>
> "We told him not to wear the shoes to school," said Michael's grandmother, Birdie Thomas. "We said somebody might like them," and he said, "Granny, before I let anyone take those shoes, they'll have to kill me."[96]

While the price tag was important to Michael Eugene Thomas, his Jordans had meaning beyond it; they represented an evolving goal, something almost unattainable yet worked toward and protected with his life. Social meaning is inextricably tied to the consumption of and violence over Js: "The brand-name goods were the trappings of inclusion. These symbols represent something meaningful for those wearing them, whether it is status through the ability to buy or status through inclusion."[97] Through the inseparable linking of the Nike Air Jordan brand with a globally recognized Black masculinity, a high markup and resale value, and limited production, Js have become synonymous with an authentic and youthful Blackness that symbolizes superior physical ability and durability, exclusive style, and class ascendance—factors and qualities that many young Black people would be both reluctant to give up and desperate to attain. Js were *ill.*

The ways that viral discourses and performances construct how the greater public understands Black people and Black bodies in discourse are slippery. Hank Willis Thomas takes the individual-as-brand concept and, using the Jumpman logo, illustrates how the individual—depicted as a brand—becomes a synecdoche for the group and thus a means of merchandising and indexing Blackness.[98] Leigh Raiford, theorist of visual culture, gender, and Black studies, coined the term "hypericonizing." It examines how the 1960s and 1970s image of American Marxist and feminist political activist, philosopher, academic, and author Angela Davis that was featured on posters, flyers, and buttons advocating for the dismissal of murder and conspiracy charges against her became commoditized and fetishized objects detached from their emotional and historical context and widely circulated in public culture.[99] These "communities of resistance" were succeeded by "communities of consumption."[100] Indeed, the public representation and merchandising of Black bodies in discourse can be the essence of racialized gender malpractice, where codes of Blackness are overdetermined and underdetermined for the sake of selling products. This background of hypericonicity and communities of resistance brings Kaepernick's uneasy relationship with Nike and abolition into greater focus.

The Last Kneeling Black Man: Colin Kaepernick's Empathy Conundrum

Murders and crimes affecting Black people over Jordan sneakers occur amid broader forms of anti-Black policing that end in public or private-turned-public murders of Black nonbinary folk, cisgender men and women, and transgender men and women at the hands of police officers or vigilantes. Only in exceptional cases are there substantial consequences for these crimes, especially for police officers, and rarely are the consequences more dire than what an average Black pedestrian would suffer for committing the equivalent crime. Kaepernick used the widely seen platform of the National Football League during the singing of the national anthem to humbly protest social injustice, police brutality, and the extrajudicial murder of Black people. He began sitting while everyone stood and eventually began kneeling on the advice of retired Army Green Beret Boyer.[101] Boyer had seen an image of Martin Luther King Jr. as he knelt during a 1965 civil rights protest and figured if Kaepernick would not stand, kneeling was the only other viable option.[102] His kneeling gesture was an attempt to appeal to or stir the pro-Black morals of a broader white populace of NFL owners, judicial officials, policymakers, and police and general spectators who watch the NFL or read the press.

Considering that the Thirteenth Amendment still allows prosecutorial officials to enslave anyone convicted of a crime, slavery is still legal in the United States amid the disproportionally Black prison population. Like abolitionist performances of Black masculinity and femininity in the past, Kaepernick performs his kneeling partially in vain. Despite the NFL's eventual rebranding of end zones to read "End Racism" and "It Takes All of Us," what we may witness is another instance of communities of resistance succeeded by communities of consumption. Indeed, anti-Black brutality, social injustice, and extrajudicial murder persist amid disproportionate arrests and surveillance of people of substantial color, and particularly Black people, in the United States.[103] Meanwhile, the NFL emerges with a moral victory without ending anything that adversely affects Black lives.

The persistence of Black people's oppression brings to the forefront the futile nature of appealing to the goodwill of those with the power and privilege to expand or extinguish one's livelihood. I say this knowing that we should not sacrifice seeking the good for waiting for a perfect solution. We need "emergent strategies"—strategies and tactics "that let us practice, in every possible way, the world we want to see."[104]

Much to the chagrin of Adidas, Nike has a rich history of generosity for athletes who are outlaws—then Michael Jordan, Bo Jackson, and Andre Agassi, and now Colin Kaepernick—that other sports industries with which Nike interplays might rather do without. The approach allows Nike to appear as a brand in touch with the intersectional awareness that Kaepernick is world renowned for and reap the rewards that come with such moral visibility. It is profitable and advantageous for Nike to appear concerned with the intersectionality of police brutality, social inequality, and extrajudicial murders against those who face anti-Black racialized gender prejudice. All the while, Nike may exploit the morals that Kaepernick represents by mentioning nothing about his particular struggles against police brutality, social inequality, and extrajudicial murders. Nike's 2018 advertisement with Kaepernick did just that.

Nike's ad features many athletes who are queer in terms of their citizenship status, racialized gender, and ability, and promotes the narrative of becoming the standard rather than the marginal to which people aspire in their respective fields. Yet Nike diminished the communities that Kaepernick represented through placement of its visual and sonic focus on the individual athlete. What I call "fractal virality" is a conceptual lens that I use to understand how today's performance is the viral afterlife of past performances at nesting scales that grow or shrink, allowing a view of the collective subtext. Thus, the Black virality of the Nike ad connects to other prior viral moments.

I illustrate fractal virality in figure 9. The lightest and largest rectangle represents the most viral performance, while the smaller, darker rectangles are what it derives from. Thus, as the largest viral performance captures our attention, like the Nike ad, it allows us to peer into the other acts within it, such as Kaepernick kneeling during games in years prior, MLK kneeling in Selma, Alabama, and the Black figure kneeling on the abolitionist seal. Therefore, the Black virality witnessed by interactors is not the only performance they see but a simultaneity of them. The opposite can happen too: a less viral performance, or the darker rectangle here, can capture our attention even though it derives from (or generates) a far more circulated performance, shown by the lighter, larger rectangle.

No matter how neutral Kaepernick seems in the commercial, he does not escape the popular imagination that he catalyzed through his stylized repetition of kneeling in protest of police brutality and social injustice toward Black people and people of substantial color during the playing of the national anthem at NFL games. When Kaepernick ends the commercial with, "Don't ask if your dreams are crazy, ask if they're crazy enough," I understand his statement to suggest that protesting police brutality and the social inequality experienced by Black people and people of substantial color and that dreaming of a world where it does not occur was considered crazy and that more craziness needed to be dreamt.[105] Yet the vagueness of his quotes, amplified by the context of Nike's advertisement, makes it easy for anyone to appropriate them for their own agenda (be it egalitarian or authoritarian). The entire ad is an open signifier and could mean whatever an audience wants it to mean. Despite Kaepernick's fractal virality and afro hairstyle that might

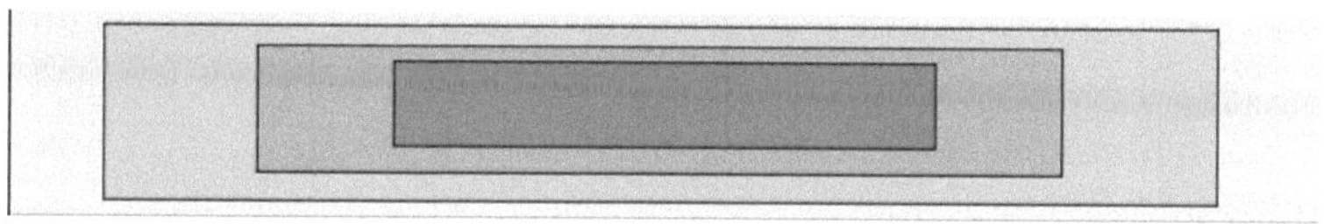

FIGURE 9 Gabriel Peoples. An illustration of fractal virality. 2023.

suggest something more rebellious and pro-Black, Nike had hypericonized him.

Neoliberalism thrives by divorcing systemic and structural oppression from politics and the economy and resting the ability to overcome said oppression on the choices of the individual. Nike performed neoliberalism through its persuasive hypericonizing of Kaepernick. Their tactic does not mean that Kaepernick had no agency in doing the commercial, but we understand how his agency was limited for this level of lukewarm branding to occur when he had been blackballed from his football career. Despite the overall message, one of the popular responses to Kaepernick's neoliberal encouragement, particularly by white men, was to burn Nikes and vow never to repurchase them. Yet, rather than inspiring a white supremacist boycott of Nike, the added attention the ad brought only led to record Nike sales for that financial quarter.

Meanwhile, the brutal police murders and anti-Black social inequalities continued. Once again, a brand sells far more than a material product to its audience. It relies on the audience's epistemologies of queerness, ability, and racialized gender to trigger affective responses whose labor correlates with decreases or, in this case, increases in capital through marketing those ways of knowing. This leaves us to rely on the goodwill of corporations as much as the morality of allies when what we need are accomplices.

I titled this section "The Last Kneeling Black Man" while reflecting on the 2022 Super Bowl. During the event, Eminem took a knee on stage, much like Kaepernick had done numerous times. However, unlike Kaepernick, Eminem did not face the same risks of being blackballed in his main career for years. In fact, he stood to gain the rewards of being embraced by rappers, activists, and progressive politicians. (I had overlooked the kneel until after the live broadcast because Dr. Dre playing piano in black Nike Air Force 1s took all my attention.) The viral moment reminds me that once some people recognize Black movements, the widespread recognition signals that said movements have moved on to other popular forms, their viral afterlives. For instance, on January 12, 2017, Paul Ryan's dabbing gesture marked the possible end of the dabbing trend, if it had not already reached its conclusion.[106]

The legacy of the kneeling Black man in antebellum and modern America is that both iterations have failed to abolish systems of anti-Blackness, as in police brutality and continued slavery through the US prison-industrial complex and its sanctioned treatment of convicted criminals as enslaved people. Yet, in other sometimes noniconic ways, these performances have at least contributed to the defanging of anti-Black geographies, for example, by making it illegal and morally reprehensible to trade in enslaved people or otherwise own them as well as popularly encouraging the defunding of the police.

• • •

Artists productively and reductively render meaning into visual "things," illuminating, unveiling, and engaging with more significant systemic issues and concerns. By Thomas's use of the traces of the reductive ways that Black bodies in discourse are or have been seen in visual culture, I insist he reconstructs their complexity, if not their wholeness. Notably, some of those reductive ways of seeing persist and haunt us in the present. Thomas's conceptual images and material objects haunt us as they contact the painful, difficult, and unsettling, which we must overcome.[107] We must acknowledge and reckon with these hauntings that saturate the structural and systemic in addition to confronting the ghosts that haunt individuals.

Inclusive of and beyond haunting, ideas of the Black body in discourse have attained worldwide recognizability in history, literature, art, film, and cultural and political discourse as lasting referents, foundations, and "scriptive things."[108] Such referents are uncontrollable, as they seem to unfold and travel of their own volition, with the subject unable to command the narrative (death of the author, indeed). Yet Hank Willis Thomas—like Spike Lee in the following chapter—refuses to allow how the Black body in discourse is popularly and fictionally used as a conduit for criminality, a locus of deep-seated fears, and as noise to be the last word. Instead, the artist conveys that the power of rescripting that which is otherwise iconic and fixed is far more generative.

CHAPTER 2

I Can't Live without My Radio

Black Viralities of Masculinity and Sound in *Do the Right Thing*

> "I tried to play my music, they say my music's too loud."
> —Isley Brothers

Spike Lee's *Do the Right Thing* debuted in US theaters on July 21, 1989.[1] In this chapter, I explore sound as a conduit of and trigger for the expression of desire and how one of the film's protagonists, Radio Raheem (played by the late Bill Nunn), manifests this in ways that implicate his and others' racialized gender and sexuality. Radio Raheem is a tall Black man who rarely goes anywhere without his boom box and lives so large that, according to a minor character named Cee (played by Martin Lawrence), "He even walks in stereo." I consider the implications of Radio Raheem's use of the boom box and his murder as a viral performance of Black masculinity and discursive subduing of the Black body.

I employ the central options of the analog tape player buttons on Radio Raheem's boom box to structure this chapter: "REWIND" delves into the material culture, history, and theory that informs the chapter. "PLAY" is a performance analysis of unfolding moments from the film proximal to Radio Raheem. "STOP" considers the implications of sound in his death and in how Radio Raheem desired others and was desired by others. The last section, "FAST FORWARD," surveys Radio Raheem's viral afterlife in popular culture and everyday life—or the legacy of the sound, breath, and life of discursive bodies and material lives beyond the peaks of their rapid popularity. Through this framing, I analyze a virtual moment that mirrors a material way that Black masculinity in the film performs and merges with a conduit for sound, namely the boom box: a historical point that played a role in transporting Black sound, and a Black imagination, across the country and perhaps even the world.

REWIND: A Material Culture of the Boom Box

Rewinding is a mechanism that allows one to reverse something on a forward path. After an analog tape ends, in the absence of an auto-reverse mechanism, REWIND is the button that, once pushed, allows its user to begin at an earlier point. It is a means for traveling back to a moment, often to recover something to enjoy or better understand in the present.

• • •

Radio programming has transformed since the second and third decades of the twentieth century, transitioning from a community-oriented news and entertainment source to a more syndicated and nationally focused source. I am deeply concerned with the trend that destroyed connections between radio stations and local communities that had access to and controlled them, which popular music scholar Charles Fairchild calls "deterritorializing the radio."[2] The deterritorialization of the radio is a valuable concept for determining how the radio's use by everyday people has changed between the radio boom earlier in the twentieth century and the late 1980s, understanding the market forces that drove broadcasting regulation and deregulation, and examining how this affected Black men's ability to express themselves through the medium of radio. The following brief material culture analysis of the radio will provide an understanding of radio's legacy in Radio Raheem's dynamic use of the boom box.

On April 10, 1912, the British passenger ship *Carpathia* responded to the distress calls of the *Titanic*. The monumental disaster of the *Titanic* colliding with an iceberg and losing over three-quarters of its passengers spawned many regulations, including those of wireless communications.[3] To prevent another such disaster, the federal government mandated radio stations, from the Radio Act of 1912 until the Radio Act of 1927, to obtain federal licenses to broadcast. The US Department of Commerce controlled the entire process. One guideline that applied to possessing a license was a directive stating that, for the public good, the licensee would prioritize any distress signal over business, news, or entertainment programming. Forewarning people of impending danger so that authorities could take measures to ensure that everyone involved was safe was the beginning of radio's widespread use.

The only caveat involving the government "regulation" of broadcasting was that the then secretary of commerce, Herbert Hoover, could not deny broadcasting licenses to any person or corporation. He could only choose the wavelength that would cause the least interference and penalize violators of federal regulations. That is, he could limit violators of regulations but not people seeking licenses.[4] The unlimited distribution of broadcasting licenses over limited frequencies created too many stations vying for the same signals. Radio congestion ensued.

Responding to dissatisfaction from audiences and broadcasters alike, the House of Representatives enacted the Radio Act of 1927, limiting the number of issued licenses the government handled. "Public interest, convenience, or necessity" were the three tenets of being granted a license by the licensing authority.[5] When the Federal Communications Commission (FCC) was created in 1934, it restricted the number of stations a single corporate or individual entity could own, abolishing the Radio Act of 1927. I will return to licensing restrictions after briefly examining how everyday people used early radio following the establishment of the FCC.

In the late 1920s, the home radio and the fireplace were central social areas for entertainment and vied for families' attention across the United States. People spent as much time fiddling with their radios as they poked at fireplace logs. They did this to achieve the maximum levels of relaxation and audiovisual entertainment.[6] The downsizing of the radio helped it become a typical console in the American home; it became more ergonomic, often disguised as a desk, a lampstand, or a small table, blending technology with multipurpose use.[7] Integrating radios into standard furniture veiled "the machine," then considered an intrusion in the home.[8] "[When] radios began to appear in American homes, music no longer was confined to one or two rooms. Victorian attempts at room specialization were gradually overridden by efforts to draw the family together and to simplify room arrangements and decor."[9] The radio played an essential part in disintegrating the distinction between private-use and public-use rooms within the American home, which Victorian designs had separated according to notions of the home as a sacred space.[10] The collapse of public and private space offered an early glimpse into how the function of the radio evolved as it became more mobile.

For many Black Americans, the public and the private were already inseparable because homes had been unavailable or unaffordable due to racial bias in home lending, or they were vulnerable to egregious intrusions, such as raids fueled by racism forged in slavery and the second slavery experienced in the postbellum United States during the long Jim Crow era.[11] Victorian notions of the home as a sacred space had to be rethought by Black Americans as they sought to create sacred spaces in public and private locations, sometimes carved out by music, prayer, and ritual.

The early uses of the radio in Chicago in the 1920s largely involved the working class.[12] Retailers and radio journalists knew that workers-turned-hobbyists constructed their radios or antennas,[13] laboring to get the maximum signal distance from their homemade devices. Listening to the radio was an active communal event whereby families listened together in 85 percent of American homes.[14] Nevertheless, second-generation youngsters frequently visited "basement clubs," "social clubs," or "athletic clubs" to elude parental supervision and socialize against the backdrop of a blaring radio.[15] Instead of bringing the family together, the radio sometimes separated it in synergy with a generational divide.

Ethnic groups in Chicago understood the radio as a means to keep their people in touch with native culture. Until broadcast deregulation, the radio thrived in long-standing relationships with local communities. Following the Communications Act of 1934, licensing authorities ensured that small, local, noncommercial radio stations dominated the airwaves because only one person or entity could own a station providing the same service in the same community, with a limit of five stations per owner—the 5/5/5 rule.

The deterritorialization of the radio turned regulated broadcasting into free-market broadcasting. Free-market broadcasting embodies a laissez-faire approach that involves less strict government regulation of broadcasting stations' corporate ownership and prioritizes the broadcasting industry's economic power. Without considering how radio stations inform their audience's choices, we assume that public preference can be measured by audience listenership or viewership.[16] The 5/5/5 rule developed into the 7/7/7 rule over twenty years, gradually increasing corporate ownership of AM, FM, and television stations from 1953 to 1974. Within ten years, the limit was almost doubled with the 12/12/12 rule in 1985. Around seven years later, in 1992, it was more than doubled with the 30/30/30 rule. By 1996, all limits were practically nonexistent via the Telecommunications Act.[17] Companies secured increasing numbers of stations, with Clear Channel going from "owning forty stations in 1996 to 1,240 in 2003."[18]

Coinciding with the rise of radio deregulation between 1975 and 1996 was the creation and wide distribution of the boom box, which tapered off in the mid-1980s. Just as the radio played a pivotal role in collapsing public and private space within the home, the boom box, or what Radio Raheem and many others of that era referred to as their "box," would significantly contribute to collapsing public and private space outside of the home due to its portability. The boom box became what Andre Torres—editor of music magazine *Wax Poetics*—called "the sonic campfire," an outdoor creation of a space where people could congregate and exchange stories and feelings through the body and sound.[19]

Unlike the transistor radio, which was portable, had smaller speakers, and could receive only AM/FM frequencies, the boom box additionally featured a tape deck—allowing its users to choose the audio content they broadcast, with superior sound quality and amplification. In the face of monopolistic corporate ownership and control of radio stations and what they could broadcast, the boom box was a device that allowed anyone to broadcast anything. While an individual's boom box was not as far-reaching a medium as the radio, anyone with a boom box could play anything recorded on a tape cassette as loudly as their speakers would permit and as far as their sound would carry.

Truly, the allure of the boom box with a tape deck stemmed from the power to control the music one enjoyed.

In the mid-to-late 1970s, hip-hop music gained popularity because people could play on their boom boxes what radio DJs and personalities (even Black ones) refused to broadcast on commercial radio. People dubbed cassettes and shared music from the DJs who played hip-hop and funk music with extended bridges or breaks to which people could dance.[20] As figure 10 featuring LL Cool J and DJ Cut Creator shows, in 1985, the *Hip Hop Hit List* advertised itself as "the first chart ever that caters only to rap music." If the *Hip Hop Hit List* was the first rap music chart (at least in the Bronx), Los Angeles's KDAY 1580 was the first hip-hop–exclusive radio station, emerging as such in the fall of 1983. WRKS and Kool DJ Red Alert played hip-hop regularly with a mixture of R & B via the 98.7 KISS FM KISS Master Mix Party.[21] And we cannot ignore the weekly radio show Zulu Beats on WHBI out of Newark, begun by DJ Afrika Islam in as early as December 1982.[22] Still, the shortage of hip-hop airplay compared with the airplay of disco and R & B grew the importance of the boom box in early hip-hop music.

Boom box production began in Japan, where living spaces were relatively smaller than in most US cities, making it difficult to accommodate the larger component systems prevalent in US homes.[23] Initially used to facilitate the next generation's living in less spacious urban dwellings, the boom box's

FIGURE 10 *The Hip Hop Hit List*, June 10, 1985, folder 44–45, Cornell Hip Hop Collection, Ithaca, New York.

unexpected popularity delivered a new frontier of audio technology in the home.[24] When boom boxes appeared in the United States in the mid-1970s, they became popular with African American and Latine youth in a different way—with kids often hoisting them onto their shoulders or holding them by their handles as they walked down the street blasting music.[25] The transportability of the boom box and its advanced tape deck made it easy to share and create music in ways that had never been possible—and to blare it as close to pedestrians as possible. The Stop and Rewind buttons were crucial controls, allowing users to replay and broadcast their tapes at will anywhere and anytime. Being able to untether entertainment from the stronghold of radio programming, share cassette tape recordings (made using the crucial Record button), and loudly play music and speeches outdoors all contributed to the boom box's viral use.

The sharing and playing of cassette tapes via boom box reached such a widespread level that it led to the creation of a comic called *Rappin' Max Robot* by New York artist and designer Eric Orr. The comic showcased a robot that rarely appeared without a boom box, whether it belonged to him or someone else. Figure 11 shows Rappin' Max Robot and the issue of dubbed cassette tapes being so illicit that a person who received one might not know

FIGURE 11 "The Big Beat" Max Robot Special Edition Zine First Printing Offset, 1986. Cornell Hip Hop Collection, Ithaca, New York.

which artists it featured. Dubbing activity via cassette tapes continued into the mid-1990s. According to Brooklyn rapper Busta Rhymes (so named by Public Enemy's Chuck D), even the late Notorious B.I.G. (Biggie) dubbed his first 1994 album, *Ready to Die*. Busta remembers Biggie freely sharing the album on cassette tapes while it played from a boom box at Biggie's Brooklyn residence. Busta recounts an occasion when Biggie told him, "If everybody playin' your shit, it makes niggas perceive that you got the hottest shit in the street, so the nigga that's not playing it looks like a dickhead." Biggie's phallic observation of what was happening in the immense line outside of his residence recognizes a kind of Black virality: "Dudes dubbing the tape for other dudes. Ha! So they were doing Big's work for him. It went viral in the street."[26]

Between the mid-1970s and mid-1980s, the production of heavier, bigger, and louder boom boxes increased alongside advancements in audio creativity and consumer demand.[27] Indeed, the mass production of thousands of models of boom boxes is inextricable from their viral stylized use by Black and Brown youth. Mechanical production interplayed with sociocultural performance, informing each other about how to exist symbiotically. Shoulder- and hand-carrying youth who blasted music from the boxes into their dwellings and along the streets were likely influencers of the demand to supply bigger and louder boom boxes. Not unlike what had occurred because of the wide availability of radios early on that produced a crowding of the airwaves, situations emerged in which, as the actor Rosie Perez describes it, the widespread use of the boom box was a nuisance and, when played in confined areas, would cause "conflicting music," with too many people playing different music all at once.[28]

The title of this chapter is a gesture toward LL Cool J's (Ladies Love Cool James) 1985 hit "I Can't Live without My Radio" from his debut album *Radio*, which featured a massive portable tape deck radio—a boom box—on its cover: the JVC RC-M90 (see figure 12). The album title suggests the pleasures and dangers involved in the entanglement of mobile conduits of boisterous sound and Black men's bodies, particularly from the mid-1970s to the mid-1980s.

DJ and radio host Stretch Armstrong notes that the cover of the record was "the pinnacle of the boom box."[29] The album established Def Jam as a record label, and the boom box helped popularize hip-hop music, which, as noted previously, radio hosts rarely played.[30] Thus, both the boom box and LL Cool J's debut album are foundational when one considers the commercial success of hip-hop music. The rapper's song clarifies the function of the boom box, which, in this chapter, I treat as a weapon and instrument of social interaction, autonomy, and entertainment. In some regards, the boom box *symbolized* Blackness—dismissed as visually and sonically noisy yet so overwhelmingly audible that one cannot help but feel it. The boom box was

FIGURE 12 LL Cool J, Radio (New York: Def Jam Recordings, 1985).

a visual and sonic attachment to an embodiment of the self that was both a blessing and a curse.

In "I Can't Live without My Radio," Cool J expresses the inseparable connection between his radio and his daily personal and cultural life and the risks associated with using it as a broadcasting tool in 1985. He raps, "Walkin' down the street, to the hardcore beat / While my JVC vibrates the concrete. . . . 'Cause I play every day, even on the subway / I woulda got a summons but I ran away. . . . See people can't stop me, neither can the police / I'm a musical maniac to say the least."[31] Through these lyrics, one can imagine the feeling of playing a boom box out loud in public spaces, the JVC vibrating the concrete. People also experienced it as an integral part of their daily routine, "[pressing] play every day." Notably, the song acknowledges that by 1985, lawmakers had criminalized the pedestrian use of the boom box—the rapper would have received a summons, but he ran away. The performance enacted by playing a boom box in public was vital and enjoyable, as Cool J risked police encounters to do so. Those who played music loudly from a boom box in the mid-1980s were maniacal because they chose to play despite the threat of the criminalizing environment, making them "musical maniac[s] to say the least."[32] The boom box's criminalization and the already criminalized bodies that wielded it for its viral and pleasurable usage outdoors were one.

Music producer and soundtrack supervisor George Drakoulias recalls a moment that touched on the pleasures of playing a boom box in public.

Drakoulias was working with Def Jam and picked up a case of product—tapes—for the *Radio* album. Seeing two kids carrying a radio half their size, Drakoulias stopped them and insisted they take a cassette; they cautiously accepted the tape and loaded it into their radio, the first track to play being "Rock the Bells." Then one kid took the entire radio they had been carrying between them and, with all his strength, hoisted it onto his shoulder and walked away, smiling, no longer acknowledging his companion. From that moment on, George knew the album would be great.[33] Indeed, many others, such as Perez, Lisa Lisa, and DJ Eclipse, reported experiencing similar pleasure from being able to blast a song they liked, whether in a small park, on the block, or in an apartment or house—and it did not have to be hip-hop. This mobile and pedestrian use of the boom box was its apex as a mode of being.

As with any pinnacle, however, a nadir is soon to follow. Despite the pleasure that the boom box generated, the criminalization of boom box playing in public spaces essentially eliminated it from public practice, and thus its production, by the late 1980s. The suppression of the pedestrian use and availability of the boom box was a reality that most would not recognize when viewing *Do the Right Thing*, in which the figure of Radio Raheem was essential to Lee's fictional Bed-Stuy neighborhood (that is, Bedford-Stuyvesant in Brooklyn).

But it was the increasing pedestrian use of the boom box that led to its demise. Considering the grievances expressed by residents throughout several northeastern states spanning from Massachusetts to New Jersey, city officials began to adopt and enforce stricter measures in the mid-1980s against individuals who played loud music in public. These punishments ranged from \$50–\$1,000 fines, impounded radios, and imprisonment. We can also imagine how these punishments unfairly targeted youth of substantial color, the kids who had begun using the boom box in a way that "wasn't meant for you to walk down the street with."[34]

Advancements in mobile technology such as the Sony Walkman and Discman, the plastic and quieter boom box, portable media players, and smartphones—all devices that maintain music's mobility yet privatize its sound—helped phase out the boom box. Without assuming that privatized sound represented an improvement over public sound, one artist, Tyler Gibney, credited such mobile music technology with creating listeners who "advertis[e] their unavailability for social interaction."[35] Other ways of broadcasting music, messages, and news had to be sought by Black and Brown people that affirmed and asserted what Black studies scholar and performance art theorist Anita Gonzalez refers to as our "Black sensibilities—stylized ways of being in relation to each other and our environments."[36]

I continue to explore Black sensibilities in relationship to the fiction of Radio Raheem that brings the meaning of the boom box to life in a way that the form and function of the object itself cannot. As historical archaeologist Paul Mullins states in *Race and Affluence: An Archaeology of African America and Consumer Culture*, "The physical attributes of an object, systemic function, and intended use loosely circumscribe the symbolic possibilities of that object, but for the most part form and function do not impose particularly profound limitations on meaning."[37] The fiction of Radio Raheem offers a lens into the meaning of his box, not only what it meant to him but also what it meant to his community. The character brings to a climax the tensions between Black men and the radio/boom box as an essential medium of being, communication, and expression in popular culture. His boom box serves the function of early regulated radio: forewarning people of impending danger so that authorities could take measures to ensure everyone involved was safe. His anthem, "Fight the Power," was an emergency broadcast not prioritized in ordinary states of emergency.

REWIND: The Performativity of Radio Raheem

The Radio Raheem character recalls haunting indexed representations of and responses to some Black men as a Giant Negro.[38] "Giant Negro" is a term that the *New York Times*, among other respected publications, used to trope Black men who stood between six and seven feet tall in fear-inducing or, rarely, awe-inspiring descriptions. The term first appeared in a *Times* headline from the September 24, 1900, issue: "Giant Negro Attacks Police: Believed He Was Called to Heaven and Cut Nephew's Throat to Carry Him Along—Officers Killed Him." This story follows a New Orleans man named Edward Gurley. His nephew alleged Gurley cut his throat after telling him, "Get out of bed, I have to die and I'll take you with me." The article describes Gurley as "crazy," of "gigantic build," and a "prisoner" (even though he was not a convicted criminal).[39] Ultimately, two policemen killed Gurley even though he was unarmed.[40] The initial criteria laid the groundwork for future uses of the term to describe Black men as deviants, dangerous, and outlaws to be contained or, more seldomly, put on a pedestal (like boxer Jack Johnson and entertainer Harry Belafonte). The *New York Times*'s use of the term peaked between 1922 and 1929 and had trailed off by the mid-twentieth century.

The early twentieth century featured yellow journalism that relied on its audience's appetite for a combination of sensational Black masculinity and gendered racism to sell newspapers, yet this is not the only backdrop that haunts Radio Raheem as a "dangerous" Black figure. Police murders of Black people in the 1980s inspired the creation of *Do the Right Thing*. Michael Stewart represents one such case—a young Black man arrested for graffitiing, or tagging, a train and beaten while in police custody, eventually leading to his death on September 15, 1983.[41] Another source of inspiration is Eleanor Bumpurs, a sixty-six-year-old Black woman who allegedly faced eviction and was shot twice and killed by a policeman on October 29, 1984, at the Bronx's Sedgwick Houses.[42] Racist vigilante mobs who terrorized unarmed Black men like Michael Griffith—who was beaten by white teens outside a pizzeria in Howard Beach, Queens, on December 20, 1986—also inspired the film. The teens taunted him with racial slurs, and the son of a police officer hit him with a car while he was trying to escape his assailants.[43] At the same time, Edward Koch (New York City mayor from 1978 to 1989) created radio-free zones in 1985 throughout Brooklyn, Queens, the Bronx, and Staten Island, where communities were targeted by armed police and vigilante violence in the policing of sound.[44]

The Black American postslavery subjects mentioned previously inhabit horrors, desires, and conditions recirculated from allegedly bygone eras that have become so normalized they are unacknowledged as monstrous. African American literary and cultural theorist Christina Sharpe coined the term "monstrous intimacies" to describe such familiar anti-Black incidents of violence and the tolerance of them.[45] The same monstrous intimacies that inspired its creation garnered both acclaim and fear for *Do the Right Thing* in 1989. Film critic Roger Ebert heralded the film for coming "closer to reflecting the current state of race relations in America than any other movie of our time."[46] Other critics, such as Joe Klein, expressed panic that the message Black audiences took from the film would "increase racial tensions in the city."[47] Scholars like Wahneema Lubiano cautioned against exalting a Spike Lee production at the cost of "other African-American filmic possibilities," particularly when Lee's efforts were lauded by Klein and Ebert as "the real thing."[48] Yet fiction is often based on its converse—reality.

Do the Right Thing channels a 1989 summer day in the life of a fictional Bed-Stuy block. In Lee's journal of *Do the Right Thing*, a noteworthy incident occurred on the actual set, where homeowners on the block held a meeting with the location manager, Brent Owens. They discussed plans for improvements on several homes, but what pleased homeowners most was shutting down a crack house described as being littered with vials, used condoms, dead animals, and feces. The film crew had to repair the block to capture it on film in a pristine state, using the expected Black virality of the film to achieve a fleeting sense of liberation from the material world beyond the film.[49]

The fictional neighborhood is home to many people, including children, retirees, activists, and business owners. Most of its residents are Black and Brown. Others are white. While the police appear white and patrol the neighborhood, Lee does not reveal where they live. One evening, following a disagreement over the playing of funk/hip-hop music in a pizzeria, all these lives clash intensely, and a police officer monstrously kills Radio Raheem.

I use this moment in Black popular culture to argue that intimate feelings, desires, and touch between humans, no matter how monstrous, are inextricable from imaginings of race evoked by sound, what I call the "racialized erotics of sound." The audience and characters in *Do the Right Thing* hear, feel, and imagine Radio Raheem's social desires through his Black hip-hop/funk sound, which bears material consequences for his life as a Black male subject.

Radio Raheem is not simply a creation of Lee for *Do the Right Thing*. Besides being inspired by the Giant Negroes of the early twentieth century and the Black people who were murdered in the 1980s by police or vigilantes, Radio Raheem originated as a real person from Lee's childhood. Everyone in the Cobble Hill neighborhood of Brooklyn referred to this man as Joe Radio. According to Lee, in the mid-1960s, Joe Radio would stand on the corner with a small transistor radio effectively attached to his shoulder, playing WMCA Good Guys or WABC featuring Cousin Brucie day and night.[50] Importantly, understanding Lee's recollection of Joe Radio and how he was never without his transistor radio undergirds the inextricability of the radio from expressions of Black male masculinity and identity in one Black community. With everyone calling him Joe Radio, he was, in effect, identified with his transistor radio. Decades later, Lee's memory of the man emerged in the character Radio Raheem.

The first time that a Raheem with a radio appeared in popular culture was almost a decade earlier on *Saturday Night Live* in the fall of 1980.[51] On the *SNL* comedy sketch "Weekend Update," Eddie Murphy is a Black basketball player named Raheem Abdul Muhammed (figure 13). In the sketch, cast member Joe Piscopo interviews Raheem about a fictional scenario in which a judge in Cleveland used a racial quota system and ruled that all Cleveland basketball teams must have a minimum of two white players. The sketch is a sarcastic gloss on the notion that basketball is a Black sport, so Black (and "Black supremacist") that it engages in systemic discrimination against white players.

Reality, however, is as strange as fiction. In real life, Cleveland judge Frank Battisti had suggested that principals and coaches make efforts at recruiting white students to predominantly Black teams (as though systemic segregation efforts were keeping white players at bay), and vice versa. This was favorable to instituting what he called "debilitating quotas" on the Cleveland school district, which was 65 percent Black.[52]

In the *SNL* parody of this scenario, a judge has proposed a racial quota to resolve basketball's alleged racial bias. Raheem, the interviewee, wears an afro and a black and yellow varsity jacket. Piscopo asks him, "What's the story, Raheem?" Poking fun at the stereotype of an unintelligent Black athlete, Raheem begins, "I been a junior at Cleveland High going on seven years now." He continues in a somewhat critical rant about racial appropriation, performing a refusal of said stereotype:

> We ain't got much, I say at least let us have basketball. Is nothing sacred? Anytime we get something going good, y'all got to move in on it. In the sixties, we wore platform shoes; then, y'all had to wear platform shoes. In the early seventies, we braided our hair; then, in the late seventies, y'all had to braid yo' hair. Now it's 1980, we on welfare, and by the end of the next year, y'all gon' be on welfare too. [The camera shows his face in closeup during rampant audience applause.] I don't see a judge saying that every two bathroom attendants got to be white. All I'm sayin' is that y'all stay on the hockey courts and the polo fields, and let us stay on the basketball courts. 'Cause if God wanted whites to be equal to Blacks, everybody'd have one of these [he pulls a huge boom box from beneath the table and places it in front of him as he glares with lips pursed, unintimidated by the camera in front of him or the news anchor to his right].[53]

This "Weekend Update" sketch exemplifies how comedic performance can make sense of how technology produces a way of understanding concepts, ideas, and even individuals and their cultural backgrounds. In saying, "If God would have wanted whites to be equal to Blacks, everyone would have one of these [boom boxes]," Murphy draws our attention to how much of a signature feature this aural conduit was in Black life, not just in Lee's childhood neighborhood, but beyond.

FIGURE 13 Screenshot, June 10, 2013, *Saturday Night Live*, "Weekend Update," season 6, episode 3, produced by Jean Doumanian (New York: Time Life Video, 1980).

From the boom box's visual culture to its derogatory nickname, films, photographs, and comic strips evidenced the frequency of Black men depicted in everyday life associated with using boom boxes to play music outdoors in the mid-to-late 1970s and 1980s.[54] The Cornell Hip Hop Collection houses a variety of artworks that reflect the pivotal importance of the boom box in the early days of hip-hop. These boom boxes came to be known as "ghetto blasters," dangerously associating Blackness and Brownness with a geographic "ghettoness" (or loudness/noisiness/ability to disturb) and the specific ways that Black and Brown people used boom boxes that diverged from white norms. Linguistically, the term intertwines the loud sound blasting from boxes with homogeneous neighborhoods that suffer from severe barriers to exit, known as ghettos.[55] The "Weekend Update" parody exemplifies the circulation of this notion of Black masculinity.

The *SNL* sketch represents Raheem's indexing in popular culture and everyday life as a disruptor of white norms, as he displays America's embarrassing racial perceptions in public and hijacks the news interview (as well as *SNL*). Importantly, this sketch set the stage for Radio Raheem's rapid rise to ubiquity in popular culture, troubling or pleasuring visual and aural fields with Black masculinity and the boom box. The Raheem Abdul-Muhammed character uses his speech for political critique while depicting his boom box as a core part of his identity and a device to amplify the accompanying affect it generates. Lee represents this character through Radio Raheem, who becomes a synecdoche for Black masculine people carrying their boom boxes in the streets. While Radio Raheem is not the first Black masculine figure to carry a boom box, he becomes the most recognizable one because of the viral mechanism of the film's mass distribution, which enables moving images to be viewed nationwide or worldwide at a quickened pace.

The radio's portability as a boom box allows its possible use as both a weapon and an instrument.[56] This potentially loud sound conduit is controllable through the user's agency in choosing the song they play (e.g., via the cassette tape). A boom box is also audible through its ability to carve out a space to exchange or express feelings and ethos created or evoked through music, sound, or speech—the aural sphere.

This rapidly commonplace performance connects us to acts of Black masculinity performed within and outside the film, gesturing toward how art imitates life and, unfortunately, vice versa. Radio Raheem performs the pushing of "PLAY" (loudly), "STOP," "REWIND," and "PLAY" (loudly)—a repetitive act of emitting his favorite song through a cassette in the tape deck of his boom box. This routine, continual playing of the song is a synesthetic act that viewers witness throughout the entire film. Every time a character hears Radio Raheem, they see him (as he walks through a door with his boom box volume maximized) or figuratively imagine him as a kind of *acousmêtre* (spectators imagine him nearby because they hear his sound).[57]

This synesthesia creates a racialized erotics of sound for the audience. The interplay of visual and aural senses anticipates the idea of Radio Raheem through his hip-hop/funk song, even when his material body is elsewhere. The performance of him playing "Fight the Power" is so frequent that he gains the nickname "Radio" Raheem.

Black Feminism, Viral Performance, and the Sound of Blackness

In her essay "Counter-Hegemonic Art: *Do the Right Thing*," the late Black feminist theorist bell hooks writes, "The narrative suggests . . . the fate of [B]lack men is solely due to racist oppression. Gender and class are not evoked as forces which shape the construction of racial identity." She also critiques Lee's erotic play with Black women in the film: "Every [B]lack female in the film . . . is constructed at some point as a sex object."[58] I do not discount these readings, yet I wish to understand dimensions of desire, intimacy, and Black masculinity through Radio Raheem, revealing how racialized gender and sexuality operate—or do not operate—in his lively interactions, as well as seal his fate.

I echo Black studies scholar and literary theorist Dwight McBride when he writes, "Whenever we are speaking of race, we are always already speaking about gender, sexuality, and class."[59] In this chapter, which I began writing on the thirtieth anniversary of *Do the Right Thing*, I take up hooks's call to consider Radio Raheem's death a "brutal murder."[60] Yet, contrary to the critique that gender and class are nonfactors in Lee's racial representations, I argue that Radio Raheem's funk/hip-hop sound facilitates the racialized erotics of sound often bound up in notions of gender and class.

For musicologist Matthew D. Morrison, Black people in US popular music foundationally produce the funk/hip-hop sound, which, inclusive of its morphing and movement, is called "Blacksound."[61] Morrison suggests Blacksound is music produced by Black people, yet once someone performs it and makes it material, it can transform into something else. This transience makes Blacksound challenging to categorize and appropriate. Once someone categorizes or performs it, like Blackness, it transforms into something else entirely.[62] I reflect on Blacksound, a sound of both terror and enjoyment, as one factor that facilitates the erotics of the film.

Even before experiencing *Do the Right Thing*, people had already heard and felt the ubiquitous and familiar racialized erotics of Blacksound. The notion that Blacksound and the material bodies associated with it are primitive, unsophisticated, loud, and lewd has been circulating widely for decades, and its legacy persists into the present. Its denigration as primitive has been extensive enough that the simultaneous celebration and questioning of the title "Black primitivism" is required to humanize Blacksound and insist upon diasporic bonds with Black subjects.[63] For example, Duke Ellington claimed rather than rejected the anti-Black term "jungle music" to describe his Blacksound in the 1920s and 1930s while imagining a connection with an Africa that he would come to know only later in life.[64] Even for Ellington, encounters with Blacksound evoked understandings, misunderstandings, imaginings, and affect around African-diasporic sounds and people.

The racialized erotics of Blacksound generate a type of Black virality where hearing and feeling Black music, such as funk and hip-hop, produces a ubiquitous Black body in discourse. Viral performances within singular acts of Black virality—fractal viralities—occur here. One Blacksound can evoke multiple discursive Black bodies, and the listener may interpret and imagine them, creating a house-of-mirrors effect where many discourses are infinitely perceived in one. Blacksound thus evokes a range of cultural understandings and misunderstandings (like the sight of giant Negroes, or Black people at leisure in antebellum Cass County, MI, or the sound of jungle music) that depend on a listener who manifests desires and affects in their encounter with Blacksound, which I explore as racialized erotics. "The music [whether physically played or otherwise imagined] is speaking on other levels, articulating and evoking affective responses that language cannot."[65] I explore the affects that language cannot express through a critical study of the racialized erotics of Blacksound in *Do the Right Thing*.

Funk and Erotics in *Do the Right Thing*

In the opening credits of Lee's film, Tina (played by Rosie Perez) fiercely dances to Public Enemy's 1989 song "Fight the Power," which is also the film's anthem and the song that Radio Raheem plays repeatedly and exclusively.[66] Tina vigorously does the Cabbage Patch, the Kid 'n Play, and the Steve Martin, among other dances. She squarely faces the camera and dances so hard that she exposes the top and bottom rows of her teeth, ducking her lips with her open mouth. A cut takes viewers from Tina in a satin robe with red boxing gloves and shoes to punching while dancing in a black leather jacket, gold hoop earrings, and a blue leotard. The entire sequence lasts four minutes, ending with her performing a series of pelvic thrusts during which she pauses with exaggeration while dancing perrea and twerking, with a powerful thrust on James Brown's "Ugh!"

Lee uses the cuts between the dancing and fighting moves and outfits to evoke a use of culture to fight. Tina's dance moves are ubiquitous

African American and Afro-Latin social dances beyond the film. The cross-referencing of dances cues the audience on a form of Black virality, pushing viewers to do something with embodied knowledge and use it to fight against more considerable powers detrimental to Black livelihoods. In combination with Public Enemy's lyrics, the viscerally rhythmic mood Tina creates leads the audience to dance, feel, desire, and imagine Black and Brown bodies in a particular way when they hear the song; the racialized erotics of Blacksound first emerges here in *Do the Right Thing*.

While Tina visually instructs the audience in the racialized erotics of "Fight the Power," the audience also feels the musical motif without sight. Ears can feel as well as hear. In *Funk the Erotic: Transaesthetics and Black Sexual Cultures*, gender and sexuality theorist L. H. Stallings centers on the nonocular components of funk's multisensorial essence or "nonvisual sensory perception (smell/odor), embodied movement (dance and sex), and force (mood and will)."[67] In attending to nonvisual sensory perception, Stallings suggests that those who encounter and summon funk must experience it in nonocular ways to understand and feel it. This necessity orients funk patrons away from the hierarchical ordering of the visual sense above the others, or ocular centricity, to understand subaltern ways of knowing, which I explore through sound. The ocular plays a role in the aesthetics of funk and erotics, but it is not pivotal.

Stallings also gestures toward funk's multidimensional essence, what American and Asian American studies scholar Elliott H. Powell theorizes as spatiotemporal engagements between past, present, and future that establish a nexus between lives and the "social formations of race, gender, and sexuality."[68] Funk disengages us from the teleological notion that knowledge or desire is linear. Funk enables a spiral of knowledge and desire that explains the coexistence of the camel walk, the Sandunguea (or whining), and the running man dances in the introductory credits of the film, despite their creation at different times and in other spaces. Knowledge and desire are interventions of the past into the present moment or the present moment into the past, with such disruptions offering new or similar constructions for the future. The Isley Brothers inspired the song by Public Enemy, haunting the listener with "fight the power" across musical eras. Unfortunately, what Radio Raheem performs in the twentieth century, and the monstrous intimacy experienced by his Black masculine body as a result, continues to haunt Black people into the twenty-first.

Attending to the circularity of time travel, Stallings, in 2015, drew from the music of Prince and George Clinton to assert that *funk* is interchangeable with *fuck*, depending on context and aesthetics.[69] Here, the profane—that which is associated with the explicit, the loud, and the sexual—is the link to what preexisted the shame around those very ways of being, a kind of maternal profane. Stallings theorizes this profanity as "funky erotixxx" and writes, "What is profane or obscene has a lineage that exceeds its destructive imperialist mandates within Western patriarchy, and that is sacred." Countering the profane by investing in modern Western and non-African diasporic sites of memory, Stallings suggests, "denies a particular history of colonization that privatized sexual desires and clothed bodies even before it physically enslaved them, and it ignores a mental enslavement that would do the same."[70] Thus, an investment in funk (or fuck) music (through listening, dancing, and feeling) can also be an investment in collectivized sexual desires and an ethos where nudity does not show vulnerability or shame.

The interchangeability of funk with a nonpatriarchal fuck opens other possibilities in the physics of sound. As Morrison shares in his description of music as an embodied process, "Sound *literally* travels through the body, as it activates many of our human faculties and senses, while we make sense out of sound(s) from our cultural experiences."[71] Sound pleasurably and unpleasurably breaches the flesh as we derive meaning from it based on our cultural experiences. Sound penetrates the body and is a container for its movement, a place inviting dance and movement. The sound thus takes on an amorphous quality that allows it to funk and fuck you and to be funked and fucked with. Sound reveals the illusion of binary divisions between public and private space and, as I argue, between the racial and the erotic.

In her book *Sex and Germs: The Politics of AIDS*, sociologist and historian Cindy Patton describes erotics as a "powerful physical longing that is contained within the imagery of sexuality [that] spills outside the purely genital to eroticize a wide range of elements."[72] Patton's wrestling with the erotic conveys how desire is complex and intertwined with dimensions of life including, but also other than, one's sexuality. While Patton does not address race directly, critical race, feminist, and queer theorist Sharon P. Holland does and expands on the notion that the erotic interplays with more than the sexuality of one's private life.

Regarding the neoliberal separation between public and private, Holland contends the erotic is one such phenomenon that too often operates on the level of the private. In *The Erotic Life of Racism*, Holland considers the historical use of the erotic as "the personal and political dimension of desire" for the individual that creates separation from the collective. The danger of isolating the erotic from other social dimensions is that it allows sexuality to emerge and be "recognized in the severance of the erotic from racist practice." Individual desire and feeling are inseparable from normative and collective influence.[73]

Here, the normative and the collective take form in how "(non)sense" is made from Blacksound through cultural (mis)understanding, (in)experience, and (conservative) respectability politics. I think about everyday people making nonsense out of expressed desires by Black bodies in discourse (e.g., mumble rap as nonsense or all Black music as jungle music). Thus, a Black person's performance of "nonsense" may function as a freeing force promising liberation from the normative, which is otherwise policing and unlivable.

The Blacksound to which Radio Raheem returns throughout the film is a funk song as much as a hip-hop song. Funk evokes a type of feeling and Blacksound that functions as the sonic backdrop for the erotics of race and racism in the film. Black people mobilize funk to be touched by, through, and in response to Blacksound. The racialized erotics of Blacksound produces a type of sound that performs tactile and affective touch, what I call "aural touch." The aural touch of Blacksound reveals the limits of the live-and-let-live ethos that *Do the Right Thing* questions. The interplay between the aural touch of Blacksound and the discursive and material body gives rise to the erotics I explore in discussing the film.

PLAY: A Performance Analysis of the Racialized Erotics of Radio Raheem's Blacksound

When you hold a boom box, PLAY is one of the many nexuses between sound and the discursive and material body, alongside STOP, FAST FORWARD, and REWIND. One presses PLAY to listen to its corresponding sonic material. Play *is a verb that denotes performance through participation in an ongoing activity, either repeatedly or ephemerally. To play is to compete against or counter another player's actions. To play is to represent something theatrically or cinematically. Play is also something used to deceive (i.e., you got played), joke about (i.e., I was just playing), or go too far with (i.e., you play too much). Importantly, to play is to engage in leisure activity, and, as Stallings reminds us, "Work society impinges upon every facet of life, even leisure."*[74] *Play is thus also labor. Play involves a dynamic interplay of the past and present as well as different aspects of the self. By pressing PLAY on a boom box and loudly broadcasting its sounds, Radio Raheem activates his participation, competition, representation, comedy, deception, relaxation, and labor, repeatedly producing erotic opportunities for social interaction, critical thought, pleasure, and death.*

• • •

Do the Right Thing's neighborhood is predominantly Black, home to African American residents and residents from elsewhere in the African diaspora. A mural titled *Bed-Stuy—Do or Die* affirms a diasporic bond (or wish) and features the Jamaican, Puerto Rican, and Pan-African flags. The neighborhood is also noticeably multiethnic. There are American descendants from unspecified places in Korea, Italy, and the broader Caribbean and southern United States. The younger and older generations of Black people recognize that there are no Black-owned businesses.

In contrast, the Italian and Korean business owners feel rightful ownership of their spaces, which creates racial tension throughout the film.[75] Race, space, and entitlement to space are important issues at the crux of many conflicts that drive the story. From the tensions raised between a group of older Black men (Sweet Dick Willie, Coconut Sid, and ML) sitting on chairs in front of a red wall, discourses concerning redlining, gentrification, and marginalization emerge that are haunting and disillusioning to Black residents, whose issues the business owners in the community dismiss.

It is possible that Radio Raheem likes "Fight the Power" enough to play it regardless of what is happening around him. However, I also decipher the Black residents' invalidation as a force that compels Radio Raheem to play his music loudly throughout the film. If those residents cannot occupy a business or a home, they can occupy Radio Raheem's Blacksound.[76] For Radio Raheem, Blacksound is a means of expressing subjecthood, desire, and ethos that is resistive to and resistant against systemic forces that limit Black people's livelihoods. He carves out an aural sphere for Black existence.

I focus on three scenes in which Radio Raheem, seen in figure 14, performs and experiences the racialized erotics of his Blacksound: a battle of the loudest sound system between him and a group of Latino men and two encounters with Sal (the owner of Sal's Famous Pizzeria, played by Danny Aiello), one that articulates the rules of Sal's space and one that enforces those rules. I navigate the politics of the public and private sphere in these scenes to think through normative erotics (which are associated with private life, inner feelings, and individual desire) and the racialized erotics that Holland pushes for, which acknowledge an individual's desires and their interconnectedness with the public, the systemic, and the collective.

While the film presents many memorable characters, I concentrate on Radio Raheem's performances and the characters he interacts with. I consider how his death represents Michael Stewart and Eleanor Bumpurs before him and Yusuf Hawkins, Jordan Davis, Eric Garner, and George Floyd, who tragically followed. My focus on how Radio Raheem performs his Black masculinity throughout the film offers a nuance to an otherwise well-known Black virality.

Scene 1: Aural and Visual Touch

Between pizza deliveries, Mookie (played by Spike Lee), Sal's Black American employee, dedicates a salsa song titled "Tu y Yo" by Rubén Blades to his Latina girlfriend, Tina. He knows what song to ask of the Black American DJ, Mister Señor Love Daddy (played by Samuel L. Jackson). In the following scene, a Puerto Rican man, Stevie (played by Luis Antonio Ramos), affirms this song's place, even as his Latino friends seem aloof about that place. He reads a definition from a book to his boys: "Salsa, música Latina—el sonido de mi país, el país mas bello, Puerto Rico." Coupled with Mookie's request, I understand Stevie's lecture as a moment when a person's ethnicity or culture does not determine that person's knowledge of said ethnicity or culture. Stevie and his boys experience joy and nostalgia when they hear salsa on the radio, even though, given his lecture, his boys know little of salsa music's origins and are not interested in being lectured about it. Here, salsa facilitates an aural touch, an intimacy beyond the ocular senses created in and through Panamanian sound.

Stevie and the other Latino men sit on a stoop and enjoy the broadcasted song playing from their boom box. The box features a miniature portrait of Jesus on a gold chain, a nod to the interplay between sound and belief systems. The boom box sits on top of a red car, behind which Mother Sister (played by Ruby Dee) sits in her window and fans herself while she observes the block. Suddenly, "Fight the Power" enters the aural sphere. The camera pans right while "Tu y Yo" and "Fight the Power" mix and blend rhythmically and seamlessly. Radio Raheem stoically stares in their direction and then offers an upward head nod (figure 14).

The scene audibly articulates a desire to recognize what jazz musician Kamasi Washington calls the "harmony of difference."[77] Even though two sets of recorded instruments play independently from two boom boxes, they coexist harmoniously. Here, Lee uses sound and panning to signal the intimacy of these Black and Brown sound cultures. This aural mix is also a synesthetic moment with viewers hearing Radio Raheem, summoning the sight of him

FIGURE 14 Screenshot, August 2, 2014, "Radio Raheem Turns Up the Volume," *Do the Right Thing*, directed by Spike Lee (1989; Universal City: Universal Studios Home Entertainment, 2009).

before seeing him. Radio Raheem does not ask Stevie and his companions to turn their music down, which would have recalled Koch-like legislation where police enforced sonic expressions of Black and Brown people. Instead, he does the diasporically possible: he raises the volume of his.

The aural encroachment enrages all the men on the stoop, and one of them shouts, "I want to listen to my salsa music!" While holding the rest of them back, Stevie yells to the group, "Chill!" He then shouts to Radio Raheem, "You think you got it like that, bro?" In support, Stevie's friends yell, "Blow it away!" Staring intently at Radio Raheem, Stevie increases the volume of the salsa music as he sips his golden can of Miller Genuine Draft. For a moment, the salsa is much louder than the hip-hop/funk music. Breaking eye contact only long enough to glance at the dials on his boom box, Radio Raheem confidently increases the volume of "Fight the Power" and resumes eye contact. Unable to compete, Stevie grinds his teeth (see figure 15), turns his volume down, and disappointingly concedes, "You got it, bro."

The long gaze between Radio Raheem and Stevie illustrates competitive masculine posturing, which gestures toward homosocial cultural practices. Yet the homoerotic lingers in this scene because of the potential for sexual desire and erotic imaginaries. Imagining where each other is from, what the other's politics are, and what else happens if the encounter escalates are all interpreted and misinterpreted through racialized gender expression, remaining elusive and unguaranteed. The heteronormativity performed throughout the film also acts to foreclose possibilities, subduing the sexual (or

FIGURE 15 Screenshot, August 2, 2014, "You Got It, Bro," *Do the Right Thing*, directed by Spike Lee (1989; Universal City: Universal Studios Home Entertainment, 2009).

flirting) and elevating the homosocial (machismo). While individuals use performative cues to show human connectivity between those with whom they share sexual desire, those cues are both real and not real to the extent that individuals perform them. The latter performativity is why the stare-down between Radio Raheem and Stevie remains an unacknowledged indicator of sexual desire or erotic imaginary. Nonetheless, the Black virality of that look and the countless times it has been "cross-viewed" stirs anticipation of physical touch that might be violent or pleasurable.[78]

With this sensual moment, Stevie and Radio Raheem vie for dominance in the aural sphere through their music. They exchange sexual and homosocial expressions across the aural sphere they create. There is as much potential longing between them, which is homoerotic, as there is desire, which is diasporic and competitive. Indeed, their staring performs the labor of intimacy—an almost constant visual touch facilitated by Blacksound—wherein they engage in a homosocial masculine tradition that leaves the machismo behind for "something [perhaps an intimacy] beyond."[79]

The competition between Radio Raheem playing hip-hop/funk music and Stevie playing salsa music is also a nod to the material uses of the boom box in Black and Brown communities. To play boom boxes as loudly as possible is to perform masculinity and machismo and to enact a general form of entertainment across ethnoracial groups. Also, Stevie's use of "bro" is double-edged, respectfully gesturing toward both Radio Raheem's Black masculinity and a diasporic masculine bonding as fictive kin.

Radio Raheem does not leave this affective diasporic bond unscathed. Moments before pushing the salsa volume up and asking Radio Raheem, "You think you got it like that, bro?," Stevie and his friend disparagingly refer to Radio Raheem as *cara chocolate*, or "chocolate face." In the erotic exchange that Blacksound facilitates afterward, this disavowal is homophobic, a racialized colorist "no homo," which repudiates (or melancholically affirms through repudiation) the presence of the homoerotic to follow. Either out of knowledge or ignorance of the Spanish language, Radio Raheem seems unbothered by it. He high-fives a Black child who witnesses his victory amid shouts of "*Pendejo!*" Then Radio Raheem triumphantly walks away from the Latino men, who assemble behind him at a safe distance in a gesture of collective intimidation.

Despite the momentary racial/sexual slight, there is a sense of respect between Radio Raheem and Stevie. When Radio Raheem turns his music up louder, Stevie responds by turning his boom box down and acknowledging, "You got it, bro." This interaction reflects a form of Black Latinidad in which Radio Raheem and Stevie participate. Black Americans and Puerto Ricans, particularly in New York, share a cultural bond.[80] My use of Black Latinidad draws from Latine performance and queer theorist Ramón Rivera-Servera's notion of "queer Latinidad." There is a collective affective bond, in this case between strangers, that emerges through encounters (here, facilitated through Blacksound) involving sundry queer cultures—in their most capacious meaning—invested in building social, political, and cultural relationships.[81] Black Latinidad's emphasis on Blackness and Indigeneity counters the erasure of each that Latinidad, in use by itself, often engenders.[82] As the film does, I leave the character of Radio Raheem and his racial and/or ethnic possibilities open yet within the scope of his Blackness.

Indeed, as I mentioned in my description of the setting, the film begins through a framework inclusive of Black Latinidad, as seen through Tina's merger of social dances and the African-diasporic mural. Through a kind of synesthesia, Radio Raheem's performance of Blacksound manifests the visual desire the mural represents and the embodied desire Tina's dance sequence demonstrates. Such diasporic relationships are more involved and riskier than simple allyship. They require a person to act as an accomplice in a harmony of difference, binding their own discursive and material body to another's fate as much as to another's pleasures. Supporting this point (and counter to his earlier anti-Black homophobic slight), Stevie returns at the end of the film to defend Radio Raheem's sainthood, which he views as tied up in Radio Raheem's livelihood.

Stevie and Radio Raheem engage in Black sensibility, too, in how their discursive and material bodies recall the combative play present throughout African-diasporic performance practices, what author, poet, and essayist Hanif Abdurraqib describes as "rituals of shared space."[83] Such performances range from carnival machete play to Afro-Brazilian capoeira and Puerto Rican and African American breakdancing. In these martial arts and cultural performances, people take and concede space to dance in time and coexist spatiotemporally. Sound functions here as a proprioceptive dance that counters ocularcentric colonialist logics of occupation, whose logic captures seen space without conceding it in return. Without this proprioceptive dance, people are unaware of their material body's position relative to other bodies in time (some might liken it to dancing or clapping on the one and three while everyone else is on the two and four).

This Blacksound scene's performance reveals aural ethics where sound and belief systems—embodied diasporic knowledge—interplay.[84] Here, Blacksound facilitates a longing for an intimacy that reduces the distance between respective Black and Indigenous diasporas, a desire to be together and to live and let live. This desire, too, is erotic. Black feminist philosopher Audre Lorde discusses the use of the erotic in creating a harmony of difference. Her essay "The Uses of the Erotic: The Erotic as Power" is a meditation on the pragmatics of the erotic, especially in her interpersonal relationships with woman-identified women. Lorde reflects on the erotic as a bridge between sharers of something affective, psychic, or discursive that helps two or more beings understand what is not shared, thus reducing potential threats that may arise from difference.[85] The desire to know something beyond yourself and the surface of another being is what Lorde pushes us toward as a means of ultimately connecting with ourselves.

Essential to the subject at hand, music is one of many activities that facilitates the feeling and desire that Lorde associates with the erotic. She writes, "Erotic connection functions . . . [i]n the way my body stretches to music and opens into response, harkening to its deepest rhythms."[86] Such an embodied and vulnerable response to music might also be a "Black sensibility," where one makes room for, feels, and embraces it—not only in its harmony and cadence but in its loudness.

The loudness with which Radio Raheem plays "Fight the Power" is just as important, if not more, as the lyrical content it contains. In *In the Break: The Aesthetics of the Black Radical Tradition*, cultural theorist Fred Moten describes the challenge to aesthetic hierarchy that Blacksound poses as the "disruption of the Enlightenment linguistic project" or how "radically exterior aurality . . . disrupts and resists certain formations of identity and interpretation by challenging the reducibility of phonic matter to verbal meaning or conventional musical form."[87] There are elements of Blacksound that are irreducible to the English tongue that funk and erotics otherwise bring forth. A lyrical or script-based content analysis would miss the myriad meanings of this scene almost entirely.

The loudness of "Fight the Power," as well as its lyrical content, is an assertion of a Black public sphere that affirms ways of knowing that manifest through affect and other nonvisual sensory experiences like funk. The Black public sphere expands on philosopher and social theorist Jürgen Habermas's concept of the public sphere, defining it first as a critical social imaginary. This imaginary "draws energy from the vernacular practices of street talk and new musics, radio shows and church voices, entrepreneurship and circulation." It also marks "a wider sphere of critical practice and visionary politics, in which intellectuals can join with the energies of the street, the school, the church, and the city to constitute a challenge to the exclusionary violence of much public space in the United States."[88] Radio Raheem's cosmopolitan Blackness represents this merger.[89] The energies of the street and the ivory tower converge into an explosion of sound and desire, articulating the Black public sphere.

Radio Raheem's blasting of "Fight the Power" asserts the will of the Black public sphere as it fills in a silence generated by Habermas's bourgeois public sphere. As media theorist W. J. T. Mitchell states about Habermas's public sphere, "The word *public* might more properly be written with the *l* in parentheses to remind us that for much of human history political and social authority has derived from a [I would add white] 'pubic' sphere, not a public one."[90] For a person to take part in Habermas's public sphere, they had to own property. In contrast, the possibility emerges of a public sphere created by those who have been infantilized and considered property in the past.

Through the broadcasting of Blacksound, Radio Raheem creates and adds to the notion of a Black public sphere by participating in a counterpublic to the exclusionary anti-Black violence of public/private spaces. As feminist critical theorist Nancy Fraser reminds us, "Virtually from the beginning, counterpublics contested the exclusionary norms of the bourgeois public, elaborating alternative styles of political behavior and alternate norms of public speech."[91] Put another way, Black aural spheres celebrate Radio Raheem's Blacksound as ill in ways that lead to its policing as disruptive in white aural spheres. Further, Radio Raheem's sound system emphasizes a broad vision of social interaction and dialogue aimed at fighting oppressive authority through volume and song. Chuck D expresses this skillfully in "Fight the Power" as he raps, "Swingin' while I'm singin'."[92]

Other erotics in Radio Raheem's Blacksound are most evident through spatial tensions with different characters in the film, who experience the erotics of his Blacksound like a serious form of play akin to slap boxing or as an offensive fight where lives hang in the balance. Both interpretations hinge on a person's sensibilities toward masculine Black people.

Scene 2: This Is a Respectable Business (or the Policing of Blacksound)

The notion of the interplay between sound and belief systems clashes each time Radio Raheem encounters Sal. Their interactions are points in the film where disagreements between white and Black performances of aural ethics and space reach the apex of their conflict. In Sal's space, Radio Raheem's music is revolting—reflecting both the resistance it incites and celebrates and the dis-ease it creates in Sal's aural sphere.

At the film's beginning, Sal's younger son, Vito (played by Richard Edson), blares music through his headphones, oblivious to his older brother, Pino (played by John Turturro), who in raising his voice to try to give Vito directions, starts an argument. After telling both his sons to shut up, Sal tells Pino, "This is a respectable business." Nonetheless, the music is heard by no one but Vito.

This scene represents a different aural sphere, privatizing the music that characters hear, affecting only the individual listening. Like Gibney asserts at the start of this chapter, listening to music through headphones closes Vito off from social interaction with his family and the block. Sal equates minimizing the loud dialogue that ensues with conservative respectability politics. His equation suggests that if a business is loud, it is disrespectful and lacks decorum.

Except for admonishing Vito for loudly arguing with his brother, Sal does not limit Vito's sound or ask him to turn off his music. Sal's nonpolicing approach sharply contrasts with the type of aural sphere and ethics that Radio Raheem experiences when he plays his music loudly in front of Sal. Unlike Vito's aural sphere, Radio Raheem's encourages social encounters (or conflicts), affects more than Radio Raheem, and interacts with and enlivens the block. Radio Raheem still hears the discourses and desires expressed around him, even when loudly playing his music.

Daylight illuminates the scene as "Fight the Power" blasts from Radio Raheem's boom box. He turns his volume down (never off) to greet Mookie, Sal's pizza deliverer. He performs a metaphorical boxing match between "LOVE," molded on his right gold knuckle-duster ring, and "HATE," molded on his left gold knuckle-duster ring (as seen in figure 16). Love wins after hate is "on the ropes." Radio Raheem relaxes his face, smiles, and tells Mookie, "If I love you, I love you. But if I hate you . . ." There is a menacing silence. Radio Raheem then admits, "I love you, bro."

While of the block, Radio Raheem reveals a beyond-the-block episteme. Lee is indeed showing off his in-depth knowledge of film. Lee's cover of a scene from the film *The Night of the Hunter* (1955), where the protagonist, Harry Powell (played by Robert Mitchum), has "LOVE" and "HATE" tattooed on his fingers (see figure 17), aligns Radio Raheem with cosmopolitan Black masculinity, which stands out from Black masculine people's popular conceptions in the streets.[93]

FIGURE 16 Screenshot, August 4, 2014, "It's a Devastating Right, and Hate Is Hurt," *Do the Right Thing*, directed by Spike Lee (1989; Universal City: Universal Studios Home Entertainment, 2009).

FIGURE 17 Screenshot, July 20, 2014, *The Night of the Hunter*, directed by Charles Laughton (1955; New York: Criterion Collection, 2010).

Radio Raheem's monologue is very much a disruption of performing the boom box–blasting, "Giant-Negro" troublemaker that he may have established as his onscreen persona thus far in the film. The performance of Blacksound here involves "the construction of a *personal front* that is part of the expressive equipment that a person deploys in performance of self and social identity."[94] The only time that Radio Raheem voluntarily turns his volume down is when he exposes this more profound side of his personhood.

Lee uses an L-cut, where the audio from the present film clip transitions into the following film clip, as he shoots Radio Raheem striding into the next scene. Radio Raheem straightens his posture, turns his volume up, and toughens his face. His facial expression is a type of "prison masculinity" where Black masculine people adopt physical aspects that embody "hard stares, large muscles, an imposing posture," while more fluid practices and performances of masculinity remain private.[95] Radio Raheem's performance of prison masculinity gestures toward the presence of the carceral state in the neighborhood, his performance of toughness anticipating the lack of authority he will experience in Sal's establishment and thus functioning as a type of defense.

In the most creative camera maneuver of the film, Lee maintains focus on Radio Raheem as he walks directly toward the pizzeria from the street. Lee then pans out into a larger shot of the interior door as Radio Raheem opens the pizzeria door. A door is the only object that separates the in from the out, the private from the public, which Radio Raheem's Blacksound dissolves as the audience hears it from the streets while the camera is inside Sal's pizzeria. Lee brings to life what Cee says at the film's beginning as the filmmaker visualizes how Radio Raheem walks in stereo.

In a close-up of his sweat-drenched face, Radio Raheem calmly says, "Two slices." Over the music, Sal loudly asserts, "No service till you turn that shit off!" He continues, "Mr. Radio Raheem, I can't even hear myself think. You are disturbin' me, you are disturbin' my customers!" Radio Raheem turns his head to the side, licks his lips, and stops the tape in his boom box, repeating, "Two slices." In the background, the audience can see a part of Sal's wall of fame, a decorative feature of the pizzeria showcasing famous Italian Americans like Frank Sinatra, Al Pacino, and Joe DiMaggio. Sal continues, "You come into Sal's, there's no music, no rap, no music, no music, no music. Capisce? You understand?"

Radio Raheem's first interaction with Sal involves a concession as he turns off his music for a slice of pizza. Still, Radio Raheem's presence is a testament to the proposition that a person cannot isolate themself from the Black sensibilities that surround them, no matter how much silence they require or how many Italian Americans grace their walls. That is, when you (settle Indigenous lands or) open a white Italian American business in a predominately Black and Brown neighborhood, there may be music, there may be performance traditions you will need to cooperate with, not the other way around. Sal frames Radio Raheem's aural sphere and ethics as disturbances, even though the customers, primarily Black, show no signs of being disturbed. Sal further defines his aural sphere and ethics in a relaxed tone to Raheem as "no music," emphasizing "no rap."

Sal establishes that the absence of music frames the parameters of his aural sphere and ethics, insulated from the consonance and dissonance of the blocks surrounding him. Sal's isolation of Blacksound from his establishment allows him to benefit from the currency provided by Black people, whether Mookie delivers pizzas or the neighborhood kids eat them, without being affected by the currents and cultures that motivate the Black residents: the essence of white privilege.

By repudiating funk, Sal expresses his determination not to fuck with or be fucked with. Unlike Stevie, Sal does not concede space but takes it by negating Radio Raheem's ability to create it through Blacksound. Lee illustrates the policing and constraining of Blacksound by white people, treating it in a manner akin to other Black expressions. Here, Blacksound also functions as an extension of Black masculinity: Radio does not exist without Raheem, and vice versa. Thus, Sal even suggests that Radio Raheem leave his expression of Black masculinity outside the pizzeria—that he dims his light so that others are not blinded by it.

Sal is the main character in the film who violently responds to being aurally touched by Blacksound. The only other person who requests silence does so nonviolently in Black street vernacular as he yells down to the street from his upper-floor dwelling, "Cut off that rap music. . . . I'm in here trying to get some mothafuckin' goddamn sle—" Before he can finish saying "sleep," Radio Raheem glances up and responds, "Yo, I'll fuck you up quick!" It only follows that Radio Raheem does not take well to Sal's policing.

Scene 3: Well, Turn It Off Then (or Challenging the White Refusal of Black Recognition)

Later that night, Radio Raheem and Buggin Out (played by the indomitable Giancarlo Esposito) partner and plan to visit Sal's pizzeria to boycott it until he puts Black people on his wall of fame. Their plot follows a moment when police officers order food for carryout and concernedly ask Sal how long he intends to stay in the neighborhood. Before telling them, "Get outta here," Sal sarcastically (or not) says he will stay long enough to build a high-rise. Referring to Trump Plaza, the police jokingly nickname Sal "Trump." The plaza they reference, constructed in 1984, had a gentrifying effect on Upper Manhattan, which explains its use as a "joke." The police frame Sal, too, as a gentrifying force in the neighborhood, and the audience witnesses their trusting rapport.

Buggin Out and Radio Raheem's earlier plot materializes as Public Enemy's "Fight the Power" plays. Black customers and Sal's sons exude distraction and disbelief even before seeing Radio Raheem or Buggin Out. To hear "Fight the Power" is to expect to see Radio Raheem or, to misquote Moten, it is a hearing that redoubles itself as sight.[96] Radio Raheem's music blares from his boom box. The characters and the audience hear it as Buggin Out spits on Sal's floor (see figure 18). Ignoring the display of disrespect from Buggin Out, Sal angrily asks, "What'd I tell you about that noise?" Buggin Out says, "We want some Black people on that mothafuckin' wall of fame *now*." Sal angrily responds to Radio Raheem, "Turn that jungle music off! We ain't in Africa!"

Sal's admonition reveals his true feelings about Raheem's music and the erotic contours of Blacksound. Beyond disturbing him or his customers, he finds the noise more disrespectful than someone spitting on his floor. For Sal, "Fight the Power" has a racial tone, timbre, and cadence, suggesting there is race in wavelengths, a seeing, being, and mythmaking that happens and comes forth in Blacksound. Sal also evokes bigoted Black viralities of Black people and the continent of Africa, referring to them, it, and "Fight the Power" as primitive, wild, and uncivilized. Funk collapses spatiotemporal boundaries and makes it possible for all these images to be projected onto

FIGURE 18 Screenshot, August 7, 2014, "Fight the Power . . . Spit," *Do the Right Thing*, directed by Spike Lee (1989; Universal City: Universal Studios Home Entertainment, 2009).

or embodied by Black lives in the present. Yet, in what he does not verbalize, Sal also inadvertently reveals how he conceptualizes his aural sphere and whiteness—as civilized and tame. In calling funk and hip-hop "jungle music," Sal emphasizes the inseparability of "cultures of visualization" from the "construction of sonic meanings."[97]

Buggin Out attempts to refocus the argument on issues of Black representation: "Why it gotta be about jungle music? Why it gotta be about Africa? It's about them fucking pictures!" Sal disagrees and says to Radio Raheem, "It's about turning that shit off and getting the fuck outta my place!" Instead of demanding representation in the form of Black businesses, Buggin Out focuses on visual recognition in Sal's wall of fame. Amid so many signs of Blackness—Buggin Out's colorful outfit of Jordan 4s, a red, black, and green leather Africa medallion and wristband, and kente shorts and shirt; photos of Malcolm X and Dr. Martin Luther King Jr. sold by Smiley (a minor character who is autistic, played by Roger Guenveur Smith); and a Mike Tyson mural—Buggin Out desires tokenism, the wall of fame, instead of robust economic involvement.

Sal is determined to regain control of his aural sphere, which Radio Raheem's sound system has infiltrated. Here, sound systems and belief systems explosively clash. Even though Buggin Out is the main speaking character in the scene, Sal screams only at Radio Raheem. Radio Raheem hardly opens his mouth, yet he dominates the point of the argument as his sound—the only thing that touches Sal—dominates the aural sphere.

Sal's son, Vito, yells, "Radio Raheem!," to which Radio Raheem replies, "Fuck you!" Sal inserts, "And fuck you too!" Radio Raheem continues, screaming at Sal, "This is music, this is my music!" In response, Sal yells, "Fuck your music!" Radio Raheem hoists his boom box on Sal's counter and challenges, "Well, turn it off then."

Here, Radio Raheem challenges Sal's facile dismissal of Blacksound as music; he also claims ownership of it amid the many things Black people do not own in his neighborhood. Leaving Sal's primitivist slight unacknowledged, Radio Raheem engages in Black primitivism, affirming Africa and the jungle as physical locations.[98] With Radio Raheem claiming the jungle music as his own, he suggests Pan-African solidarity and acknowledges Africa's performance legacy into the present moment.

Unlike Stevie's interaction in scene 1, which embraces Black performance, the phrase "fuck you" quickly transforms into "fuck your music," intertwining anti-Black sentiments with disdain for Blacksound. Sal's assault on Radio Raheem's music is an assault on his Blackness, and by extension, is also a white man's response to a perceived assault on whiteness. For Sal, immediate proximity to Radio Raheem's Blacksound only reminds him that feelings and sounds of whiteness do not surround him in the African-diasporic environment of Bed-Stuy.

Buggin Out intensifies the hostility of the moment, screaming, "We're closing you guinea bastards for good . . . until you get some Black people on that motherfucking wall of fame!" Deeply offended by the threat of closing his business and the Italian racial slur, Sal responds directly to the camera, "You fucking close me?" After this dare of a question, he grabs his bat and yells at Buggin Out, "You Black cocksucker. I'll fucking tear your fucking [takes a deep breath] . . . nigger ass!" His inhalation represents a hesitation in the escalation of racial and sexual epithets. Everyone else in Sal's confrontationally responds, "Oh, we niggas now?!" Then, looking at Buggin Out, Sal yells, "You Black cocksucker!" Looking back at Radio Raheem, Sal shouts, "You nigger motherfucker!" Sal then smashes Radio Raheem's boom box with a wooden baseball bat (see figure 19), in effect destroying Raheem's identity. The boom box blared throughout the film as something resistive to the violent and ever-encroaching white supremacy that manifests as zero investment in Black businesses and oppressive police surveillance. With everyone standing silent in disbelief, Sal confirms, "I just killed your fucking radio."

Sal reestablishes, this time through more violent means, the policing of pleasure that he does not sanction. His reaction to an Italian racial slur erupts into a racist, homophobic rant. Sal uses the act of fellatio between Black people as a denigration, threatens to rape Buggin Out, and suggests that Radio Raheem is a Black breeder. Sal's disparaging remarks demonstrate a heteronormative racial epistemology, as he uses heteropatriarchal insults. It is notable that he stereotypically directs "Black cocksucker" toward the man

FIGURE 19 Screenshot, August 10, 2014, "You Nigger Motherfucker," *Do the Right Thing*, directed by Spike Lee (1989; Universal City: Universal Studios Home Entertainment, 2009).

wearing the most colors and "nigger motherfucker" toward the largest Black man. His denigration of imagined (read: stereotypical) racialized sexuality is "the terrifying, irrational reaction to the erotic which makes individuals and society vulnerable to psychological and social control in cultures where pleasure is strictly categorized and regulated"—what Patton calls "erotophobia."[99] Here, erotophobia suggests Sal feels aurally touched by Radio Raheem's Blacksound, enough to cause a visceral panic and destructive response.

Despite conducting business in a Black neighborhood, Sal—with his aural ethics—sanitizes the pizzeria as pleasureless for Blacksound, Black sensibility, or Black representation. Racism interplays with erotophobia, casting Raheem and Buggin Out as "too close to their sexuality, too passionate, out of control."[100] Their Black virality—Raheem as every boom box–wielder and Buggin Out as every Afrocentric activist—flirts with the metaphor of contagion, where they become overwhelming viral bodies whose destruction becomes necessary to human, read white, survival. Raheem and Buggin Out are fatalistically embedded by discursive structures that render them licentious troublemakers long before they arrive on the scene.

STOP: The Consequences of Blacksound at the Nexus of Desire and Death

One presses the STOP button to cease all leisure, competitive, and representative activity that ensues when allowing music to play. After stopping, one may never play again, refusing to engage further with what they already experienced by playing. To stop means to have had enough. To stop limits the possibilities of what lies ahead. It is also a moment to reflect on to take in everything that preceded it, a praxis to prepare for what will follow when the activity is resumed.

• • •

Blacksound is inextricable from Blackness, so, in damaging a conduit for Blacksound, Sal should be destroying Blackness. Blackness cannot cease, however. Nor can virality. While inextricable in some ways, when Blacksound stops, the Blackness and Black virality associated with it continue, not because they are indestructible but because they are resilient. Also, Blacksound's fluidity ensures that it changes even when it seems to be destroyed.

Sal's confirmation, "I just killed your fucking radio," is an affirmation to the Black and Brown residents of that block to stay in their place as consumers (never producers), occupants (never owners), tokens (never belonging), and silent (never loud or expressive). In destroying Raheem's sound system, Sal destroys (an essential part of) Raheem's belief system. It represents the erasure of agency in how Black and Brown youth broadcast their music. Indeed, Radio Raheem symbolizes a bygone era where commercial radio did not play rap music, so children and young adults turned to boom boxes to play the music representing them. Many discovered certain musical acts listening to other people's mobile sound systems, such as boom boxes and car stereos. This Black broadcasting, too, never stops; it just changes form. Thus, the "fucking radio" continues to reproduce in queer ways through, for example, pirate radio, internet radio, and streaming.

Sal destroys a piece of technology that materializes counterspaces to the monstrous intimacies that residents in Raheem's neighborhood experience. This familiar violence of unbelonging includes disproportionate police surveillance, which dispels any sense of residents safely belonging in their neighborhood, and redlining, which prohibits them from acquiring leverage to buy property in their community. Sal destroys the aural medium of Raheem's desire and pleasure and the erotics and socialities it facilitates—a "fucking radio" indeed. Raheem now must "live" with a desire that can no longer be felt or heard by others through the specific loudness of his boom box, which may not be living at all for him. Again, the use of *fucking* with *radio* suggests the slipperiness between *funk* and *fuck* that Stallings suggests depends on context and aesthetics.

None of Sal's insults urge Radio Raheem to fight with his hands. Seeing his boom box destroyed and Sal's proclamation over its destruction, however, pushes Raheem to choke Sal inside and outside the pizzeria, telling Sal, "You don't fuck with my box!"

Da Mayor (a nickname, not an occupation, played by Ossie Davis) yells, "Break it up!" Pino yells, "You're gonna kill him," as he unsuccessfully tries to choke Raheem from behind. Despite the attempts at stopping him, Raheem keeps his hands wrapped around Sal's neck, and Sal's breath hangs in the balance between the LOVE and HATE knuckle-duster rings on Raheem's right and left hands.

The entire neighborhood gathers for the fight between Raheem and Sal on the sidewalk in front of the pizzeria. This fight is a touch and desire premeditated by Blacksound, a battle between characters and sensibilities, symbolizing a clash of aural ethics, touches, and spheres.

Just as Sal's face turns red in his struggle to breathe, the police arrive and perform the all-too-quotidian subduing of Raheem. Some officers pull Pino away from choking Raheem, after which they leave Pino untouched. Officers, including Ponte (a Latino man played by Miguel Sandoval), Long (a white man played by Rick Aiello), and a plainclothes officer (a white man), then grab Raheem from behind and peel him from Sal's neck. The circular flash of red and white lights reflects off Officer Long's sweaty skin while he chokes Raheem with his police baton, taking Raheem's breath as Sal regains his.

Long's position of dominance from behind reinforces Raheem's nonconsensual submissive position and the surveillance the police officers perform in the neighborhood. Even after Raheem stops resisting, Long continues to choke him—no longer choking another human—as though, in his fear, he is choking cisgender Black male masculinity to death. After the many scenarios that this fictional moment in the film is based on, the NYPD continues to deploy the choke hold today, even though it was banned long after this film's main run (in 1993).[101]

The camera zooms in on Raheem's Nikes, kicking as his body writhes for air. This shot recalls scenes of mob violence against Black people, yet instead of a voluntary white audience, an audience predominantly made up of Black and Brown people witnesses this lynching. Contrary to the assertions of Justice Clarence Thomas and Donald J. Trump, lynching is not a social encounter where one is ideologically outnumbered; it encompasses the execution, and representation of execution, of human life to send a monstrously intimate message to the larger collectives that that life represents.[102]

Raheem's lynching petrifies the onlookers. Neighborhood residents sense that interfering with the monstrous intimacy they are witnessing between Long and Raheem will render their bodies as vulnerable as Raheem's. The intimacy of their two bodies is instructive: these are the consequences that arise for Black and Brown people in such proximity to police.

Recognizing fragility where the police officers see only brute strength, Coconut Sid yells, "Goddamn it! You're killing him. Let him go!" He exclaims this, even though Sal has already killed "Radio Raheem"—as the Black man whose boom box was an extension of his desire. When Sal destroys Raheem's machine, as though cyborg, Raheem cannot (or perhaps is uninspired to) live without his radio. Sal does not interject, nor does Pino, as he has done earlier on Sal's behalf. Neither father nor son expresses any concern that the police are killing Raheem. Their silence articulates their complicity: Sal and Pino want Raheem dead. Their aural ethics align them with the same white supremacist capitalist heteropatriarchy that requires the exploitation of Black people, their unowned resources, and their premature deaths to remain supreme.

The last person to touch Raheem drops his lifeless body onto the sidewalk, and I wonder, rhetorically, what is Blacksound without breath. His right hand and the knuckle-duster ring that reads LOVE lie equally lifeless in front of his face. What is breath when the struggle to breathe constitutes resisting arrest? At this moment, I am reminded of a quote from Black feminist and performance and sound studies scholar Ashon T. Crawley regarding Eric Garner: "If he could not breathe it was because of the violence of white supremacist capitalist heteropatriarchy, a violence that cannot conceive of black flesh feeling pain, a violence that cannot think 'I can't breathe' anything other than ploy, trick, toward fugitive flight."[103] Raheem is as inviolable as his perceived Black masculinity—inviolable not because he is invulnerable but because there is (grossly assumed to be) nothing to violate.

Following this logic, Officer Ponte, instead of calling for an emergency medical technician, kicks Raheem's side, screaming, "Quit fakin' it!" This act suggests that Raheem's brute strength and Goliath-like appearance are too great to be subdued by a baton choke hold—an unfortunate overestimation of Raheem's Black masculinized body that (to them) justifies their use of excessive force. Raheem represents the Giant Negro their grandfathers before them had read about in the *New York Times*. Officer Ponte's racial subjectivity demonstrates how anyone, regardless of their perceived powerlessness in the eyes of the state, can wield the state's authority to take Black lives.

As the performance of subduing Raheem ends, the officers all act as though he is still alive, as one officer murmurs "Get him to the car" to hide their indiscretion from the rest of the community. After the incident, the police depart with Raheem's lifeless body resting in the back seat. Meanwhile, the concerned neighborhood residents trail the vehicle on foot, determined to follow as long as possible. They refuse to let go of their worry and fear for what the police have done to one of their own.

Enraged Black and Brown people surround Sal's place. Cee bursts out, "Damn, man! It ain't safe in our own fucking neighborhood." Coconut Sid (played by Frankie Faison) replies, "Never was. Never will be." Sid's revelation signals his sense of residential vulnerability as an older Black person disillusioned by his neighborhood's apparent unattainability of security or safety. This moment emblematizes how the performance of erotics is bound to safety along other dimensions of Black life. Indeed, had Raheem lived in a safe environment absent of state surveillance with financial support that affirms Blackness, would he have felt the need to express himself by blasting "Fight the Power"? And even if he had felt the need to do so, if Stevie's sensibilities had been more commonplace, would Raheem's violent encounter have occurred? Black safety and sensibility are a necessity if the racialized erotics of Blacksound is to not end in death.

Stevie claims, "It's murder. They did it again, like Michael Stewart." Ahmad (another neighborhood youth, played by Steve White) chimes in: "Murder. Eleanor Bumpurs. Murder." Later, Ahmad angrily blurts out, "You see how they had him in a choke hold, man? I know that choke hold. It kills people, man." With these recitations of Black murders, Lee references Black viralities within the already viral moment of his film—fractal virality. His characters enact this move by breaching the fourth wall with knowledge of the material world outside the film's diegetic symbolism. Stevie's and Ahmad's interferential knowledge of the choke hold and of Black men and women whom police had killed testifies to the repeated murderous acts they have witnessed more than once: enactments of the Black virality involved in subduing Black people.

Eleanor Bumpurs's murder is haunting for its fit within the index of the murders of Black women and girls in their homes—Nina Pop, Breonna Taylor, and Aiyana Stanley-Jones.[104] Counteracting the erasure of Black women caused by the Black virality of Black men due to male privilege (as with the "man and a brother" abolitionist seal), the film *Do the Right Thing* acknowledges and remembers the lives of Black women at this moment. Stevie's and Ahmad's examples of racial performativity suggest that Black men's livelihoods are bound to Black women's livelihoods, neither taking precedence over the other.

Still, the figurative Black viralities in popular culture that occupy the American imaginary are not divorced from these material police practices. The same imaginaries that incite a police officer's brutality toward and disregard for Black people (and their allies and accomplices) reflect understandings of Black people as inherently well endowed, superhumanly strong, and possessing a rapacious appetite for sex, violence, and criminality. These bigoted notions emerge from rumors about and encounters with mass-produced images of Black bodies in discourse. As cultural theorist Stuart Hall suggests, Black life is not a lived experience outside of representation.[105] Representations of Black people inform them of their personhoods as much as they reveal other people's perceptions of them. Thus, a lived Black experience interplays with representation in generative and detrimental ways. The material costs of representation raise the significance of Buggin Out's insistence on being represented on the wall of fame, which for him constitutes a liberated world—yet another "emergent strategy" that fighting back requires.

Mookie punctuates Stevie and Ahmad's recital of Black murders by throwing a garbage can through Sal's window (perhaps the fictional depiction of

Lee's wish for what should have occurred instead of a silent prayer at the pizzeria site of Michael Griffith's murder in Howard Beach).[106] The neighborhood then rebels en masse, looting and destroying Sal's pizzeria. The camera pans across the top of Sal's outdoor windows, which feature the words "Pizza Heroes Calzones Sausage." Sal, held back by Da Mayor, yells, "What the fuck are they doing? . . . That's my fucking place." Pino disapprovingly shakes his head, saying, "Fucking niggers." Smiley is the last protester to leave Sal's Famous Pizzeria as he sentimentally lights a match and drops it. The neighborhood chants, "Radio, Radio, Radio, Radio! . . . Howard Beach, Howard Beach, Howard Beach!" Having witnessed Radio Raheem's encounter with Stevie earlier, Mother Sister screams, "Burn it down! Burn it down!" Firefighters and more police arrive, alternately cuffing and blasting protesters with water. After many disperse, Mother Sister wails toward the burning building like the quintessential Black mother mourning a murdered child, a scene depicted in countless Hollywood films.[107] Da Mayor's chest muffles Mother Sister's cries of "No!" as he consoles her.

Every moment of the rebellion that Mookie encourages gestures to a greater phenomenon. The looting and burning of Sal's does not arise in a vacuum and gestures toward the Black lives looted and consumed by white supremacy referenced throughout the film. As the words "Pizza Heroes Calzones Sausage" shatter and burn, viewers face not only the food lost but also its heroes. The protest chants of "Radio!" and "Howard Beach!" cue the audience to the fractal virality of the fictional moment and how it links to earlier iterations of nonfictitious Black virality. The juxtaposition of Mother Sister's cries with Sal's shouts after the police drive away with Raheem's dead body and as residents destroy Sal's pizzeria is an open signifier of the shrill frictions that burn between the permanent loss of human life and the temporary loss of an insurable business.

Who is Raheem to Mother Sister? This question haunts her screams, as we learn nothing in the film about Raheem's age, family, or guardians. In this way, the screams articulate the complex personhood and intertwining of Mother Sister's and Radio Raheem's lives, if not as blood family, then chosen family. Her cries capture the loss that the community feels, performing a racialized erotics that expresses desire, longing, and loss through sound. In the spirit of lynching plays, even though Radio Raheem is now lifeless, Lee portrays the ineradicability of a community that lives on and honors him in mourning and rebellion.

Following the destruction of the visual source of Blacksound (Raheem's boom box consumed by flames), Lee employs an acousmatic recording of "Fight the Power" as a symbolic representation of a Blacksound born in flames, mirroring the technique used in Tina's initial street scene, where the song is played from an imaginary source.[108] The presence of "Fight the Power" articulates the resilience of Blacksound as it reverberates off the tiles of Sal's walls before playing loudly in the soundtrack's foreground. Smiley wanders into the pizzeria without being accosted by the police or blasted by water from the firefighters. Sal's wall of fame still burns—but not before Smiley exerts the righteously loud will of Buggin Out and Radio Raheem and puts "some Black people [Malcolm X and Dr. Martin Luther King Jr. specifically] on that motherfucking wall of fame."

FAST FORWARD: Black Masculinity and the Viral Afterlife of Radio Raheem

FAST FORWARD brings one to the most present performance of a recorded act. Fast forward allows one to skim through things quickly, to survey them instead of capturing every element. One can also hear how, even through the distorted pitch of the original act winding almost out of control, the performance remains in the loop. Every fast forward on one side of the tape rewinds the other, producing a concurrent back-and-forth in time.

• • •

Radio Raheem—just like the Black boom box–wielders that he references—proves to be an undying performance of Blackness and Black masculinity. His survival and revival in the popular imagination and Black popular culture signal his meaning in African American communities as a folk hero.[109] His character continues to be performed and retold. People almost reject the idea of his fictional death or perhaps relate to the essence of his life: the determination to listen and be heard. In popular culture, people persist in performing and retelling how he was perceived—as a disturbance, unarmed yet dangerous.

For instance, the adult cartoon *The Boondocks,* which is based on the comic strip of the same name and follows the unfolding drama/life of the Freemans—a Black family that has moved from Chicago's South Side to settle in the fictional white suburb of Woodcrest, Maryland—(re-)presents Radio Raheem's narrative on an episode titled "The Block is Hot."[110] During an unusual winter heat wave "hotter than the barrel in Dick Cheney's gun," Huey Freeman (a fictional version of the Black Panther leader Huey Newton as a child) walks out of his aluminum-sided house dressed in a peacoat and scarf. He plays Public Enemy's "Fight the Power" from his boom box, which looks like a suitcase.

Figure 20 showcases a brief portrayal of the opening of this scene. As the music blasts, white people are running and walking for exercise and walking their dogs—acts that have quickly become commonplace with white privilege, entitlement, and leisure. Riley (Huey's brother), reanimating Punchy's character from *Do the Right Thing,* opens up a fire hydrant, attaches a can to its opening, and aims it across the street to his white neighbors' dismay, yelling, "C'mon everybody, what you waitin' for!" Huey highlights race and class differences as reflected in the contrasts between urban density and suburban spaciousness inherent to Riley's performance, reminding his younger brother, "White people have pools!" Amid all of this, Uncle Ruckus (a Black white nationalist) tells Riley, "You quit playin' with the white man's water, boy," and then tells Huey to "Turn off that goddamn BlackAfrican-Congo-jungle noise!," emulating both Officer Long—to a lesser extent—and Sal—to a greater extent—but as an older Black American. Uncle Ruckus then calls the police on Riley only to be mistaken, ironically, as the threatening Black male he tries to identify at the scene. This case of mistaken identity due to racial profiling echoes countless instances of the sort in the United States that have ended in the deaths or arrests of Black and Brown people, such as Leon McCray and Ricardo Diaz-Zeferino. Recalling Amadou Diallo's execution by police, as Uncle Ruckus pulls out his wallet to show identification, an officer yells, "Gun!" Everyone shoots at Uncle Ruckus, who responds by not identifying as a Black person: "Wait, not me, I got Indian in my family." The police officer's reaction signifies the notion of Blackness as arming, a visual embodiment that alerts one to the presence, or the possibility, of a threatening weapon. As a Black virality of Radio Raheem, *The Boondocks* not only repeats his narrative with a signal difference, it also expands on and reduces its meaning, giving us a short satirical glimpse into what could unfold after transplanting Radio Raheem's Black performance to the modern suburbs.

FIGURE 20 Screenshot, July 25, 2014, "The Block Is Hot," *The Boondocks*, directed by Kalvin Lee (Culver City, CA: Sony Pictures Home Entertainment, 2006).

Radio Raheem is often mentioned in the first verses of hip-hop songs that revere him for standing up against the polarizing forces of anti-Black racism and white entitlement and for asserting an unapologetically loud expression of himself that was not concerned with outward gazes. For example, the first verse of the song "Pump Up the Volume" by The Cool Kids begins

> Feel like summer '89 in Do The Right Thing
> Got a big ass radio walking down the street
> With the Spike Lee Nikes on Buggin Out the streets
> Hand full of gold rings like Radio Raheem[111]

This rap group—comprising Chuck Inglish and Mikey Rocks, both born in the 1980s—was interested in bringing that decade back and evoking Radio Raheem's memory to do so. Here, Radio Raheem is not only an index of the Black men who came before him blasting radios in the streets but also of the 1980s era.

Radio Raheem appears again in the first verse of the song "Good Morning" from Kanye West's third album, *Graduation*, which is part of a three-album series that uses school—dropping out, registering, and graduating—as a theme. He raps, "I mean, did you ever see the test / You got Ds motherfucker Ds!"[112] In his verse, West recalls the situation where Radio Raheem's boom box stops playing because its batteries are low. Radio Raheem communicates his need for D batteries—"D motherfucker, D!"—to the Korean store owners, who do not understand him. West, however, evokes this scene to explain a school report card, referencing Radio Raheem over fifteen years after the release of *Do the Right Thing*.

J Dilla's posthumously released album, *The Shining*, references Radio Raheem on the song "E=MC²." In the second verse, Common raps, "Since the early 80s I rocked the planet daily / Radio Rasheed this is how I do when I write things / The party for your right to fight scenes."[113] Common merges his and Radio Raheem's identity into one, "Radio Rasheed," identifying with him as someone who travels the earth executing great parties and concerts, which are necessarily loud. Playing on the title, *Do the Right Thing*, Common uses the homonym *write* to play on *right* and to talk about his writing as a hip-hop artist. His line, "The party for your right to fight scenes," blurs the line between leisure activity and political resistance, recalling the idea of "singin' while swingin'" from Public Enemy's "Fight the Power."

On Danny Brown's *The Hybrid Mixtape*, Danny raps, in the first verse of his song titled "My Father's Gun," "Brown ain't good no reason for a theme / So do the right thing or get Radio Raheem'd / 'Cause little nigga you pop tart."[114] The entire song is a machismo boast, but what stands out for my purposes in this chapter is how Radio Raheem becomes a verb in his viral afterlife. Turning someone or something into a verb requires certain recognizability (think: Airbnb, Zoom, Google). This verbification suggests that what happened to Radio Raheem is recognizable enough to make his circumstance into a verb and fit it into a couplet. Being Radio Raheem'd entails being senselessly assassinated (in this context, analogous to being a pop star in the company of Brown).

In a song titled "Tell Me" on Hassaan Mackey and Apollo Brown's *Daily Bread* album, Mackey raps, "They say the music is too loud but / Radio Raheem's thing / Is keeping Hassaan attached to his dreams."[115] His lyrics suggest that the loudness at which he plays his music, which he associates with Radio Raheem—indicative of audacity, boldness, and courage—resounds with Hassaan more than those who would have him turn down the volume, this freedom of expression inspiring Hassaan to pursue his goals in life.

In Jarren Benton's "C.R.E.A.M '17 (feat. Nick Grant)," the artist raps,

> You can't win when you got haters on the team
> They did that nigga Eric Garner like he Radio Raheem
> No D batteries they train 'em at academies
> No empathy for niggas just wet up their whole anatomies
> Sadly another casualty.[116]

Benton recognizes the parallels between how Radio Raheem was killed in *Do the Right Thing* and how Eric Garner was killed in Staten Island. Further reflecting on the police, Benton notes their lack of empathy. They see Raheem as a threat, even while holding him in a choke hold, while in those same moments, his neighbors see him as threatened. Moreover, Benton shares how police are trained to riddle Black people's entire bodies with bullets, which recalls how police used racially Black-appearing targets at shooting ranges in Farmington Hills, Michigan, and Villa Rica, Georgia.[117]

A more recent rap that Radio Raheem was named in is Rapsody's song "12 Problems," one of several promotional singles from a curated Roc Nation compilation called *Reprise: A Roc Nation Album*. The album intends to "bring awareness to social justice issues," with a portion of the "proceeds [going] to funding organizations [like the NACDL Foundation for Criminal Justice, Until Freedom, and Grassroots Law Project] that support victims of police brutality, hate crimes, and other violations of civil rights."[118] In the song, the artist raps, "Get ya shit straight, mr. Police / Did the same thing to Cochise / Did the same thing to Raheem / Did the same thing in our reality, y'all bogus." Like the viral violence that Stevie narrates, Rapsody recalls the Indigenous resistance to colonialism that Cochise, an Apache chief, carried out and tethers it to the Black resistance to gentrification and police brutality of Radio Raheem's performance. In *The Black Shoals*, Black feminist and Indigenous studies scholar Tiffany Lethabo King refers to the legacy of Rapsody's "mr. Police," whose violence haunts Cochise and Raheem as the "conquistador-settler" whose possession of land is one of many violent strategies for controlling Black and Indigenous people, perpetuated in what Rapsody calls "our reality."[119]

Radio Raheem inhabits the realm of visual art, too. For the Mandela Poster Project, which honors Nelson Mandela's lifelong contributions to humanity, self-taught South African and Zimbabwean artist, graphic designer, activist, and contemporary illustrator Sindiso Nyoni (aka R!OT) submitted a cutout design called *The Boxer* (see figure 21). In the image, which merges Mandela's features with signature elements of Radio Raheem, Nyoni gives Mandela a high-top fade, places a boom box on his shoulder, depicts the words "Fight the Power" in the corner, and creates a gold knuckle-duster ring on his fist that reads *UTHANDO*, which means "love" in Zulu. The image gestures toward how love defeats hate, a part of Radio Raheem's and Nelson Mandela's ethos. Of seven hundred submissions, Nyoni's design made it to the final ninety-five. In the work, "95" replaces the "gh," of *fight*, which is the year of Mandela's presidency when he established the Truth and Reconciliation Commission

FIGURE 21 Sindiso Nyoni, *The Boxer,* 2013, from "The Boxer (Mandela Poster Project)," Behance, accessed July 18, 2013, http://www.behance.net/gallery/The-Boxer-(Mandela-poster-project)/9346799.

with chair Archbishop Desmond Tutu to begin the process of healing from the many thefts of apartheid. Here, we witness Radio Raheem's cosmopolitan Black masculinity being transnationally communicated by an artist who sees a similar strength, courage, and love in the late international figure in the fight for humanity—Nelson Mandela.

In 2014, Chicago's Daniel S. Wentworth Elementary School featured an installation dedicated to Radio Raheem. Figure 22 shows the installation, titled *Black Wall 2*. Led by the teaching, visual, and performance artist Avery R. Young (since appointed the first poet laureate of Chicago), students used images and texts to examine hip-hop context, culture, and audience. These children, born over a decade after the waning of the popularity of *Do the Right Thing*, are not paying homage to Mookie, who indecisively throws the garbage can through Sal's window, or to the elders like Mother Sister, who watches over the neighborhood, and Da Mayor, who drinks beer and protects the neighborhood in his own way. Instead, the students pay homage to Radio Raheem, who lived to express himself loudly and resist placation, who died because of how he was popularly perceived—a superhumanly strong, Black, and dangerous disturber of the peace.

In 2015, visual artist Brandan "BMike" Odums curated what he called the "largest street exhibit in the American South," a graffiti exhibit called *ExhibitBE*. It was open on Saturdays from November 15, 2014, to January 25, 2015, in an abandoned apartment complex known as Bridge Plaza and renamed De Gaulle Manor at 3010 Sandra Drive in Algiers, New Orleans. At the exhibit's heart lies a two-story recreational building facing those apartments. Among images of historic Black leaders like Harriet Tubman, MLK,

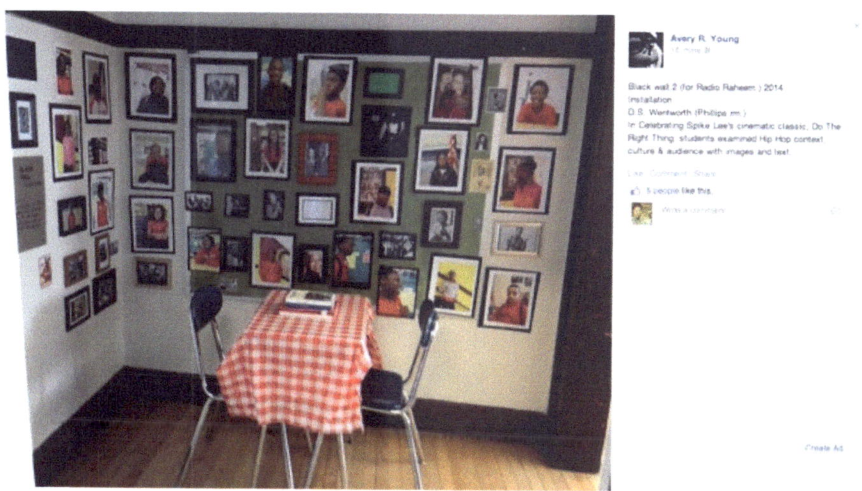

FIGURE 22 Screenshot, June 14, 2014, Avery R. Young, "Black Wall 2 (for Radio Raheem)," from D. S. Wentworth (Philips Rm), Facebook.

and Assata Shakur, BMike had spray-painted a mural of Radio Raheem onto a tall panel on one face of the four-sided column at the center of the domed building. At the nexus of the roof arches, Raheem stares off to his left while holding his boom box with his right hand. Atop a background of red, a bold yellow circle haloes his head. The work, completed May 15, 2014, is in good company. To Radio Raheem's right, on a nearby wall, is a picture of Muhammad Ali.[120]

In a more haunting representation of Radio Raheem's legacy, on July 18, 2014, Spike Lee posted an unlisted YouTube video to Facebook titled "NYPD Puts Deadly Chokehold on Staten Island Man," visually and sonically drawing parallels between Eric Garner's and Radio Raheem's deaths.[121] Lee did not publicly list the link, which means that it had to be actively clicked to see the video rather than it playing passively or unintentionally through a Facebook feed. (Because such an exposure could trigger unnecessary psychic trauma, I refuse to include a still from the video here.) To create the chilling video, Lee mainly used a cutaway film technique to alternate abruptly between the scenes leading up to and including Eric Garner's and Radio Raheem's deaths to highlight their similarities.

Both Black men had the air choked out of them after their Black and Brown neighbors had seen them surrender and the sense of emergency had dissipated. But white police officers still saw a loud, large, and superhumanly strong Black masculine figure, characteristics they considered life-threatening. Unlike Raheem, though, Garner was not physically threatening anyone. Yet his resistance to being seized by police officers who did not announce they were arresting him and, what is more challenging to prove, this antagonism over his Black masculinity provoked the undertaking of a similar deadly response to subdue his body. In this response, even the fight for breath is resisting arrest.

The routine nature of the deadly responses to both Garner and Raheem cannot easily be distinguished from the racial fantasies and indifference toward Black life that influenced the behavior of these NYPD officers, both in material and figurative ways. The criminalization of both men, driven by systemic stereotypes of their Black masculinity, guided the officers in how to handle them. Almost like agents from the precrime criminal justice agency—an agency from Philip K. Dick's science fiction novel *Minority Report*—which punishes people for crimes before they have committed them—police officers apprehended both Black men in deadly ways that Garner's and Raheem's actions did not conjure.[122] Blackness, then, becomes false yet believable evidence of crimes that will be committed by Black people who, "if allowed to remain free [or alive], will at some future time commit felonies [or misdemeanors]."[123]

As with many other people and concepts that populate *Do the Right Thing*, Radio Raheem existed long before he arrived on the scene and, as such, will persist long after the scene ends.[124] Whether as Joe Radio, Raheem Abdul Muhammed, or the drum's keeper, Radio Raheem embodies all these figures, using the beat for every aspect of existence: creating (life, harvest, and celebration) and destroying (war and death).[125] His murder echoes the unfortunate violence experienced by Black people and foreshadows the violence that Black people to come will experience. Radio Raheem's murder was the consequence of the Black virality of excessive force enacted to subdue Black bodies.

During the remote graduations of 2020, forced due to the ravages of the COVID-19 pandemic, I tuned in to Huron High School's virtual commencement address on Zoom to witness my cousin's graduation. It featured a discussion of Radio Raheem as arguably one of film's most compelling and vital characters. The speaker, English teacher Sean Eldon, emphasized, "It's not just in the past. Radio Raheem is George Floyd and Breonna Taylor. This is not just in a thread or social media stream. The anger and mass protests are not new. . . . It is the America into which you are graduating."[126] With these words, Eldon conveyed the fractal virality that Radio Raheem represents, which requires the interplay of fiction with reality.

Indeed, in the ending scenes of *Do the Right Thing*, Stevie, who concedes the aural sphere to Radio Raheem earlier in the film, shouts out, "It's murder. They did it again, just like Michael Stewart."[127] His assertion, "They did it again," is crucial to an understanding of viral violence—this incessant doing again that, through repetition, becomes the natural and inhumane way of subduing Black people. The lack of consequences that police (and civilians) experience time and again after using excessive force instructs them as much as the viral violence toward Black people they witness.[128] A Black man then shouts, "Murder. Eleanor Bumpurs. Murder!"[129] What emerges are citations that reference the unnecessary and egregious killing of Black people. If characters from the fictional neighborhood were to persist, they would inevitably arrive at our present moment, shouting out names like Latasha Harlins, Renisha McBride, Aiyana Stanley-Jones, Mike Brown, Trayvon Martin, and, with a poignant relationship to Radio Raheem's death, Jordan Russell Davis.

Radio Jordan: See-Jaying Visceral Realities with Visceral Fictions of Black Masculinity

Figure 23, titled *Radio Jordan*, is an image that manifests certain feelings that I experienced during the moments I first heard about seventeen-year-old Jordan Davis, the mistrial following his murder, and the "loud-music trial" of Michael Dunn. I was already incorporating Radio Raheem into my work, and Jordan's encounter haunted me as a frightening instance of life imitating art. The mistrial, nevertheless, inspired me to see-jay—or sample

FIGURE 23 *Radio Jordan*, photograph by Gabriel Peoples, February 26, 2014.

and remix familiar images that summon the sonic and visual—*Radio Jordan*.[130] Renowned author and journalist Ta-Nehisi Coates's reflection on the mistrial after his interview with Jordan's mother, Lucy McBath, captures the unwritten rules implied in the court that day: Black lives are inviolable (in the sense of not being able to be broken rather than being protected from breaking). Coates writes, "The killer was convicted not of the boy's murder but of firing repeatedly as the boy's friends tried to retreat. Destroying the black body was permissible—but it would be better to do it efficiently."[131] Dunn was later convicted of first-degree murder in the retrial on October 1, 2014. Still, before and after the retrial, my feelings centered on the interrelationship of the Black viralities of Black masculinity and the Black viralities of excessive force undertaken to subdue Black lives.

Radio Raheem's music was deemed more disturbing than Sal's racial slurs and more violent than Sal's act of killing his radio. And Raheem's perceived brute strength and criminality induced Officer Long to choke the life out of him. Likewise, I witnessed how Jordan's music was deemed more threatening, his visible identity as a young Black teen more troubling than the ten shots fired by a white man, Michael Dunn, at a Dodge Durango filled with four unarmed Black masculine teens. Dunn, like Sal, could not separate the (Chicago drill) music he heard from the life of the young teenager he saw.[132] Despite Jordan's cosmopolitan Blackness, the music that Dunn encountered reinforced the expressions of the street thugs he associated with the thumping bass, leading him to imagine the presence of a shotgun. Playing loud music, something that gave Jordan and his friends so much enjoyment, was inaccurately used to profile them as dangerous figures, even if only as precriminals.

During the loud-music trial, Dunn's fiancée, Rhonda Rouer, testified that, on the evening of his confrontation with Jordan Davis, Dunn had said, "Oh, I hate that thug music."[133] What Dunn said substantiates my earlier claim about the inseparability of cultures of visualization from the construction of sonic meanings. As the title of my first chapter states, people hear what they see. Dunn saw criminal Black masculinity based on what he associated, not with the lyrics, but, in his own words, with "just bass."[134] Similarly, without distinguishing the diversity of lyrics and issues addressed in "Fight the Power," Sal understood hip-hop music as jungle music, which escalated into his calling Radio Raheem a "nigger motherfucker." Sound is negligently assessed and displaced onto a visual Blackness in ways that call into question the moral basis for using music in criminal trials or making snap judgments based on sound in everyday life.

The "thug music" that Dunn heard was Jordan and his friends playing Chicago drill music, whose themes (similar to trap music) are not only a reflection on street life but also a premeditation of scenarios (i.e., selling drugs, murdering a specific person or group, having sex or being in a relationship with a person, and making something of yourself), which makes it both a representation of life and potentially real life. The term *drill* originated from Pacman, a late rapper from Chicago, and it was used to signify retaliating against an adversary. The Chicago rap duo L.E.P. Bogus Boys describes drill as slang for various meanings, from women beautifying themselves to street wars.[135] The music, which varies from trap- and twerk-oriented rhythms to ghettotech/juke rhythms prevalent in places like Chicago, Detroit, Baltimore, and New Jersey, is unique for integrating all these rhythms. Repeated sonic features of drill songs include heavy bass, gunshots, and the haunting rings of tolling bells, their slow ringing often associated with death. The name also recalls the repeated exercise and inundating nature of its lyrical and sonic content. "Beef," by the rap artist Lil Reese and featuring Fredo Santana and Lil Durk, was the drill song Jordan and his friends were playing that led to the altercation with Dunn.

In *Radio Jordan*, I merge Jordan's face with Radio Raheem's, suggestive of how people in Jacksonville, Florida, specifically Dunn, saw him as a fictional larger-than-life young Black masculine figure, which was, unfortunately, alarming even though Jordan was unarmed. Similarly, although Radio Raheem was physically large, his music made him physically larger, increased his sonic volume. But no matter how Goliath-like or thug-like music makes a person in another's imagination, it never justifies treating them as actual Goliaths or thugs with imagined superhuman strength and deadly projectile weapons. This assumption doomed both Radio Raheem and Jordan Davis.

In the piece, Davis wears an OBEY hat, "an experiment in Phenomenology." Shepard Fairey, the creator of OBEY fashion explains: "Phenomenology attempts to enable people to see clearly something that is right before their eyes but obscured; things that are so taken for granted that they are muted by abstract observation."[136] Considering this definition, the OBEY hat Davis wears comes to signify much more than a fashion symbol. What is clear but concurrently obscured is that figurative perceptions have dire material effects on Black people's lives. White entitlement maintains the subjugation of Black people and their representations. Therefore, obedience to maintaining peace will not change how other people see and hear Black people. "OBEY," in this juxtaposition with Black masculine bodies materially affected by how white and white-passing people have figuratively seen and physically heard them, acts as sarcasm, encouraging disobedience in the face of anyone or any system requiring them to turn their volume down.

I made the *Radio Jordan* photograph black and white to suggest that this type of loud expression, as well as violence toward Black people, is old, yet its legacy extends into 2012 and beyond, from 1989 and before. Twice I witnessed the shock of an eavesdropping passerby noticing the scene on my laptop where police killed Radio Raheem. To paraphrase, two people asked me, "Again?" The repetitiveness of this violence toward Black people blurs the distinction between 1989 and the present, indicating its long-standing existence. The black and white of the photograph also signify the racial bodies involved in both death-bound encounters—Jordan Davis being Black, Michael Dunn being white, Radio Raheem being Black, and Sal being white. Whiteness also haunts the scene in its absent presence.

While some similarities between Radio Raheem's and Jordan Davis's stories prompted me to render the image, their lives are very different. Radio Raheem, of course, is fictional and merely representative of real Black masculine bodies. Alternatively, Jordan was real and representative of a Black masculine person. In *Do the Right Thing*, we never know who Raheem's parents or guardians are or what his goals and ambitions are beyond Mother Sister's bellowing cries for him and his playing of "Fight the Power" all day. In contrast, Jordan's mother described him as cosmopolitan. His family included Mexicans, Panamanians, and white people. He lived in a three-story home in the suburbs, and he was aware of the level of consciousness in Jacksonville—likely the same consciousness that rendered him illegible as the young Black person he was.[137]

Radio Raheem and Jordan are similar, however, in telling ways. Based on how McBath raised him, she imagines he defended his friends. In response to being asked by Dunn to turn his music down, she imagined and shared that he likely critically asserted, "We're not bothering you. We don't know you. You don't know us. Why can't we play our music as loud as we want?"[138] Raheem and Davis were loudly playing music, not just for themselves but for their blocks/cul-de-sac, their friends, and for the line of Black people before them who asserted themselves through the aural sphere for everyone to hear. Despite their awareness of the racism present in their respective worlds, both Radio Raheem and Jordan refused to let others' hatred or entitlement suppress their agency.

What began as a form of Black sensibility, playing loud music with friends, became a counter to Dunn's entitlement to the gas station they both rightly occupied. Taking the circumstances in the gas station into account, even a song like "Beef" can be understood through Davis's cosmopolitan Blackness as resistance to, camaraderie against, and declaration of the symbolic dismantling of white entitlement.[139] Jordan was in line with an underlying intent of drill music: to retaliate against an adversary—an enemy, including Dunn, that had loudly assaulted his space, his expressions, and his existence as a Black person in the United States long before he arrived at the gas station. Retaliation against Dunn's assault took the form of unapologetically turning the music up loudly in the face of his false politeness and white entitlement.

Jordan's and Radio Raheem's lives inspire us to turn the music up. As an example, during the first day of the loud-music trial, @swhiteAKA3 wrote on Twitter, "I will be playing my radio very loudly on purpose today #NeverForget #JordanDavis."[140] That Jordan was a bright young man with a promising future was not the only reason we will #NeverForget him. It is also because of circulating his photos online, indexing him with other Black men who have suffered similar precrime fates, and his not compromising himself to satiate white entitlement. Despite the real danger that exists from being Black while playing music as loudly as desired, the audacity to do so exercises freedom, which I define as the absence of fear with an awareness of danger—an act that both Jordan and Raheem performed in their lives that we have come to know. They both dared to refuse to turn down their volumes to make others comfortable.[141]

Radio Jordan imagines Raheem's legacy in the things that affect Black livelihoods and reflects how his boom box travels, transforms, and mutates. Also related to loudly playing music outdoors, car and truck speakers, too, are used in performances of Black masculinity. After lawmakers had criminalized loudly playing the boom box, the next logical focus, always there, became the sound systems of cars and trucks. The cultural act of loudly playing mobile sound systems in public indeed counters the deafening loudness of white entitlement, white privilege, and anti-Black racism that masks itself in silence. Laws, practices, and prices that violently exclude Black and Brown people and their expressions from spaces possessively invested in whiteness contribute to the amplification of assaults on Black wellness. Turning our volume up to disrupt the silence around the presumed precrime of Black and Brown people, the disproportionate surveillance of Black and Brown people, white privilege, white entitlement, and white nationalism is one of many things we must do to be heard.

Radio Jordan is the unlisted upload I never uploaded, the comment I never posted, and the critical rumor I never circulated. By framing *Radio Jordan* with my thoughts, I disengage from the type of circulation that can easily lead to amnesia around the circumstances that birth Black performances before they become uncontrollable. By centering the burden, I deliberately anticipate circumstances under which audiences engage with everything except the burden. In this way, although I engage in the Black virality of Black masculine boom box wielders, I am also raising the visibility of their noniconic vulnerability, their seeking of pleasure, and their challenge of power through the capacity of Blacksound.

To be sure, making the image is also a mode of critique, remix, or repetition with signal differences, not to mention mourning. Remixing is a critical technique for thinking, revealing, and exploring ideologies. It reminds us to persistently combat not just the structure of authority but those in authority, using the strength of our sound systems, encompassing not only our boom boxes and car stereos but also our voices and creativity, electronic posts and reposts, and mediums that allow us to spread wellbeing and social engagement. Broadcasting vessels continue to be crucial to struggles against racism and discrimination of all sorts, and even though Sal (read: white supremacy) destroys Radio Raheem's boom box, the Internet may contain much hope for amplifying his message: fight the power!

CHAPTER 3

Woman Wakes Up to Find Intruder in Her Bed

A Critical Discourse Analysis of a Rape Attempt Gone Viral

> "This actually aired on my local news today. 'Obviously, we have a rapist here . . . so hide yo kids, hide yo wife, and hide yo husband 'cause dey rapin' e'rybody out here."
> —panhead

In July 2010, I was a graduate student living in Atlanta, Georgia, for the summer. I recall how hot it was and trying to save money by leaving the central air conditioner off until the evening. The apartment windows remained closed to keep the cool air inside. While lurking on the web that hot summer, I encountered a story about an attempted rape that had circulated quickly and widely, goin' viral.[1] I was lurking only because a friend had shared a link to its remix video, which made me want to research whether it had been staged. I questioned its validity because the scenario of news media reporters seeking Black people for testimony was overdone ("Who all seen the leprechaun, say yeah!").[2] Shortly after going down that rabbit hole, I concluded: that shit happened!

The viral story began when a local news station reported the home invasion and attempted rape of Kelly Dodson, a Black cisgender (cis) woman, in the Lincoln Park public housing projects of Huntsville, Alabama. Reporters interviewed Kelly Dodson and her brother, Antoine Dodson, a Black cis man who had thwarted the rape, causing the assailant to flee the scene. The Dodsons' story gained popularity when Huntsville's NBC-affiliated WAFF 48 News broadcasted it under the title "Woman Wakes Up to Find Intruder in Her Bed," and it became their most frequently viewed video in 2010 (with upwards of two hundred thousand views before someone removed it from the station's website for unspecified reasons). Each remix that followed, perhaps taking cues from the original newscast, relegated Kelly Dodson further to the margins, reducing her to sound bites, diminishing her personhood, and centering her brother's testimony. The story's rapid and broad circulation marginalized the Black woman at its center.

My return to this media event reflects a broader issue—the never-ending violence against Black cis women, Black trans women, and queer Black men, and their simultaneous viral circulation and marginalization. The neglect of these groups of Black people also plagues current social media–based movements, despite Black queer or cis women's centrality to their emergence. Given the past popularity of the #MeToo movement, it is important to acknowledge that despite Tarana Burke's creation of the phrase as a response to a Black girl's sexual trauma, Black women often experience erasure in its overindexing. Therefore, it is worth revisiting the viral circulation and subsequent erasure of Kelly Dodson's narrative, the event of which occurred over a decade and a half ago.

To explore the meaning of the Black virality of the Dodsons and the cultural mechanisms through which interactors circulated it, I examine the textual and (audio)visual details of a select group of viral sources. My examination unveils how textual, visual, and audiovisual material adapts to and adopts the Dodsons' story of domestic and discursive violence. Using critical discourse analysis, I focus on the original newscast to illuminate how interactors script the Dodsons, how the Dodsons have scripted themselves, and what the tensions between scripted and scripter reveal in an atmosphere where interactors have circulated an aspect of the Dodson's lives to the point of being commonplace. This critical discourse analysis reveals how the Dodsons, Black womanhood, Black femininities, and Black masculinities come into being in popular culture and everyday life through their transformation into mass-produced "things"—including objectified things and things inspired by what is unlivable—and move toward new possibilities for livability.

I argue that the rapid mode in which racialized gender knowledge of Black people circulates to the point of being commonplace—Black virality—often marginalizes Black women who experience sexual assault. My use of Black virality clarifies how I arrive at a concept that fits under its umbrella, the Ghetto Witness, which I explore later in the chapter.

In this chapter, I converge on three points of inquiry: (1) an analysis of the visual language and sonic vocabulary of WAFF 48's news coverage of the rape attempt and its trivialization of Kelly Dodson's experience of violence; (2) how Kelly Dodson's erasure occurs through what interactors include, exclude, and foreground in the story of her rape attempt; and (3) the foregrounding of her brother, Antoine Dodson, as it plays a crucial role in (re)scripting their racialized sexualities and genders, doing Black feminist work, and goin' viral.[3] My investigation reveals the chaos and order inherent to Black viralities, exemplified by the uncertainty of knowing when or how the next person will interpret, remix, or spread a Black performance.

In the second phase of my argument, I examine the "Woman Wakes Up to Find Intruder in Bed" news broadcast. The viral broadcast serves as an example of the noniconic: something pedestrian encountered by spectators with the viral remix video forever appended to it. In this chapter, I focus on that newscast rather than its far more widely circulated viral remix video counterpart, which I explore in the following chapter. Concentrating on the newscast allows a sharper focus on Kelly Dodson, whose erasure continues to structure its viral afterlife. Unfortunately, the comedy that structures her erasure simultaneously suggests there is nothing remarkable about a Black cis woman's perceived straightness or the fact that a stranger almost raped her. Racialized sexuality contributes to the social amnesia and misogynoir of these movements and moments that originate with Black women and end with their erasure.[4]

According to literary and cultural theorist Abdul R. JanMohamed, we are already discussing race when we talk about sexuality, and vice versa, and there are racial ways that sexuality becomes differently expressed, pathologized, and policed, particularly when thinking about a Black woman's body in discourse.[5] Thus, when discourses treat Black women as subjects who are inviolable (read: ineligible for violations that would be transgressions against white women), the single Black woman–led family as always public, and Black men as the most visible victims or survivors of violence (except for rape), Black women's racialized sexuality and gender are circumscribed.[6] These limitations shape the social forgetting that erases Black women's traumas and pleasures. Thus, Black women have no virtue to be dishonored or broken, and their households hold no rights to privacy when intruded upon by the state or vigilantes, and no joy to protect from violence. As violence against Black men is more openly recognized and commonly seen, observers neglect violence against Black women, a case of misogynoir.[7]

The danger for Black people when their representations go viral is two-sided. Anyone can access discourses that abound within interfaces, thus transforming Black virality into a pedagogical tool that teaches interactors what to do and what not to do in encounters with Black life. This story, for example, taught us that an intruder can get away with attempted rape in Lincoln Park without worrying about accountability. However, the visibility that interfaces like the news and YouTube allow are also used by activists as leverage for social justice (as in aiding Marissa Alexander's receiving a reduced sentence for aggravated assault).[8] Thus, Black virality is both a tool and a weapon.

Black virality turns Black beings into "things." Things include the mainstream definition on one side, which is a type of violent objecthood; however, my differentiated use in quotes centers on the other side, wherein they are objects that stand out by their visibility and are worth paying attention to, owing to their livability (this type of memorability is involved when someone asks, “Is that a *thing* now?”). What is livable demands dignity affirmed by the individual “thing” and the society that surrounds that “thing.” I focus on what we should keep, where an intentional liberatory force is at the center of objects, which performance historian Uri McMillan calls “(Black) objecthood.”[9] Here, by standing out from the mundane, objects like viral videos that feature Black life become “things” and need not always be mute commodities or derogatory objects but “things” that can speak to their complexities and counter their reducibility.[10] “Woman Wakes Up to Find Intruder in Bed” is one such “thing.”

The Forgotten Kelly Dodson: Black Virality and the Interplay of Excess and Erasure

On July 28, 2010, at 3:10 am, Kelly Dodson was sleeping in the Lincoln Park projects when she awakened to find a stranger in her bed attempting to rape her.[11] She screamed, and hearing this, her brother, Antoine Dodson, ran upstairs to help. Seeing the intruder’s hands wrapped around Kelly’s neck, Antoine pulled him off. While Antoine attended to Kelly, the man escaped.[12] The Dodsons called friends and family first to alert them that someone had broken in. They then called the police. After the police arrived and questioned them about the attack, they went to a relative’s home. At 8:00 a.m. the same day, Kelly and Antoine returned to their home and reported to housing management what had happened, which “thought it was a joke . . . was making fun of it and was actually laughing in [their] face[s].”[13] Later that morning, WAFF 48 News of Huntsville arrived to cover the home invasion. The Dodsons welcomed the news crew and, at this point, were eager to tell their story.[14]

On the following day, July 29, 2010, WAFF 48 published a live news story online chronicling the events under the aforementioned title, “Woman Wakes Up to Find Intruder in Her Bed.” On *r/funny*, a Reddit community that shares humorous stories on Reddit.com, an interactor who went by “panhead” posted a link to WAFF 48’s online video of the story.[15] (The referenced post has since disappeared from the news station’s website.) The link posted by panhead read, “This actually aired on my local news today. ‘Obviously, we have a rapist here . . . so hide yo kids, hide yo wife, and hide yo husband ’cause dey rapin’ e’rybody out here.’”[16] The post showed that 93 percent of the voting Reddit interactors had upvoted the post. Like Facebook’s likes and Twitter’s retweets and favorites, upvoting increases the visibility and popularity of Reddit posts, in this case, WAFF 48’s interview. Shortly after panhead’s post appeared, YouTube interactor Z01D1111 posted the news station's interview video on YouTube.[17] From WAFF 48 News to Reddit to YouTube, the live interview spread uncontrollably, goin' viral.

In thc unedited news broadcast, Kelly Dodson (almost inaudibly) tells the white female news reporter, Elizabeth Gentle, that her daughter was with her when the stranger sexually assaulted her, revealing the intergenerational trauma that resulted from this rape attempt.[18] But the edited sound bite heard most clearly in the live broadcast comprises Kelly Dodson proclaiming, "I was attacked by some idiot out here in the projects." Then, rolling her neck, she asserts, "He tried to rape me. He tried to pull my clothes off."[19] Despite the seriousness of this home invasion and the rape attempt, most of the story focused on Antoine Dodson.

In his interview with WAFF 48, as seen in figure 24, Antoine Dodson emphasizes the intruder did exist and was not a figment of his sister's imagination: "Well, *obviously*, we have a *rapist* in Lincoln Park!" He then cautions others about the rapist: "He's climbin' in yo' windows, snatchin' yo' people up, so y'all need to hide ya kids, hide ya wives, and hide ya husbands 'cause they rapin' e'rybody out here!" He then offers a passionate, odd, and threatening warning to the perpetrator involved: "We got yo' t-shirt, you done left fingerprints and all, you are so dumb, you are really dumb, for real." He continues, "You don't have to come and confess that you did it, we lookin' for you, we gon' find you. I'm lettin' you know na," and reinforces that warning with the confrontation, "So you can run 'n' tell that . . ." He rolls his eyes to his left, ". . . homeboy."[20]

What followed was a cascade of viral online coverage of the news story by "grassroots intermediaries,"[21] the most popular being "Auto-Tune the News: Bed Intruder Song!!!" by the Gregory Brothers. The song was uploaded on July 31, 2010, garnering 74,000,000+ views within its first year and 147,358,044+

FIGURE 24 Screenshot, October 18, 2014, "Antoine Dodson. This Is Just Too Funny!," originally from an interview by WAFF 48 News, posted August 3, 2010, by iloveWSHH, YouTube, 2:03, https://www.youtube.com/watch?v=VXPgjsB0Xm0.

views as of July 2019 (this number always updates to consider views by bots). The number of views accumulated may not seem significant today, but it was a notable achievement for a 2010 grassroots video. Since then, the Gregory Brothers have renamed the song twice—"Auto-Tune the News: Bed Intruder Song!!! (Now on iTunes)," and then simply "Bed Intruder Song!!!"[22]

A parallel video by the Gregory Brothers with the same publication date but with fewer views, "Bed Intruder Song – Full Version (on Spotify, Apple, and Your Microwave)," signaled the transition to an era of streaming music from cloud servers. Considering the increased usage of mobile devices to stream video content and the introduction and growth of unique media platforms such as Instagram, TikTok, and Snapchat, YouTube is no longer the primary platform for accessing and sharing digital videos hosted on data servers or "the cloud." YouTube is still a significant platform, however, for social video aggregation.

From 2010 and beyond, "Bed Intruder Song!!!" and its extraordinary attention in popular media inspired observers to react in various ways. Some dressed up as Antoine Dodson for Halloween (wearing a red bandanna and black A-shirt); the artist Dave MacDowell produced a painting titled *Hide Your Husbands!*, depicting Antoine Dodson in a dress holding a lit cigarette in his right hand and a Colt 45 brew in his left;[23] and RobotKristen14 turned the song into a metaphor for claiming tributes, as in the film *Hunger Games*.[24] Capitalizing on his viral popularity, Dodson began selling outfits resembling what he wore on July 28, 2010, created a sex offender tracking application, and performed the song on the 2010 *BET Hip Hop Awards* show with one of the Gregory Brothers (where some in the audience, primarily Black women, mouthed the words and danced to the song). In a sea of grassroots viral videos, from "Double Rainbow"[25] to "Best Cry Ever"[26] to "Ya Dun Goofed,"[27] Antoine's discursive and material body became a commodity like none before him as he commodified himself by performing Black objecthood. He became an icon of queer Black femininity in the American imaginary while his sister Kelly Dodson, a feminine Black cis woman, faded into the background.

In the newscast, from which the most viral grassroots video of 2010 derived, Kelly and Antoine Dodson performed that "specific unspecificity,"[28] that "jawn," that "whatchamacallit"—a performance that stands out from the pedestrian even as it names something that is an everyday occurrence. The siblings emerge as a digital video that is rewound, fast-forwarded, paused, and played like a cassette on a tape deck. The video's spectacular circulation moves it from the background to the vanguard of popular consciousness. Those popular ideas and discourses about an object that emerge after encountering it make it a "thing." The "thing" and the object's simultaneity means that "the thing seems to name the object just as it is even as it names some thing else."[29] Discourses generated by the Dodsons' interactions in and out of the newscast and their newfound fame make their digital video a "thing" even as it remains an object or something pedestrian and in the background of our consciousness. In all of its objective specificity as a televised newscast-turned–YouTube video, the news story "Woman Wakes Up to Find Intruder in Bed" points to many other unspecified "things" regarding racialized gender and sexuality.

Janet Jackson's YouTube

YouTube's origin is one unspecified "thing" connected to this moment of Black virality: the voracious online search for something that trivializes a trauma a Black woman has experienced. Super Bowl XXXVIII took place on February 1, 2004. However, readers of this text may recall it as "Nipplegate." Without a doubt, Janet Jackson dominated the Super Bowl halftime show with her unforgettable performance of chart-toppers like "All for You," "Rhythm Nation," and a duet with Justin Timberlake titled "Rock Your Body." Until Timberlake (wearing khakis similar to those of the IT guy from the Intel ad) sang, "Gonna have you naked by the end of this song," it was what you would expect from a Super Bowl halftime show. Then, grasping the upper-right portion of Jackson's black patent leather bustier, beneath which peeked a red lace bra, he ripped away the entire right cup of the bustier and red lace bra. In making this move, Timberlake exposed her right breast, which she had covered with only a shining star nipple pastie. To reduce the viewing of her nakedness, the producers, who had zoomed in on the performance duo, faded the stage to black and then zoomed out to a larger panoramic shot. That moment was referred to as Nipplegate or "Janetgate" and described as a "wardrobe malfunction" by spectators and popular media.

"Janet Jackson" became the most heavily searched term of the twelve months that followed the performance.[30] However, soon-to-be cofounders of YouTube—PayPal employees Chad Hurley, Steve Chen, and Jawed Karim—admitted it was challenging to find a place online with footage of either Jackson's breast from that February or the Indian Ocean earthquake and tsunami from that December.[31] Their admission was a formative moment in 2004. Besides the disastrous earthquake that produced the Boxing Day catastrophe, a Black woman's nakedness and its viral afterlife were the haunting inspirations for the YouTube we know today.

Even though viral broadcast footage of Rodney King's beating, the Los Angeles riots, and the September 11, 2001, World Trade Center collisions were part of the world's memory in the early 2000s, Nipplegate preceded today's concept of viral videos originating in formal media. Video footage was not a conveniently spreadable medium unless film companies distributed it widely in cinemas and projected it on screens where many could view it, just as was done with *Do the Right Thing*. People could not rewatch the performance unless they had recorded the moment on TiVo or VHS, been given a physical copy, or been invited to watch a recording on one of those sources. Thus, YouTube became a primary mechanism enabling interactors to relive or witness the 2004 Super Bowl performance a year later.

YouTube was an object before it was a "thing." In fact, Alphabet acquired it in November 2006, nearly two years after its birth. Beyond cat videos, rebroadcasts of Nipplegate fueled YouTube's early popularity among interactors online, transforming it from object to "thing." YouTube was no longer a platform operating in the background of widespread awareness, but in its foreground, functioning as a site to generate or consume audiovisual phenomena as people had done with stories around the fireplace and radio broadcast events. Google monetized YouTube only after acquiring it. Its monetization was a signal that Google, partly through the currency of Black virality, recognized a company that could generate substantially greater revenues based on its viewership and format.

The search for Jackson's moment of nakedness on YouTube involved racialized erotics. It required individuals to envision Black women's bodies in public-facing performances along with their desires, disgust, or curiosity about that envisioning. Searching for it required an epistemology that emerged from so many people spectating Jackson's nakedness and spreading their knowledge of it via word of mouth, news outlets, and personal recordings that interactors would later upload to YouTube. Otherwise, how would anyone know to search for her in the first place? To be sure, artists experience a spike in album sales after Super Bowl performances, but this was a different level of demand that continued long after the halftime show and into the following year's Super Bowl.

YouTube's slogan and ideology has always been "Broadcast Yourself." From its inception in 2005 through 2009, that slogan was part of the logo, as seen in figure 25 (Google dropped the slogan in 2010). YouTube emphasized allowing individuals to broadcast themselves, forever democratizing audiovisual broadcasts. Anyone could establish an online channel with specified content for a targeted or untargeted audience. The Gregory Brothers, for instance, started their channel, schmoyoho, where they featured their *Auto-Tune the News* show and broadcasted the Dodson incident, integrating themselves into the video.

As the example of 2011 YouTube shows in figure 26, the platform's background was an antiflash white color.[32] Right of the YouTube logo was a search field, and next to the field were links for browsing or uploading. These links encouraged visitors to find or share their content, in that order. When a user

YouTube Broadcast Yourself

Sign Up | Log In | Viewing History | Help

Videos Search

Home Videos Channels Groups Categories Upload

My Videos | My Favorites | My Friends | My Inbox | My Subscriptions | My Playlists | My Groups | My Profile

Join YouTube

Sign Up

Joining YouTube is free and easy. Just fill out the account information below. (All fields required)

Are you a musician? Sign up for a musician account. NEW

Email Address:

User Name:

Password:

Confirm Password:

Country: ---

Postal Code: Required for US, UK & Canada Only

Gender: Male Female

Date of Birth: --- --- ---

Sign me up for "The Weekly Tube" email

- I certify I am over 13 years old
- I agree to the terms of use and privacy policy

Sign Up

Log In

Already a Member? Login here

User Name:

Password:

Log In

Forgot: Username | Password

What Is YouTube?

YouTube is a way to get your videos to the people who matter to you. With YouTube you can:

- Upload, tag and share your videos worldwide
- Browse thousands of original videos uploaded by community members
- Find, join and create video groups to connect with people with similar interests
- Customize your experience with playlists and subscriptions
- Integrate YouTube with your website using video embeds or APIs

To learn more about our service, please see the Help Center.

Advertise With Us | About Us | Help Center | Safety Tips | Developers | Terms of Use | Privacy Policy | Jobs

Copyright © 2006 YouTube, Inc. RSS

FIGURE 25 Screenshot, October 14, 2024, "YouTube in 2006," February 16, 2018, https://www.webdesignmuseum.org/gallery/youtube-2006.

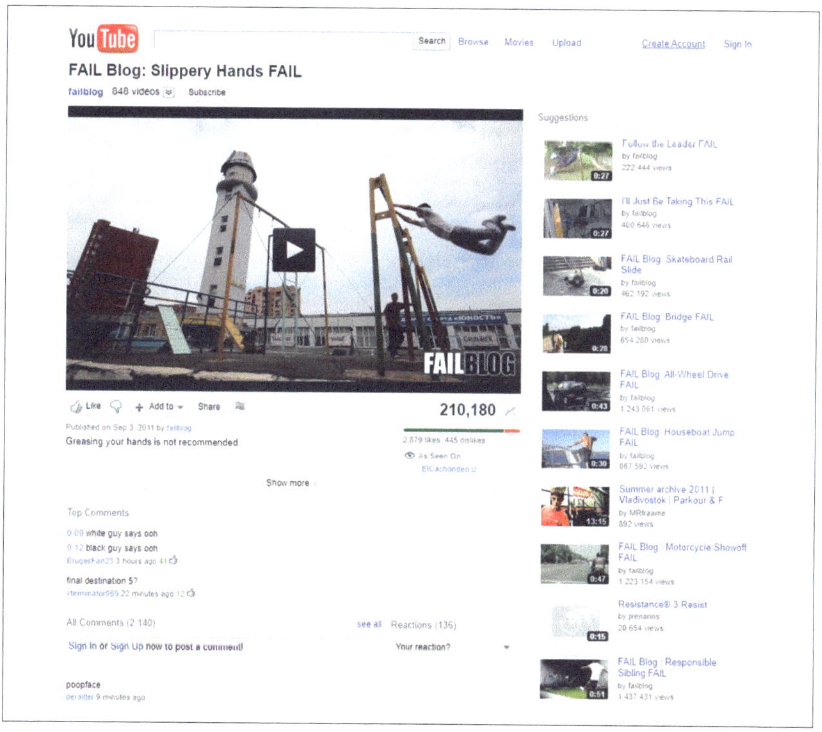

FIGURE 26 Screenshot, October 14, 2024, "YouTube in 2011," December 20, 2022, https://www.webdesignmuseum.org/gallery/youtube-2011.

signed on, the username appeared in the upper right with an option to sign out. Interactors customized their avatars with a chosen image, including the default light-blue square with a human body's basic silhouette. By allowing users to interact through an account they set up through Gmail, YouTube oriented itself as a social network for video sharing and subscriptions rather than as a space solely for video aggregation.

The central, gray-outlined white box was labeled "All Comments." It included a link to "respond to this video." Again, the locale for all comments was at the nexus of the video and previous comments. That location encouraged engagement with both the video and commenters. Once interactors commented or uploaded a video, any YouTube account owner could like or dislike the comments and video. They could also move comments to the top or bottom of the feed for that day, or even boost the video's position in the pane showing suggestions. By doing so, they could increase or decrease the visibility of a video or comment to anyone browsing. These dynamics encouraged interactors to make comments and videos either "liked" or risk obscurity.

To the right of the central boxes was a column of recommended videos, "Suggestions," showing a snapshot of related videos, their length, an uploader, and the number of views they had attracted. A sociotechnical algorithm determined what an interactor might want to watch and curated the related videos. The haunting aspect of the algorithms is that their engineers rendered them to appear that they are race-neutral technical systems. But algorithms are like black boxes hiding their processes as commercial secrets and outputting phenomena that can also be understood as coded inequity.[33] Whether an interactor allows YouTube to use their viewing history affects the results of the sociotechnical algorithm. Although my related videos had little relevance to the newscast, I noticed the algorithmic suggestions became more precise once the newscast had been remixed. This happened even with my viewing history turned off. Over time, both Kimberly "Sweet Brown" Wilkins and Charles Ramsey, other Black performers, came up as suggested videos, indicating that the algorithm, engineered to learn patterns, had noticed what I had been attentive to as a scholar of performance: the tendency of news media to sensationalize racial expressions of vulnerability to advance their viewership.

Janet Jackson's performance laid the groundwork that enabled YouTube to become a universe of racialized gender knowledge. In this later universe, interactors think they know more than they do about the racialized people they witness. Kelly Dodson's broadcasted trauma is a continuation of everything Jackson's performance and the layout of YouTube set into motion, projecting a different nakedness for her and her brother to experience and for the greater public to trivialize.

Trivializing the Attempted Rape of Kelly Dodson

Conspicuously, "Woman Wakes Up to Find Intruder in Her Bed" does not feature the woman. Instead, in the news broadcast, Kelly Dodson's brother Antoine is the dominant feature. This misrepresentation and representation set in motion an entire stream of uncontrollable performances, which not only saw the Dodsons goin' viral but also trivialized the rape attempt Kelly Dodson had experienced. The restrictive frames of racialized gender performances minimized her. This created a scenario where even resistance to oppressive phenomena, such as Antoine Dodson's recorded defense of her, also contributed to Kelly Dodson's silencing.

WAFF 48's newscast began with an announcement by a white male anchor wearing a suit and tie: "Terrifying moment for a woman who woke up to a strange man in bed with her." Using "strange man" brought attention to the criminal's features rather than the crime. His emphasis on the man's strangeness started the work of deemphasizing and trivializing the strangeness and horror of the home invasion and attempted rape of Kelly Dodson.

With the unsettling progression of normalizing a home invasion and sexual violence, WAFF 48 visually enlarged a digital satellite map to showcase the crime scene. It began by zooming in from a macroscale view of Alabama to a microscale view of a street in the Lincoln Park public housing project, seamlessly following the scene. WAFF 48's efforts to depict scenes of violence, combined with the nonchalant manner in which they do so, have had the unintended effect of normalizing the invasion of private space. This portrayal perpetuates the notion that public housing is always public, thus undermining the need for the same level of security provided to private housing. It is worth noting that the state already treats poor Black people as outsiders to privacy, making them susceptible to surveillance. This viewing perspective, from above, reinforces a class hierarchy. It implies a sense of intrusion and penetration, whether through the lens of a camera used by the news media or by a potential rapist's easy access to a bedroom.[34]

The production team of WAFF 48 News chose to zoom in on the crime scene. Unfortunately, carrying out this decision revealed the location of the insecure housing, causing a heightened sense of insecurity for the survivor and other locals. My concern was that a potential future perpetrator might recognize it as an easily penetrable location. Alerting people to danger without further revealing the structural weaknesses of the site where a stranger had committed a crime requires more sensitive critical practices by reporting agencies. Indeed, the spatial conditions under which the assault had occurred already heightened residents' vulnerability to environmental racism and sexism.

The geography of Huntsville's Lincoln Park public housing project has all the markings of neglect that Black geography scholars Katherine McKittrick and Clyde Woods identify as the effects of "hegemonic spatial practices"[35]: fitted out with single-paned windows, unrefurbished since its opening in 1961,[36] and built on the floodplain of Pinhook Creek.[37] Here, hegemonic spatial practices converged to make a bedroom easier to break into and its occupier more vulnerable to being further violated than the environment already allowed.[38] Huntsville hosts several massive defense corporations, such as Boeing, Lockheed Martin, and Raytheon, yet the residents of Lincoln Park experience insecurity.

WAFF 48 reporter Elizabeth Gentle was at the crime scene and locked eyes with the camera with investigative authority. Gentle recounts the Dodsons' struggle with the intruder and remarks that the man had left evidence of his "visit." But her referring to the intrusion as a "visit" reinforces the effects of a "strange man" while superimposing casualness on a violent act. Gentle's remark narrates the Dodsons' residence as a space of Black inviolability, and the satellite image illustrates it. WAFF 48 News renders Lincoln Park a place where no violation is possible because, as a public housing "project," it is already available for and accessible to the public.

Space, race, gender, and sexuality intertwine here as one arrives at a scenario where Kelly Dodson cannot be intruded upon. This is a situation where the interests of the state and the public supersede the privacy of her bedroom and the "inalienable" privacy of her material body. This discourse travels into perceptions of Kelly Dodson's Black female body as already public and thus unable to claim protection through sexual consent or domestic privacy.[39] Black inviolability monstrously assumes that Black lives and Black homes are impervious to violation (and pain), nullifying paths that would evidence a violation (and pain/trauma) when it happens.

As the Dodsons are public housing tenants, the state owns their family's residence, amplifying the systemic collapse of the distinction between public and private space that already afflicts African American spheres. WAFF 48's phrasing and visual framing sustain the narratives, suggesting that the spaces where Black people find themselves and the places they carve out of those spaces do not deserve security, care, or privacy. These populations are "subject to highly spatialized forms of surveillance and control."[40] Thus, the collapsed public/private terrain was ripe for the type of dismissal that the Dodsons experienced, first with their housing management, then in their news interview, and finally, on the comment walls of video aggregation sites like YouTube and WorldStarHipHop and through derisive memes on Reddit, which I explore at greater length in the following chapter.

Discussing the collapse of African American public and private space, historian Elsa Barkley Brown cites the examples of bullpen confinement and raids on Black homes in Richmond, Virginia, at the turn of the nineteenth century.[41] As time progresses, the state regulates Black people and the spaces they live in, making them public and subject to its interest. Or, as McKittrick aptly writes, "Geographies in the diaspora are accentuated by racist paradigms of the past and their ongoing hierarchical patterns."[42] The legacy of state-sponsored violence in Black lives and their geographies persists in a wide range of forms. Such violence ranges from the Tuskegee experiment in Macon County, Alabama, to the stop-and-frisk policies of the New York Police Department, to minor offenses targeting Black people (such as Manner of Walking violations) in Ferguson, Missouri. Geography is integral to conceptions of race, gender, and the indiscriminate ways civilians and the state violate and police Black lives.

Gentle uses enframing to narrate Kelly Dodson's struggle with the intruder. WAFF 48's camera pans across the bedroom, revealing broken items on the bed and floor. Gentle then describes Antoine Dodson's intervention in the scuffle, but the postproduction editing of the segment gives him more airtime. Using a "vox pop" aesthetic, while Gentle remains unseen, the camera's frame renders her microphone in front of Antoine Dodson's face. He disses and threatens the sexual assaulter. What follows is an S-shaped twist of his neck, hand gestures that extend his speech, and a roll of his eyes to the left. Audiences witness how "stancetaking and styling can operate as both verbal and embodied tools in the production of a form of covert denigration."[43] As sincere as his queer defense is, we also bear witness to a representation of a Black queer stereotype—the feminine Black man as comic relief—which represents a perfect distraction from a Black woman's daunting reality.[44]

By centering on Antoine Dodson, WAFF 48 News relieves the audience of the need to make sense of or even acknowledge the attempted rape that Kelly Dodson experienced. The spectacle of her brother's femininity as comic relief functions to ridicule feminine Black performances and ways of being. American popular culture has a lengthy history of such demonstrations, often intertwined with the mocking of Black trans women and feminine men. These histories began as early as nineteenth-century minstrel shows with white men dressed as Black women and have continued almost unabated into more recent acts such as "Men on . . ." from *In Living Color* (1990–1993), *To Wong Foo, Thanks for Everything! Julie Newmar* (1995), and *Big Momma's House* (2000), among many others (not to mention Madea). Notably, the latter examples are all comedies featuring cis heterosexual men who play butch queens or straight Black women. This rendition highlights the issue of miscasting Black and Brown men, which frequently happens when producers choose to whitewash or "ablewash" roles by selecting white or nondisabled actors instead of nonwhite or disabled actors. In this case, however, the trivialization extends to femme Black women, their femininity undermined as producers cast straight Black and Brown cis men.

We can center Antoine Dodson because Black queerness goes viral, not only by standing out from norms of gender, sexuality, and race but also by spreading quickly and achieving wide recognition. Black virality enframes the material Black queer body as contagious and ill. I use the Black vernacular version of *ill* here, less to suggest sickness and more to gesture toward an undeniably appealing way of being. Here, WAFF 48's nonconsensual enframing of all the Black subjects involved appears consensual yet minimizes the circumstance's weight and seriousness by relying on the illness (i.e., undeniable coolness) of Antoine Dodson's queerness and the trope of the feminine Black queer body as comic relief.

In my critique of the trivialization of the attempted rape of Kelly Dodson, it may seem that I am also critiquing Antoine Dodson's domination of the spotlight. That interpretation of my analysis would pit a gay Black man against a Black woman in ways that double down on the wrongheaded myth of gay men as woman-hating.[45] WAFF 48, not Antoine Dodson, reinforces this myth by setting up and investing in the conditions for him to perform as comic relief in a Black woman's traumatic circumstance.

In response to the trivialization of their experience, the Dodsons employ various forms of interaction or disaffection. For example, Antoine Dodson grants interviews during and after the newscast, whereas Kelly Dodson refuses to allow news personnel to interview her any further—disallowing future platforms for her sympathy or ridicule.[46] Although executed differently, these tactics embody liberated worlds that both Dodsons long for, "emergent strategy." These worlds include an awareness of fractal virality in Black life and doing something with that awareness to improve Black livelihoods. They also encompass the longing for personal safety in terms of one's body, surroundings, and community, without infringing on the humanity of others. These worlds, too, hold the hope of being able to live undisturbed and left alone.

Each of the Dodson's approaches to this moment of Black virality articulates a distinct liberatory strategy. Antoine Dodson uses Black objecthood to capitalize on how his body functions as comic relief. Kelly Dodson knows the sustained racial, sexual, and class climate toward Black lives like hers and her brother's and expects that the media attention will, in her words, "make him [Antoine] look like a fool."[47] Well aware of this tendency of media outlets, she resists using Black objecthood as a strategy and instead removes herself from the spectator's sight. She engages in a freedom practice that counters racializing surveillance and surveillance capitalism, engaging in what Black and surveillance studies scholar Simone Browne calls "dark sousveillance."[48]

It would be naive to understand WAFF 48's reporting as the genesis of the enframing of this Black virality that later spread to other domains of popular culture. I gesture to a long history of the collapse of Black public and private life and Black queer femininity as comic relief. This newscast is one moment in an array of Black performances that resemble this form of trivialization, violation, and ridicule. Histories of racialized Black sexuality and gender inform WAFF 48's ethos as they enable the newscasters to make contemporary Black people available for viral circulation in trivialized ways. That is, viral performances exist within singular acts of Black virality—fractal virality.

A Meme of a Meme of a Meme: The Fractal Virality of Black Performance

While informed by racial performativity, fractal virality is a lens through which to understand how yesterday's performances nest within today's, the descending and ascending scales of performance referents, or how a Black virality comes into being in relationship to current social and political structures. For example, the musical *Hairspray* remixes "Run and Tell That" from Denise LaSalle's 1972 funk song "Now Run and Tell That," which derives from the same African American vernacular expression. Yet many people today likely know the latter phrase through Antoine Dodson's performance. Thus, beginning from a quantitatively more circulated Black performance, we can trace and understand how similar phenomena repeat at an increasingly smaller scale. Meanwhile, the most recent performance supports and counters its earlier referents, telling a story with material repercussions in the present. Fractal virality is a perspective that situates Black people as goin' viral before their present performance, suggesting that singular performance is an illusion. A singular performance coexists in a multitude. This counters the illusion of singular performances. In this observation, fractal virality evidences the collection of discursive and gestural performances from which a Black virality derives and to which it generates. Fractal virality suggests no original viral performance or stand-alone act of Black virality exists.

Unlike a purely discursive lens, fractal virality provides a way of analyzing beyond and through written and spoken communications, focusing on rapidly and widely circulated "things." It also offers a sense of a spectator's awareness of a performance, an awareness influenced by the viral mechanisms available in an era (i.e., word of mouth or the telegraph versus sharing a digital video or making cellular phone calls) and the human population that is alive to witness it. Thus, public reactions to the Dodsons are never only about their stand-alone performances but all that they recall and foreshadow.

The fractal virality of the moment shapes reactions to the Dodsons, which underscore the preceding instances of Black virality that the performance encounter evokes. Other performances enframe Black communities long before the Dodsons arrive on the scene, hence, my recognition of this moment as one of many in a litany of Ghetto Witnesses.[49] Furthermore, the fractal virality of public/private collapse in Black communities, like the raids on Black homes and their ongoing connections to Black women killed in or near their homes, reveals an ongoing recurrence and trivialization of Black women's traumas. Considering the prevalent trivialization, the continual reenactment of the erasure of Kelly Dodson, or WAFF 48's foregrounding of Antoine Dodson as comic relief, appears more strategic than happenstance.

The Dodsons engage in Black feminist solidarity work in their distinct ways, even as they confront the actions of WAFF 48. This news outlet perpetuates white supremacist capitalist patriarchy by exploiting Black virality to marginalize Black women for profit. Simultaneously, it uses the struggles of Black women to attract an audience and advertisers. Yet, given all the attention the Dodsons generated for WAFF 48 News, I still wonder what, if any, royalties they might have received from the news station they could have used to continue the Black feminist work they started.[50]

The Noniconicity of Black Feminist Work

If comic relief exists in using queerness to disrupt the expected or routine, people also employ the spectacle of comic relief as a tool to shed light on the noniconic. Here, the noniconic is illegible and nearly indecipherable. It exists, but not readily. Indeed, the noniconic is a type of dark matter, "invisible and unknowable, yet somehow still there."[51] As Black feminist theorist of visual culture and contemporary art Tina M. Campt asserts, "Attending to the infraordinary and the quotidian reveals why the trivial, the mundane, or the banal are in fact essential to the lives of the dispossessed and the possibility of [B]lack futurity."[52] Exploring what is not viral within Black virality expands commonplace understandings of Black performance to include "the density of Black life," a density enlivened by a focus on the livable and noniconic conditions of viral performances.[53] Kelly Dodson's testimony was not only turned into a comedic spectacle by the positioning of her brother's defense, but it also led to the marginalization of her voice by WAFF 48. However, amid this spectacularity and marginalization, other noniconic aspects of her subjectivity, as well as her brother's, emerged, revealing the Black feminist work of this viral performance. Black feminist work resists and counters assumptions about the oppression of marginalized discursive and material bodies. It actively or passively protests the conditions that influence their pathologization, which are often unrecognized.

Amid the Black virality of the newscast (and remix video, to which I gestured earlier in this chapter), audiences forget or never encounter some noniconic interviews. In an NPR interview following this story, Antoine Dodson reveals that people contacted him, complaining that he "was making their city look bad."[54] In another interview on *Judge Alex*, Dodson discloses that Black communities were saying, "Oh, he's slow, he's dumb . . . he's ghetto, he shouldn't represent the community in this way."[55] Given their lack of specificity regarding what "looking bad" meant, these interactions suggest the exclusion of feminine Black men from Blackness, which summons a question about authenticity in the popular imagination about Black performance. These responses also cue spectators to observe what the body "*does* once it *is* constituted and the relationship between it and the other bodies around it" and push a reconsideration of the stakes of racial performativity in the present.[56]

Notably, the critical reactions to Antoine Dodson's Black street vernacular performance reflect the reification of public performances of Blackness that reduce Black communities to a monolith. Popular media outlets support this myth, to the great embarrassment of Black people. A vicarious vulnerability to this Black performance by the Dodsons and the performance of Blackness by WAFF 48 lies at the root of provoking or evoking responses from Black communities.

Indeed, performance "affirms and denies" the "fictional ontology" of race and gender.[57] Some things happen "for display" (as in WAFF 48's editing of the narrative) and "despite display" (as in the Dodsons' genuine reactions to multiple efforts of gaslighting), and performance accounts for all those possibilities.[58] Consequently, race and gender are fictional acts made real to the extent that people perform and experience them.[59] The palpability of fractal virality to Black onlookers (where they see many other Black performances that this one conjures) recalls the "efficacy of meanings that repeat the initiating moments" of marking the material body.[60] To see this newscast as a Black person in the United States is a reminder of that which collectively stigmatizes Black people redoubled as news.

The moment of the news interview was a discursive "remarking" of a collective Black body because this was not the first or last performance conveying the visual and sonic cues that abounded. Kelly and Antoine Dodson are the first examples, however, of a repetitive theme that has such an explosive effect on popular culture and everyday life. The recurrent media motif, which I call the "Ghetto Witness," often, but not always, involves people of African descent who use the intimate street vernacular of their larger racial group, irrespective of their audience, to describe a sensational event or theory from their deeply personal perspectives, clarifying, verifying, and producing a larger narrative. They are weaponized by social and news media by being "regularly cast and highly visible despite their usual narrative marginalization."[61] I use the motif as a retronym of "#ghettowitness" to recognize and analyze it before it became a hashtag. Moreover, I examine its existence prior to, during, and beyond the popularity of "Bed Intruder Song!!!"[62] The concept of the Ghetto Witness represents a form of "ghetto fabulousness" that, when embodied, centers not on materialism but on rejecting or disregarding external validation and conforming for the sake of others' comfort.[63]

My definition of Ghetto Witness follows a small digital index. An interactor named L3M0NP3PPA on Twitter created this index under #ghettowitness.[64] The latter use of #ghettowitness was unknown to me in August 2010 and referred only to the remix video, "Bed Intruder Song!!!," which derives from the "Woman Wakes Up to Find Intruder in Bed" performance. Yet perusing that index revealed that interactors, like me, were not engaging with each other but had used the hashtag to index the performance independently of one another. While "Woman Wakes Up to Find Intruder in Bed" is not the only performance of a Ghetto Witness (one can quickly point to Bubb Rubb,[65] Crichton Leprechaun,[66] Kimberly Wilkins,[67] Charles Ramsey,[68] and Walter Bankston[69]), it is such a Black virality that it becomes the rallying point around which interactors understand other past and future Ghetto Witnesses. By signaling to the Black virality that preceded and would follow it, Kelly and Antoine Dodson, as Ghetto Witnesses, are a *part* of Blackness yet conditioned to represent the *whole*—living synecdoches.

WAFF 48's Gentle responds to the accusations of Black shame regarding remarking the collective Black body as Ghetto by cleverly separating the news station from the staging of events. She notes that "some have contacted our newsroom saying that interviews with people like Antoine reflect poorly on the community. To that I say censoring people like Antoine is far worse."[70] It is essential to think through how racial sincerity and authenticity perform here to understand the self and others. Anthropologist and filmmaker John L. Jackson Jr. suggests that intent and the greater community's acceptance are components of racial sincerity, whereas authenticity relies upon an arbitrary authenticator.[71] Employing this ethos, I understand the interactors who are ashamed of this performance as exercising a double consciousness, wherein they see Antoine Dodson through the eyes of the heteronormative racialized Other, the authenticator. In contrast, Gentle understands the Dodsons through their intent and emphasizes the sincerity of their racialized performance. Given her position of authority, however, Gentle's focus on intent and racial sincerity divorces WAFF 48's responsibility from a greater community's vulnerability to derisive media representations of Black people. Therefore, Gentle's advocacy for freedom of speech sabotages any possibility of arriving at an understanding of racial sincerity.

Gentle's freedom-of-speech gesture is an insincere move. Here, television management offers the illusion that their representations are nuanced and even expansive, yet they do so in an unsophisticatedly immutable way, a "simplified complex representation."[72] By suggesting that the Dodsons deserve dignity while presenting them one-dimensionally, Gentle weaponizes respectability politics and aims it at the witnesses who gave their testimony and the critics of those witnesses.

Certainly, those marginalized by race reoccur in certain narratives more often than in others.[73] I suggest that WAFF 48 was drawn to the currency of Blackness, specifically of the Ghetto Witness, which motivated its perceived need to pursue and edit this story.[74] This intent goes unsaid by Gentle and allows for the perpetuation of anti-Black surveillance and rendering. Without more complex coverage of events such as these, media outlets maintain reified perceptions of Black life, as seen in the Ghetto Witness, that threaten the wellness of discursive Black bodies and material Black lives.[75]

Kelly Dodson recognized the media's power in derisively positioning her brother's appropriately abundant performance and understood how his degradation in that positioning was also hers. Antoine Dodson's response is not excessive but abundant in passion, defense, and Black feminist thought.[76] Kelly performed dark sousveillance to counter the racializing surveillance of WAFF 48 she was keenly aware of. She engaged in a "performance of counterpublicity."[77] As a result, the deployment of optic and aural opacity, or "Black data," of her material Black body and voice intentionally resisted the all-too-easy denigration her brother experienced as this performance traveled beyond the newscast.[78]

Despite Kelly Dodson masking her subjectivity in later appearances (whether by choice or imposition of media outlets), because of her initial unguarded response to WAFF 48, she did not perfectly counter the Black virality she experienced. In fact, in the later versions of this emotional performance, the Dodsons' observers intensely scrutinized it. They felt embarrassed by it, as they were vulnerable to discourses that circulated about Black racialized genders and sexualities. This vulnerability inspired the crucifixion of the Ghetto Witness, a crucifixion experienced far more viscerally by Antoine than by Kelly Dodson, thanks to her performance of dark sousveillance and her erasure by other media outlets.

This archetyping, especially this Bed Intruder brand, made Antoine Dodson visible while remaining illegible, another noniconicity. I use *illegible* to describe lives that do not "serve the historical fictions of American culture."[79] The tension between the high visibility and illegibility of Dodson's body connects the two. Like the bling aesthetic of diamonds, his spectacularity "literally blinds audiences (and critical readers) to the complexities that 'lay in the cut.'"[80] His noniconicity retained realities that troubled historical fiction, like that of the "culture of poverty" or the "welfare queen," which interactors in the United States already hold knowledge of in their encounters with Black viralities.[81]

Preceding and fanning the flames of Antoine Dodson's inflammatory outburst, what "lay in the cut" beyond the purview of the spectacular news broadcast is a girl on the sidelines. She seemed to live in Lincoln Park, but WAFF 48 News never interviewed her. According to Antoine Dodson, the unidentified girl responded to the reporter to maintain her honor: "Oh, well, this had never happened to us in this neighborhood—nuh uh, this had only happened to y'all."[82] His retelling recovered her unrecorded response, which suggests that the Dodson family somehow enabled the rape attempt. The girl's response blames the survivor and strips the perpetrator of responsibility and anything systematic (like housing insecurity), sanitizing relationships in Lincoln Park as innocent and peaceful and skewing this crime as anomalous.

The broadcast reached not only Black people worldwide but also another person present during the interview who was apprehensive about the news media's depiction of her and her surroundings. This girl, whose identity is undisclosed, engaged in conservative respectability politics that echoed the discourses of other Black individuals who expressed dissatisfaction with Antoine Dodson.[83] Conservative respectability politics operates on the wrongheaded notion that the salvation of Black lives depends on the righteousness with which white lives perceive them (as though the persistence of white supremacist patriarchy would cease through speaking the King's English and following Victorian levels of etiquette). If nothing else sparked Antoine Dodson's reaction, her response *obviously* sent him into a frenzy.

Despite bringing sexual violence in Black communities to the forefront of popular culture and mass media, challenging the restrictive parameters of Black gender expression, and resisting the white normative gaze, Antoine Dodson's excessive visibility indirectly rendered Kelly Dodson invisible. Furthering this invisibility, a few days after the interview, Gentle emphasizes that both the siblings were victims and "like any victim, they have the right to speak out."[84] Yet the producers of WAFF 48 News facilitated Antoine Dodson's speaking out. Without specifying what the Dodsons had been victims of, Gentle also insensitively conflates their victimization into identical forms. Her conflation suggests that enduring a rape attempt is equivalent to using self-defense in a home invasion.

I must emphasize that WAFF 48, not Antoine Dodson, essentially erased Kelly Dodson's narrative by enframing the scenario and choosing what to include and exclude. Their narrative and illustrative choices offer a glimpse into how normative gender roles, condoned by WAFF 48, structure Black women as marginal. WAFF 48's structural actions (or linguistic and visual renderings) edited out Kelly Dodson's ability to speak prominently as the one who had experienced the rape attempt and edited in Antoine's performance, centering the opportunity to talk on the one who had thwarted the rape attempt. By emphasizing their "right to speak out," WAFF 48 News engaged in a neoliberal gesture that distanced structural responsibility from personal responsibility;[85] thus, it removed itself from the performance and gave viewers the illusion of choice and autonomy in depicting Kelly Dodson's story, which focuses more intently on her brother's rage than on her distress.

Antoine Dodson's rage was a breaking point lodged in a long history of repressed knowledge of intracommunal sexual violence, particularly Kelly Dodson's, his, and his community's encounters with sexual violence. Not only does his rage disrupt notions of conservative respectability politics, but because the assaulter is a stranger who breaks in through a window, the usual questions that marginalize Black and Brown women's experiences—"What were you wearing? Do you have sex with multiple partners? And were you flirting with him?"—do not apply. These questions typically dismiss the legitimacy of Black women's claims of sexual violation and shift responsibility from the violator(s) to the victims. Despite the gravity of the situation, WAFF 48 downplayed its seriousness. Instead of highlighting Kelly Dodson's emotions following a rape attempt while her daughter was present, the focus was exaggerated on Antoine's anger.

In the gap between the formality of the WAFF 48 News reporting and the informality of Antoine Dodson's rage, Black street vernacular, and stylized gestures lies another dimension contributing to the Ghetto Witness's Black virality: comedy. WAFF 48 deliberately highlighted this gap, making a spectacle of Antoine Dodson's take on the story and transforming Kelly Dodson's misfortune into comic relief. Antoine Dodson focuses on what is not funny as an act of refusal to others who position him as comic relief amid the monotony of the standard WAFF 48 news broadcast. At one point in his NPR interview, he states, "It's been a lot of complaints, even before my sister's attack; it's been a lot of people complaining about how people was getting raped in the projects and people just sweeping it under the rug and not talking about it."[86] Rather than isolate and sensationalize the sexual assault on his sister, Antoine Dodson raised a more systemic issue of rape in Lincoln Park public housing. After pointing out this preexisting viral violence, he asks, "What do we need to do as people to keep our community safe?"[87]

By referencing "community," Antoine Dodson suggests that everyone in Lincoln Park public housing is vulnerable to sexual violence, with "we" offering to address the issue with a community accountability model rather than a punitive model. Supporting this notion, in a CBS interview with Shira Lazar, Antoine reveals that he, too, was a "rape victim."[88] Thus, when Antoine warned viewers of the news broadcast that someone could rape their husbands, he was pointing toward his own direct or indirect experiences with sexual violence. In this way, he kept an ethos of sexual violence that fell outside of heteronormative patriarchal presumptions and activated broader rape activism. He did this by addressing the structural conditions that made rape possible rather than focusing on the singular, anomalous criminal often portrayed in dominant news media and the law. This particular and punitive focus on individuals, such as this intruder, is the "perpetrator perspective."[89] WAFF 48's neoliberal gesture focusing on and sensationalizing the specter of a singular bad actor was a distraction from addressing the racially oppressive conditions that intersected, in this instance, with spaces that increased individuals' vulnerability to sexual violation.

Besides its emphasis on the single bad actor, WAFF 48 News also attempted to maintain a "homopatriarchy"[90] by leaving patriarchal systems intact and reaping the fiscal benefits of exploiting a queer Black male subjectivity in which Antoine Dodson defended Kelly Dodson and was edited to speak for her. Yet homopatriarchy is also a means of survival, particularly in Black and Brown communities "in the face of mounting economic marginalization and state-enacted racial violence."[91] The father's rule (as breadwinner and protector) is not neatly abolished but strategically deployed alongside realities that queer how it is experienced, such as maintaining same-sex desire while "butching up" one's presence to appear as less of an easy target of homophobic femme violence.[92] Thus, this antagonistic circumstance fostered some alliances that would otherwise be debated. Antoine Dodson's performance unties the Black femme from a cis female body, further theorizing Black viralities of male femininity that disrupt heteronormative gender performance. He also challenged homopatriarchal and masculine norms by responding to and publicly raising awareness of sexual violence against all lives in public housing, particularly in Lincoln Park. Antoine Dodson broadcasts this awareness of sexual violence even while maintaining his quintessential patriarchal role as protector, with his gendered performance suggesting that protectors can be femme.

Antoine Dodson believed Kelly Dodson was a survivor, validating her assertion that the perpetrator was an idiot when he declares, "We got your fingerprints . . . you are really dumb, for real." The defense of his sister's honor operates against notions of Black women's sexual inviolability that reflect false assumptions about their inherent promiscuity and aggressiveness, which is, in the end, Black feminist work.[93] While honor, as a Western European myth of feminine purity, is not an aspirational ethos for the Dodsons or anyone else who requires no external validation, the subject of Kelly's dignity surfaced through Antoine's spirited defense. Antoine Dodson's act of protection before the news aired occupies a historical void found in Black feminist sociologist Anna Julia Cooper's plea on behalf of "colored girls of the South," about whom she wrote were "often without a stronger brother to espouse their cause and defend their honor with his life's blood."[94]

Running counter to the Black feminist work advanced by Antoine Dodson's unfiltered performance, reactions to his appearance that criticized him for "making the city and community look bad" maintained the silence around sexual acts of violence that he suggested were "swept under the rug."[95] This silence reflected a salvific wish to keep up a conservative and respectable public facade despite the violence Black and Brown women experience in their inner lives, which both Dodsons exposed.

Exploring intervention strategies with battered Black and Brown women, Black feminist scholar and foundational critical race theorist Kimberlé Crenshaw foregrounds narratives that frame the victims as criminals. Popular discourses link a victim's criminality to older, bigoted ideas concerning the barbarism (easily extendable to the ghettoness) of Black and Brown people in the United States. Battling racism forced women to sacrifice their racialized gender priorities. In exchange, they made their communities appear absent of the intracommunal violence that plagues every racial group to improve their collective racial image and reduce racialized surveillance. Thus, to combat the larger racial narrative of violent and savage Black and Brown communities (as well as to avoid deportation for being undocumented), women take on the burden of silence around the violence, sexual and otherwise, they experience at the hands of Black and Brown men.[96] Concerning this phenomenon, Black women have also strategically desexualized their personas to protect the sanctity of their inner lives from oppressors while offering performances of selective disclosure that make the collective look "good," perpetuating what Black feminist historian Darlene Clark Hine calls "cultures of dissemblance."[97]

Antoine Dodson bravely confronted the strategies that inadvertently sustain silence around domestic violence and racism. He refused to conform to the expectation of presenting himself, his sister, or his community as desexualized personas. In his powerful statement, he boldly declares, "Dey rapin' e'rybody out here." By speaking out, Antoine Dodson publicized the acts of the perpetrator of the rape attempt and the violence inflicted, but he also stood up for his Black sister's dignity and acknowledged her vulnerability to sexual violence. Through his words, he brought attention to the fact that these acts of violence were not isolated incidents but part of a systemic problem affecting "e'rybody."

The revelation of sexual violence that everyone experiences also functions as a performance of disclosure that protects the Dodsons' inner lives by eschewing lurid detail and refusing to hypersexualize them, arguably embracing as much as rejecting the culture of dissemblance. The Dodson siblings' refusal to be silent in this moment of testimony provided a popular venue, namely broadcast television and, centrally, YouTube, with the opportunity to talk or at least think about sexual violence. Here, sexual violence is beyond, but also specific to, Black gender, its social links to masculinity and patriarchy, and its structural ties to (a lack of) security and the inaction of the state in spaces like US public housing.[98]

Antoine Dodson layers his statement with the cadences of southern African American speech, stylized gestures, and queer perspectives on sexual violence, situating himself within a queer performance of Black femininity. In part, his queerness challenges how people see what they hear, what dramaturg and theater and performance studies scholar Faedra Chatard Carpenter calls "racialized synaesthesia."[99] Dodson's Alabamian African American vernacular belies any thought that he is acting white. Additionally, his pursuit of an associate degree in business administration at Virginia College counters misunderstandings of him as undereducated that many would associate with his speech, dress, and location. His caution toward his neighbors and warning to the perpetrator tests and transgresses the bounds of African American norms around gender expression and silence concerning intracommunal sexual violence. Dodson also supports protective paternalism, albeit through the actions of WAFF 48, practicing Black patriarchal norms that reinforce the subordination of Black feminine voices. While he refrains from weaponizing paternalism—a livable abstinence—it has been historically inaccessible to Black queer bodies like his, rendering his restraint noniconic at that moment. Still, a performance's noniconicity does not always guarantee it will be generative or livable.

Kelly Dodson's increasing reluctance to claim the spotlight and her subsequent rendering to the background of her story also points toward her awareness of "the annihilating objectifying force at the core of all oppressions," what poet, performer, and sound artist Duriel Harris calls "thingification," of Black life goin' viral.[100] Unlike her brother, she eschewed the spotlight, a resistance that manifested through distancing herself from this performance spectacle, a "critical Black female spectatorship."[101] As a result, no one produced costumes based on the outfit Kelly Dodson wore that day and very few remixes center her fractal virality (a benefit of her unfortunate marginalization by WAFF 48 and deliberate withdrawal from the story), so she was less derisively memeified than her brother was.

I do not wish to imply that the commodity form cannot counter the annihilating forces acting upon it or that the only way to withstand them is to not become a commodity, a thing, in the first place. In a recounting of *Narrative of the Life of Frederick Douglass, An American Slave,* cultural theorist, performance studies scholar, and poet Fred Moten discusses Douglass's Aunt Hester's screams as Captain Anthony whips her.[102] Enslavers use and insure enslaved African lives as commodities (they are considered property). Unlike political theorist, economist, and historian Karl Marx's notion that commodities do not speak and objects do not resist, Aunt Hester's screams imply they do. I insist that refusing the commodity form and the commodity works to reveal what is insignificant yet must not be ignored. Thus, by experiencing a rape attempt yet refusing the spectacularity of how knowledge about it unfolded, Kelly Dodson comes to embody the noniconic.

Before goin' viral, as a Black cis woman, Kelly Dodson would not have come to mind in the popular imagination as someone likely to be raped because of pervasive discourses regarding Black women as inviolable and hypersexual. Still, an attempt to rape her occurred, forcing a reconsideration of her as a violable subject. It is heartbreaking that one can only imagine a Black woman's violability through a violent act or be forced to imagine it because of it goin' viral.

The queerness of this Black virality, from interactors understanding Kelly Dodson as feminine and violable to Antoine's twisting his neck with a high inflection in his voice while remaining strong and protective, also rescripts their genders. This performance both challenges and leaves unchallenged hegemonic masculine and feminine US norms. It questions what it means to be a protector, a woman, or a man, as well as who deserves protection. The lives of white masculine cis men and white feminine cis women popularly occupy these roles.[103] Upheld, however, are notions of man as protector and woman as intrinsically sanctified, therefore needing protection. These are not inherently aspirational gender roles. They are fictions that continue to be touted as normative, natural even, yet have remained unavailable to Black Americans because of the horrors of slavery and its widespread legacy.

Referencing this horror, Angela Y. Davis suggests that the Black family's pejorative framing as matriarchal overlooks laws created by the same American culture that separated enslaved African families by selling their members across states. Those laws dictated that the child's status followed that of the mother and ignored how the nonexistence of hierarchically gendered slave labor was coupled with domestic sexual and gender equality that countered normalized gender roles.[104] The incongruence is just one of many examples of the ravages of slavery that racialize gender, sustaining a troubled legacy that continues to plague Black communities in the United States today. Remarkably, the gendered legacy of US Black people's unpaid, exploited labor signifies "being out of the way of traditional symbolics of female [and male] gender."[105] This legacy is closely connected to how both Kelly and Antoine Dodson trouble the visual and aural fields of gender and sexuality. The siblings exist within an American landscape where their material and discursive bodies are viral products of the Middle Passage, which is also a form of Black virality.

The disturbance of gender roles in the past and in this performance further signifies the nonnormative ways that kinship and gender operate in Black communities. Antoine Dodson's Black gender performance seamlessly sustains masculinity and femininity, expressing "the power of 'yes' to the 'female' within."[106] Although his sexuality remains unknown as he defends his sister, gesturally, Antoine Dodson enacts a "Butch Queen" performance.[107] The siblings perform a "[survival strategy that a] minoritized subject practices in order to negotiate a phobic majoritarian public sphere that continuously elides or punishes the existence of subjects who do not conform to the phantasm of normative citizenship."[108] The strategy, when deployed against popular imaginings of Black womanhood and Black manhood, where each embraces fierce femininity and pushes back against the normative idea that this fierceness and strength cannot coexist, is a form of what critical theorist and performance studies scholar José Esteban Muñoz calls "disidentification."[109]

These disidentificatory performances of strong and protective femininity and protection-deserving femininity also contradict the ease with which Black manhood and Black womanhood are popularly aligned with normative masculinity.[110] In this performance, there cannot be an assumed strength where it may not exist or an inherent strength that does not need protection. Antoine Dodson's act of protection queers his sister, offering femininity and violability to her Black womanhood, which has not been historically presumed or accessible.

While WAFF 48's rendering of the rage in Antoine Dodson's performance silences his sister and makes a spectacle of him, it also creates a counterspectacle. His counterspectacle, which is attached to the visibility of his Black virality, insists that news media no longer "sweep" acts of sexual violence "under the rug" in Black communities, or at the very least in Lincoln Park.[111] "Hide ya husbands" is a nonheteronormative call to activism that counters patriarchal aims by articulating every gender as violable subjects (and, indeed, husbands do not have to be men). Yet this call remains part of the noniconic Black feminist work Black virality achieves, forever appended to its most viral elements while rarely acknowledged. Antoine Dodson's testimony and warning affirm Kelly Dodson's honor, expose issues around sexual violence in the Lincoln Park community, and challenge normalized conceptions of gender roles.

CHAPTER 4

Suggestions

"Bed Intruder Song!!! (Now on iTunes) . . . 157M views"
"Annoying Orange – Kitchen Intruder (Bed Intruder Spoof) with AutoTune Remix! . . . 15M views"
"Sweet Brown – Ain't Nobody Got Time for That (Autotune Remix) . . . 71M views"
"Dead Giveaway! . . . 37M views"; or, The Travel of The Ghetto Witness

> "This song will never die."
> —AwesomeAostin

If an algorithm had a uniform sound, it would be Auto-Tune. This now-popular sonic formation is an algorithm created by Andy Hildebrand with math similar to what he used in reflective seismology to locate fuel deposits for Exxon, except he adapted the algorithm's use to digitally adjust or "correct" a sound's pitch. This notion of correction assumes that something was imperfect about the pitch of the initial sound. Yet, to a casual listener, pitch correction disguises the "original," sometimes already digitized, recorded sound. In place of the initial sound, a musician creates a kind of dissonance and consonance, which *Pitchfork* contributor Simon Reynolds notes as revolutionizing the sound of popular music.[1] The influence of R & B musician T-Pain (short for Tallahassee Pain) on the widespread blatant use of Auto-Tune in US popular music in the early 2000s cannot be overstated. While T-Pain was not the first—among others were Cher (1998) and Daft Punk (2001)—his success in 2005 (and the copious musicians who followed his lead) pointed to the profitability of auto-tuning music. There were so many auto-tuned songs that in 2009, Jay-Z was compelled to make the song "D.O.A. (Death of Auto-Tune)," rapping, "You're T-Paining too much."

Jay-Z's warning may have given more life than death to Auto-Tune, as I now shift my attention from the "original" story, "Woman Wakes Up to Find Intruder in Her Bed," to focus on its auto-tuned remix, "Bed Intruder Song!!!," and popular remixes of the song.[2] Here, I seek to understand the impact of the transmission of Black virality on the individuals it features, the collectives it represents, and the people who interact with "Bed Intruder Song!!!" and its remixed performances. The chapter title, "Suggestions . . . ," underscores the YouTube suggestion panel that uses algorithms to recommend videos based on what an interactor has just watched.[3] Through an interactor watching "Woman Wakes Up to Find Intruder in Bed," for example, the input generated in YouTube's algorithmic process affects what the platform suggests are related videos.

The later remixes show how responses to the attempted rape of a Black woman can become uncontrollable performances of epic proportions that function to denigrate and erase her while transforming her brother into a jester of himself. I focus on the noniconic aspects of this story to highlight less popular perspectives. By examining the additional layers that emerge during the performance, we can delve deeper into the humanity of Kelly and Antoine Dodson. This exploration serves to rethink these figures, often subject to derision, as generative of Black livelihood. To achieve this, I consider the racialized gender knowledge generated online within specific contexts and spaces, treating it with the seriousness it deserves.

Viral mechanisms amplify the simplicities and complexities of performances. They serve as one of many lenses that "call attention to the complexities inherent in the production of cultural artifacts, particularly those surrounding Black people."[4] I use netnography and critical discourse analysis to consider how queer Black femininity is framed and unframed through viral mechanisms, such as sharing links from video aggregation sites, commenting on walls built to archive discourses on the performance, and generating memes that are crucial to understanding how the Dodsons are both understood and misunderstood.

The democratization of technology and the increasingly interactive ways that interactors produce media online—through personal blogs, YouTube with its early slogan to "Broadcast Yourself," and unsolicited responses to online broadcasts through Twitch, TikTok, and other platforms—have blurred the boundaries between presenter, expert, and audience. That blurring necessitates new ways of interrogating the discourses that emerge within Black viralities. To respond to these newer modes of production, I communicate some of what interactors have said, what rumors they have circulated, and what discourses they have generated in select online spaces regarding WAFF 48's initial coverage of the Dodsons. What interactors say and suggest online through comments and memes produces and re-creates racialized gender knowledge. I examine this knowledge through what Robert V. Kozinets calls "netnography."[5]

Researchers first used netnography, or the study of communities and cultures over the World Wide Web,[6] in marketing research to explore consumption and cultural activities online. Combining cultural anthropology conventions, namely ethnography and cultural studies concerns, makes netnography possible. It employs participant observation in situated websites online to gather data about computer-mediated cultural or communal ways of knowing. As such, netnography is instructive in my research, enabling me to examine how people interact with and produce "things" in situated spaces online that affect and are affected by everyday life outside of those situated spaces.[7]

I take on the role of a lurker. Notably, a lurker can later become a more directly involved member of an online community, evolving into such roles as newbies, makers, interactors, and networkers.[8] Often, these roles exist in varying degrees in online communities, and netnographers must choose which roles they will participate in to gather data. I observe interactions on the video aggregation sites of YouTube and WorldStarHipHop in what Kozinets calls "cruising communities"—"online gatherings known for their weaker social relationships and the low centrality of any particular kind of consumption activity."[9] As such, interactors tend to comment on something that a maker posts or another interactor comments on, then they move on to interact with something completely different. Thus, interactions in cruising communities are sustained over brief periods.

The transient nature of the discussions and the delocalized framework of the websites justify my relationship with cruising communities as a lurker. Unlike cruisers, however, I repeatedly return to the sites I lurk on. Repeated returns to performances are also a necessary part of the process needed to make a performance viral. In that sense, my research has affected the virality of this performance, increasing its viewership.

The interactions I observe unfold in online spaces where users disguise or reveal their identities through discourses, usernames, and avatars—or digital representations via images or names of users' selves in real life ("IRL," as it is said online). As such, along with their usernames, I often indicate interactors' race and gender neutrally with "they." My subscription to using "they" regarding racialized gender blends and collapses popular associations with the use of pronouns to describe gender alone.[10] Representation by avatar or username requires me to analyze the discourses between interactors online, as their avatars or names may not indicate an identity-grounded IRL. As a result, I will not identify interactors beyond what they share at their discretion, and even that sharing is questionable. My refusal does not mean that racialized gender and sexuality or other supposedly visual, cultural, and behavioral cues do not influence interactors. It also does not mean that interactors do not reveal racialized gender when considering how they make sense of what they produce and respond to. Indeed, interactors' discourses construct and maintain relationships with race, gender, sexuality, and class in salient ways that are as enriching as visible or sonic cues.

For my purposes, I use netnography to examine people's relationships to online content, critically expounding on cultural phenomena. The remix video, "Bed Intruder Song!!!," gained popularity by remixing an already in-demand newscast ("A Woman Wakes Up to Find Intruder in Bed") into a palatable form. Additionally, the video's longer shelf life is attributable to the interactive comments and subsequent sharing and sampling by interactors. All these actions are necessary elements for the virality of performance. Indeed, a performance's virality is "produced in and by the relationship between audiences and performers and not aroused in listeners [and watchers] by the performer alone."[11] Therefore, netnography allows me to gain insight into the relationship between interactors and this performance on select sites where this video, and its related content, has gone viral.

By observing how news reports, music videos, memes, and interactors dialogue with one another, I capture the interreferential discourses of the Dodsons. Furthermore, I explore the intersections between sexism, racism, classism, and gender normativity and the interplay of sexuality, race, class, and gender through the mediums. Understanding the travel of this complex performance and its performatives in the domain of mass media (WAFF 48 News) and popular social media (YouTube, WorldStarHipHop, Reddit, and Bossip—an online magazine covering Black popular culture) requires a close examination of Black virality across these spaces. Interactions with these media produce an understanding of this performance and a more extensive cultural comprehension of race, sexuality, gender, and class.

The travel of the Dodsons' performance is a powerful example of how a singular performance can morph into an act representing multiple communities' responses to a violent offense. Many people witnessed Antoine Dodson not only as the primary eyewitness to the attempted rape of Kelly Dodson but also as a representation of how a Black queer subject looks and performs. I explore how online spaces that traffic in popular news and provide commentary on world events about Black representation and Black people engage the Dodsons as Ghetto Witnesses.

Tracing performances and ideas through online cultures allows me to trace how the Dodsons' bodies and performances move iteratively, with a signal difference, across virtual online communities. "Bed Intruder Song!!!"—the

Gregory Brothers' remix video of the initial Dodson newscast—gained more currency and travel across social media online than any other grassroots video at that time.[12] As the YouTube interactor remarks in the chapter's epigraph, "This song will never die." Importantly, as the song gained traction, people thought it had plagiarized another viral media product that had actually followed it: "Annoying Orange – Kitchen Intruder (Bed Intruder Spoof) with AutoTune Remix!"[13]

The Contrapuntal Time of Black Virality

"Annoying Orange – Kitchen Intruder," pictured in figure 27, is a news story narrated by a red bell pepper anchor and eggplant newscaster about an attempted slicing. A fruit named Nancy Nectarine was sleeping on her counter when someone came into the kitchen with a butcher knife and tried to "slice her peel off." Her friend (not brother), Annoying Orange, wanted to save her by spitting seeds but could not before the knife-wielder had sliced through a kiwi and three limes. Annoying Orange, dressed in a red bandanna, finally responds, "Well, obviously, we have a knife in the kitchen." He warns people to hide their kids, wives, and husbands because he's "slicing everybody out there." He then threatens the knife-wielder, calling him an apple.

FIGURE 27 Screenshot, October 20, 2014, "Annoying Orange – Kitchen Intruder (Bed Intruder Spoof) with AutoTune Remix!," posted November 23, 2010, by Annoying Orange, YouTube, 2:14, https://www.youtube.com/watch?v=pezdRcVe04c.

After the news version of the story, the auto-tuned remix appears, featuring a sped-up version of the same trap music from "Bed Intruder Song!!!":

(Chorus)
He's climbing in your windows
Choppin' your people up
Choppin' choppin'
So you better
Hide your kids
Hide your wife
Hide your kids
Hide your wife
Hide your kids
Hide your wife
And hide your husbands
Cause he's slicing everybody out there
(Bridge)
You don't have to come and confess
We're looking for you
We're gonna find you
We're gonna find you
So you can run 'n' tell that
Run and tell that
Run and tell that
Knife, knife, knife, knife,
Knife
(News reporter interrupts)
I guess that's just one
more good reason why you
should lock your doors at night
Ah, ah, ah, aaaah
(Eggplant newscaster line)
The knife got away, leaving
behind evidence
(Nancy Nectarine line)
I was attacked by some idiot in
the Kitchen
(Annoying Orange verse)
You're an apple
You're an apple
You're an apple
Knife
(Chorus repeats once)[14]

As of October 21, 2014, this remake of the remake, understood to be an original by some interactors, garnered 12,962,665 views on YouTube. Mentions of the "Annoying Orange – Kitchen Intruder" video on the comment feed of the "Bed Intruder Song!!!" video revealed that interactors were not only led to the Gregory Brothers' remix (perhaps by the suggestion panel) but also believed the groups' remix mimicked Annoying Orange's.

Interactor queries open essential discussions of the origins and adaptations of Black virality. Black virality reorders knowledge, making what came first look like an unsatisfactory simulacrum of itself. Hence, the "Kitchen Intruder" remix of the Dodsons' WAFF 48 News broadcast and its auto-tuned remix appears to be the original by happenstance whenever an interactor encounters that video first. This relativity situates the Dodsons as a mere imitation of a thing, an orange.

Even though YouTube was the first site to host "Bed Intruder Song!!!," its viral circulation raised many questions about what was original, what the Gregory Brothers remixed, and how interactors should distinguish the two. There can be no original when everything known about the "original" is created from existing elements. In the essay "Imitation and Gender Insubordination," gender theorist Judith Butler examines the idea of the original gender that a drag performance imitates. She writes, "There is no original or primary gender that drag imitates, but *gender is a kind of imitation for which there is no original. . . .* [Gender] produces the very notion of the original as an *effect* and consequence of the imitation itself."[15] Butler posits that beyond putting on clothes and enacting the behaviors popularly associated with other genders, drag performers demonstrate all genders are reenactments.

In a similar cadence, Black virality is a technology of racialized gender. It complicates the notion of an origin from which a viral performance of Blackness emerges while enacting an "absent Black presence" of Black performance.[16] Annoying Orange's performance reminds witnesses of a sight and sound not accessible sonically or visually here.[17] Indeed, even YouTube interactors expressed confusion over the video's origin, and this continued well into 2014, highlighting the nonlinearity of Black virality and showing how viral performances of the Black body in discourse can exist in contrapuntal time or have independent points of origin.[18]

Expressing confusion and confidence over the video's origin, YouTube interactor blezard2011 remarks, "This is the song from the annoying orange :@."[19] Having seen Annoying Orange's video first, blezard2011 mistakenly thought "Bed Intruder Song!!!" was the parody and the anthropomorphic orange was the source. Another interactor named jackred5 responded to blezard2011, noting "@blezard2011 it's the original one; annoyingorange took it."[20] Like fractal virality, Black virality disguises points of origin, conceals necessary narratives, and complicates the rumors that construct public attachment—an exponential collapse of context. The difference reveals another aspect of fractal virality: instead of beginning at the most viral moment and connecting that huge moment to increasingly minor iterative moments, a smaller performance can be the path to encountering the largest performance (recall figure 9 in chapter 1).

Here, the stakes for Antoine and Kelly Dodson depend on the proxies for their material bodies—an orange and a nectarine. Unfortunately, these parodies eliminate all signifiers of the racialized sexuality, gender, class, and geography that are crucial to the virality of that from which they derive. The Dodsons' Black lives thrive in the shadow of this performance, an absent Black presence. However, the presence of Black bodies in discourse is vital for productive discussions and comments examining how power structures influence Black life in this performance. By turning Antoine into Annoying Orange and Kelly into Nancy Nectarine, we witness cues taken from WAFF 48 News' coverage of the Dodsons' story to make light of a traumatic situation.

Besides sound bite, the makers of Annoying Orange use caricature as a memetic, reductive, and trivializing method that results in comedy. The makers transform the Dodsons into things again—from an online news video to an online hip-hop video to fruits—simplifying or altogether erasing their humanity. Indeed, such thingification depoliticizes a performance produced from the interplay of race, gender, sexuality, class, and geography. Like Auto-Tune, Black virality distorts and alters the pitch of the Dodsons' geography and racialized gender. This phenomenon removes the siblings from their original context, undermining their personhoods, which are required for comprehending the significance of their performance. Memeification further obscures the origins of Kelly and Antoine Dodson's story, making recognizing its true source even more challenging. Yet, as discussed in the first chapter of this book, sometimes what lies outside a performance frame can tell us more about what lies within the frame.

YouTube interactor Zceed received thirteen likes when they wrote, "Thumbs up if Annoying Orange bring'd you here [to the 'Bed Intruder Song!!!']."[21] The consensus, indicated by the likes that Zceed's comment receives, shows an important aspect of Black virality: an adaptation brings one closer to a source. Apart from including "spoof" in the title, which could pique the curiosity of interactors about the target of the parody, the "Bed Intruder Song!!!" video was in the suggested videos column to the right of the Annoying Orange video. This provided a point of entry for viewers to explore the cited performance. Thus, YouTube's algorithmic design created interreferential frameworks that sustained Black virality while instigating a performance's contrapuntal time.

Undoubtedly, the hip-hop sampling method helps me understand this contrapuntal time. For example, producers make new music from derivations of older sounds. Even though I may be unfamiliar with the sampled music, I have discovered entire recordings this way. A hip-hop song may have sampled only seconds of older recordings, but I enjoy them as much as their remix. Similarly, I may have never known of the Dodsons' moment had it not been for interactors, like the Gregory Brothers and panhead, sampling or copying the newscast. Thus, while Black virality may be contrapuntal in its origins, its interreferencing can connect it to other viral performances, amplifying their visibility and currency. Here, interactors use mimesis, which generates new meme material of the performance it derives from and produces a novel Black virality by repeatedly consuming that memetic thing (listening to, viewing, and sharing it). While hip-hop music is not alone in its use of sampling in the recording industry, the central role sampling plays as a catalyst for hip-hop makes its cultural spaces ripe for Black viralities. It is essential to highlight that the sampling we commonly consume as mash-ups and remixes here involves the audiovisual. We might consider this splicing of visuals that conjure sound and vice versa as a kind of see-jaying.

Netnographies of the Most Viral Grassroots Video of 2010 on WorldStarHipHop and YouTube

With the synergy between Black virality and hip-hop sampling, one space where I lurk is WorldStarHipHop—a space for video aggregation inflected with hip-hop tonalities. Because interactors sample "Bed Intruder Song!!!," it travels into many web spaces. Here, I focus on interactors' marginal and popular responses to the music video on the YouTube and WorldStarHipHop websites and their relationship to considerations of racialized class and sexuality. I perform a netnography of "Bed Intruder Song!!!" on YouTube and the reposted version of the same video retitled "Antoine Dodson – They Rape'n Everybody Out Here (Auto Tune Edition),"[22] which has received over four hundred thousand views on WorldStarHipHop.

The Dodsons' narratives gained significant traction on YouTube and WorldStarHipHop. The spaces reveal how varying interactors interpreted this moment of Black virality. I am especially concerned with how interactors' commentaries amplify the attention focused on Kelly's sexual inclinations as a Black cis woman and Antoine's vernacular queer Black femininity. Interactions on comment walls reveal what happens outside any performance frame as fervently as, if not more than, the enframed performance does. In discussing audiovisual Black viralities, interactors' discourses reveal pressures and issues that the Black lives featured within the camera's field of vision do not readily uncover.

Hank Willis Thomas's *Frames* series is a contemporary exemplar of what lies within and without the frame.[23] To make the series images, Thomas has someone hold frames in front of people or objects, and then he takes pictures that include the frame and what is outside the frame. In his demonstration, Thomas reveals the limitations of the camera's focus on the center or what is within the frame. Its narrow viewpoint provides an incomplete picture, as it cannot capture other important factors that script the enframed performance. For example, in one image from Philadelphia's Million Woman March, *Three*, three women smile at the camera. They center themselves within a wooden frame, outside of which everyone else's attention is elsewhere.[24] If viewers saw only the frame with the three figures, they might imagine that the women played a crucial role in the Million Woman March. Yet, interpreting the picture beyond the frame shows how inconsequential the three women might have been, with many other attendees surrounding them inattentive to their pose.

Here, the Dodsons' performance functions like that of the three women smiling at the camera while the interactors' attention is both there and elsewhere, on- and off-platform. Exterior factors script what the camera captures.

Indeed, interactions call attention to minor and major details within and outside the remix video that WAFF 48 or the Gregory Brothers did not center. Nevertheless, these factors shape the discursive perception of Antoine and Kelly Dodson. The repeated ways Antoine's performance travels beyond the camera's frames (or video box) also contribute to the remix video's success as a Black virality. While certain perceptions and mechanisms frame and limit the racialized gender and sexuality of the Dodsons' performances, they are also unframed by the same technologies.

Undoubtedly, sampling or incorporating preexisting music, styles, and bodily gestures in hip-hop cultural spaces creates something "original" and brings the past into the present. The Gregory Brothers use hip-hop to remix the WAFF 48 newscast and tap into a tradition where composition unsettles origin stories as much as creates them. The framing and unframing of Kelly and Antoine perform differently on YouTube, described in the previous chapter, and WorldStarHipHop because each website's design was unique in 2010 and continues to change.

The Architexture of WorldStarHipHop

The WorldStarHipHop and YouTube websites featuring the Gregory Brothers' remix encourage discussion; video sharing and aggregation are central. Yet the associated interactions carry a contrasting tone and ideological framework depending on which website they generate within. Interactions vary between the sites because each had a unique *architexture*—or physical (structure of the space) and ideological frame (that encompassing the texture of the space)—in 2010.[25] Indeed, design is never neutral. An interactor's comment reflects as much on the ideology of a site, what it allows and disallows, as it does on the interactor's ethos. In this section, I briefly explore the physical and ideological designs of WorldStarHipHop and YouTube to prepare for the following netnography.

WorldStarHipHop, dubbed by its late president Lee O'Denat as the "CNN of the Ghetto," is a video aggregation site that enables its interactors to communicate with its videos and each other through sharing in comment boxes their thoughts about the videos and each other.[26] After YouTube signed with Google, O'Denat was inspired by YouTube's success to follow suit. Respecting the "DVDs in the hood," he began WorldStarHipHop.[27] O'Denat's vision frames WorldStarHipHop as concerned with the interests and everyday joys and perils of life in socially and economically marginalized communities. Although CNN coverage should not be expected to solely emphasize joy or peril, peril appears to be its most sensationalized, and WorldStarHipHop follows a similar path. However, WorldStarHipHop differs from CNN in one significant way: it lacks an anchor to guide the audience through its sensationalized perils. In 2010, WorldStarHipHop was one of the best aggregate online sites for visual hip-hop with original and exclusive content, such as music videos and documentaries. WorldStarHipHop's position made it a fitting setting to examine varying perspectives on "Bed Intruder Song!!!" from those who traffic in such music online.

The videos I observed on WorldStarHipHop were created by interactors who used recording devices like cameras and smartphones. These interactors sought to capture everyday life and preserve these moments in audiovisual form. After interactors shared these moments with WorldStarHipHop moderators, the moderators, if they chose, featured them in video boxes on the site. Some posted recordings tended toward the amateur, like the footage from a man selling DVDs of novellas in a barbershop. The site also featured quasiprofessional recordings, such as musical performance videos. To share a video in 2010, one uploaded it to a file-storage site (such as SendSpace or WeTransfer) or video-sharing site (such as YouTube) and sent the video link and description to a WorldStarHipHop email address. WorldStarHipHop administrators and moderators then subjectively determined whose upload got selected and posted to WorldStarHipHop. Once administrators posted a video, interactors could discuss it and respond to one another in its comment boxes.

In 2010, interactions could occur only anonymously, immediately disguising an interactor's identity with "guest" instead of as a unique designator. That anonymity likely encouraged interactors to post unfiltered opinions, altering the bluntness and care with which they shared ideologies about WorldStarHipHop's content. This design has encouraged the unfiltered responses expected within WorldStarHipHop's comment section since the website launched in 2005.

WorldStarHipHop's overall color scheme emphasized shades of black with contrasts of white and red, as seen in figure 28. It featured a space-gray background with a gradient into black from top to bottom. A video box overlaid the background gradient in a thin black frame to the left of the center. The video box's top border carried the title in a white Impact-style font over a dark gray backdrop. With a glowing red and white center, the WorldStarHipHop logo featured a five-point star followed by "WorldStarHipHop," also in an Impact-style font, and it branded each video in the lower-right corner of the page. The star and letters featured a light gray gradient sparkling with red animations followed by a smoking bullet hole (or ash burn). WorldStarHipHop's logo, like its infamous content, evoked violence.[28]

Beneath the video box, viewers saw buttons enabling them to share their videos via Twitter or Myspace and to "like" videos via Facebook, all of which turned interactors into tastemakers. These were also social-marketing tactics to attract people to videos by expanding the networked culture. Beneath the buttons was an area marked "Leave a comment," with a white comment box beneath it, under which one could see every previous comment. The

FIGURE 28 Screen featuring 2010 WorldStarHipHop layout, "World Star Hip Hop Freaks," sbmotorparts.com, August 10, 2010, http://3.bp.blogspot.com/_6bw5m6fZShl/Swn9AXiSxql/AAAAAAAACqs/fpyKDbfQvCs/s1600/worldstarhiphop.png.

comment box's position at the nexus of the video and prior comments encouraged interaction with the video and other interactors. To the video box's right was a similarly designed detail box containing a description of the video's contents, noting the day and time WorldStarHipHop administrators had added the video and its total number of views. It also showed an advertisement. Under the description inside the detail box was a similarly designed layout containing a list of recommended videos.

Compared with all internet users, in the first quarter of 2012, WorldStarHipHop viewers were "disproportionately African-American."[29] The users also "tend[ed] to be childless, moderately educated men in the age range of 18–24 who browse from school and home."[30] A 2011 comprehensive study by the Opportunity Agenda, "Media Market: Media Consumption Trends among Black Men," provides insight. The study revealed that, besides reflecting the habits of the general adult population (visiting YouTube, ESPN.com, and Yahoo!, for example), WorldStarHipHop was one of four music sites in the top ten mass-media, Black-oriented content sites that were the most popular among African American men.[31]

WorldStarHipHop's visual design, while not radically altered, now resembles YouTube's, most evident in the transition of its home page background from a black gradient to an antiflash white. To interact, a user must adopt an avatar name through Disqus, a website that enables the user to interact and comment on many other online platforms through a standard interface and unique avatar. Even though a user can still create an online identity separate from their IRL identity, the requirement to adopt an avatar complicates the preservation of anonymity that existed when administrators published "Antoine Dodson – They Rape'n Everybody Out Here (Auto Tune Edition)" on WorldStarHipHop.

The Currency of Blackness and Appropriating Black Virality

In 2014, YouTube reached more US adults ages 18–34 than any cable network. Eighty percent of its traffic came from outside the United States.[32] YouTube's personalities, who carry channels with subscribers to their videos, had been disproportionately "minorities," unlike what is on mainstream television, where the stars are primarily white.[33] In 2012, Hayley Tsukayama, a reporter for the *Washington Post*, wrote, "Among the 20 most-subscribed-to channels on YouTube, eight feature minorities. Most are Asian American. Many more Black and Latino shows populate the top 50."[34] Performances by nonwhite YouTube users and invited features have attained significantly high consumption by online interactors and spectators.[35] These statistics are telling when six out of ten of the top video uploads on the Gregory Brothers' YouTube channel, schmoyoho, featured Black Americans or their voices (as of August 2014). If schmoyoho had not capitalized on the profitability of commodifying Black performances and transforming them into marketable products, the Gregory Brothers' channel would not have achieved its particular viral success.

Unlike WorldStarHipHop, where administrators must approve videos before they upload them to the site, on YouTube, interactors bear a significant burden for sustaining the broadcasting; thus, before anyone could view their video, the Gregory Brothers, like any other interactor, needed only to log in to their YouTube account and upload it. Three days after the WAFF 48 news report on the Dodson family aired, the Gregory Brothers turned the already sensationalized framing of WAFF 48's news story on the rape attempt of Kelly Dodson into an episode, "12b," of their *Auto-Tune the News* series without having secured permission to do so.[36] Auto-Tune, like its mathematical genesis, functioned to search for (Black) material to mine and refine to fuel other aspirations.

Other interactors see-jayed the newscast and the auto-tuned version into a mélange of fan-edited videos, but none reached the popularity of the Gregory Brothers' rendition.[37] The Gregory Brothers further narrowed WAFF 48's focus on Antoine Dodson by making his rage even more of a spectacle and deepening Kelly Dodson's silencing. Indeed, this change further trivialized the seriousness of what had happened to Kelly and transformed her story into an "almost forgotten strand in the narrative."[38]

Eventually, the Gregory Brothers contacted Antoine Dodson (it is unclear if they spoke with Kelly Dodson) and asked him if he wanted to receive half of the iTunes song's profits. Initially, Antoine hesitated. His hesitation was crucial in that it conveyed his awareness of the varying stakes between making money from, mocking, and creating an understanding of his family's pain, rage, and courage.

Less than a year after everyone, including Antoine Dodson, had made a fair sum of money, someone at a press conference with him and the Gregory Brothers asked him to share his first reaction to the song. Anticipating Antoine's response and announcing his awareness of the staging of the passionate performance in the queue of their comical news representations, one of the Gregory Brothers insisted, "It's okay if you say we were jerks." Antoine's response was, "Is somebody trying to be funny? Is they taking this to be a joke?" His response allowed the pain and seriousness of the news interview to be known.[39]

His latter rhetorical question echoes the sentiments in Antoine Dodson's first (and earlier) Facebook fan page post he created two weeks after the publishing of "Bed Intruder Song!!!" In the post, he declared, "HEY GUYS! Today I just want to say for the people who think that they can make me look crazy or hurt my image. THINK AGAIN I don't care how much you offer. You are not going to make me or my family look stupid so runandtelldat homeboy."[40] His comment had received 644 likes by February 2014. These two pivotal comments reflect the vulnerability and cultural currency of the Dodsons as Ghetto Witnesses. African American studies scholar and performance theorist and practitioner E. Patrick Johnson discusses the attraction to, and currency of, Blackness, which helps consider the incentives to memeify this Black performance. He writes, "For their part, whites construct linguistic representations of [B]lacks that are grounded in racist stereotypes to maintain the status quo only to then reappropriate these stereotypes to affect a fetishistic 'escape' into the Other to transcend the rigidity of their own whiteness, as well as to feed the capitalist gains of commodified [B]lackness."[41] After other failed (or less viral) attempts at performing Blackness, it is possible that the Gregory Brothers recognized this performance as a perfect entry for a profitable fetishistic escape into the Other.[42]

Meanwhile, the form of the Dodsons' sincere testimony is ready to be sampled by interactors as comedic and, as Aisha Harris—a *Slate* culture blogger for *Brow Beat*—phrased it, "derisively memeified." Their derisive memeification stems from their sonic and optic dissonance in the normalized field of vision and sound of news broadcasts. Indeed, the Ghetto Witness emerges as an aesthetic through the technological ability to visualize and sonically project a vernacular recounting of traumatic or otherwise events in documentary formats that appear live, informal, and unadulterated. Antoine Dodson's Facebook comments indicate he was aware of this aesthetic.

Despite this awareness, Antoine Dodson agreed to split all profits fifty-fifty between him and the Gregory Brothers. Here, the Gregory Brothers use their class, racial privilege, and musical expertise in memeifying through Auto-Tune to exchange the Dodson family's pain, rage, and courage for fiscal gain. America has a historical trend of showcasing and consuming Black people in pain, profiting through anything from public atrocities to popular sports.[43] Indeed, YouTube is a contemporary site where all people perform and consume spectacles of pain (and pleasure) in differing ways. White men still claim a significant stake in the staging and consumption of this pain and pleasure, whereas Black people experience and remember the moments, storing them for later opportunities to counter the memory.

However, the Dodsons' performance is also traumatic for many who view it. This performance haunts spectators with yet another instance of sexual assault, Black life accompanied by casual violence, and feminine Black men reframed into comic relief. Even though WAFF 48 News staged the event, the Gregory Brothers became collusive in that staging. They distributed it, with auto-tuned and see-jayed differences, to a broader audience, monetizing its value.

Their rendition of the newscast, "Bed Intruder Song!!!," sold more than three hundred thousand copies on iTunes and became the most widely viewed grassroots YouTube video of 2010.[44] On April 10, 2014, the song received platinum certification.[45] The contract between the Dodsons and the Gregory Brothers indeed complicated understandings of the song's intended message. Antoine Dodson called it "a positive message, like an alert." However, he and the Gregory Brothers turned the song into a product that sold far more than it raised awareness about sexual assault.[46] The profits from Dodson's business investments—including songs, T-shirts, a sex offender application—helped him move his family out of public housing. This upward class mobility was one instance of how, in Antoine's words, "a blessing came out of a bad situation."[47]

Many of the YouTube interactors engaged in one of four behaviors. First, some sarcastically commented on the remix video. Second, others distastefully accused those who disliked the video of being "rapists." Third, some agreed on disliking the video after 1:15 of its running time. Or last, they repeated what is said in the video. Many WorldStarHipHop interactors engaged in one of three discourses. First, some mentioned their desire to use the song as a ringtone. Second, others emphasized how hilarious they found the video. Last, interactors repeated the words verbatim from the video. One can imagine how investigating the racialized gender knowledge of the most common behaviors and discourses regarding this remix video gets us critically nowhere. Indeed, that which is viral and occupies most of the attention economy may not be the richest site of generative knowledge. So, instead, I question the politics of race, class, sexuality, and memeification that arises in some of the marginal and noniconic comments from interactors reacting to the performance. The issues concerning derisive representations of Blackness in popular culture and the challenge to those notions come up in such instances of Black virality as this. These two tensions lead me to consider how technologies and aesthetics amplify the pejorative and simultaneously breed and sustain ideas situated in livability and complexity.

It's Just That, Trap: A Netnography of a Black Virality as Trap Muzik

By presenting the Dodsons as Ghetto Witnesses on YouTube, the Gregory Brothers used audiovisual techniques to shape how viewers perceived and misunderstood the siblings. This leads to more questions, concerns, and hot takes, magnifying the Gregory Brothers' remix and ultimately assisting its circulation into increasingly wider audiences. The Dodsons' visual representation in the WAFF 48 newscast acts as an aesthetic cue for what is associated with trap music's sound: Black lives, thugs, drugs, poverty, violence, and a desire to overcome the struggles that arise from those conditions, positions, and access. I shift here to investigate the see-jaying of the WAFF 48 newscast into a trap music video, "Bed Intruder Song!!!," and consider how it makes Kelly and Antoine Dodson highly visible, illegible, and legible.

The music video sampled the incidents from the newscast and was my first path to the incidents that WAFF 48 covered. Just as Annoying Orange led some interactors to "Bed Intruder Song!!!," the same "Bed Intruder Song!!!" led me to the WAFF 48 newscast I discuss in the previous chapter. The Gregory Brothers' remix video then memeified the television interview.

One glaring difference between the interview and the remix is that the remix begins and ends with snippets of Antoine Dodson's interview, with Kelly Dodson appearing only briefly in the remix video (with, literally, one line). Recall that the initial newscast features Kelly Dodson first. Thus, the Gregory Brothers further subtract her from the video. This erasure reveals that, while Black virality amplifies its performers' visibility, it also distorts it, almost effacing them from the narrative.

Antoine Dodson opens the music video with these words said during the interview: "Well . . . *obviously* we have a *rapist* in Lincoln *Park*!" The catchy trap music comes in on a 4/4 rhythm with mid-seventy beats per minute, buzzing electronic bass and staccato piano keys at the forefront, sparse kick drums and sprinkled snares in the backdrop, and handclaps. Following that intro, the choral auto-tuned motif (integrated with the Gregory Brothers' voices) begins:

(Antoine Dodson chorus)
He's climbin' in yo' windows /
he's snatchin' yo' people up /
tryin' to rape 'em /
so you need to /
hide ya kids / hide ya wife /
hide ya kids / hide ya wife /
hide ya kids / hide ya wife /
and hide ya husbands /
cause they rapin' e'rybody out here /
You don't have to come and confess /
We lookin' for you /
We gon' find you /
We gon' *find* you /
So you can run 'n' tell that /
Run 'n' tell that /
Run 'n' tell that homeboy /
Home, home, *homeboy*
(Antoine Dodson verse)
We got yo' t-shirt
and you left fingerprints and all /
You are so dumb /
You are really dumb /
For real
(Elizabeth Gentle)
The man got away
leaving behind evidence
(Kelly Dodson)
I was attacked
by some idiot in the projects
(Antoine Dodson)
So dumb / So dumb / So dumb / So!
(Chorus repeats once)[48]

Throughout the song, the Gregory Brothers transform gestures that express the no-nonsense attitude and queerness Antoine Dodson performs in the newscast, such as using the eye and neck roll with his blown-out afro. After video editing, his face almost functions as a bouncing ball, assisting spectators as they follow the unwritten lyrics. The song breaks down into a bridge at the close of the second chorus and, through repetition, musically emphasizes a performance laced with Black street vernacular.

Antoine Dodson delivers his threat to the sexual predator using this vernacular. It is not just his slang that is street and Black but also his commanding presence. He encroaches on the camera space, rolls his eyes and neck to his left, and firmly states, "Now you can run 'n' tell that, homeboy." This gesture and phrase are the stance and words that precede a Black street fighting ritual. Beyond a reference to Denise LaSalle's 1972 song "Now Run and Tell That" or a song in the 2007 musical *Hairspray,* here we see how Antoine suggests that the sexual predator should inform his family of Antoine's threat and bring them so that they can get their "asses beat" too. This stance recalls and amplifies moments where an assailant provokes a fight, leading to the involvement of the perpetrator's entire family in a brawl. Yet the Gregory Brothers set this threat to trap music.

Trap music, a term coined in 2003 by rap artist T.I. as "Trap Muzik," denotes a southern United States (Texas, Georgia, and Tennessee) style of hip-hop music inspired by the struggles of making/dealing drugs that have defined an unofficial genre of music since the early 1990s. Trap music's rap lyrics often range from paranoid to megalomaniacal, reflective of the states of mind that can emerge from a lifestyle informed by drug dealing. The word *trap*, before it became the name of a music genre, represented the location where dealers mixed, packaged, and dealt drugs and the lifestyle that came with the job. Musically, trap is characterized by "booming 808-style subbass kick drums" and "sixty-fourth-note hi-hats" created on drum machines, deep synths, and "cinematic strings."[49]

The term also functions as a critique of the dead-end nature of that business. As Big Boi from the Atlanta rap group Outkast reflects, "So now you're back in the trap / Just that, trapped / Go on and marinate on that for a minute."[50] For this moment, trap resembles what novelist, African American literary scholar, and sound studies scholar Regina Bradley insists to be "a framework for recognizing the grief and grievances of young southern black men [and women, in this instance] who feel unseen or are deemed unworthy of recognition elsewhere."[51] Instead of the Dodsons choosing trap as a medium through which to testify, the Gregory Brothers had already selected it.

Trap music is derived from situated (often blighted) places and the psychic, spiritual, and physical struggles of certain (Black) lives to survive within those places; as such, trap music functions as a witness to kinds of life in the African diaspora and represents how that seeing/imagining sounds. The visual summons the aural—what Fred Moten describes as "a seeing that redoubles itself as sound" or "visible music."[52] Here, the use of trap music by the Gregory Brothers further ties race to both bodily and aural signifiers, a performance of their racialized erotics.

From a perusal through the Gregory Brothers' other *Auto-Tune the News* videos, I did not always find a correlation between the identities of the content and the music. But the Gregory Brothers' use of trap music to represent the Dodsons' testimony and warning deserves attention. The music group linguistically and gesturally represents Blackness by repeatedly highlighting certain sections of the newscast, including "run 'n' tell that." Indeed, they amplify this Black performance by setting it in a trap music soundtrack and harmonizing with that representation—clapping while singing "You can run 'n' tell that"—forever attaching themselves as part of the Other's (read: the Dodsons') entourage. As I consider Antoine Dodson's performance of the Ghetto Witness, I also wonder why the Gregory Brothers chose trap music instead of another musical form.

In a later interview, the Gregory Brothers reveal that they found the musicality of Antoine Dodson's warning attractive.[53] Their attention to the cadence of his speech and their familiarity with trap music signaled how the Dodsons could fit within a trap-themed video. Because other interactors also recognize how well the interview integrates with trap music, they echo and promote the Gregory Brothers' attraction to Antoine Dodson's rhythm, directness, and vivid particularity. Indeed, trap music, a viral Black American musical subgenre of hip-hop, increased the Black virality of the performance. Viral material—the Dodsons' performance—met a viral music genre—trap—and created a coconstitutive viral product that translated into money and fame.

One YouTube interactor called MaNgAnlmE stated, "this is why i love black guys. They can rap even when they dont realize it."[54] After posting this comment, MaNgAnlmE received seventeen likes, making it one of the top comments for "Bed Intruder Song!!!" on the afternoon of January 26, 2011. Through their likes, these other unnamed YouTube interactors affirmed the assumption that there is an inherent quality in how Black men speak that genetically predisposes them to rap. This notion is inseparable from inaccurate ideas about Black lives as proxies for entertainment. Beyond the belief that Black people are naturally inclined to be musical or rappers, MaNgAnlmE also found Antoine Dodson's speech particularly captivating and appealing because of its distinct musicality, encompassing a specific rhythm, melody, and tonality. Reminding others of the musicality of the WAFF 48 newscast, YouTube interactor airstrike141 received three likes after commenting, "The original video actually sound like hes trying to rap already."[55] One can get lost in the rhythm as he moves his head from side to side—as if to accent his syllables—and achieves varying pitches. Yet Antoine Dodson's gestures express his affect regarding his sister's violation and his disdain for the conservative respectability politics of the girl on the sidelines, not his intent to be melodic or speak with rhythm.

The trap music decided on by the Gregory Brothers for the background of this remix video commodifies and caricatures the Dodsons' location, class, and racialized gender, transforming and masculinizing the siblings into unintentional singing rap artists. The remix artists draw inspiration from an African American music genre that emerged from the income-driven necessity to sell drugs in the southern United States.

In an interview, Michael Gregory reveals a little-known fact about the *Auto-Tune the News* series: "Sometimes in our videos, we include a lot of singers, and when we do, we might arbitrarily use a beat that we're going to shape them all to. But Antoine, you know, he kind of owned the song—this was going to be all him—so I wanted [the beat] to be specific to that."[56] In essence, Gregory saw confidence and heard a song in the Dodsons' interview, highlighting Antoine (not Kelly) Dodson. Rather than making a random musical selection, Gregory deliberately opted for a trap motif to maintain the "authenticity" of Antoine Dodson's performance. Thus, the Gregory Brothers dangerously correlate the ordeals of a young, Black, working-class Alabamian family with the sound of trap music.

Trap music represents poverty, masculine Blackness, and blighted locales, effectively embodying these classes, racialized genders, and geographies through its widely shared lyrics and imagery. It capitalizes on viral mechanisms like video-sharing websites, applications, (connected) television broadcasts, and music streaming services to reach a broader audience. This viral genre does unspoken work for the Gregory Brothers in trapping Antoine Dodson in something legible. Still, the Gregory Brothers also trap him in illegibility: the bodies associated with trap music rarely exhibit performances of queer Black femininity. Through this "miscasting," the Gregory Brothers create comedy.[57] What operates as a trap of representation inadvertently liberates the spectrum of lives that can effectively perform (or fail at performing) trap music. Admittedly, this trauma transforms into an interview, now inseparable from hip-hop music, as Antoine Dodson's address to an unnamed intruder—with a minor interjection from Kelly Dodson—becomes the lyrics to the latest trap song.

She Doesn't Look Like a Rape Victim: The Black Femme Body in Discourse as Promiscuous

Many other interactors on WorldStarHipHop and YouTube have responded only to the trap song video and not to each other, praised the song for its brilliance and coolness, asked others if they stopped watching the video at 1:15, and wondered whether anyone found the intruder. These remarks outnumber the responses I interrogate here and speak to the Gregory Brothers' talent for making the gravely serious comedically palatable. Nevertheless, the interactions that lurk in their shadow suggest that this Black virality is outstanding and trendy in ways that affect Black wellness. A closer look at comments that are marginal to most reveals haunting assumptions about Kelly Dodson's sexual desires. Here, I explore how interactor responses on WorldStarHipHop both challenge and support the racist, sexist, and heteronormative discourses surrounding her Black womanhood. I also produce a netnography of YouTube that distills similar discourses from the first year's comments and explores how conceptions of the sexual desires of Black women couple with notions of the sexual desires of Black men.

Soon after WorldStarHipHop published "Antoine Dodson—They Rape'n Everybody Out Here [Auto Tune Edition]," an interactor commented on the dynamics of rape in connection with Kelly Dodson, posting, "his sis doesnt look like a rape victim . . . she probably wanted it."[58] Such a comment implying that she had welcomed the assault evokes the stereotype of the promiscuous Black woman who can never be sexually assaulted against her will.[59] The notion of Kelly as Antoine's sister, again, situates her only in relation to him, enabling viewers to witness an effect of what WAFF 48 News had set in motion: emphasizing Antoine and deemphasizing Kelly. Also, suggesting that Kelly does not "look like a rape victim" symptomatizes the popular image of a rape victim. The suggestion also reveals the difficulty in perceiving Black women's bodies as vulnerable to sexual violence. The significance of the comment is that another interactor questioned it, starting a dialogue that broke up other monologues on the comment wall.

While the ideology of racialized sexuality used to justify sexual assault here is disturbing, an interactor faced it and challenged the notion that Kelly Dodson desired her sexual assault. In response to the comment about Kelly's not looking like a rape victim, another WorldStarHipHop interactor commented, "What Kinda cr*p is that? Seriously? Who WANTS to be raped? . . . JERK!!!!"[60] By not limiting rape to genders or races, they do some critical work in considering rape beyond the standard white heteronormative cis women discourse and in questioning who fits the description of a rape victim. They also take the previous person to task for treating force and violence like consensual sex. Kelly Dodson's scenario—where an uninvited stranger invades her home and assaults her—eliminates the possibility of rape fantasy. The remark that no one aspires to be raped by another person demonstrates how Black viralities amplify issues related to the denigration of racialized gender and class. These Black viralities also create conditions whereby one can learn of and challenge that very slander.

Even though comment walls (more on YouTube than on WorldStarHipHop) prioritize comments with the most likes or replies, comment areas on such websites make it possible for other interactors to encounter alternative perspectives. This possibility is where the perspective-altering potential that affirms Black life lies in the domain of memeified Black virality. In *Modern Dance, Negro Dance: Race in Motion*, dramaturg and performance studies scholar Susan Manning explores race, gender, sexuality, and, of particular interest here, spectatorship and reception in mid-twentieth-century American theatrical dance. Manning describes a process she terms "cross-viewing." Cross-viewing elaborates on how performance spectators understand other subjectivities from alternative social locations. Such an act enables observing the same performance in dissimilar ways, inducing cross-viewers to interpret bodies in motion or watch them differently. Cross-viewing is the watching of other people watching to inform viewing practices and ways to exist in the world.[61] This cross-viewing, she writes, "has the potential to alter how publics read bodies in motion and thus to effect social and artistic change."[62]

Comment areas on video-sharing sites provide a platform for interactors to engage in acts of cross-viewing. In this context, interactors can observe and respond to each other's comments and witness instances of abusive power. These interactions can reinforce, challenge, or transgress the content they are cross-viewing. However, despite my optimistic viewpoint, the WorldStarHipHop and YouTube comment sections of videos such as the Dodson video often contain numerous sexist, racist, classist, and homophobic comments.

These comments pose a challenge to critical antiracist discourses and create a hostile environment.

The overwhelming number of likes or comments on a video also suggests a level of endorsement for its discriminatory discourses. This indicates that interactors read comments but are often uninterested in conversations with others or being engaged by someone else. On platforms like YouTube, other interactors validate commenters by liking their comments. Moreover, it is essential to note that the number of views typically outweighs the number of comments. This suggests that many interactors exhibit antisocial behavior when engaging with the video. Understanding that watching an online video does not automatically count as social engagement is crucial. While a view can be as social as a group gathering around a radio to listen to a broadcasted event, pressing Play or autoplaying a video does not guarantee active online social interaction. Also, counting a view does not guarantee that someone saw the material. A view could result from an interactor pushing the Play button or passively autoplaying after actively viewing a related video. And even if they are playing it, muting the video may prevent someone from hearing it. While a view quantifies virality, engagement, and affective labor, it also masks their factual execution.

Thus, the comment areas on video-sharing sites provide a space for countless instances of cross-viewing and interaction that is not always captured by the indicated amount of views of a video. These spaces hold the potential for liberation from perspectives that limit the humanity of others, made more powerful through virality. However, the prevalence of discriminatory comments, the engagement disparity between views and comments, and the significance of likes all contribute to a complex social dynamic within these spaces that does little to guarantee liberation.

As recorded in my field notes, I repeatedly observed that a particular concept had received many likes that emerged only from YouTube commenters, which alarmed me. For example, there is a little Black baby boy in the background of the WAFF 48 coverage of Kelly Dodson's story who interactors label as the rapist. Numerous top comments refer to seconds 0:41 through 0:43 of the video, alerting others that they can see the rapist during that period. Other users liked these comments. Indeed, the original newscast's rendering centered a small Black boy in a grey-and-yellow-striped shirt at the precise moment when Kelly Dodson says, with one hand on her hip, "I was attacked by some idiot in the projects." (See figure 29.) The little boy opens the door to the cadence of "projects." Playing off the "hide ya wife, hide ya kids, and hide ya husbands" phrase of Antoine's, which the Gregory Brothers had transformed into a mantra, YouTube interactor Laplap9370 received sixty-eight likes for asking, "did any body notice that little boy from 0:41 to 0:43 he is the rapist!!! he is trying to rape the others . . . so, ya need to hide

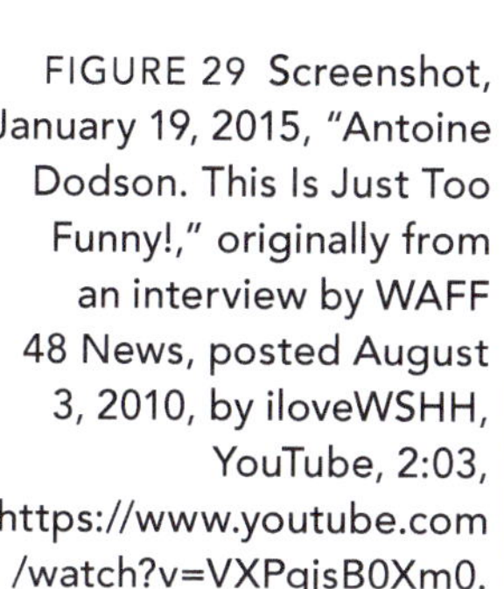
FIGURE 29 Screenshot, January 19, 2015, "Antoine Dodson. This Is Just Too Funny!," originally from an interview by WAFF 48 News, posted August 3, 2010, by iloveWSHH, YouTube, 2:03, https://www.youtube.com/watch?v=VXPgjsB0Xm0.

you kid . . . just your kid . . . home boy!"[63] Describing what the Black baby is doing, Irockgame1 received twenty-four likes after remarking, "at 0:42 there is a rapist entering the house. lol."[64] Linking the video's title to the little boy, baradona10 received fifty-nine likes after posting, "0:41 the little kid is the bed intruder!!!!!"[65]

The consensus around these remarks posits the small Black boy as the rapist. They also collude the YouTube comments with the pejorative comment on WorldStarHipHop depicting Kelly Dodson as desiring her sexual assault (with the assumption she could easily defend herself against a small child). Discussing the link between Black women's perceived promiscuity and Black men's perceived compulsive sexual urges, Black feminist theorist Patricia Hill Collins suggests that the stereotype of Black men as rapists reinforces the archetype of the Black woman as whore.[66] These twin conceptualizations, coupled with the remarks about the very young Black boy in the backdrop of the news story, demonstrate how Black baby boys are socialized not to experience childhood, with society denying them the experience and instead expecting them to mature while prematurely imagining them as accountable (or, in this case, criminal) adults.

Discourses of racialized gender and sexuality criminalize and sexualize Black boys before they can tell the difference between right and wrong or express sexual desire.[67] These comments, as a result, function to reinforce the mythical Black rapist and Black whore archetypes. At this moment, the Dodsons are survivors of trespassing—of their home and their bodies. Yet interactors criminalize the Dodsons and make them the agents of their own trauma. This framing and reframing of Kelly Dodson as a sexual predator also amplifies her vulnerability as sexual prey.

He's Not Gay at All: Racialized Sexuality and Class as Black Performance

I continue my netnography of the dangerous knowledge interactors on WorldStarHipHop and YouTube produce and reproduce. I shift attention to comments concerning Antoine Dodson's sexuality, which compound and trouble popular notions associated with Black gay lives. In my analysis of the WorldStarHipHop comments, I am particularly cautious of the neoliberal impulse to label Black cultural spaces as overly homophobic, making Black groups responsible for structural homophobia (often resulting from settler sexuality) of which they are a part and not the absolute whole.[68] Based on my survey of the first year of top-rated comments on YouTube and WorldStarHipHop, interactors used "gay" and "fag" in denigrating ways. Indeed, a spectrum of interactions repeats itself, which signals an ideological consistency I cannot ignore, all broadcasted behind an avatar that reads "guest." As critical race scholar Matthew W. Hughey and digital sociologist Jessie Daniels posit, "Given that racist [and homophobic] language has (1) changed form to become more subtle and (2) moved backstage to private areas, one might view the intersection of racist [and homophobic] discourse and the internet as a third space betwixt and between the public and private spheres."[69] The subsequent comments showcase the inclination to publicly degrade others. They also reveal how YouTube and WorldStarHipHop interactors betray the anonymity that online identity ostensibly provides by using discourses from bodies IRL.

On November 3, 2010, YouTube interactor jcords400z received two likes for commenting, "He's not gay at all . . . Lmfao."[70] The user's attention to Antoine Dodson's sexuality is denigrating, as the sarcastic tone of "he's not gay at all" is followed by the comedic "lmfao." If part of comedy emerges from placing the abnormal in a typical scene (as is done in miscasting), and Black feminine men do not traffic in the US imagination as able to protect anyone, including themselves, this performance creates a perfect storm for a laugh. While wrongheaded, it is possible to comprehend why jcords400z finds it amusing, as the Dodson family requires protection, and the role of protector is fulfilled by a Black feminine man.

Nonetheless, the purportedly comedic remark concerns the ease with which the interactor, and popular culture by extension, understands sexuality. Masculine expressions of gender are not only dysphoric, inconsistent, and subject to failure, but the men who show them are compulsorily collapsed into possessing heterosexual desire—just as Black feminine men, as in jcords400z's comment, are misleadingly collapsed into possessing homosexual desire. For this interactor, Antoine Dodson's femininity gives away his sexuality. Even though people enact gestural behaviors to signal their social position and sexual desire to others (with elongated glances, a lingering shoe under the bathroom stall, or a wink with a pursing of the lip), there is no natural correlation between femininity or behavior and sexuality.

The openness of, and attention to, commenting on Antoine Dodson as gay suggests an inability to understand race as always constitutive of gender, class, and sexuality (among many other dimensions of people's lives). Indeed, jcords400z's disaggregation of gayness from Blackness compounds the assumption in racial discourse that the authentic Black subject is masculine and heterosexual.[71] This compounding recalls African American literary theorist Marlon Ross's contention of "a persistent gender ideology that views the sissy [misread as feminine, male, and failing at Blackness] as a danger to proper masculine [misread as stoic, cisgender, heterosexual, and, thus, succeeding at Blackness] conduct and character, even if the particular nature of that danger varies with the changing conditions of racial and gender entitlement."[72]

The remark by jcords400z also encompasses Black gay men within the trope of "Negro Faggotry" that filmmaker, activist, and poet Marlon T. Riggs describes as caricature at the expense of the humanity of Black gay men, "entertaining us in the castles of our homes—like court jesters, like eunuchs—with their double entendres, their dead-end lusts, and, above all, their relentless hilarity in the face of relentless despair. Negro Faggotry is all the rage! Black Gay Men are not."[73] Indeed, in viewing Blackness and homosexuality together through the lens of cinematic and televisual representations, a trope exists that enframes Black gay men as comic relief: Negro Faggotry. Antoine Dodson's sexual desires become most visible and laughable to his audience in a scene of despair, with the assaulter still unaccounted for. Dodson entertains, transforming a dangerous situation into one of amusement that reflects the incapacity of onlookers to reconcile that which has never been estranged: Black male femininity. It is a gender expression that onlookers struggle to comprehend, often leading them to compound gender with sexuality and to understand Dodson as gay.

Instead of disaggregating Blackness from sexuality, a circa 2010 WorldStarHipHop interactor considered Blackness and sexuality inseparable, albeit in casting an insult, commenting, "WHY DO THIEY SHOW THESE IGNORENT BLACK f*gS ON TV MAKI BLACK PPL OOK BAD!!!!!!"[74] As this interactor shares his embarrassment about, or observation of, Dodson, he echoes the sentiments of conservative respectability politics that other Black people hold in the previous chapter. This rhetorical question interplays with class contentions by labeling Dodson ignorant while labeling him Black. The question is also an insult to his perceived sexuality.

The interactor's use of "fag" violently compounds gender with sexuality and dangerously situates male femininity within a homophobic understanding of queer sexuality. There is both congruity and incongruity between behavior and sexuality: "Because femininity is always already devalued in patriarchal societies, those associated with the feminine are also viewed as inferior. Given the ways in which effeminacy in men is read as a sign of homosexuality, particularly in the United States, it follows that homosexual men are devalued."[75] Interactors devalue Dodson's behavior by focusing on his femininity and inferring his sexuality based on visible and auditory cues, misinterpreting him as gay.[76]

We must also understand this devaluation as trivializing Antoine Dodson's Blackness. For this WorldStarHipHop interactor, Dodson's portrayal of Black gender, which is also delivered with classed inflections, is detrimental to the image of Black people. The idea of "looking bad" is rooted in a feeling of racial embarrassment caused by seeking the approval of the white (hetero)normative gaze. Such humiliation threatens the pride of Black heterosexual masculinity and undermines the salvific wish for collective dignity. However, Dodson's threat is unconcerned with the approval of any white power structure, and undue attention to his perceived Black sexuality obscures the Black feminist work of his performance.[77]

While aspects of Antoine Dodson's performance summoned politics related to conservative respectability and racialized masculine pride, one WorldStarHipHop interactor offered an alternative view. Responding to the interactor who referred to Antoine (and possibly Kelly) as ignorant, they say, "I don't think the individuals were ignorant. He came correct." This interactor expresses a ghettocentric ideology that recontextualizes perspectives from "a collective identity shaped by class consciousness, the character of inner-city space, police repression, poverty, and the constant threat of interracial violence."[78] Through ghettocentric constructions, negative stereotypes of Black men become contextualized, and in this instance of witnessing, a WorldStarHipHop interactor used fearlessness to quantify masculinity and intelligence.[79] Their comment is a ghettocentric view of the siblings' performance, their standpoint offering a lens through which Antoine Dodson correctly approaches the situation with respect not only for his sister but also for racial and class pride.

Another WorldStarHipHop interactor praising the aesthetic value of the video around 2010, wrote, "THIS SONBG IS A CERTIFIED BANGER!" The interactor then takes a surprising and insulting turn, writing, "YOU NAPPY HEADED JIGGABOOS ALWAYS GIVE ME A LAUGH ON THIS MONKIE SITE!—JOHN BOY."[80] John Boy deploys "jiggaboos"—a derogatory early twentieth-century characterization of a Black person with clichéd Black attributes, such as wooly hair, dark skin, and big lips—to derisively label those who are popularly featured in WorldStarHipHop videos, in particular "Antoine Dodson—They Rape'n Everybody Out Here [Auto Tune Edition]."[81] The interactor describes WorldStarHipHop as a "monkie site," implying that the website's content/design is unsophisticated and its interactors are untamed and uncultivated relative to other online sites and their users. Indeed, the construction of WorldStarHipHop and the remix video as a simple space and production evokes characterizations of sites trafficked less frequently by Black interactors—and therefore judged as "less Black"—as cultivated, tamed, and high-tech, relegating Black discourses to their margins.[82] Here, one guest commenter renders WorldStarHipHop and its interactors as operating outside of the human.

John Boy confirms that as raceless and genderless as their interactors can represent themselves through anonymous or disguised profiles, digital spaces still "have ethnocentric inflections when [the World Wide Web is] uncritically presumed to be a kind of universal reality."[83] Scholars have discussed virtual worlds as locations where interactors can abandon bodily subjectivity (including prejudice) because they can be whoever they want to be, even if they are only known as "guest," as on WorldStarHipHop back in 2010.[84] Yet virtual interactions, no matter how disembodied, chart discourses that emerge from collectives IRL that experience privileges and inequalities that drive choices concerning whether they can interact and how they interact in virtual life once they do.[85] As anthropologist and media scholar Shaka McGlotten so euphorically suggests, we respond to the virtual world, and the virtual world responds to us. Indeed, we give life to one another, a phygital existence.[86]

Evidently, as media scholars Lisa Nakamura and Peter Chow-White state, "the Internet and other computer-based technologies are complex topographies of power and privilege, made up of walled communities, new forms and platforms of economic and technological exclusion, and both new and old styles of race as code, interaction, and image."[87] In this case, John Boy communicates a white supremacist discourse arising from the experiences that emerged when white lives came in contact with Black lives IRL in the nineteenth and twentieth centuries (and, of course, before). The corresponding discourse betrays gendered, racial, and, at the very least, sociopolitical positionality. John Boy's unopposed comment reveals the xenophobic, or at least the antidialogical, architexture between interactors. Interactors might share John Boy's perspective, condone it by not caring enough to counter it, or not find expressing their disagreement a valuable investment of time.

Bigoted comments may seem figurative with little or no impact on the real lives they reference. Yet the comprehensive Opportunity Agenda study on media representations and the lives of Black men and boys reveals that the "distorted pattern of portrayal" of Black people generally, and Black men particularly, has causal effects on public attitudes toward them.[88] Truly, "The caricature of Black masculinity has long been both the thing that excuses white oppression and stimulates the fear that motivates it," a sentiment to which Black people are not immune.[89]

In correlation, the federal investigation of the Ferguson Police Department conveys how less flagrant public attitudes, such as the belief that African Americans in Ferguson lack "personal responsibility," cause African Americans to "experience disproportionate harm under Ferguson's approach to law enforcement."[90] The investigation revealed how discursive bias and stereotyping influence behavior in policing, which adversely affects African American residents. These adversities in Ferguson range from the issuance of multiple citations during a single incident to municipal judges' infrequent dismissal of cases regarding excessive force used at disproportionately high rates.[91] It is dangerous to believe that because lawful racial discrimination ended in juridical ways, we live emancipated and can be complacent about racism's discursive existence and causal relationship to anti-Black behavior, whether spoken, emailed, or posted on a comment wall.[92] At the same time, I like to recall, as Stuart Hall posits, "Popular culture commodified and stereotyped as it often is, is not at all, as we sometimes think of it, the arena where we find who we really are, the truth of our experience. It is an arena that is *profoundly* mythic."[93]

The Viral Afterlife: A Perpetual Ghetto Witness in Popular Discourse

The performances I discuss—from the Dodsons' original performance on a local news station to its Gregory Brothers trap remix to the Annoying Orange remix—continued to travel beyond their first year, taking on a viral afterlife. My centering of Black virality demands an African-diasporic cosmographic consideration of life: a viral afterlife does not signal the death of a Black virality but its simultaneous birth. Yet, consistent with each iteration of the viral afterlife of "Woman Wakes Up to Find Intruder in Bed," interactors render Kelly Dodson further from the center of the performance while Antoine Dodson gains visibility. She mutates into a gendered racial subtext, an increasingly absent Black presence in these performances of Blackness. Yet, along this viral journey, her performance takes on an interior quality whose quiet functions as a queer freedom practice, refusing the oppressive forces that thingify beings, haunting us with what we will never know about her experience.[94]

The mechanisms contributing to the rapid spread of Black virality, such as memeing, sampling, and citing, also provide opportunities to examine Black lives in a broader context. These mechanisms allow for the indexing of Black lives, enabling us to generate new ways of critically understanding them as integral parts of larger phenomena, such as the aesthetic of the Ghetto Witness. Turning Black lives into "things," like the Ghetto Witness, has been integral to the processes of commodification and the production of Blackness, affecting how Black people identify and disidentify.[95] I continue to pay attention to the viral afterlife of "Bed Intruder Song," focusing on how people frame it through memetic racialized gender knowledge and to what comedic ends.

Memes function as shadows. They both perform beyond a frame and derive from the performance within the frame, constructing a new framework through which to understand the so-called original version. Memeifying, which involves creatively deriving new content from a performance with slight variations, serves to amplify the visibility and hear-ability of Antoine Dodson's performance. This brings attention to new lives proximal to him and sets up a genealogical conversation for the Ghetto Witness.

Tracing the circulation of derivations of the Gregory Brothers' remix exposes an aesthetic where interactors distill certain behaviors for media consumption. Here, I examine how interactors have visually and vernacularly memeified Antoine Dodson. I conduct a brief critical discourse analysis of a meme concerning Dodson in a different YouTube remix video, "Sweet Brown – Ain't Nobody Got Time for That (Autotune Remix)"; next, I perform a critical discourse analysis of an image that a Reddit user curated from the most popular Ghetto Witnesses from 2010 through 2013; last, I close with a brief critical discourse analysis of a vernacular derivation of "Hide ya wife, hide ya kids, and hide ya husbands," used as a tagging mechanism on the Bossip website. As interactors remix performances, it becomes essential to decipher them because digital media represents livable and unlivable things about race, class, gender, and sexuality that pervade everyday cultural experiences both online and IRL.

The Dead Giveaway of Ain't Nobody Got Time for That

NBC news affiliate KFOR 4 interviewed Kimberly "Sweet Brown" Wilkins, a Black woman from Oklahoma City, because she lived in one of five units in an apartment complex that had caught on fire. Smiling every so often, she recounts the following in the interview: "I woke up to get me a cold pop. And then I thought somebody was barbecuing. I said, 'Oh Lord Jesus, it's a fire!'" At this point in her brief interview, her son, Stanford Wilkins, walks into the background, covers his entire face, and then removes his hands, shaking his head as if to say no. As her gold tooth glimmers in the camera, she continues, "Then I ran out; I didn't grab no shoes or nothing, Jesus." Shaking her head and gesturing her index finger toward her feet, she says, "I *ran* for my life!" Stanford Wilkins walks back, and he locks eyes with the camera, cheeks raised, not laughing. Clutching her chest, she continues, "And then the smoke got me. I got bronchitis." She shakes her head in disbelief, adding, "Ain't nobody got time for that!" Once Wilkins finishes her testimony, she bursts into laughter as she looks to her right toward her son.[96]

There is something about this video that is not easily absorbed and popularized, and it lies with Stanford Wilkins. He casually roams in the background while she amusingly, and even smirkingly, shares her side of the story with the news reporter during her testimony. As he paces, he expresses the helpless shame that children feel when their parents humiliate them in public. He also represents the embarrassment that Black communities feel toward the iconicity of such performances that, even though they may be sincere on that individual's level, come to be symbolic of their entire racial group. Essentially, we have the absent presence of the humiliated group and the person performing what that group is ashamed of in the same performance, which rarely, if ever, happens in the index of Ghetto Witnesses. While Stanford Wilkins's shame and embarrassment are probable, it is also possible that he is still in shock from escaping the fire.

Kimberly Wilkins's nickname summons a consumable and addictive Brown. It places her in a more direct relationship with what food studies scholar and literary theorist Kyla Tompkins calls the "trope of [B]lack edibility" and the associations of Blackness with sweetness.[97] Black edibility conjures the image of the Black body when "metaphorized as food."[98] However, Sweet Brown is the name Wilkins goes by, not what a YouTube or WorldStarHipHop interactor named her. Thus, at the most critical juncture, Wilkins's self-application hints at an awareness of the historical consumption of Black bodies in popular culture (which her son visually performs) or, at the most pedestrian, hints at her personality as a kind Black woman.

After the initial newscast went viral, the Parody Factory—a YouTube channel specializing in parodies—posted a gospel-themed music video mash-up.[99] Its use of gospel music was a nod to Wilkins's Blackness and her references to Jesus throughout her interview. Gospel music was a "byproduct of the late nineteenth- and early twentieth-century black 'folk church.'"[100] The declarations of Ghetto Witnesses fit within the gospel tradition, where "the official doctrine of the folk church encourages spontaneous expressions through improvised song, testimonies, prayers, and praises from individuals."[101] Instead of trap music being used to set the scene for the remix of this Ghetto Witness's testimony, gospel music is used to prepare listeners for a particular embodied verbal testimony, one of triumph over obstacles. Indeed, gospel music often precedes, occurs during, and follows a testimony in church. Employing handclapping, foot stomping, and a choir during Wilkins's testimony, the Parody Factory taps into this tradition in its remix video of the KFOR 4 news interview. Gospel music acts as a sonic witness to testimonies of those who struggle to overcome obstacles to live righteously or, in this case, to just live.

The video also features clips from dozens of movies and obscure videos filled with people clapping their hands, people and monkeys dancing, and, most notably for my current analysis, Antoine Dodson barbecuing with Don

FIGURES 30–32 Screenshots, June 11, 2014, "Sweet Brown – Ain't Nobody Got Time for That (Autotune Remix)," posted April 13, 2012, by The Parody Factory, YouTube, 1:56, https://www.youtube.com/watch?v=bFEoMO0pc7k.

King, as seen in figures 30, 31, and 32.[102] While this video contains a plethora of material to interrogate, particularly the use of dancing monkeys, I stay with the topic of the memeification of "Bed Intruder Song!!!," observing that the appearance of Dodson barbecuing with Don King in the middle of "Sweet Brown – Ain't Nobody Got Time for That (Autotune Remix)" struck me. The memeification of Dodson in the video featuring Wilkins centers him in the aesthetic of the Ghetto Witness. Not only do these memes populate the viral afterlife of Antoine Dodson's tirade, but with each reproduction, they reinforce his body as the primary referent for the Ghetto Witness while further erasing Kelly Dodson's.

The image of Antoine Dodson emerges as a thought bubble from Wilkins as she muses, "I thought somebody was barbecuing." King and Dodson stare at the spectator. Their photoshopped heads onto other Black men's bodies suggest that Black male bodies are interchangeable. This photoshopping tactic recalls the duplication mechanisms of the Intel advertisement discussed in the introduction or the seal of slavery abolitionists and the wanted posters of proslavery advocates whose rendering frame visuals of Black men's bodies as anonymous. Dodson and King represent Black men from the 'hood whose masculinities, not to mention blown-out hair, stand out in queer ways in mainstream media. Their presence as a fighter and his promoter suggests a secret plan to arrange a boxing match against the man who assaulted Antoine Dodson's sister. Black virality is nothing if not intertextual. The Parody Factory deploys the cultural capital of Dodson's visual imagery to enhance the viral energy of Wilkins as an organic witness to and survivor of trauma. These two images—exemplary of the Ghetto Witness—operate in the public sphere as fodder for the public consumption of comedy and the candor of Black street vernacular.

The Parody Factory inserts Antoine Dodson into the Sweet Brown remix like a Black collectible. It becomes clear how "culture as commodity carries its past into its present in ways that insist that we reckon with the logics of [B]lackness."[103] The thought bubble emerging from Wilkins citationally connects her to Dodson. This reference situates his past in Wilkins's present moment, urging us to reckon with how his body and Kelly's absence perform in popular culture two years after they first appeared on the newscast. This rendering shows how digital mechanisms allow images to perform contrapuntally, a time indicative of Black subjectivity, disrupting the linear chronologies that European cultures claim.[104]

YouTube interactors on the Parody Factory's page also note how Antoine Dodson's body enframes Kimberly Wilkins's in particular ways. After the first month of the remix, interactor MadXMaverick commented that "she's the new bed intruder guy."[105] The interactor points toward the Dodsons' remix video, with the Sweet Brown video as its reincarnation, when they refer to Wilkins as the "bed intruder guy." MadXMaverick's framing prioritizes Wilkins's race and street vernacular as traits that tie her to Dodson. Another user, mynameissparkle1, later posted, "The new Antoine Dodson."[106]

In their reference to Kimberly "Sweet Brown" Wilkins as the new bed intruder guy, MadXMaverick compounds ideologies about Black women as masculine or queerly feminine. We encounter this notion in chapter 1 regarding the seal of the kneeling Black woman and her simultaneous bustiness and muscularity. We also observe this enframing in chapter 3 regarding a unique female masculinity linked to historical practices of slavery in the United States that regressively rendered Black women inviolable (since they could carry out the tasks given to men, this made them unable to be violated as women). At the same time, given Antoine Dodson's failures at performing heteronormative masculinity or femininity, there is potential to understand what Wilkins performs as a queer femininity—one that transgresses normative expectations of femininity for something raspier, smokier, and less rehearsed. At the very least, the way Wilkins performs femininity may not neatly align with widespread US expectations.

Such comments convey "Bed Intruder Song!!!" and Antoine Dodson as proxies for the archetype of the Ghetto Witness. Still, Dodson is only one point along an extensive line of Ghetto Witnesses. The newscast titled "Woman Wakes Up to Find Intruder in Bed," and its auto-tuned remix rapidly became commonplace through interactor activity. This included uploading and sharing, commenting and re-presenting, and critiquing and historicizing the performance, ultimately making it increasingly accessible across different audiences. Due to this development, Dodson's performance transformed into something interactors could queue up, rewatch, and study (as I have). All this activity enabled it to become more referential than previous Ghetto Witnesses. Indeed, the new Ghetto Witness always becomes the new Antoine Dodson. Further cementing my assertion that Dodson has become the exemplar, one interactor curated the most viral Ghetto Witnesses between 2010 and 2013, framing them into one image.

Dead Giveaway: Ghetto Witnesses as Antiheroes/-heroines

One Reddit user, suparboysean, created the image *The Justice League* (figure 33), uploaded it to Imgur—an online image hosting service—and shared its hyperlink on Reddit on May 11, 2013.[107] *The Justice League* features Antoine Dodson, Kimberly "Sweet Brown" Wilkins, and Charles Ramsey alongside each other, all frozen in moments of disheveled viral public testimony.[108] Antoine's facial expression appears to catch him in the middle of saying, "You are really dumb." Wilkins appears to be saying, "I got bronchitis." And Ramsey seems to say, "Dead giveaway"—potentially his reference to Shalamar's 1983

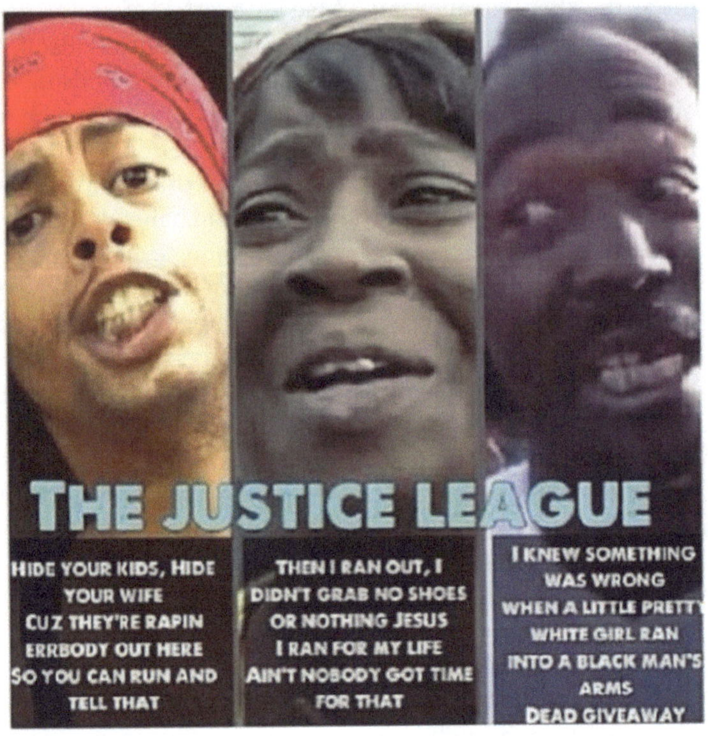

FIGURE 33 Suparboysean, *The Justice League*, Reddit, May 11, 2013, http://www.reddit.com/r/funny/comments/1e4zjf/the_justice_league/.

song of the same title. In the practice of see-jaying, suparboysean's post serves the purpose of indexing the trope of the Ghetto Witness. They achieve this by memeifying various other Black viralities found in popular culture. One example is the creation, sharing, and upvoting of *The Justice League*. Like "Sweet Brown – Ain't Nobody Got Time for That (Autotune Remix)," this image is a visualized commentary on the trail of discourses following "Woman Wakes Up to Find Intruder in Bed," and although Reddit interactors generated very critical comments, I alone examine this visual as racialized gender knowledge with which to engage.

While *The Justice League* meme visually evokes notions of the Ghetto Witness as an American superhero or superheroine, its indexing also mocks and challenges those notions. If anything, here the image represents America's antiheroes and antiheroines—the forgotten, the perceived criminals, the welfare recipients on the grind—people who do not occupy the role of protector or savior in the popular imagination. They become the joke because, with their racialized class, genders, and sexualities, they cannot be the heroes and heroines they reference, barely able to keep their families, let alone their dignity, from harm.

Instead of receiving the hero, we are presented with a Black queen. But this queen is not just any queen; he is a feminine Black male, serving to both affirm and challenge our preconceptions of Black queer men. Similarly, instead of encountering a heroine, we face a figure resembling an aunt wearing a headscarf and reinforcing our limited perception of a mature Black woman in her pajamas. And rather than being introduced to a hero, we are confronted with a self-described "scary looking black dude," further solidifying our narrow understanding of a mature Black man.[109] These figures are antiheroic because they visually and sonically trouble popular fantasies of a white heterosexual male protagonist.

As antiheroes and antiheroines, Dodson, Wilkins, and Ramsey function to critique America, exposing it as an unsafe place where we need to be protected from sex offenders, to run for our lives from fires, or to know that something is wrong when a white woman shows unsolicited affection or need to a Black man she does not know. They come to us as they are, without masks or uniforms, and they reflect, as plainly as possible, on pivotal moments in their lives. They alert us that no hero will be there to save anyone—not the ambulance, the police, or the fire truck will respond in time because of who they are responding to or where the people in need are located or live. They alert us that people will perish if they do not save or fend for themselves.

These are not the American, Amazonian, and Atlantean heroes and heroines representative of the Justice League; these are US casualties from Huntsville, Cleveland, and Oklahoma City, who represent the detrimental ways media conglomerates and everyday people perceive pedestrian Blackness. If anything, they are in an entirely different comic universe: they are X-Men. Scratch that. Considering how white, male, heteronormative, and integrationist the main cast has been and continues to be, Dodson, Wilkins, and Ramsey are the Morlocks of the X-Men. Indeed, "They're actually not the type of people we're used to seeing or hearing at all."[110] They are mutant (illegible) bodies, the marginalized of the marginalized, standing as Others to society and Other to Black people—Others who trouble the popular visual and aural fields of perception, who challenge and raise critical questions about society. They do this even as the disenfranchisement that makes them so spectacular creates problems for them as individuals and groups. The mechanisms of Black virality that amplify their optic and aural dissonance also neglect Dodson's, Wilkins's, and Ramsey's socioeconomic and sociocultural conditions. Their hypericonicity allows them to sustain our attention while being severely overlooked and underheard.

These antiheroes/antiheroines are situated in and highly concerned with matters closest to home. The high barriers to exit, which make the ghetto such a trap, intensify their situatedness and, by extension, make the Ghetto Witness possible. Indeed, Antoine Dodson, Kimberly Wilkins, and Charles Ramsey each have such an intertwined relationship with and vulnerability in their communities that what happens in their neighborhoods, whether a sexual assault, fire, or kidnapping, directly affects them. The news reporters are also witnesses, editing the facts and audio to convey the witnesses' stories. But Elizabeth Gentle, or other reporters who sometimes go unnamed, can exit the site of trauma and go to the next story. The Ghetto Witness must live with and be thingified by the narrative for which they have become known.

Witnessing Viral Black Vernacular in a Popular Culture Magazine called BOSSIP

Ghetto Witnesses become known by spectators for, among other things, the vernacular phrases they (re)produce. Wilkins popularized "Ain't nobody got time for that!" Ramsey popularized "Dead giveaway!" And Dodson coined and popularized "Hide ya kids, hide ya wife, and hide ya husbands."

True to the chaos of Black virality, Dodson's phrase was memeified, this time into Bossip categories—tags used to index news items on Bossip.com. Bossip, an online magazine whose name merges "gossip" with "Blackness," centrally reports on events concerning or that might have currency among Black people in the United States. The result extends this Black virality through the reporting of gossip and rumor. By using the "hide ya" phrase, Bossip demonstrates how Dodson's body is understood through his Black queer vernacular and extends this understanding beyond the enframing of his performance on WAFF 48 News.

While the Hide Ya Kids titles feature a superabundance of news articles dating back to 2020 (including an article about Roald Dahl's *The Witches*, in which they try to turn children into mice) and Hide Ya Wife titles are plentiful until 2022 (when Drake retributively followed a husband's wife on Instagram after said husband derided his son), titles under the tag Hide Ya Husbands were almost nonexistent. Through 2014, Bossip used tags as indexing mechanisms for news, but that format has since changed.

The Hide Ya Kids tag featured news with titles such as "Funny or Foul? A Gallery of Armed Fathers Posing with Daughter's Prom Date," "Another Day, Another Female High School Teacher Popped for Being a Freak," and "#BringBackOurGirls: Michelle Obama Joins Social Media Movement to Return Kidnapped Nigerian School Girls via Twitter." The tag Hide Ya Wife featured news with titles like "For Discussion: If You Caught Your Friend's Husband Kissing Another Man . . . Would You Tell Her?," "Smooches Hooches: WNBA Baller Diana Taurasi Plants a Juicy Kiss on Opposing Player during Game! [Video]," and "What the Hell?? Racist and Drugged Up Dad Axe

Murdered His Family with Brown Eyes, but Spared Youngest 'Pure Aryan' Daughter!" Even though Hide Ya Husbands was not a featured tag used to index news on the site, there were two titles that mentioned it: "Hide Ya Kids And Hide Ya Husbands! Sisqo (The Dragon) Is Back!!! [Video]" and "Ho Sit Down: Kirk's Alleged Jacuzzi Jumpoff Claps Back after Being Put On Blast for Creepin' with A Married Man – 'Just Hide Your Husbands'"—both titles about Black men predicated, respectively, on Sisqó's assumed gay sexuality and the difficulty of controlling Kirk Frost's infidelity on *Love and Hip Hop: Atlanta*. Importantly, the volume of news in each category (children, women, men) decreased as topics on adulthood and maleness increased, with seventy-eight pages of news tagged under Hide Ya Kids, twenty-one pages of news tagged under Hide Ya Wife, and none tagged under Hide Ya Husbands as of June 3, 2014.

The limited volume of news that Bossip featured, or could evidence, reflects the egregious stigma that remains associated with the violence that men experience, particularly sexual and physical violence, which reduces the likelihood they admit to being survivors.[111] The shortage of news under the Hide Ya Husbands category signals that accounts of sexual violence involving mature adult men are not reported frequently enough to index. If this is true, it is probable that the reason for the absence is that men (or those who identify as husbands) are reluctant to disclose their experiences of sexual and physical trauma. This reluctance may stem from the societal expectation that husbands should embody an unbreakable sense of "masculinity" and from men and husbands often being in the position to cause, not succumb to, such sexual traumas.

The tags and titles of the aforementioned stories evoke a disconcerting association, with Antoine Dodson being portrayed as the rapist of his sister. This raises the disturbing idea that his perceived "deviant" sexuality makes him the one from whom protection is required, despite his efforts to encourage his community to safeguard their families from sexual predators.[112] Indeed, the subtexts in each news story under the tags protecting kids and wives follow this sickening logic. The stories are reminders of how news and opinion outlets use so-called deviant desires, sexualities, and races to tag as scapegoats or proxies for the world's ills. Media technologies make those proxies conveniently available in simplified ways.

While the phrase was a verbal and embodied tool used by Antoine Dodson as covert denigration of Kelly Dodson's perpetrator and naysayers, Bossip shows how news and opinion outlets can weaponize a covert denigration and use it to disparage embodiment and street vernacular, turning stance taking and styling on its head. The phrase "Hide ya kids, hide ya wife," and perhaps the entirety of Antoine Dodson's warning/defense, became reworked and deployed as a category for serial rapists, pedophiles, LGBTQI drama, and infidelity (all things misguidedly associated with Black gay men). WAFF 48's enframing of the Dodsons did not communicate a sincere concern about finding the rapist, so it makes sense that the viral afterlife of that moment followed suit.

• • •

A profound story about a sexual assault that summoned discourses about sexual violence in Black communities developed and devolved into Black viralities concerning Antoine Dodson's sexuality, the threat and fear of homosexuality, a Black man's queer femininity as comic relief and entertainment, and the memeification of Black gender. Dodson used the clout of the initial performance and generated a sex offender tracker application, an iTunes song, T-shirts, and Halloween costumes. He also landed a cameo in Tyler Perry's *A Madea Christmas* (where he played the same Ghetto Witness). Filmmakers Jenner Furst and Julia Willoughby Nason used a screenshot of Dodson's neck twisting and signature red bandanna in their documentary *Fyre Fraud* (2019), with the narrator describing him as part and parcel of the viral influencer culture that created the Fyre Festival failure.[113] Today, the Gregory Brothers continue to traffic in highlighting Ghetto Witnesses and making the Black pedestrian sensational. More recently, they songified an interview from the web channel Recess Therapy by a little boy named Tariq and made it the newest viral hit, "It's Corn – Songify This Ft. Tariq and Recess Therapy."[114] This song and scenario never die; instead they are reborn as new "things." Indeed, the number of representations I have just named in this paragraph alone are worth a thorough examination.

Yet these representations would never signal the sexual assault of a Black woman in public housing. They show us how Black virality acts to erase and brand Black people in stereotypical and generative ways. We also see how Black virality sustains acts into perpetuity. Whenever someone comments on a comment wall, shares the link to the newscast and remixes, or uses a performance out of context, they ensure that the Dodsons' performance will never die. At the very least, the uncontrollable resurfacing kept the siblings and, one would hope, the traumas they faced and overcame at the forefront of the popular imagination.

Still, the visibility of this Black virality also amplifies factors affirming Black life by challenging norms and expectations of Black womanhood, masculinity and femininity, and Blackness. For instance, I expound on the many ways that interactors' affective labor drives them to respond through antiracist, antisexist, and anticlassist discourse to other interactors' denigrations of Blackness, sexuality, and class. Thus, the spaces where these interactions occur are locales where generative cross-viewing can take place, which can alter perspectives on Black life in life-affirming and liberatory ways.

Through creating mobile applications, making celebrity appearances, and generating enough capital from his Black virality to move his family out of public housing and into a house and beyond, Antoine Dodson has made a career, or at least a side hustle, out of the rage inspired by his sister's sexual assault. A fictional Black male Ghetto Witness, Walter Bankston from the Netflix original series *Unbreakable Kimmy Schmidt*, warns about the flip side of the resulting notoriety and flows of capital: "After my viral video, I got a taste of fame . . . but there's a darker side to fame. . . . The other shoe is gonna drop."[115] Indeed, by capitalizing on the currency of the Ghetto Witness, Dodson becomes a minstrel of himself, what Black performance scholar, practitioner, and activist Amber Johnson calls the Homo Coon—a sexualized form of the zip coon that frames Black gay masculinity negatively and memeifies a stereotype that denies its authenticity by reducing it to coonery. He forever recalls his own earnest performance, albeit as this queer caricature that he can never escape.[116] However, unlike minstrelsy, which performs popular and derisive ideas about Blackness, a slight separation exists between those ideas and Dodson's organic self, as the first performance was sincere. A complex negotiation of the tensions between agency and the way capitalism compels performance unfolds. His ongoing performances also cue us in on his awareness and recycling of "the nervous joke making, a laughing to keep from talking—or to hide otherwise awkward silences" that so many interactors revealed through their lols, LMFAOs, and silence.[117]

With each instance of the representation of Antoine Dodson's performance, his sister's voice gets further lost in the narrative and the audience risks losing sight of the seriousness and importance of the event. Nonetheless, as much as the news and social media coverage of Dodson reifies notions of Black people as a monolith, creates comedy out of poverty and Black queer femininity, and reinforces sexual and patriarchal normalcy, he "still remembers what's important . . . and [stays] grounded in the reality of what started it in the first place."[118] Thus, before we get to Antoine Dodson performing at the BET Awards, making a sexual predator application, going platinum, reappearing as the progenitor of influencer culture on the Fyre fraud documentary, becoming a Black Hebrew Israelite, and denouncing his gay sexuality—apologizing to queer communities afterward—we have this sincere opportunity to place the Black woman, Kelly Dodson, at the center of this traumatic moment.

In observing Black virality, we, as critics, also contribute to determining what becomes visible in any performance. Our critiques establish our role as interactors. Our comments draw audiences to sites of performances, enabling fresh interactors to see our remarks through the perspectives in which we frame, critique, and praise those performances. The unlivable normative (read here as embodied in acts of racism, classism, and sexism that are both unbearable and common enough to be pedestrian), which we critique, becomes understood in ways that enable what is livable (acts of joy, acts of countering oppression, and unapologetic agency that does not limit another's wellness) to continue to be undertheorized.[119] Hence, the news has the potential to marginalize Kelly Dodson while the insufficient analysis of her deliberate noniconic position persists. Similarly, Antoine Dodson may enact a minstrel version of himself while his agential possibility of using Black objecthood for upward class mobility is unacknowledged.

In acknowledging the homophobic misogynoir that Black virality makes most visible, it is vital to spend time with performances of the noniconic. Dark matter, Black data, and the noniconic contrast with and remain appended to Black virality. Performances that remain out of easy reach gain visibility by being a less acknowledged part of what has quickly become commonplace. Dark matter, Black data, and noniconicity challenge the unlivable normative, which has a marginalizing and policing effect uninhabitable by the fluidity and improvisation of everyday life. Refusal of the spotlight that results from virality can generate a livable queerness. Black women, queer people, and the queerness and Trans*-ness of Blackness itself constitute a noniconicity that can generate, and have generated, livable worlds. That truth continues to be omitted, however, by a myopic focus on the excesses of the loudest and most visible.[120] The Black viralities of Kelly Dodson's brother represent one of many examples.

With far wider accessibility and reach, online social media has become the great broadcaster that the radio once was. Online social media provides a spectrum of perspectives on many situations and emergencies concerning the greater public, leaving it to the audience to decide what knowledge to absorb and act upon. Yet, unlike what we observe regarding the news that follows journalistic standards, there is sometimes no anchor or frame to this viral media, leaving much of its literacy at the whims of the interactor.

CODA

They Killing Him, Look

The Viral Afterlife of a Justice at Odds with a Liberation

> They're only interested in drawing the biggest crowd that they can. It's psychological emotional rubbernecking. People are driving by a burning car on the freeway, they have no intention of helping, they just want to see the blaze. They're perverting a human need to watch spectacle.
> —Yasiin Bey

The epigraph above is a critique of professional (career-aware) clout chasers that traffic in an environment described by Yasiin Bey (formerly known as Mos Def) as a Gladiator Circus—a kind of staged conflict of characters we know are fictional (until we do not). The snippet is a part of a larger counter to white supremacist voices (one of which received a Medal of Freedom in 2020 from the forty-fifth president of the United States) that have flooded the Web with hatred, misinformation, disinformation, and spectacle on numerous news and social platforms. I find it useful as a concise metaphor to describe the tragedy of chasing virality at the expense of material and discursive human lives. This tragedy might be avoidable through withnessing, understanding how aspects of yourself are caught up in another's experience (like Stevie and Radio Raheem), to the point where you must be an accomplice in witnessing, ensuring, and preserving their livelihood. I often notice the converse to withnessing in Black viralities, where you are so disconnected from the Black lives you capture that you do not know how to engage them beyond their spectacle, beyond thingifying them. This may look like screaming "WorldStar!" into the air (to your anticipated followers) before asking the one who is central to your recording if they are safe or intervening to ensure they will be.

How interactors enframe a spectacular tragedy after observing it unfold limits or makes way for differing forms of liberation in the viral afterlife of the spectacle. In previous chapters, I focus on how particular news media seek witnesses for the content they provide and the currency they will produce for a specific news channel. Here, someone for whom news media is not their job records a moment as it unfolds, creating content and currency for the platform they eventually broadcast to. I shift my attention from meditations on Black virality and its tragically comedic effects toward understanding how a grassroots enframing of a spectacle can minimally operate as leverage for justice, and more hopefully, liberation. Indeed, this possibility recurs throughout the earlier chapters: using visual culture to call on onlookers to question historical and contemporary performances and rumors of Black bodies in discourse and Black people; using mass-distributed fictional film to critique police brutality, examine racial inequality, and articulate the racialized erotics of sound; and increasing the visibility of sexual violence in Black communities by confronting it publicly in hopes of eliminating its recurrence. Yet, I ask, what else might *goin' viral* and *liberation* mean, and how do those meanings surface in the murder of Derrion Albert in 2009 and his viral afterlife in the decade following?

Near Christian Fenger Academy High School on the far South Side of Chicago, a massive fight occurred between young men from Altgeld Gardens (a public housing community) and "the Ville" (the southern area of Chicago's Roseland neighborhood)—a fight in which Derrion Albert became an innocent victim.[1] On September 24, 2009, Derrion, a sixteen-year-old sophomore on the honor roll, was killed by his peers. On September 27, 2009, a video titled "Tragic: Teens Give a Chicago Student from a Rivarly [*sic*] Hi [*sic*] School a

FIGURE 34 Screenshot of WorldStarHipHop warning preceding the video "Tragic: Teens Give a Chicago Student from a Rivarly [*sic*] Hi [*sic*] School a Deadly Beating with Huge Wooden Boards! *Warning* (Very Graphic) (R.I.P. Derrion Albert) (This Has To Stop)," World Star Uncut digital video, 2009. URL delisted.

Deadly Beating with Huge Wooden Boards! *Warning* (Very Graphic) (R.I.P. Derrion Albert) (This Has to Stop)" surfaced on WorldStarHipHop, where I happened upon it while browsing the website. It began with a notice (see figure 34): "Warning: The following footage is graphic and violent. If you can identify any people allegedly involved in the death of Derrion Albert, please call the Chicago Police Dept. at 312-747-8272."

Following the notice, the video begins inside a car from which a person with a voice in a lower register documents the fight and exits the car to gain a closer view. The brawl in the frame involves twenty-plus high schoolers in brown khakis and black golf shirts walking or jogging around and brutally punching each other in the street. As a vehicle honks its horn, people holler and scream indecipherably. A young man equipped with extra-large wooden planks pummels another young man with them. A person with a voice of higher timbre [likely the one that had been driving the car] yells, "Zoom in!"

A different young man grabs a wooden plank, and a second young man who is being assaulted in front of a car by a small group speedily runs away. Derrion is walking amid the chaos, and the young man running away brushes Derrion's body. Instead of absorbing his velocity, Derrion quickly intercepts him and defensively deflects the boy into the angle he is already running. This move destabilizes Derrion, turning him around. While Derrion turns his head, the other young man, still holding the wooden plank, swings it down on Derrion's head. A young man in front of Derrion backs away with his hands up as if to signal surrender to the one with a plank. Someone yells, "Damn!" All audio drops for a few seconds as Derrion tries to stand. The audio returns as a young man punches Derrion to the ground. Then another young man kicks him. As the camera turns and focuses on other fights happening in the street, someone screams, "Yeah, put that nigga to sleep!"

In the camera's corner view, Derrion is trying to sit up. Someone blurts out, "Oh my God, get closer." Anticipating the impact of another blow from a wooden plank, Derrion puts his hand out as another young man stands above him holding a plank. Mercifully, the young man does not follow through and walks away. Other young men begin surrounding and punching Derrion while another runs at him holding a wooden plank and swings it twice at his body. Subsequently, horrifying screams echo through the surroundings. The entire scene is frantic as young men run away and a woman runs toward Derrion Albert's body and fearfully utters, "They killing him, look."

As a small group carries Derrion's body into a building entrance, a girl pleads, "Get up, Derrion, please!" The camera turns away, and a man says, "We got a kid down in here. We got a kid down. They beat him to death." Meanwhile, the person with a lower voice register holding the camera says, "Damn, look, they still down there goin' at it," and chuckles.[2] Even though many encountered this moment through a digital video, because of the way

WorldStarHipHop enframed it, there was no mistaking this was an actual murder.

Something that haunts me about viral violence—which is summoned by the brutality in this video and the ways it circulated—is how the currency of an act eclipses the lives featured in it. Why press Record before dialing 911 (not that police may not have escalated the situation)? Until Derrion appeared lifeless, no one urgently reacted to his situation or the circumstances. The people recording may not have felt safe, but it is equally possible they invested in the moment of violence for the resulting clout from the views, likes, or retweets it might receive. A high value is placed on raw emotion (as in the response of the Dodsons), liveness (as in the visceral performances in *Do the Right Thing*), and spontaneity (like the chaotic violence in this brawl). This value eclipses the concern for another's or one's own life and codifies what is spreadable. Except for cute videos of babies and cats, there is a supply and demand for danger, from brawls to police chases to severe weather, that interactors reward with ratings, views, and listens that fatten the pockets and increase the visibility of the maker despite the risk to the performer. This aspect of the attention economy provokes me to ask rhetorically: Would you risk life or health, including yours, for the reward of being seen by a large public?[3]

As I surmise in the Radio Raheem chapter, what I hope does not happen with viral products like these is their being used to justify excessive force against Black people. I also want to avoid conflating Derrion Albert's defensive behaviors in the video or the behaviors of others with something "staged" in my use of performance. My capacious use of performance includes the unintentional ways we exist in, anticipate, and are interpreted by others in the world. My use of Black virality as a concept of performance here addresses how interactors rapidly share, rewatch, and comment on the cellular footage because of spectacle and racialized gender knowledge. Derrion's memory became commonplace in 2009 and meaningful to countless lives through that circulation.

Yet Derrion's memory also aligns his sainthood with normative notions of gender and sexuality in a way that projects them into the future. What Ta-Nehisi Coates writes in *Between the World and Me* rings true here: "When the young are killed, they are haloed by all that was possible, all that was plundered."[4] Yet what troubles me is that there is only a heteronormativity and masculinity to all that was plundered and possible.

The ubiquity of the Derrion Albert video motivated Nas, a world-renowned and lyrically brilliant Queens, NY, rap artist, to write a letter he titled "Open Letter to Young Warriors in Chicago." In Nas's letter, he paternally addresses and empathizes with all the young men in Chicago involved in Derrion's murder as "soldiers" and "warriors" while emphasizing that this kind of violence needs to stop. Moreover, he includes Derrion in a group characterized by its fortitude, writing, "Everybody knows Chicago breeds the strongest of the strong."[5] While being soldiers and warriors does not determine sexuality, there is a subtext that relies on the epistemology of "Don't ask, don't tell" and what a city that expelled the Potawatomi can reproduce. The anticipation around sexuality depends on performing heteronormativity, even if a warrior or soldier exists otherwise. The masculine heteronormativity projected onto Derrion in his viral afterlife influences his gendered and sexual possibilities, affecting how interactors remember him.

Derrick Sanders's short film *Perfect Day* (2013), which circulated at gatherings like the Pan African Film Festival and Boston International Film Festival, is one way to remember Derrion Albert through visual culture.[6] It illustrates how pedestrian the school day may have been and shows the suddenness and confusion of the violence that Derrion encountered. Yet, regarding gender, it picks up where Nas leaves off, with a nuance. Desmond, who represents Derrion, is an intelligent kid with a crush on another character named Asha. Sanders does not represent Desmond as a soldier. Thus, even though Desmond counters the military masculinity that Nas prescribes, he continues the notion that Derrion's sexuality, had he remained among the living, would be heterosexual.

The hegemonic spatial practices within Chicago, which structure rival groups and individuals to attend the same schools together, are suspended in the background of Nas's neoliberal conservative respectability as reflected by his observation that "you have the ability and mindpower to change the way we are looked at." Nowhere in the letter does Nas mention the racial segregation that concentrates Black residents into subsidized housing like Altgeld Gardens and neighborhoods like the Ville.[7] Nor does Nas mention the destruction of subsidized housing by the Chicago Housing Authority's Plan for Transformation that dispersed residents across the city who were also in rival gangs. Nas's letter also neglects to mention that plans like Renaissance 2010 have resulted in school closures.[8] Beyond the individualized militarization of Chicago adolescent masculinity, these are all issues in Chicago that anyone addressing this circumstance would need to centralize to inform a critical understanding of the structural factors that set up this brawl.

Unfortunately, those responsible for these macrosocial conditions scapegoated Derrion, symbolically laying Chicago's sins upon him and casting him out into the wilderness of the afterlife. Teens murdered him with the same neglected railroad debris from the train tracks that functioned as a border (an unofficial safe zone that was ignored on the day of the brawl) between Fenger High School, the Ville, and the one bus on Michigan Avenue that could transfer Altgeld Gardens' teens south to their home.[9] People from Agape Community Center took him in from the street brawl. They witnessed and protected him as he lay unconscious.

President Obama sent members of his cabinet to Chicago to speak with Mayor Richard M. Daley about the violence there. Altgeld Gardens' teens attended Fenger Academy High School in the first place because Carver High School, their local school, had been designated by then CEO of Chicago Public Schools, Paul Vallas—a noted education privatizer and charter school advocate—as a military high school. Fenger was the alternative to military school for residents of the Altgeld Gardens community. Fenger teens from Altgeld were trying to be something other than soldiers and warriors.

The decision to repurpose or demolish George Washington Carver Area High School echoed decisions like the Plan for Transformation that redistributed rather than deconcentrated poverty throughout Chicago. Neither decision followed through with one-to-one replacements for residents. So Altgeld teenagers had to leave their neighborhood for the limited education options that compelled them to enroll in Fenger High School, located north of their home. Ironically, Arne Duncan, who later became President Obama's secretary of education, served as CEO of Chicago Public Schools after the school was renamed George Washington Carver Military Academy. Arguably, he supervised the circumstance, and President Obama assigned him to rectify it. Responding to Duncan's decision and the attention to Derrion's murder, among other things, Daley said: "The day that the city of Chicago decides to divide schools by gang territory, that's the day we've given up the city."[10]

While violent and racist sentiments about this too-familiar tragedy circulated online through diverse means, including news articles, video footage, and comments, those means also made the life of this young Black man further valuable. Due to the shared cell phone footage, public evidence of Derrion's murder existed, and the pressure to find his killers grew. Witnesses identified the young men in the video who had murdered Derrion Albert; later, a judge convicted them of first-degree murder.

By framing the video through a notice, WorldStarHipHop functioned as a twenty-first-century version of the nineteenth-century antebellum wanted posters discussed in chapter 1. WorldStarHipHop's framing solicited information about the perpetrators of the murder it portrayed. The Black boys in the wanted video followed the visual culture strategies of proslavery advertisements: they were in motion, out of control, and intent on causing alarm and harm. However, glaring differences between the nineteenth-century stereotyped cut and the WorldStarHipHop video are that the video was live footage, the Black boys were committing acts of violence, and nothing recorded was fictional. The literal purpose of the video's framing was to identify and enslave them into the prison industrial complex as convicted criminals.

Yet the witnessed murder occurred within a scene of structural confinement and hegemonic spatial practices. Altgeld Gardens (where the young men who killed Derrion live) sits upon a raw sewage landfill. Historically, it housed African Americans working for the Acme Steel Plant and Pullman

Factory. Like many deindustrialized areas, it suffers from water and air pollution. Unlike other Chicago Housing Authority sites, its location—described by resident and environmental activist Hazel Johnson as "self-contained"—and ecological toxicity made it an unlikely candidate for "mixed-income" development. Residents were being exposed to cyanide in the drinking water, lead paint, and leaking underground storage tanks, among many other environmental hazards near Altgeld Gardens. And one understocked and overpriced grocery store existed in the neighborhood in 2014.[11] Residents called the area a "toxic donut," an explicit acknowledgment of being encircled by the country's largest concentration of hazardous waste sites.[12] These circumstances convey the violence residents were already engulfed in before the fateful day of Derrion Albert's murder.

But once witnesses identify the boys in the video, what does it mean to incarcerate Black boys in a prison industrial complex that disproportionately houses Black men?[13] Indeed, what might be justice for Derrion's family is an illusion that fuels further investment in our system of criminal punishment and pushes everyone further from liberation. This system of mass incarceration based on retributive justice has proven ineffective at addressing the crimes it supposedly seeks to address, "correct," and prevent from happening in the future.[14] What might restorative or transformative justice look like for Derrion's family? Would sincere and apologetic accountability for his murder and naming the harm caused be a start? Might those who caused the harm be required to undergo a lifelong restitution period? Might we extend this restitution to the interplay between institutions and political decisions that harmed those whose fighting led to Derrion's murder? In this accountability for trauma and the associated restoration (that truly can never be achieved), might there be healing—not the erasure of a wound, but a scabbing? In this antiretributive process, might there be a divestment from and eventual abolition of the prison industrial complex?[15]

A boy who was arrested in 2009, charged with the murder of Derrion Albert as a juvenile at fourteen, and sentenced to thirty years but released under the condition he would not commit any other crimes was again arrested in 2019 on felony charges of unlawful use of a weapon.[16] Gaining possession of a gun in Chicago should be highly difficult, given that gun shops are illegal. However, Indiana, a state with some of the least restrictive gun laws in the country, sits only thirty minutes or fewer away, guaranteeing it will never be challenging to obtain a gun in Chicago. Structural causes that have yet to be addressed underlie the young man's activity and exceed neoliberal blame on his individual actions, choices, and squandering of the resources offered in the past by juvenile courts.

Even by changing the trajectory of the convicted boy's life, without expungement, his felony conviction in Chicago would effectively disqualify him on the job market (increasing the chance of recidivism in his case), erect a high barrier of entry for the approval of rental space, and block him from voting, among other difficulties. Furthermore, Derrion's parents voiced their anger that the boy had been released and were already beyond considering nonretributive justice, whether restorative or transformative. Justice, at odds with liberation, takes on the normalized perpetrator perspective; meanwhile, the underlying issues regarding environmental racism, public housing, gentrification, displacement, and gang or neighborhood violence remain.

Even in these obvious moments of excessive violence toward Black people by Black people, there is a swelling of those who through their sharing of the moment refuse to forget such incidents. Contrary to opinions that undermine the importance of addressing systemic racism by using examples of intracommunal Black violence to deflect attention from movements against police brutality and for defunding the police, WorldStarHipHop, a site that traffics in Blackness, was actively uncovering this instance of intracommunity crime. Also, WorldStarHipHop broadcasted this tragedy without the need to counter any momentum against police brutality. People were unwilling to stay silent and let experiences where civil rights were violated, even between other Black people, remain unresolved. Highlighting instances of violence within a Black community runs against the grain of discourses that suggest Black people care only when white cops kill their children with malice. Rap artist and activist Immortal Technique spoke to another nuance of this discourse on Amanda Seales's *Small Doses* podcast, saying, "It's also belittling to the parents of the child that has died because you're basically telling them that you don't care about your own child, that somehow the limelight is what you're really after."[17]

It is essential to recognize that these incidents of violence are not isolated acts committed by individual suspects but rather are symptoms of larger systemic issues. By individualizing the problem, we fail to address the root causes and structural processes that contribute to the perpetuation of such violence. This systemic illness requires systemic solutions rather than placing blame solely on individual perpetrators. We must also create the capacity to imagine and dream in ways that allow for possibilities of queerness, even in one's afterlife.

Black Viralities from a Past to a Present: Black Performances in the Civil Rights Movement, Black Power Movement, Movement for Black Lives, and Beyond

Black performance studies provides me with a theoretical framework within which to examine performance in Black life that does not disavow Black women; lesbian, gay, and transgender people; or genderqueer people from Blackness. Still, I incorporate certain moments known through the hashtag #BlackLivesMatter into my theoretical analysis. While writers have likened #BlackLivesMatter movements to the spawning of a new civil rights movement, they differ by upholding lives across the full spectrum of Blackness, including marginalized sexualities, genders, and classes.[18] Historically, popular references to American Blackness and political movements have excluded other Black voices and Black futures, thereby dangerously homogenizing Blackness to cis heterosexual men.

The mass-produced images and broadcasts of the civil rights movement of the past and the movements for Black lives in the present reveal the spread of certain Black viralities, amplifying those visual and sonic products to create leverage for liberation. While the photos and videos produced within the movements display the containment and, in a sense, quarantining of Black people in the United States, they also appeal to the ethical instincts of those who empathize with the plight of Black people on a global scale. So much of the visual culture from the civil rights movement echoes the discourses present during the abolition of slavery in Western Europe and the United States: appealing to the sympathies of morally aligned people and positioning Black as cisgender and male. #BlackLivesMatter counters that singular-dimension gendered discourse through an expansive consideration of Blackness. Advocates of #BlackLivesMatter also continue making demands through protest, organizing, and policy creation, but without seeking sympathy or empathy and instead moving toward anything that manifests liberation from and despite material and discursive anti-Blackness.

Following George Zimmerman's verdict of not guilty on July 13, 2013, interactors used the #BlackLivesMatter hashtag to index countless violent crimes against a spectrum of Black people. The endless proliferation of these crimes had a chaotic frequency. Still, hashtags brought order to the chaos of the many stories by organizing them, increasing public access, and enhancing the searchability of such information. The hashtag targets political agendas and raises awareness through stories that everyday people and extraordinary people have categorized. I, too, have attempted to create my archive of phenomena through hashtags, with occasional #Blackvirality posts on Twitter. Through these public indexes, global patterns visibly emerge, and it becomes evident how anti-Black violence is, and has been, goin' viral in the United States and beyond.

Hashtags on Twitter and Facebook (e.g., #ICantBreathe, #IfIDieInPolice Custody, and #BlackLivesMatter) and video-aggregation/sharing sites and applications (e.g., YouTube, WorldStarHipHop, and TikTok) have been used to index, crowdsource, and document stories that center Black people. A hashtag's use brings unprecedented visibility to the visceral intimate effects of popular immaterial perceptions of Black people, that is, racialized erotics. Principally, these conscious and subconscious biases have hinged on assumptions about the criminality of Black people based on things like the music they play (Jordan Davis), the clothes they wear (Trayvon Martin), or their inability to be subjects in rather than assumed perpetrators of crisis (Renisha McBride). Black gender biases, when acted upon, have led to material deaths.

For instance, in reaction to Sandra Bland's death, where a routine traffic stop ended in her dying in police custody (purportedly a suicide by hanging)—and which echoed the deaths of many other Black people in police custody (Michael Stewart, Latandra Ellington, Kimberlee Randale-King, Dejuan Brison)—Black interactors on Twitter, or at least interactors with their avatar featuring a Black body, created the hashtag #IfIDieInPoliceCustody. Interactors were incessantly using hashtags, almost as periods, to punctuate posts about interwoven issues, bringing visibility to any post's content, as anyone could search for and through the hashtag. Here, the hashtag summoned the participation of other interactors and revealed individuals' skepticism and fear of police arrests concerning them as Black people.

April Reign, a popular Twitter interactor and managing editor of Broadway Black, garnered one of the heaviest retweets after tweeting, "#IfIDieInPoliceCustody know that they killed me. I would do everything in my power to get home to my family. So never stop questioning."[19] That, and many other tweets, revealed a deep distrust of police and correctional officers: "know that they killed me." I also witnessed a premeditated willingness to live despite an expected confinement: "I would do everything in my power to get home to my family." The tweet is also a call to action and investigation—"never stop questioning"—around the circumstances of Bland's arrest and July 13, 2015, death. Beyond individual skepticism, the collection of these stories in one ongoing virtual archive creates an irrefutable consensus regarding the obstacles faced by Black people, both collectively and in more nuanced intracommunal ways.

The combined visual material and indexed stories provide evidence that activists can use to harness the power of Black viral content for liberation. For example, the Black Panther Party newspaper circulated four hundred thousand plus copies at its weekly peak in the late 1960s, making them quickly commonplace via print and visual culture.[20] On the one hand, Emory Douglas of the Black Panther Party for Self-Defense used visual propaganda to evoke the image of police as unclean (i.e., "pigs") and whose anti-Black corruption would become acts around which to rally.[21] One particular image features a tearful Black woman sprawled on the ground, a pig in a police uniform exposing her breast in a suggested sexual assault. Behind her is a crying pig in a uniform with a badge holding a baton with its hands up. Meanwhile, two Black men in all black with berets hold the pig at gunpoint with shotguns while yelling, "You're under arrest . . . you pig."[22] The pervasive pig image centers intercommunal violence against Black women, highlighting the intracommunal defensive virtues of the Black Panthers. This viral image was also a part of the legacy of their first issue, in which Denzil Dowell's mother raised awareness about his likely murder by police (another fractal virality of Radio Raheem).[23]

Detractors also use the consensus generated from Black viralities as evidence to justify an anti-Blackness that is unjustifiable. In contrast to using visual culture to illustrate corruption in police, a government counterintelligence program used public media like the *Los Angeles Times* and *Newsweek* to circulate a rumor from an undisclosed source that high-ranking Black Panther Raymond Hewitt, had impregnated a white actress, Jean Dorothy Seberg, in an act of adultery. Given her support of various radical causes, including those of the Black Panthers, Seberg was a perfect target, the rumor intended to discredit both the actress's and the party's morals. The racialized erotics of that story was a lever that challenged the goals of Black nation building espoused by the Black Panther Party and Seberg's fidelity to her husband to a greater public. To vilify the Black Panthers and disgrace a white ally, myths around white purity, white women's innocence, and Black men's voracious sexual appetites were weaponized (recalling discourses at play in Hank Willis Thomas's *Jordan and Johnnie Walker in Timberland Circa 1923*). To disprove the rumor, Seberg held an open-casket funeral to show the skin tone of her premature newborn child.[24]

With a different impetus for displaying the death of a loved one, Mamie Till allowed the visuals of her son Emmett Till's open casket to circulate, propelling the civil rights movement forward. In 1955, Emmett, a Black youth from Chicago, Illinois, visited Money, Mississippi, where witnesses falsely accused him of physically and verbally threatening a white woman named Carolyn Bryant, possibly because of his speech impediment. Bryant's husband and his half-brother hunted down and brutally killed Emmett, enforcing a vigilante policing of Black men who dared to breach the norms of race and sexuality.

Discourses surrounding Black men's deviant sexuality and aggression, coupled with the innocence and passivity of white women's sexuality, buttressed their torture of the fourteen-year-old boy, who was beaten to a pulp, tied to a cotton gin, and left to sink in the Tallahatchie River.[25] John H. Johnson published the posthumous photo of Emmett Till in *Jet* magazine. Johnson's publication of the photo turned it into an iconic representation of the violent and disposable ways Black people were treated in Mississippi and throughout the United States. The image of Emmett's mangled and waterlogged face in a coffin ignited an already brewing civil rights movement.[26]

Contrasted with the visual propaganda of Seberg's open casket, the posthumous image of the teen was based on a reality that surpassed the creative attempts of someone aiming to convince an audience. Emmett's open-casket photograph is far less persuasive, far more of an invitation to feel the loss of a Black child mutilated by white men and to feel the mourning of a mother living with that loss and trauma. The image is a visual of a visceral reality, necessitating a tenderness in those who witness him, a withnessing. Is it even accurate to characterize the visual of the death of another person as propaganda? Might that visual of death be something that gestures beyond propaganda and toward a will to live and the unfulfillment of that wish? Derrion Albert's death, suggested by then US attorney general Eric Holder to be a wake-up call for the country, was a significant contemporary example of this will and unfulfilled wish.

Black Viralities: Other Suggestions

Engaging with and reflecting on Black viralities is exhausting, mainly because of how uncontrollable performances become. As such, I could discuss so much more, but I gesture to it only at short length here. While completing *Goin' Viral: Uncontrollable Black Performance*, so many things were goin' viral that fed into my conceptualizations. I expect that people using today's iteration of social platforms, video-aggregation sites, and applications, not to mention artificial intelligence that uses algorithms based on large language models and people-backed content moderation, will find crucial cultural insights from what I examined more than a decade ago in the early phase of the influencer era. Here, I suggest some Black viralities that unfolded while I wrote that I hope might pique the interest of future scholars, prompting them to engage with the Black viralities critically.

Early on, people used the concept of digital blackface, or "twisted love of Black culture through caricature" or minstrelsy in cyberspace, to think about Black masculine representations in the 2004 video game *Grand Theft Auto: San Andreas* or used Black GIFs to express digital reactions and emotions.[27] Blackness became so commonplace in posts by interactors using certain mediums and performances on social platforms such that it was no longer Black Vine, it was just Vine, or Black reaction GIFs, just reaction GIFs.[28] Regarding the moment I examine, auto-tuning "Bed Intruder Song!!!" is an example of digital blackface.

Digital blackface experienced a resurgence on TikTok during the COVID-19 pandemic lockdown in the United States. Black TikTokers rebelled on the platform in response to ongoing uncited performances of their dances, particularly those posted by white TikTokers with sponsorships and large numbers of followers.[29] These white dancers consciously avoid the offensive practice of blackface while maintaining a white privilege that appropriates and steers the representation and interpretation of Black performance.[30] From 2019 into 2020, the renegade dance (done to Atlanta rapper K Camp's song "Lottery") was one of many dances created by Black girls, yet the girls were routed through algorithms in ways that rendered them to the background of that which they, as creators, should have been centered.[31] Jalaiah Harmon became the absent Black presence of the performance she began. This recalls the recurring pattern of Black femme erasure that I note with Kelly Dodson that preceded and followed her testimony. I was excited to find that a book had been written about not just the renegade dance's theft but its pleasures as well.[32]

Speaking of digital blackface and TikTok, I was intrigued by Factory New cofounders Anthony Martini and Brandon Le's digital robot rapper named FN Meka. The virtual robot attracted over ten million TikTok followers, and Capitol Music Group signed them on August 14, 2022, only to drop them from the label ten days later because of the racist masculine tropes they visually and lyrically materialized and parodied. One of those instances is an Instagram photo that features FN Meka clothed in an orange jumpsuit and being beaten by a police officer. In another instance, FN Meka uses the offensive derogation "nigga," despite being a programmable subjectivity themselves, raising questions about its use by those who can choose (or program) their Blackness.[33] FN Meka displays a partially shaven head with green braids, brown skin with facial tattoos, a gold nose ring, glowing green LED eyes, and gold teeth, all generated by Martini and Le's use of artificial intelligence that had used popular songs and video games as source material. Before Capitol dropped them, they had collaborated with Atlanta rapper Gunna on a single called "Florida Water."

This viral moment informs a case for the uncompensated and undercompensated human labor behind artificial intelligence, the results of which the consumer experiences as automated and free of the labors and creativities of the flesh (like "the cloud" relative to the material life of its data center). The creators of FN Meka had used the lyrics and pitched-up voice of a Black Houston rapper, Kyle the Hooligan, without compensating him.[34] The embarrassment caused in Black communities made to look bad by this avatar echoes that of Kelly and Antoine Dodsons' audience, except that the siblings' reality and sincerity contrasts with FN Meka's socially fabricated reality and insincerity. Indeed, FN Meka embodies the same racist sexism I noticed in comment sections on YouTube and WorldStarHipHop.

Others have noticed a similar phenomenon with technologies trained by the data fed to them. Suppose the indexes, models, and data used to represent or recognize people in virtual worlds are anti-Black. In that case, those who are marginalized and affected by anti-Blackness will continue to experience anti-Black stigma when virtual knowledge interplays with their material world. Thus, we must examine and modify the source material that perpetuates anti-Blackness and misogynoir, which programmers often use to train artificial intelligence and algorithms. To do so, we must equip ourselves with the knowledge and awareness to identify instances of anti-Blackness and misogynoir when we come across them in any media, including the first media technology: our eyes and ears. By using technologies powered by artificial intelligence, or algorithms, it becomes essential for us to actively interrogate and transform the material that influences these technologies, ultimately working toward a more equitable future.[35]

Despite Black virality's downsides in the previous examples about appropriation by different names, the next example posits far more livable possibilities within its scope. On August 5, 2023, during a weekend when I was repotting my plants and DJing, a violent encounter happened that my Instagram algorithm brought to my attention days after my being disconnected from the Web. (I hope someone writes a chapter or a book about how everything unfolded and traveled.) By Monday or Tuesday, interactors had playfully dubbed it the "Montgomery brawl" or "Montgomery uprising."

A Black cocaptain, Dameion Pickett, asked the white owners of a pontoon boat to move it forty-five minutes after his captain had made the same request to them several times over an intercom. The space from which the tiny pontoon boat refused to move was reserved for their 227-passenger ship, the *Harriot II*.[36] Following his captain's instructions, Pickett moved the boat, but its owners assaulted him.[37] As a white mob beat Pickett, a young man named Aaren Hamilton-Rudolph, a passenger on *Harriot II*, fearlessly leaped into the water. In the video someone yells, "They wrong for that now . . . that boy swimmin' his ass off over tha . . . Gaaaaaaawd dayum . . . that boy finna help that boy."[38] Sixteen-year-old Aaren intended to swim over and prevent any further harm from befalling Pickett, who appeared to be blocked from escaping by a white woman deliberately standing in his way. People intervened and separated the mob of white people beating Pickett, *Harriot II* docked, and some passengers who witnessed everything unfold appeared to rage against anyone who countered the cocaptain.

Referring to the brawl/uprising, a friend asked me, "How you reading this in relation to your work?" In my text to him, I wrote, "I think I was scared for that man's life." Regarding my research, I shared, "It conveys what I mean by rapid ubiquity." Then I offered why I had found out about it so late: "I was repotting and DJing all weekend and missed it. But it came across my IG feed. Then, a friend shared a meme of it in my IG messages. I had to search for the original footage. But it's at the point where the echo is more intense than the origin. While I was searching, I found a Detroit remix of it." I texted him the first meme regarding the brawl/uprising that I encountered on my Instagram feed and asked, "Have you seen the *Good Times* credits for it?"

With the help of visual composer Premimathieu Sterlin, the Detroit-based fine artist James Charles Morris had see-jayed the *Good Times* theme song, sung by Sondra "Blinky" Williams, Jim Gilstrap, and a gospel choir, with select visuals of the Montgomery brawl/uprising. As the credits roll, they unapologetically label every Black individual or group by category: "starring A Brother Doing His Job, costarring Michael Evans Phelps,[39] with The Bruhs, Unc With The Chair, The Aunties, and The Brothers of Alabama as The Crew, created by Consequences & Repercussions, produced by The Ancestors, developed by James Charles Morris."[40]

Like the opening credits of *Good Times*, the meme concludes with a visual representation of joy and amusement depicted by Ernie Barnes's 1976 acrylic painting, *The Sugar Shack*. I saw the unfolding of a scenario that could have ended in a white mob lynching a cocaptain doing his job. What I encountered instead were ghettocentric perspectives that the standoff was a symbol of camaraderie and the defense of Black lives, one Black cocaptain's life and those representatively tethered to his. The words of Aaren Hamilton-Rudolph, who would later be dubbed "Black Aquaman," remain with me as an intervention in the spectacular from this moment and the epigraph I use to open this coda: "Before y'all start recording and joking and laughing, how about think and help people? He could have gotten injured or worse."[41] I cannot help but wish his withnessing ethos had been present for Derrion Albert, whose onlookers recorded the violence instead of intervening.

Thus, a danger and benefit of goin' viral lies in that it does not produce knowledge—instead, it quickly centralizes already-circulated knowledge in ways that evidence it as a pattern. More specifically, there is a recurring pattern of disproportionate violation and caricature of Black people. The Ghetto Witness, for example, has long been a Black virality. Still, processes such as sharing videos, posting memes online, and generating hashtags expose a pattern: a tradition whereby news media gathers information from people within (or of the diaspora of) ghetto communities who perform subjectivity in ways that trouble normalized expectations—where the expectation itself is trouble. This is a well-known phenomenon and is sometimes sought to gain the currency that comes with Black virality.

So Black viralities are a news source, broadcasting informative and misleading knowledge about Blackness, the world, and the challenges and pleasures that interplay with them. Unlike a news source, however, interactors and algorithms index Black viralities in ways others can use as evidence to leverage liberation with or subjugate those directly or indirectly featured. While there seems to be no cure for what pathologizes the Black lives related to Black virality, the labor and leisure toward liberation (from and despite pathology) maintain freedom as an unfinished and fleeting possibility of Black virality that I hope to see further explored.

Notes

Introduction

1. Keeling, *Witch's Flight*, 24; Marks, *Skin of the Film*, 22, 170. That night on the bus was an indirect example of what the Black feminist film theorist Kara Keeling describes as the culturally informed affective labor that goes into processing televisual images and representations framed and circulated by cinematic machines. I say *indirect* due to my processing of other people's affectual labor between them and their cinematic machines. This affectual process is how acts transfer from representation to embodiment and memory. This is also discussed by film theorist Laura U. Marks as "haptic visuality"—a kind of predisposed vision that functions haptically because of one's cultural understanding.

2. Keeling, *Witch's Flight,* 25. The affect that is required to live in and make sense of the world (crying from sadness, laughter from joy, and furrowing from anger, for example) is the same embodied way of knowing that is required to process news media directly and indirectly.

3. Peoples, "We Are Not Expendable," Twitter, July 13, 2013, https://twitter.com/Gofthepeoples/status/356242125328891904.

4. Sharma, "Black Twitter?," 50. See also Craft, "Afrofuturism," 386.

5. My use of the term *discourse* is influenced by the broad and performative ways that theater and performance scholar Michael Issacharoff thinks about it in *Discourse as Performance* (3): Discourse ranges from "verbal utterances to nonverbal uses comprising the visual elements, including gesture, facial expression, movement, costume, players' bodies, properties, and décor." Discourse, in this formulation, is a set of performances.

6. Gene Demby, "Combing through 41 Million Tweets to Show How #BlackLivesMatter Exploded," *NPR*, March 2, 2016, http://www.npr.org/sections/codeswitch/2016/03/02/468704888/combing-through-41-million-tweets-to-show-how-blacklivesmatter-explodednews.bbc.co.uk.

7. Trymaine Lee, "Eyewitness to Michael Brown Shooting Recounts His Friend's Death," *MSNBC*, August 12, 2014, http://www.msnbc.com/msnbc/eyewitness-michael-brown-fatal-shooting-missouri.

8. I use the term *interactors* in *Goin' Viral* to connote people participating within their situated interfaces. People interact with each other through discourses and content such as videos, images, and texts. They execute these interactions through (re)producing, uploading, or posting said content and commenting on other people's posts and comments and other forms of media, such as academic texts.

9. Francesca Chambers, "Dem Representatives Make 'Hands Up, Don't Shoot' Motion on House Floor as They Discuss What It's Like to Be 'Black in America,'" *Daily Mail Online*, December 2, 2014, http://www.dailymail.co.uk/news/article-2857549/Dem-Congressman-makes-hands-don-t-shoot-motion-House-floor-African-American-lawmakers-discuss-s-like-black-America.html.

10. Jeremy Gordon, "The St. Louis Rams' 'Hands Up, Don't Shoot' Protest," *Wall Street Journal*, December 1, 2014, http://blogs.wsj.com/dailyfix/2014/12/01/rams-protest/.

11. Michelle Ye Hee Lee, "'Hands Up, Don't Shoot' Did Not Happen in Ferguson," *Washington Post*, March 19, 2015, http://www.washingtonpost.com/blogs/factchecker/wp/2015/03/19/hands-up-dont-shoot-did-not-happen-in-ferguson/.

12. Fine and Turner, *Whispers on the Color Line*, 18.

13. US Department of Justice Civil Rights Division, *Ferguson Police Department*, 4.

14. Populo Iratus, "#CecilTheLion," Twitter, July 30, 2015, https://twitter.com/cmahar3/status/626753864612638720?lang=en. Account suspended.

15. Jay Detroitcast, "Mike is coming over for a meeting. Doesn't know Russ and Manny are waiting in bushes with airsoft guns. #TheDetroitCast #handsupdontshoot," Twitter, July 30, 2015, https://twitter.com/JayDetroitcast/status/626762336888471552?lang=en.

16. Conservative Pelican, "A narrative crumbles. #PantsUpDontLoot #IStandWithDarrenWilson #NoBill," Twitter, November 15, 2014, https://twitter.com/TheHappyPelican/status/533747484745797634; Trader for Trump [previously known as Paper or Plastic], "@kendricklamar puts #Ferguson protesters on the cover of his new cd. NICE! #pantsUpDontLoot @mikerotond086," Twitter, March 15, 2015, https://twitter.com/eshropshire1/status/577272106062389248; and Jeff, "#pantsupdontloot," Twitter, June 17, 2015, https://twitter.com/12voltman60/status/611306079503425536.

17. R. L. Jackson, *Black Masculine Body*. Communications scholar and Black masculinity theorist Ronald L. Jackson II uses the notion of a racialized gender "scripting" to understand the process involved in assigning meaning to Black masculine bodies and what that exercise reveals about contemporary mass-mediated stereotypes. As I use it, *resistive* is that which resists unintentionally. That is, one's behavior is resistive when one is minding one's own business, and yet that behavior can be codified as an act of resistance even though one is not consciously concerned with countering any force. Resistive is a disposition rather than an act. I appreciate Black feminist media studies scholar and queer theorist Moya Bailey's distinction in *Misogynoir Transformed* (24–25) between "defensive digital alchemy" and

"generative digital alchemy" for its similarities to what I put forward here. While the first form responds to and recalibrates against violence, the second is an ongoing, productive force, whether in the face of violence or not, focused on a livable world for one's self and community that does not imperil others.

18. R. L. Jackson, *Black Masculine Body*, 74.

19. Velotron, "#cosby Would Say #pantsupdontloot," Twitter, December 30, 2014, https://twitter.com/308husker/status/549804263774240768.

20. Chuck, "#PantsUpDontLoot IS NOT RIGHT," Twitter, December 13, 2014, https://twitter.com/ChuckSleep/status/543872099371061248?lang=en.

21. Rugged Amethyst, "White cops coerced Stinney's confession. He was executed by the state at 14. He was exonerated 70 years later #PantsUpDontLoot," Twitter, December 17, 2014, https://twitter.com/GrooveSDC/status/545301898798981120?lang=en.

22. Demby, "Combing through 41 Million Tweets."

23. Carpenter, *Coloring Whiteness*, 197–202.

24. Gordon, *Ghostly Matters*, 4–5. Sociologist Avery F. Gordon coined the term "complex personhood." The Black viralities that I analyze are constructed and made knowable through visual technologies, and as such, there will always be something unknowable about their acts, something outside of the allowed frame. This unknowability reveals that "'we'—whether in our various disciplines, or languages, or geographic locations throughout the Americas—do not simply or unproblematically understand each other [or ourselves]." Taylor, *Archive and Repertoire*, 15.

25. Kimbwandende, *African Cosmology*, 33.

26. Gates, *Signifying Monkey*, xxiv; and Baraka, *Black Music*, 232. Like placing one mirror in front of another, no matter which is stared into first, the posterior mirror always appears to reiterate infinitely at progressively smaller scales. This is the "signifying" that literary critic, African American historian, and filmmaker Henry Louis Gates Jr. refers to, or the "changing same" that poet, playwright, music critic and essayist Amiri Baraka suggests—the indirect and direct ways that Black bodies in discourse convey, critique, and compound meaning in the form of the referent. In the prologue of *Darkening Mirrors* (xvi), Batiste, too, discusses the memory of being in a house of mirrors and the moment where she saw her material Black body in infinitely repeating, yet descending, form. Batiste uses this concept and metaphor to name an African American form of mirroring—"darkening mirrors"—which upholds and challenges normative representations and aesthetics, and which belongs to both African Americans and their larger culture.

27. Eglash, *African Fractals*, 4.

28. Moraga and Anzaldúa, "Entering the Lives of Others," 19.

29. Althusser, *Reproduction of Capitalism*, 190; and Spillers, "Mama's Baby, Papa's Maybe," 79–80. If, as Marxist philosopher Louis Althusser suggests, that ideological representation is done so seamlessly that the subject must come to it, must come to discourse, disidentification becomes virtually impossible. Indeed, how does one embrace current discourses and strive for something beyond that which socially exists? If the flesh or prediscursive subject did not exist, there is nothing that social gendering or racializing undoes. However, as flesh and prediscursive subjects, we

desire recognition, which requires social legibility and labeling. Black feminist scholar and literary critic Hortense J. Spillers counters Althusser's inescapable ideology and discusses the possibility of existing beyond traditional symbolics and possessing the ability to name rather than be interpellated into preordained syntax and semantics.

30. Butler, *Undoing Gender*, 91.

31. Schechner, *Performance Studies*, 14–20. Peggy Phelan even mentions her fascination with two men giving birth.

32. S. Jackson, *Professing Performance*, 13.

33. Phelan, *Unmarked*, 146 (italics in the original).

34. W. Benjamin, "Mechanical Reproduction."

35. Butler, "Performative Acts and Gender Constitution," 528.

36. Butler, 519.

37. Schechner, *Performance Studies*, 28–29.

38. Diamond, *Performance and Cultural Politics*, 1.

39. B. Brown, "Thing Theory," 4.

40. B. Brown, 5 (italics in the original).

41. Bernstein, "Dances with Things," 67–70.

42. Zien, "Sidelong Glances," 368.

43. Taylor, *Archive and Repertoire*, 2.

44. Campt, *Black Gaze*, 23. I recognize how vulnerability to anti-Black and white supremacist discourses constitutes Black people; however, those discourses should not be the primary way of knowing them.

45. E. P. Johnson, "'Quare' Studies," 10; and Manning, "Katherine Dunham," 489.

46. Trader for Trump, "@kendricklamar puts #Ferguson protesters on the cover of his new cd. NICE! #pantsUpDontLoot @mikerotond086."

47. Campt, *Black Gaze*, 39.

48. "Kendrick Lamar, 'To Pimp a Butterfly,'" *Rolling Stone Australia* (blog), July 19, 2024, https://au.rollingstone.com/music/music-lists/-64137/kendrick-lamar-to-pimp-a-butterfly-4-64226/.

49. McBride, "Can the Queen Speak?," 377.

50. Adeyemi, Khubchandani, and Rivera-Servera, *Queer Nightlife*, 3.

51. E. P. Johnson, "'Quare' Studies," 12.

52. Adeyemi, Khubchandani, and Rivera-Servera, *Queer Nightlife*; see also E. P. Johnson, "'Quare' Studies," 1–6.

53. Muñoz, "Disidentifications."

54. Auslander, *Liveness*, 56. In a tongue-in-cheek way, performance studies scholar Diana Taylor also affirms the liveness of mediated performance, or the "archive," by unsettling the notion that the mediums often relegated to being archival, instead of embodied and of the repertoire, are unchanging. She writes that "documents, maps, literary texts, letters, archaeological remains, bones, videos, films, CDs [are] *supposedly* resistant to change." Taylor, *Archive and Repertoire*, 19 (italics mine for emphasis).

55. "This liveness means that we spectators cocreate the photograph's meaning, rendering it an event, an intersubjective duet, and thus allowing new interpretations

to arise apart from the intentionality of the portraits' sitters and production team." Zien, "Sidelong Glances," 368.

56. Campt, *Black Gaze*, 17.

57. Campt, 2.

58. Keeling, *Witch's Flight*, 25.

59. Viral Blackness "works to erode borders/boundaries that inhibit the free flow of [B]lackness." Wade, "'New Genres of Being Human,'" 38.

60. See Felton-Dansky, *Viral Performance: Contagious Theaters*.

61. Jenkins, Ford, and Green, *Spreadable Media*, 4–6.

62. Fine and Turner, *Whispers on the Color Line*, 18.

63. Fleetwood, *Troubling Vision*, 33. See also Scott, *Domination*, 19, 27. Note that this goes beyond what anthropologist James C. Scott has called "infrapolitics," or hidden transcripts, as there can be an intentional resistance or unintentional resistiveness whereby the substance of the noniconic performance is unconcerned with countering discourse or being secretive in response to domination, even though it can exist as such.

64. Gaunt, "YouTube, Twerking and You," 265.

65. X (Twitter) is a shortform-text-oriented online social network to share thoughts, links, and visual media. Meta Platforms' services includes WhatsApp, which allow users to send text, voice, and video messages as well as electronic documents, links, and location; Instagram allows similar functionality to WhatsApp, with the addition of a more visual culture-oriented network; Threads functions similarly and as an alternative to X; and Facebook is a social networking service that achieves all of the above without specializing in any one way to share and consume information. YouTube is an online social network centered on video and audio sharing.

66. Scientists have linked the sociological spread of contagious media viruses and memes—online images and thoughts that have gone viral—to the various ways contagious biological viruses and genetic material spread. Douglass Rushkoff's *Media Virus* draws direct connections between a virus's function in biology and in media networks. Richard Dawkins's *The Selfish Gene* describes memes as devices communicating and replicating cultural information, like genes reproducing genetic material. I find these approaches obfuscating.

For example, how biological viruses, like COVID-19, affect economically, racially, and sexually stigmatized and marginalized people does not correspond with how a media virus circulates within and across those communities. Media viruses frequently circulate in ways that are not fatal or harmful, are affected by context collapse, and are confined to those who can access rumors, printed materials, websites, or application data. Viruses are agential and infect and replicate to thrive in that or variant forms. Whereas a TikTok video does not care whether interactors share it, its creators and TikTok—a business whose algorithms curate aggregated videos enabling interactors to participate in the attention economy—do. Truly, any TikTok video will fall into oblivion unless an audience vulnerable to what the video transmits acknowledges, shares, and replicates it.

This shift to metaphor also compromises the mechanics of viral material as I use it. Unlike COVID-19, a media virus remains unaffected by isopropyl alcohol or the antibody response—it continues to exist despite attempts to eliminate it. Our discursive notions inform a media virus or event that perpetuates and mutates through other people's perceptions of and vulnerability to said discourse. Indeed, inequalities magnify risks to the livelihoods of marginalized and stigmatized groups that are vulnerable to a media virus because pejorative perceptions about them are already commonplace. By goin' viral, this already-existent virality generates a compounding effect.

During my work on this book, the biological COVID-19 virus was ravishing communities across the globe without discrimination, and all the while, rapidly commonplace racist ideas about Black communities in the United States put their members in even more precarious positions. While racism might be viral, it did not infect otherwise progressive people whose immune response generates antiracist antibodies to neutralize racist antigens. As much as I wish for it, reducing deaths and hospitalizations from racism will not result by introducing weakened versions of racism to its hosts, as happens with a vaccine. In fact, to presume that something like racism is biological imagines an otherwise innocent world and excludes the agential, institutional, and systemic ways people culturally and politically constitute, perpetuate, and privilege racism. Likening culture to biology can dissolve the agency and responsibility of the people and institutions that enact racist ideas and policies. Attributing racism to genetics assumes an inherited condition that infects otherwise innocent minds. Maintaining that culture is biology is a determinist gesture toward neoliberalism, the idea or belief that civil society operates independently from our political and economic worlds.

When I use *viral* for what becomes or became culturally rapidly commonplace, it is with the latter limitations in mind. My usage is far more conversational and adapted from a phrase that everyday people use in social interactions and that my online interactors have adapted from sources ranging from grassroots social media to the most blatantly corporate media. Therefore, my use of the term does not affirm that what is happening with biological viruses is what we are witnessing when something cultural becomes rapidly commonplace. While epidemiology allows for the containment of a biological contagion, the same does not apply to the viral fallout I am describing. Black viralities travel uncontrollably. We cannot contain Black viralities as we can a virus because Black viralities leave an imprint in their wake that changes the material and representative grounds on which we stand. Furthermore, Black virality is not inherently harmful and can be generative for the wellness of the individuals and groups it centers.

Yet the biological study of viruses is crucial for understanding Black virality's reproduction, spread, and recognition. For example, as a virus attacks parts of the body, causes inflammation, and multiplies itself, the immune system produces antibodies to counteract the virus's effects; metaphorically, Black viralities spread through their digital and analog environments, irritating their audiences into eliciting responses that multiply the viral acts and critiques. The exponential spread of Black virality increases our vulnerability, inundation, and resistance to it. From grassroots campaigns to top-down marketing campaigns run by big-budget corporations, the Black virality I study helps us understand acts of transfer between performers, objects, and interactive audiences.

67. Diekmann, Heesterbeek, and Metz, "Infectious Diseases," 365–66. An epidemic exists where each infected person shares the infection with at least one more susceptible person, creating many secondary infections, or where a basic reproduction ratio that is greater than one. Sickness is the state of being ill, which both signifies disease and, of particular interest, is what I call "illness"—a Black street vernacular term for an expression or way of being that is undeniably appealing, communicable, and enduring. Thus, Black bodies redeploy illness, and Black virality can be ill, not because of something pathological, but because it is fresh, cool, and popular. Lil Wayne articulated this idea adroitly in his song "A Milli," where he boastingly announces, "Mothafucka I'm ill!" See *Tha Carter III*, audio CD, Cash Money, 2008. For other examples, see Nas, *Illmatic*, audio CD, Columbia, 1994; Foxy Brown, *Ill Na Na*, audio CD, Def Jam, 1996; Red Cafe, "I'm Ill," *Red October*, MP3 audio, Howie McDuffie Music Group, 2010.

68. Benjamin Lawless, "Intel, Racism Inside," *Penciled In* (blog), July 19, 2007, http://penciledin.com/wp/?p=688. URL delisted.

69. Wily Ferret, "Intel under Fire for 'Racist' Ad: White Men Can't Run," *The Inquirer*, August 10, 2011, http://www.theinquirer.net/inquirer/news/1004060/intel-racist. URL delisted. The small print in the bottom portion of the Intel ad reads, "Multiply computing performance and maximize the power of your employees. Intel® Core™ 2 Duo Processor. 40% more performance for business. Boasting 40% more performance with improved energy efficiency,* 64-bit capable Intel Core 2 Duo desktop processor delivers unparalleled multitasking capability. Now you can boost productivity and efficiency by running multiple computing-intensive applications at once. Learn more about why great business computing starts with Intel Inside. Visit intel.com/dualcore. *Performance measured Intel® Core™ 2 Duo desktop processors compared to Intel® Pentium® D Processor 805 on SPEC_intbase2000 and SPEC_int_rate_base2000 (2 copies). Actual performance may vary. Visit intel.com/performance ©2007 Intel Corporation. Intel, the Intel logo, Intel. Leap ahead, Intel. Leap ahead. Logo, Intel Core and Core Inside are trademarks of Intel Corporation in the United States and other countries."

70. For a list of stereotypes of Black people in film and stage performance, see Mapp, *Blacks in American Films*, 30–31.

71. Artificial intelligence is unable to appropriately moderate complex scenarios due to an inability to process context. Thus, humans must intervene in these moments, as their decisions and inputs create a feedback loop for algorithms to learn the difference between acceptable and flagrant content. In addition to being underpaid ($1.46–$3.74 per hour in Nairobi, Kenya) for the background labor of algorithms and artificial intelligence, the discourses and images workers must process daily take a toll on their mental health. See Drootin, "'Community Guidelines,'" 1215. See also Niamh Rowe, "'It's Destroyed Me Completely': Kenyan Moderators Decry Toll of Training of AI Models," *Guardian* (US edition), August 2, 2023, sec. Technology, https://www.theguardian.com/technology/2023/aug/02/ai-chatbot-training-human-toll-content-moderator-meta-openai.

72. Sociologists Michael Omi and Howard Winant describe that applying an ethos of white ethnic history to racial groups enables white people to appear variegated, whereas Black people—as well as Asian, Latine, and First Nations

people—"all look alike." This ignores "intra-racial distinctions" in favor of "lumping." Omi and Winant, *Racial Formation*, 44.

73. Through a discourse analysis of the Geek Squad's website and nerdcore music, Lori Kendall conveys the "difficulty in expanding the nerd identity to include people who are not white or not male" when attempts at challenging the normalized nerd role require access to science and tech that are still "guarded by the unmarked signifiers of whiteness and male gender." Kendall, "'White and Nerdy,'" 505, 510.

74. See Sirmans, "Legal Status of the Slave," 465.

75. Intel, *Intel's Efforts to Achieve a "Conflict Free" Supply Chain*, May 2014, https://www.intel.com/content/dam/doc/policy/policy-conflict-minerals.pdf.

76. I am thinking here of the three pillars of white supremacy that feminist scholar Andrea Smith outlines and how, even by writing against and critiquing white supremacy, I may still participate in oppressing others through my engagement with capitalism (i.e., buying an Intel-powered laptop through which to critique conflict minerals). See Smith, "Heteropatriarchy."

77. As ethnographer and performance theorist Dwight Conquergood writes, "It is no longer easy to sort out the local from the global: transnational circulations of images get reworked on the ground and redeployed for local tactical struggles [and purposes]." Conquergood, "Performance Studies," 145.

78. CRN Staff, "Intel Apologizes for 'Insulting' Ad: Critics Charge Racial Insensitivity," *CRN*, August 1, 2007, https://www.crn.com/news/components-peripherals/201202249/intel-apologizes-for-insulting-ad-critics-charge-racial-insensitivity.htm.

79. In the comment section of Keith Boykin's blog post, an interactor named Jas writes, "ALSO I DON'T THINK IT'S A TECHNICALLY GOOD AD. IT'S A DEMEANING WAY TO PORTRAY YOUR EMPLOYEES, EVEN IF THEY HAD BEEN WHITE GUYS, AND IT LOOKS LIKE THEY'RE ABOUT TO RUN INTO EACH OTHER." Boykin, "Is This Ad Racist?," keithboykin.com, accessed January 20, 2012, http://www.keithboykin.com/arch/2007/08/17/is_this_ad_racist. Website discontinued.

80. Schrøder, "Media Discourse Analysis," 79.

81. Gray, "Black Masculinity and Visual Culture," 402.

82. Keeling, "Passing for Human," 248. See also Muñoz, "Disidentifications," 12. I use *disidentification* here to touch on how we can disagree with stereotypes yet simultaneously use them in a critique or a nuanced account of them.

83. I use the essence of the original to suggest a starting point, a performance that spawned many others or recalls those types of acts. Inasmuch as acts that precede a performance also compose it, however, performance nullifies the notion of an original.

84. See Brandon Moore (@youngbusco), Instagram, June 14, 2015, https://instagram.com/p/36y_adBPK3/. "What are those?!" is a question that comedian Young Busco created to call attention to ugly shoes. He became known for the phrase while documenting a Bay Area police arrest on his cell phone. Young Busco says to the police officer, "Officer, I got one question for you . . ." His cell phone camera aims at the sky and then swoops down to the officer's shoes as he screams, "What are those?!" Both everyday people and popular artists, like Soulja Boy Tell

'Em and Ludacris, have referred to his act. After five weeks, it had garnered 4,473 likes on Instagram as of July 21, 2015.

85. Shawn Setaro, "Episode 146: Phonte," March 14, 2016, in *The Cipher*, produced by Josh Kross, podcast, MP3 audio, 1:33:40, https://soundcloud.com/thecipershow/146-phonte. Phonte, a rapper from the groups Little Brother and Foreign Exchange, defines the sample succinctly in saying, "[Samples] . . . are a way to recontextualize something and put it in a way that is more palatable to an audience that may not have gotten the first thing."

86. *30 Americans*, Corcoran Gallery of Art and College of Art + Design, accessed August 10, 2013, http://www2.corcoran.org/30americans/explore. URL delisted.

87. "The Wedgwood Anti-Slavery Medallion," Victoria and Albert Museum, January 17, 2024, https://www.vam.ac.uk/articles/the-wedgwood-antislavery-medallion.

88. Fairclough, *Media Discourse*, 57.

89. Fairclough, 57–58.

90. Fairclough, 63.

91. Fairclough, 144.

92. Kozinets, *Doing Ethnographic Research*, 34.

93. Gregory Brothers [schmoyoho], "Bed Intruder Song!!!"; and "Tragic: Teens Give a Chicago Student from a Rivarly [*sic*] Hi [*sic*] School a Deadly Beating with Huge Wooden Boards!"

94. As a Black virality, Thomas's sculpture *The Embrace* (2023) certainly challenges my suggestion of the virality of his art by itself.

95. Aisha Harris, "The Troubling Viral Trend of the 'Hilarious' Black Neighbor," *Slate*, May 7, 2013, http://www.slate.com/blogs/browbeat/2013/05/07/charles_ramsey_amanda_berry_rescuer_becomes_internet_meme_video.html. Harris also picked up on this viral trend, referring to it as the "Hilarious Black Neighbor," as she discusses how "derisive memeification" and the desire to see Black people perform surpasses the heroism and courage of Charles Ramsey, Kelly and Antoine Dodson, and Kimberly Wilkins.

96. Madison, "Performance Ethnography," 151.

97. Adeyemi, *Feels Right*, 101.

Chapter 1. People Hear What They See

Epigraph: Kurt Streeter, "Kneeling, Fiercely Debated in the N.F.L., Resonates in Protests," *New York Times*, June 5, 2020, Sports, https://www.nytimes.com/2020/06/05/sports/football/george-floyd-kaepernick-kneeling-nfl-protests.html.

1. Lindsey, *America, Goddam*, 26.

2. Kelley, "Burning Symbols," 103.

3. Branding is the act of labeling one's own self with or being labeled by a specific logo, gesture, or sound, and is used by individuals to symbolize ownership of or belonging to organizations and ideas or is used by organizations to symbolize a product or idea.

4. Neal, *Looking for Leroy*, 7.

5. Lindsey, "Post-Ferguson," 236. The #BlackLivesMatter movement was begun by three queer Black women activists, Alicia Garza, Patrisse Cullors, and Opal

Tometi, who were seeking to use "Black" to affirm the many (queer, disabled, undocumented . . .) lives within the Black spectrum of existence.

6. S. Hall, "Notes on Deconstructing," 187.

7. Here, I use "remember" to connote the process of piecing together disconnected parts and stories, a striving to both achieve and challenge wholeness.

8. Fine and Turner, *Whispers on the Color Line*, 21–23.

9. See Connor, "Edison's Teeth," 172. My use of *synesthetic* here derives from the idea that what stimulates one sensory mode can be experienced in another sensory mode, as in smelling sounds, hearing a mute image, or tasting a color.

10. Phelan, *Unmarked*, 2.

11. R. L. Jackson, *Black Masculine Body*, 98; and Bernstein, "Dances with Things," 70. Scripts assign roles to bodies, and these roles also instruct bodies in how to exist; Jackson uses the notion of racial and gendered "scripting" to understand the process of assigning meaning to Black masculine bodies. Bernstein uses "script" as a verb, which instructs the way in which bodies operate socially.

12. *30 Americans*, Corcoran Gallery of Art and College of Art + Design.

13. See M. O. Wallace, *Constructing*, 8.

14. Wallace, 8.

15. See Gates, *Signifying Monkey*, xxiv.

16. Barthes, *Camera Lucida*, 32.

17. See Moten, *In The Break*, 172. Moten uses salient sensual elements discussed in an essay by Lee Edelman, "The Part for the (W)hole," to explore how the aural emerges in its fullest possibility through the visual—hearing a character most clearly by seeing a character—and how the visual emerges in its fullest possibility through the aural—seeing a character most clearly by hearing a character.

18. Barthes, *Camera Lucida*, 32.

19. See the timeline circa 1787 at the Black Cultural Archives in Brixton, London.

20. Cobb, *Picture Freedom*, 20.

21. Committee for the Abolition of the Slave-Trade, *Remarks*, 62–63.

22. See Fleming, *Black Patience*, 1; and Hartman, *Scenes of Subjection*, 116.

23. "The Wedgwood Antislavery Medallion," Victoria and Albert Museum, accessed January 17, 2024, https://www.vam.ac.uk/articles/the-wedgwood-antislavery-medallion.

24. Bey, "Trans*-Ness," 275–95.

25. Nicole Fleetwood's definition of iconicity applies to the "iconic" nature of the broadside: "the ways in which singular images or signs come to represent a whole host of historical occurrences and processes." Fleetwood, *Troubling Vision*, 2.

26. Concerning the number of people on the broadside of a ship like *Brooks*, the Plymouth Committee and their chairman, William Elford, wrote that this depiction was an understatement and the ship could have carried 609 enslaved Africans, as it had done in one past voyage.

27. Papers of John Bishop Estlin, record view 17562/1, Bristol Archives Catalogue, accessed November 8, 2012, http://archives.bristol.gov.uk/Record.aspx?src=CalmView.Catalog&id=17562%2f1&pos=1.

28. Fleetwood, *Troubling Vision*, 19. Fleetwood observes that considering the outline or shadow of bodies that occupy the field of vision, or affective framework,

can be more helpful than the visible bodies themselves when gathering information about the absent referent.

29. "Meet Hank Willis Thomas," *NowThis News*, accessed July 16, 2013, http://www.nowthisnews.com/news/meet-hank-willis-thomas/?autoplay=true. URL delisted.

30. Lipsitz, *Possessive Investment*, 1.

31. Finley, "Committed to Memory," 12.

32. For a plethora of examples, see AbsolutAd.com, "Absolut Gallery: Singles," 2009, accessed October 15, 2015, http://www.absolutad.com/absolut_gallery/singles/.

33. Staddon, *Women and Alcohol*, 45–63.

34. Kendrick Lamar, "Swimming Pools," MP3 audio, Aftermath/Interscope Records, 2013.

35. Foucault, *Foucault Reader*, 265.

36. "Black men, especially those under the age of 30, are more likely to be victims of alcohol-related homicides than were either white men or women or Black women in that age group." Gary, "Drinking, Homicide," 24. This was particularly true of lower-income Black men and related to coping mechanisms to deal with larger structural issues and prevalence of liquor stores in proximity to where they live.

37. Douglass, *Narrative*, 116.

38. Staddon, *Women and Alcohol*, 123.

39. See Gilroy, *Black Atlantic*, 4. Sociologist and cultural studies scholar Paul Gilroy uses the slave ship to think through the Middle Passage as a transnational formation, this Black Atlantic that facilitates the exchange of artifacts, politics, ideas, and culture.

40. Fleetwood, *Troubling Vision*, 10.

41. Evans and Rydén, *Baltic Iron*, 172.

42. Gumbs, *Dub*, 18. See also Shakur, *Assata: An Autobiography*, 176–78.

43. Lhamon, "Optic Black," 112.

44. Eradication of the form of slavery specifically involving noncriminals is a point that must be emphasized, as slavery is technically permitted in the United States if one is convicted of a crime. See the first clause of the Thirteenth Amendment to the US Constitution.

45. "Context," Centre for the Study of the and Legacies of British Slavery, accessed August 25, 2022, https://www.ucl.ac.uk/lbs/project/context/.

46. Estes, *I Am A Man!*, 2.

47. Estes, 2 (italics in the original).

48. The reference comes from the full title of the 1982 book by Gloria Hull, Patricia Bell Scott, and Barbara Smith, *All the Women Are White, All the Blacks Are Men, but Some of Us Are Brave: Black Women's Studies*.

49. Spillers, "Mama's Baby," 72–73 (italics in the original).

50. Primo, "Visual Arts 1."

51. See "Africans in America: Part 3: Historical Documents: Specimen of Modern Printing Types, No. 844, 1845," PBS, accessed October 22, 2024, https://www.pbs.org/wgbh/aia/part3/3h1586.html. It should be noted that as early as 1826, members of the Ladies Negro's Friend Society of Birmingham, England, used the image of a strong, modestly busty, supplicating enslaved African (presumed to be a woman),

her wrists in chains, her fingers intertwined, and face to the sky, to raise money to relieve enslaved Africans, particularly women. Some reproductions, particularly in the United States, contained a slogan beneath her that read, "Am I Not a Woman and a Sister?" Over thirty years after this figure was sketched, the image was finally used interchangeably with the image of the supplicating enslaved African man, yet the same issues with essentialization remain.

52. Hugh McCall, a retired US Infantry major, made references concerning the unique physiology of Africans, which "seemed" to make them uniquely fit to endure the labors of slavery. He writes, "Agriculture was the prime object, and the culture of rice, which held up the most promising source of wealth, could not be carried on successfully without the assistance of Africans, whose constitutions seem formed by nature to bear the heat and exposure of a climate most favorable for its production." McCall, *History of Georgia*, 5. Also, Black people were treated so cruelly by white people that they eventually, almost as a way to cope, "accepted their master's claims about the rightness, the power and the sanctity of whiteness and the degradation, the powerlessness, and the shame of Blackness." Blassingame, *Slave Community*, 303.

53. Hartman, *Scenes of Subjection*, xxiii.

54. Again, for more information on the legality of slavery for criminals in the United States, please read the first clause of the Thirteenth Amendment to the Constitution.

55. Genovese, "Rebelliousness and Docility," 312.

56. Yao, *Disaffected*, 2. Stated differently, see also Hartman, *Scenes of Subjection*, 24–25.

57. Cobb, *Picture Freedom*, 168.

58. The idea that enslaved Africans were happy in confinement is related to what Hartman calls in *Scenes of Subjection* (31) "an interested misreading of the interdependence of labor and song common among the enslaved." See also Cobb, *Picture Freedom*, 50.

59. American Anti-Slavery Society, *Anti-Slavery Record*, 73.

60. LaRoche, *Free Black Communities*, 1. Historic preservationist and archaeology scholar Cheryl LaRoche calls such images biased and suggests they are not representative of the collective involved in assisting escapees from slavery in the United States, inclusive of free Black communities, Black churches, and fraternal societies like Freemasonry.

61. Van Deburg, *Slavery and Race*, 17.

62. *The Underground Railroad*, "Chapter 9: Indiana Winter," written by Jihan Crowther, Barry Jenkins, and Colson Whitehead, directed by Barry Jenkins, aired May 14, 2021, on Amazon Prime Video.

63. McGinnis, *Michigan Genealogy*, 200–201.

64. Cobb, *Picture Freedom*, 180.

65. "Strategic essentialism," a term coined by the postcolonial scholar Gayatri Spivak, uses the group as the foundation for struggle while "debating the issues related to group identity within the group." Wolff, "Strategic Essentialism," 4797–99.

66. Kelley, "Burning Symbols," 103.

67. "Truffle Butter," featuring Drake and Lil Wayne, MP3 audio, track 10, on Nicki Minaj, Cash Money/Motown, 2015.

68. "Money Trees," featuring Jay Rock, MP3 audio, track 5 on Kendrick Lamar, *good kid, m.A.A.d city*, Aftermath/Interscope, 2013.

69. "Nobody's Perfect," featuring Missy Elliott, MP3 audio, track 11 on J. Cole, *Cole World: The Sideline Story*, Columbia/Roc Nation, 2011.

70. "Detroit State of Mind," MP3 audio, track 2 on Elzhi and Will Sessions, *Elmatic*, XXL, 2011.

71. "Nothing Lasts Forever," MP3 audio, track 4 on Nas, *The Lost Tapes*, Columbia, 2002.

72. "Bout It, Bout It II," featuring Mia X, MP3 audio, track 13 on Master P, *Ice Cream Man*, No Limit/Priority, 1996.

73. Newman, "Web Postings Turn Writers into Anonymous," *Detroit Free Press*, July 3, 2001.

74. Rich Buhler and Staff, "Poet Maya Angelou Highlights Corporate Racism-Fiction!," TruthOrFiction?, accessed December 16, 2011, http://www.truthorfiction.com/rumors/m/mayaangelou.htm#.VM7SLmTF_JI.

75. Michel Marriott, "Out of the Woods," *New York Times*, November 7, 1993, Style, https://www.nytimes.com/1993/11/07/style/out-of-the-woods.html. In an interview with the *New York Times*, the then CEO of Timberland, Jeffrey Swartz, was quoted as saying that "hip hop kids" were not his "target customer" and that instead "honest working people" were. Violet E. Gill from Queens wrote the editor almost a month later, saying, "I would like Mr. Swartz to know that the majority of the African-Americans in the inner city are 'honest working people.' Wake up, Timberland. If you don't want our money, some other establishment will gladly accept it." *New York Times*, December 5, 1993, Style, https://www.nytimes.com/1993/12/05/style/l-letters-to-the-editor-timberland-message-323093.html.

76. Woods, *Development Arrested*, 6.

77. The oak tree is known for its density and as a symbol of strength, and it appears only in the Northern Hemisphere. North America contains the greatest number of oak species in the world.

78. Rice, *Witnessing Lynching*, 89.

79. Fedo, *Lynchings In Duluth*, xxii.

80. Mitchell, *Living with Lynching*, 24.

81. See Eric Wilson, "Fashion's Blind Spot," *New York Times*, August 7, 2013, http://www.nytimes.com/2013/08/08/fashion/fashions-blind-spot.html.

82. P. Turner, *I Heard It*, xv–xvi.

83. A copy of the auctioned piece *Jordan and Johnnie Walker in Timberland Circa 1923 from the Series Branded*, 2006, inkjet print on canvas, 61.3 cm x 53.7 cm, can be seen here: https://www.artnet.com/artists/hank-willis-thomas/jordan-and-johnnie-walker-in-timberland-circ-aa-LnJqdTFPNHXFY09KpjxIbg2, accessed October 22, 2024. A more detailed image is found in Thomas's *Pitch Blackness*, 62.

84. Mitchell, *Living with Lynching*, 3 (italics in the original).

85. Guterl, *Seeing Race*, 64.

86. Guterl, 47–49.

87. See Maxine Jones, *A Documented History of the Incident Which Occurred at Rosewood, Florida, in January 1923*, Florida Board of Regents, December 22, 1993, http://edocs.dlis.state.fl.us/fldocs/regents/rosewood.pdf. The Rosewood massacre took place during the first week of January 1923 in rural Levy County, Florida. It began when a group of white men from towns nearby lynched a Rosewood resident, Sam Carter, over unsupported accusations from a white woman in Sumner, Florida, that a Black man had robbed and raped her. When other Rosewood residents defended their lives against a white mob, members of the mob began acting without restraint, hunting Black people and burning every structure in Rosewood. Even though they were aware of the violence, state and local authorities made no arrests.

88. Thomas, *Jordan and Johnnie Walker in Timberland Circa 1923*; and Thomas, *Pitch Blackness*, 62.

89. Mitchell, *Living with Lynching*, 4.

90. Mitchell, 8.

91. Mitchell, 69.

92. Nike, "Michael Jordan 'Banned' Commercial," posted December 12, 2007, by shahtoosh, YouTube, 0:32, https://www.youtube.com/watch?v=zkXkrSLe-nQ.

93. Todd Boyd, "The Holy Grail of Basketball Shoes," *ESPN*, January 25, 2008, http://sports.espn.go.com/espn/page2/story?page=boyd/080125.

94. See archived Nike annual reports from 1987–90. "Investors: News, Events and Reports: Annual Reports," Nike, Inc., accessed October 10, 2024, https://investors.nike.com/investors/news-events-and-reports/default.aspx.

95. See Alexander, *New Jim Crow*, 102–5. This trend of us (white suburban Americans) and them (Black Americans) in news stories around sneaker violence also occurred within and alongside news stories that disproportionately featured images of Black drug criminals, which, in the related discourse, led to the inseparability of sneaker murderers, drug criminals, and Black people.

96. Telander, "Senseless," *Sports Illustrated Vault*, May 14, 1990, p. 1, accessed December 15, 2011, https://vault.si.com/vault/1990/05/14/senseless-in-americas-cities-kids-are-killing-kids-over-sneakers-and-other-sports-apparel-favored-by-drug-dealers-whos-to-blame.

97. Coleman, "Classic Campaigns," para 38.

98. We can see that the individual-as-brand notion has a strong presence in earlier propaganda, such as with the seal of the Society for Effecting the Abolition of the Slave Trade.

99. Raiford, "Restaging Revolution," 220–22.

100. hooks, *Black Looks*, 33.

101. Peña, "Protest to Movement," 191.

102. Streeter, "Kneeling, Fiercely Debated."

103. I use "people of substantial color" to suggest that white people must deal with the consequences of race as well and cannot escape racialization by being the invisible racial default. This presumption is part of what fuels white privilege in the first place. At the same time, I wish to be able to name how skin tone can act

as a kind of mark or stigma, prohibiting people from the privileges of whiteness to varying degrees.

104. brown, *Emergent Strategy*, appears in the section "So, ok, but what EXACTLY is emergent strategy?," approximately 39–40.

105. KPIX | CBS News Bay Area, "Kaepernick Nike Ad: New Ad Featuring Former San Francisco 49ers QB Colin Kaepernick," September 5, 2018, YouTube, 2:05, https://www.youtube.com/watch?v=jBnseji3tBk.

106. CNN, "Paul Ryan: I Know What a "Dab" Is," January 12, 2017, YouTube, 1:02, https://www.youtube.com/watch?v=0KWeQeaB4c8.

107. See Gordon, *Ghostly Matters*, 23. Gordon argues that acknowledging the ghost is the best way to move beyond the ghost, the best way to no longer be haunted by it, even if for only that moment of recognition/reconciliation. Her analysis of the ghost as a haunting in the motion picture *Beloved* (1998) is useful in many ways, especially for thinking of how fiction can fill in the blanks of slave narratives—specifically thinking here about how Thomas's concepts fill in voids in the history of enslaved Africans both in the United States and abroad.

108. Bernstein, "Dances with Things," 69.

Chapter 2. I Can't Live without My Radio

Epigraph: "Fight the Power (Part 1 and 2)," MP3 audio, track 1 on The Isley Brothers, *The Heat Is On*, Sony, 1975/2015.

1. Lee, *Do the Right Thing*.
2. Fairchild, "Deterritorializing Radio."
3. Ryan, "Internet's *Titanic* Moment," 3.
4. See Hoover v. Intercity Radio Co.
5. Radio Act of 1927, Pub. L. No. 632, § 11, 15 (1967).
6. Foy, "Home Set to Music," 58.
7. Foy, 59.
8. Foy, 59.
9. Foy, 77.
10. Foy, 66.
11. Lipsitz, *Possessive Investment*, 13; and E. B. Brown, "Negotiating and Transforming," 119.
12. Cohen, "Encountering Mass Culture," 155–58.
13. Cohen, 155.
14. Cohen, 155.
15. Cohen, 155–56.
16. Andrew Graham, "Broadcasting Policy in the Digital Age," *The Aspen Institute*, accessed June 20, 2014, http://www.aspeninstitute.org/policy-work/communications-society/programs-topic/digital-broadcasting-public-interest/broadcasting-. URL delisted.
17. Fairchild, "Deterritorializing Radio," 553.
18. Chang, *Can't Stop*, 442.

19. Owerko, *Boombox Project*, 153.

20. Owerko, 47.

21. Red Bull Music Academy, "Kool DJ Red Alert Talks the Bronx, Grandmaster Caz and DJing, August 22, 2017, YouTube, 1:23:12, https://www.youtube.com/watch?v=Aap7Vkdp3pM.

22. "Zulu Beat: WHBI (105.9 FM), New York, NY, USA," HipHop Radio Archive, December 1982, https://hiphopradioarchive.org/show/392.

23. Browne and Browne, *Popular Culture*, 110.

24. Owerko, *Boombox Project*, 24.

25. Browne and Browne, *Popular Culture*, 110.

26. Reggie Ossé, "Biggie Stories | The Combat Jack Show (Busta Rhymes, Styles P, DJ Premier) on Complex," March 12, 2014, YouTube, 10:39, https://www.youtube.com/watch?v=uIkUugqYiuY.

27. Owerko, *Boombox Project*, 24.

28. Owerko, 153.

29. Owerko, 89.

30. LL Cool J asserts that rap was still a regional genre because it was broadcast so infrequently: "You know, a lot of stations play rap when they want to raise their ratings, then drop it once they get there. They should stay with it. When people hear it, they like it—and that's the only way we'll go national." David Hinckley, "Let's Stop Giving Them a Bad Rap," *New York Daily News*, December 27, 1985. A year following these comments, Cool J cited racial differences in radio play that contributed to rap's regionalism: "Black radio is definitely doing rap justice. . . . They play rap. As far as pop radio is concerned, they don't really play it as much as they should. The record has to be a 'double-trillion hit' for them to even play it a little bit. Sooner or later they'll open up." Bob Pfeiffer, *Washington Post*, December 25, 1986.

31. LL Cool J, "I Can't Live without My Radio," CD audio, from *Radio*, Def Jam, 1995.

32. For example, Mayor Ed Koch created "radio-free zones" on certain beaches and city parks in Brooklyn, Queens, the Bronx, and Staten Island. See "N.Y. Beaches Ban Boomboxes," *Star News*, July 26, 1985, http://news.google.com/newspapers?nid=1454&dat=19850726&id=KuBOAAAAIBAJ&sjid=zBMEAAAAIBAJ&pg=4605,7604220. Another article discusses how the signs designed to limit noise levels in Jersey City convey that boom boxes, instead, are illegal and subject to fines of up to $1,000 and/or imprisonment. It also reveals how the laws targeted youth who sold crack and used the radio at early hours in the morning to announce that crack was for sale. See Albert J. Parisi, "4,2>Noise Ban Angers Ice Cream Vendors," *New York Times*, September 4, 1988, N. Y. / Region, http://www.nytimes.com/1988/09/04/nyregion/42-noise-ban-angers-ice-cream-vendors.html.

33. Owerko, *Boombox Project*, 90.

34. Owerko, 90.

35. Owerko, 96.

36. DeFrantz and Gonzalez, *Black Performance*, 8.

37. Mullins, *Race and Affluence*, 29.

38. Undercover Black Man, "Attack of the Giant Negroes!!," *Undercover Black Man* (blog), July 10, 2007, https://undercoverblackman.blogspot.com/2007/07/attack-of-giant-negroes.html.

The writer blogs about the Giant Negro phenomenon by highlighting specific stories from its ongoing use in the early to mid-twentieth century to describe tall Black men committing crimes or playing sports. Many thanks to Dr. Mashadi Matabane for bringing this phenomenon to my attention!

39. Special to the *New York Times*, "Giant Negro Attacks Police: Believed He Was Called to Heaven and Cut Nephew's Throat to Carry Him Along—Officers Killed Him," *New York Times (1857–1922)*, September 24, 1900. https://www.nytimes.com/1900/09/24/archives/giant-negro-attacks-police-believed-he-was-called-to-heaven-and-cut.html?searchResultPosition=1.

40. I use *unarmed* elsewhere in this book descriptively and work against any notion of this term as a default trope when describing Black people who are murdered by police or vigilantes. That is, Black people are allowed to be armed, and this should not preclude them from protection or the presumption of innocence.

41. Sam Roberts, "When Police Are Accused of Brutality: An Examination of Cases Involving Charges of Police Brutality This Year; McGuire's Response to US Hearing Raises Questions as Well as Answers." *New York Times (1923–Current File)*, October 27, 1983, https://www.nytimes.com/1983/10/27/nyregion/when-police-are-accused-of-brutality.html. Seven of eight stories Roberts examines feature pictures of Black men.

42. Selwyn Raab, "Autopsy Finds Bumpurs Was Hit by Two Blasts," *New York Times (1923–Current File)*, November 27, 1984, https://www.nytimes.com/1984/11/27/nyregion/autopsy-finds-bumpurs-was-hit-by-two-blasts.html.

43. Robert D. McFadden, "Black Man Dies after Beating by Whites in Queens," *New York Times (1923–Current File)*, December 21, 1986, https://www.nytimes.com/1986/12/21/nyregion/black-man-dies-after-beating-by-whites-in-queens.html.

44. See "N. Y. Beaches Ban Boomboxes."

45. Sharpe, *Monstrous Intimacies*, 2, 3, 13, 26.

46. Ebert, review of *Do the Right Thing*, June 30, 1989, https://www.rogerebert.com/reviews/do-the-right-thing-1989.

47. Klein, "Spiked?," *New York Magazine*, June 26, 1989, 14. If *The Dark Knight* (2008) and the recent *Joker* (2019) films are any indication, the other seems to be true: that a white man responded violently to seeing a white-passing male figure on screen victimized by society at large and could do so again.

48. Lubiano, "Compared to What?," 256.

49. See Lee and Jones, *Spike Lee Joint*, 83.

50. Owerko, *Boombox Project*, 5.

51. Chuck D, "Eddie Murphy," Twitter, September 22, 2011, https://twitter.com/MrChuckD/status/116749836535074816?lang=en.

52. Bart Barnes, "Schools Must Reconsider Racial Quotas," *Washington Post*, December 26, 1980, https://www.washingtonpost.com/archive/sports/1980/12/26/schools-must-reconsider-racial-quotas/0dad8823-9b29-4a4a-b7ef-e2cb03dd14f7/.

53. "Weekend Update," *Saturday Night Live*, directed by Dave Wilson (New York: Time Life Video, 1980), VHS.

54. See Rodgers, "'What Constitutes Life?,'" 510. Discussing this interplay of technology with identity, feminist historian and sound studies scholar Tara Rodgers explains that varying forms of embodiment are constituted in forms of audio technology and in what they are called.

55. See Rothstein, "Don't 'Sanitize,'" interview by Terry Gross, May 14, 2015, http://www.npr.org/2015/05/14/406699264/historian-says-dont-sanitize-how-our-government-created-the-ghettos. Historian Richard Rothstein discusses a similar definition of ghetto.

56. The radio's evolution into the boom box is crucial, because with the boom box, owners can control what they listen to or desire other people to listen to without depending on a prescheduled program. This agency contrasts with radio in the home: "Bringing music as well as other programs into the home, the radio also diminished the individuality of the music heard. People were bound by the programming available at a given time." Foy, "Home Set to Music," 76.

57. Carpenter, *Coloring Whiteness*, 215. *Acousmêtre* is the shadow associated with the sound when the associated body remains unseen.

58. hooks, *Yearning*, 177, 182.

59. McBride, *Abercrombie and Fitch*, 58.

60. hooks, *Yearning*, 174.

61. See Morrison, "Sound(s) of Subjection," 18.

62. E. P. Johnson, *Appropriating Blackness*, 2.

63. See Batiste, *Darkening Mirrors*, 10.

64. Teal, "Beyond the Cotton Club," 123–27.

65. White, *Jim Crow to Jay-Z*, 48.

66. Public Enemy's "Fight the Power" (1989) is the musical motif of *Do the Right Thing*. It was recorded for the film before their highly acclaimed album *Fear of a Black Planet* (1990). Along with Perez's opening credit sequence, the film's mass distribution functioned to make "Fight the Power" go viral after being seen and heard communally by many viewers in theaters. The song also became an anthem through the Bomb Squad's (Public Enemy's producers) unique pastiche of sound, including Syl Johnson's "Different Strokes," Sly and the Family Stone's "Sing a Simple Song," James Brown's "Funky Drummer," the Soul Children's "I Don't Know What This World Is Coming To" (featuring Jesse Jackson), and, last, the Isley Brothers' "Fight the Power." This sound that the Bomb Squad executed is also known as funk music.

67. Stallings, *Funk the Erotic*, 4.

68. Powell, "Ghosts Got You," 2–4.

69. Stallings, *Funk the Erotic*, 4.

70. Stallings, xv, 177.

71. Morrison, "Sound(s) of Subjection," 16 (italics in the original).

72. Patton, *Sex and Germs*, 104.

73. Holland, *Erotic Life*, 9, 47, 60.

74. Stallings, *Funk the Erotic*, 188.

75. "Historically, non-African American merchants have dominated the economy of African American communities." Kim, *Koreans in The Hood*, 44.

76. I am adopting the concept of occupying sound from a School of Sustainability lecture during Milan Design Week wherein the creative director of sound for BMW Group, Renzo Vitale, asked the question, "How can we inhabit sound?" (lecture, Salone Del Mobile, Milan, June 12, 2022).

77. Kamasi Washington, *Harmony of Difference—EP*, Young Turks, 2017.

78. Manning, *Race in Motion*, 10.

79. J. Johnson, *Killing Poetry*, 14. See also M. M. Bailey, "Queerness of Touch," 60; and Marks, *Skin of the Film*, 22, 164, 192–93. I use *visual touch* from a phrase from Black queer theorist Marlon M. Bailey, later published as "touching as seeing," regarding *Moonlight* (2016) and how "mutual recognition" between Black men in the film is a type of touch. Importantly, Bailey's distinction happens within the film between characters rather than between the film and spectator.

80. In *Hip Hop Heresies* (15), artist and Black popular culture theorist Shanté Paradigm Smalls writes on how certain hip-hop formations in New York city produce Blackness in ways that might not be "rendered by people who are racialized as Black." I am pointing toward this through Stevie's obvious Puerto Rican pride and Raheem's racial and ethnic possibilities that the encounter generates.

81. Rivera-Servera, *Queer Latinidad*, 3.

82. See Miguel Salazar, "The Problem with Latinidad," *Nation*, September 16, 2019, https://www.thenation.com/article/hispanic-heritage-month-latinidad/. Normative discussions of Latinidad are silent regarding the Spanish conquest of African and First Nation cultures, the voicing of which might enable that legacy to be a unifying force rather than a solely Indigenous and African-diasporic legacy of knowledge and culture. *Latinidad* is a contested term, but when I use *Black Latinidad*, I am attempting to engage in a queer and Black way of imagining it as part of the African diaspora. See also Rodriguez, "Afro-Latinx at NYU."

83. Abdurraqib, *Little Devil*, 97.

84. To acknowledge Black sensibilities is to commit to embodied knowledge as a legitimate way of knowing. Embodied knowledge is especially significant in the face of acts of anti-Blackness that continue to be difficult to prove by what prosecutorial agents legitimate as evidence.

85. Lorde, "Uses of the Erotic," 341.

86. Lorde, 341.

87. Moten, *In the Break*, 6–7.

88. Black Public Sphere Collective, *Black Public Sphere*, 2, 3. For more on this, see Habermas, *Structural Transformation*.

89. See Neal, *Looking for Leroy*, 99. African American studies scholar and popular culture theorist Mark Anthony Neal discusses Black masculinity and cosmopolitanism in relation to the character Stringer Bell from HBO's *The Wire* and how his cosmopolitanism—how he is seen as a citizen of the world—was mostly illegible in the context of the masculinities articulated on the block. Similarly, I contend that Radio Raheem, and many other Black men who allude to him, (in)voluntarily perform cosmopolitanism, broadcasting a sort of performance that disrupts the normalized expectations of their perceived masculinities.

90. W. J. T. Mitchell, "Violence of Public Art," 887.

91. Fraser, "Public Sphere," 8.

92. Public Enemy, "Fight the Power," CD audio, track 1 on *Music from Do the Right Thing*, Def Jam, 1989.

93. The film is about a misogynist serial killer, but I am drawn to the fact that Radio Raheem knows of this 1955 black-and-white film in what is a disidentificatory performance.

94. White, *Jim Crow to Jay-Z*, 34 (italics in the original).

95. Shabazz, *Spatializing Blackness*, 95.

96. Moten, *In the Break*, 200. Moten describes a synesthetic experience in seeing Emmett Till's death in a picture and discusses being able to hear the mourning, "a seeing that redoubles itself as sound."

97. Rodgers, "'What Constitutes Life?,'" 517.

98. Batiste, *Darkening Mirrors*, 10.

99. Patton, *Sex and Germs*, 103.

100. Patton, 12.

101. Thomas Tracy, "Cops Involved in Fatal Confrontation with Eric Garner Were Asked to Crack Down on Illegal Cigarette Sales: Bill Bratton," *New York Daily News*, January 9, 2019, http://www.nydailynews.com/new-york/nyc-crime/cops-involved-eric-garner-confrontation-asked-target-illegal-cigarette-sales-bratton-article-1.1901612.

102. CSPAN, "'High-Tech Lynching': Thomas Denies Anita Hill Harassment Allegations," September 18, 2018, Video, 0:58, https://www.washingtonpost.com/video/politics/high-tech-lynching-thomas-denies-anita-hill-harassment-allegations/2018/09/18/370097aa-bbae-11e8-adb8-01125416c102_video.html; Allen Smith, "Lawmakers Outraged after Trump Compares Impeachment Inquiry to 'a Lynching,'" *NBC News*, October 23, 2019, https://www.nbcnews.com/politics/trump-impeachment-inquiry/trump-compares-impeachment-effort-lynching-n1069906; and Ore, *Lynching*, 3–30. The Thomas and Trump examples are different from the "end-of-lynching discourse" that Black feminist rhetorician Ersula J. Ore identifies as being used by organizations that believed the geographies that produced lynching ended. The notion that lynchings are of the past make it so that people who continue to encounter lynching today cannot name lynching as such. Those gaslighting realities pushed the NAACP to adopt a more "capacious" meaning of lynching. In pointing this out, I am exposing how conservative voices weaponize to their advantage the capaciousness that has been given to the definition of lynching to make exploitative uses of the lynching trope in popular discourse.

103. Crawley, *Blackpentecostal*, 2.

104. "#SayHerName: Black Women and Girls Killed by Police," *NewsOne*, March 21, 2021, https://newsone.com/playlist/black-women-girls-police-killed-photos/.

105. S. Hall, "What Is This?," 111. Hortense J. Spillers seconds this, writing, "Material values engender symbolic and discursive ones (and vice-versa) in perfect synecdochic harmony." Spillers, *Black, White, and in Color*, xiii.

106. Ronald Smothers, "1,200 Protesters of Racial Attack March in Queens," *New York Times*, December 28, 1986, sec. New York, https://www.nytimes.com/1986/12/28/nyregion/1200-protesters-of-racial-attack-march-in-queens.html.

107. Indeed, this trope has been portrayed to a point of ubiquity, compelling the parody film by Paris Barclay and Keenen Ivory Wayans, *Don't Be A Menace to South Central While Drinking Your Juice in the Hood* (1996), to feature a scene depicting just this.

108. See Carpenter, *Coloring Whiteness*, 215. The acousmatic is defined by dramaturg and theater and performance studies scholar Faedra Chatard Carpenter as "sounds that are heard but not seen." For more on the acousmatic, see Eidsheim, *Race of Sound*.

109. J. W. Roberts, *Trickster to Badman*, 5–6. Folk heroes are defined as figures who at critical moments in time offer certain qualities or behaviors that enhance culture building (or the ability to protect group identity and values in the face of threats) and are therefore embraced as heroes by the groups whose identities they share.

110. "The Block Is Hot," *The Boondocks*, directed by Kalvin Lee (Culver City, CA: Sony Pictures Home Entertainment, 2006), CD.

111. "Pump Up the Volume," MP3 audio, track 4 on The Cool Kids, *Totally Flossed Out EP*, C.A.K.E., 2007.

112. "Good Morning," MP3 audio, track 1 on Kanye West, *Graduation*, Roc-A-Fella Records, 2007.

113. "E=mc²," featuring Common, MP3 audio, track 2 on J Dilla, *The Shining*, BBE Records, 2007.

114. "My Father's Gun," MP3 audio, Danny Brown, *The Hybrid Mixtape*, no record label, 2009.

115. "Tell Me," MP3 audio, track 9 on Hassaan Mackey and Apollo Brown, *Daily Bread*, Mello Music Group, 2011.

116. "C.R.E.A.M 17 (feat. Nick Grant)," MP3 audio, track 2 on Jarren Benton, *The Mink Coat Killa*, Benton Enterprises, 2017.

117. "'It Doesn't Look Good.' Chief Speaks after Pictures Show Shooting Range Targets as Black Men," *WXYZ 7 News Detroit*, July 26, 2022, https://www.wxyz.com/news/farmington-hills-police-to-conduct-review-after-gun-range-targets-show-only-black-men; and Kiara Alfonseca, "Police Department in Georgia Apologizes over Image of Black Man Used for Target Practice," *ABC News*, June 22, 2023, https://abcnews.go.com/US/police-department-georgia-apologizes-image-black-man-target/story?id=100302417. The same visual targets of a black-and-white image of a Black man dressed in a beanie and a jacket while aiming a handgun near his hip were found at Farmington Hills and Villa Rica police shooting ranges.

118. Jem Aswad, "Jorja Smith Drops 'By Any Means,' First Song From Roc Nation's Social-Justice-Themed Album 'Reprise' (Listen)," *Variety* (blog), July 30, 2020, https://variety.com/2020/music/news/jorja-smith-by-any-means-roc-nation-social-justice-1234720877/.

119. King, *Black Shoals*, xi.

120. bmike2c, "As high as the stakes get when paint get low | #paintwhereitaint #RadioRaheem #streetart #graffiti #dotherightthing #spikelee #montanacolors #projectbe," Instagram, May 16, 2014, https://www.instagram.com/bmike2c/p/oCdaj9Am2a/; Times-Picayune and Doug MacCash, "'ExhibitBE,' a Spectacular Outdoor Graffiti Environment, on View Saturday Only," NOLA.com, November

12, 2014, https://www.nola.com/entertainment_life/arts/exhibitbe-a-spectacular-outdoor-graffiti-environment-on-view-saturday-only/article_6ec8d7f8-0501-5d15-98ee-514689cf8340.html; and Leland Kent, "Exhibit Be," *Abandoned Southeast* (blog), June 30, 2019, https://abandonedsoutheast.com/2019/06/29/exhibit-be/.

121. Spike Lee, "NYPD Puts Deadly Chokehold on Staten Island Man," 2014, https://www.youtube.com/watch?v=CS_rm3ai90g&feature=youtube_gdata_player. URL delisted.

122. In Dick's novel, Precrime is a criminal justice agency that uses precog mutants who are able to see up to two weeks into the future. These mutants produce cards that are interpreted by the agency to stop future criminals before they commit crimes.

123. Dick, *Minority Report*, chap. 9.

124. For example, Mother Sister was the old Black lady who watches everything on the block, Da Mayor was the wino, the white guy (self-proclaimed Brooklynite) was the yuppie who moved in to escape the high rent in Manhattan.

125. Adisa Banjoko in Owerko, *Boombox Project*, 61.

126. Sean Eldon, Huron High School commencement address, Ann Arbor, MI, June 17, 2020.

127. See Isabel Wilkerson, "Jury Acquits All Transit Officers in 1983 Death of Michael Stewart," *New York Times*, November 25, 1985, N. Y. / Region, http://www.nytimes.com/1985/11/25/nyregion/jury-acquits-all-transit-officers-in-1983-death-of-michael-stewart.html. Twenty-five-year-old Black graffiti artist Michael Stewart of Brooklyn was arrested on September 15, 1983, at which point he was in transit to police custody for spray-painting graffiti in a Manhattan subway. He was bruised, hogtied, and comatose when admitted to Bellevue Hospital. He died thirteen days later. All six white male transit officers involved with his arrest and accused of permitting Michael to be beaten while in their custody, were acquitted. This incident, in which the police officers went unpunished, echoes the murder of Freddie Gray of Baltimore.

128. Kimberly Kindy and Kimbriell Kelly, "Thousands Dead, Few Prosecuted," *Washington Post*, April 11, 2015, http://www.washingtonpost.com/sf/investigative/2015/04/11/thousands-dead-few-prosecuted/.

129. See Selwyn Raab, "State Judge Dismisses Indictment of Officer in the Bumpurs Killing," *New York Times*, April 13, 1985, N. Y. / Region, http://www.nytimes.com/1985/04/13/nyregion/state-judge-dismisses-indictment-of-officer-in-the-bumpurs-killing.html. Eleanor Bumpurs is the sixty-six-year-old African American woman living in the Bronx's Sedgwick Houses who was shot twice with a shotgun by New York City Police who were enforcing a city-ordered eviction notice. Eleanor was waving a knife at the officers, and one of them shot her hand, shattering the knife and her hand in the process. She was then shot in her chest, with the officer claiming that he continued to feel threatened. The judge dismissed the indictment on manslaughter charges.

130. Young, "Posthumans: Rise of the See-J," 49. Scholarartist John Jennings has referred to himself as a "See-J."

131. Coates, *Between the World and Me*, 112.

132. See Lucy Stehlik, "Chief Keef Takes Chicago's Drill Sound Overground," *Guardian* (US edition), November 16, 2012, Music, http://www.theguardian.com/music/2012/nov/16/chief-keef-chicago-drill-rap#start-of-comments. Chicago drill is a South Side style of music that emerged in early 2010 during what was called a "homicide crisis." It celebrates camaraderie, money, love, and lust, reflects on and premeditates violence, and discusses selling drugs to survive as well as thrive. Stehlik describes the sound of drill as the sonic cousin to footwork, southern hip-hop, and the 808 drum style of trap music.

133. Michael Dunn, "'Loud Music' Shooter Testifying," interview by Cory Strolla, *CNN Newsroom*, February 11, 2014, http://transcripts.cnn.com/TRANSCRIPTS/1402/11/cnr.04.html.

134. Dunn, "'Loud Music.'"

135. Paul Meara, "It's a Drill! The Sound That Has Music Labels Flocking to the Windy City," *AllHipHop*, August 23, 2012, http://allhiphop.com/2012/08/23/its-a-drill-the-sound-that-has-music-labels-flocking-to-the-windy-city/.

136. Shepard Fairey, "Manifesto," Obey Giant, April 18, 1990, http://www.obeygiant.com/articles/manifesto.

137. Ta-Nehisi Coates, "'I Am Still Called by the God I Serve to Walk This Out,'" *Atlantic*, February 25, 2014, http://www.theatlantic.com/politics/archive/2014/02/i-am-still-called-by-the-god-i-serve-to-walk-this-out/284064/.

138. Coates, "'I Am Still Called.'"

139. "Beef," featuring Fredo Santana and Lil Durk, MP3 audio, track 5 on Lil Reese with DJ Drama and Don Cannon, *Don't Like: A Gangsta Grillz Exclusive*, 2012. In the scenario where Dunn asks Jordan and his friends to turn down their music, and they do so only to turn it up again, "Beef" must be read differently. For example, "Ain't playin' fair so we keep them things" alludes to the way that the odds have been stacked against Jordan and his friends as Black men, requiring them to metaphorically even the odds with figurative weapons. "Fuck nigga you don't want no Beef" is suggestive of how white men who tout their white entitlement are immediately relegated to being unlikeable while insisting that they do not want conflict with Black folks like Jordan and his friends. "Run up on 'em you better think again" builds on the previous idea that white men had better think twice before provoking conflict with and flashing their entitlement in the faces of Jordan and his friends. "Free all of my niggas" points to a sense that not only are there Black men locked up for crimes they did not commit but also there are Black men suffering from the same white entitlement and privilege smothering Jordan and his friends in their confrontation with Dunn.

140. swhiteAKA3, Twitter, February 3, 2014, http://www.twitter.com/swhiteAKA3.

141. Black, gender, and performance studies scholar Vershawn Ashanti Young discusses how Black men are feared and how our knowledge of this level of legibility inspires varying performances of quieting down or "testing out just how equal our society is by speaking out freely instead of shape shifting." V. A. Young, *Average Nigga*, 144.

Chapter 3. Woman Wakes Up to Find Intruder in Her Bed

Epigraph: panhead, "This actually aired on my local news today. 'Obviously we have a rapist here . . . so hide yo kids, hide yo wife, and hide yo husband 'cause dey rapin' e'rybody out here,'" Reddit, July 29, 2010, http://www.reddit.com/r/funny/comments/cuvn3/this_actually_aired_on_my_local_news_today/.

1. In *Going Viral* by information scientists Karine Nahon and Jeff Hemsley (35), the concept of going viral is explained as a remarkably new possibility made feasible by the sharing of information across digital social networks at an alarming speed and with a previously unattainable reach, standing out in a "sea of content." While this suffices as a definition, it does not tell us how (a modicum of) this virality is sustained over longer periods—which can explain how past viral performances continue to resurface—their "viral afterlife"—albeit sometimes at smaller or slower rates of virality.

2. See WPMI, "Leprechaun in Mobile, Alabama," posted March 17, 2006, by botmib, YouTube, 2:03, https://www.youtube.com/watch?v=nda_OSWeyn8; and "The Branding," streaming video, 22:00, *Key and Peele* (New York: Comedy Central, February 21, 2012), https://tv.apple.com/us/episode/the-branding/umc.cmc.dkawielqhsf2berci7cfnx85?showId=umc.cmc.3zn0d5n33p17buheotza10yfs. In 2006, shortly after the creation of YouTube, the WPMI NBC 15 news station sought the testimonies of Black Americans in the Crichton area of Mobile, Alabama. In an episode titled "The Branding," Keegan-Michael Key and Jordan Peele performed a parody of the moment, but instead of a leprechaun, it was Pegasus. That is to say, the trope was quite common.

3. I use "goin' viral" to emphasize Black virality through an African American vernacular English.

4. See moyazb, "They Aren't Talking about Me . . . ," *Crunk Feminist Collective* (blog), March 14, 2020, http://www.crunkfeministcollective.com/2010/03/14/they-arent-talking-about-me/; M. Bailey and Trudy, "On Misogynoir," 762–68; and M. Bailey, *Misogynoir Transformed*, 1.

5. JanMohamed, "Sexuality on/of the Border," 112–13; Higginbotham, "African-American Women's History," 251–74; M. M. Bailey and Stallings, "Antiblack Racism," 614–21; and Vidal-Ortiz, Robinson, and Khan, *Race and Sexuality*, 44–59.

6. See Lindsey, "Post-Ferguson," 232–37. Black feminist theorist Treva B. Lindsey advocates for a "herstorical approach" to what she calls "Black violability" so that Black women do not continue to be rendered by others as unable to be scathed by state-initiated and sanctioned violence against them. See also Hartman, *Scenes of Subjection*, 137–97; King, "Black 'Feminisms,'" 76; and Moore and Pipkin, "Are *All* the Blacks?," 33–34.

7. Treva B. Lindsey, "The Lack of Mobilized Outrage for Police Killing Black Women Is an Injurious Erasure," *Bustle*, June 3, 2020, https://www.bustle.com/p/the-lack-of-mobilized-outrage-for-police-killing-black-women-is-injurious-erasure-22953764.

8. See Ransby, *Making All Black Lives Matter*, 45–46. We see how virality is used as leverage for liberation in the Free Marissa Now campaign.

9. My use of "(Black) objecthood" builds on how McMillan rescrambles the binary between objectified bodies and the embodied subject, with "[B]lack objecthood" being a means toward agency rather than "a primal site of injury." Surely, McMillan writes, "the borders between subjectivity and objecthood are not nearly as distinct as we pretend they are . . . and never have been." McMillan, "Performing Objects," 9–10.

10. Bernstein, "Dances with Things," 67–94; and Foster, *Reinventing Hoodia*, 88–100. "Things," such as a racist coloring book, are analyzed by cultural historian Robin Bernstein in a way that limits them to pejorative connotations of Blackness. It is essential to analyze such denigrations, yet such an analysis can miss the aspects of the things that may be generative of critical meanings of the pejorative. Taking these contentions outside of the human, African and gender studies scholar Laura Foster's examinations on hoodia's politics in South Africa show how the plant, commodified by companies for weight loss, chemically resisted being transformed into the object that scientists and corporations desired.

11. Antoine Dodson, "Antoine Dodson NPR Interview," posted September 4, 2010, by The truth?, YouTube, 8:19, https://www.youtube.com/watch?v=4r2poH70YPA.

12. Elizabeth Gentle, "Woman Wakes Up to Find Intruder in Her Bed," *WAFF 48 News*, July 28, 2010, https://www.waff.com/story/12883477/woman-wakes-up-to-find-intruder-in-her-bed/.

13. Dodson, "Antoine Dodson NPR Interview."

14. Elizabeth Gentle, "Overnight Internet Sensation Reacts to New-Found Fame," *WAFF 48 News*, July 30, 2010, https://www.waff.com/story/12901080/overnight-internet-sensation-reacts-to-new-found-fame/.

15. Reddit is a social news website, then known as the front page of the Internet and now understood as a community of communities.

16. panhead, "This actually aired on my local news today. 'Obviously, we have a rapist here . . . so hide yo kids, hide yo wife, and hide yo husband 'cause dey rapin' e'rybody out here.'"

17. "Antoine Dodson / Bed Intruder," added July 30, 2010, created by Chris Watson, Know Your Meme, http://knowyourmeme.com/memes/antoine-dodson-bed-intruder. The oldest video footage of the original newscast can be found here: WAFF 48 News, "Woman Wakes Up to Find Intruder in Her Bed," posted July 29, 2010, by iKING, YouTube video, 2:02, https://www.youtube.com/watch?v=uzKtPezPsqE.

18. WAFF 48 News, "Bed Intruder *Original Extended Version* (Woman Wakes Up to Find an Intruder in Her Bed)," posted August 6, 2010, by Matt Kolditz, YouTube video, 2:51, https://www.youtube.com/watch?v=W91wh8J33pw (URL delisted); and Jamie Loftus, "Hide Your Kids, Hide Your Wife Pt 1," Sixteenth Minute (of Fame), accessed May 11, 2024, https://omny.fm/shows/sixteenthminute/hide-your-kids-hide-your-wife-pt-1?in_playlist=sixteenthminute. Antoine Dodson shares that Kelly Dodson, her daughter, her sister, and their mother all had nightmares, sometimes waking up and screaming out of their sleep.

19. WAFF 48 News, "Woman Wakes Up."

20. WAFF 48 News.

21. "Grassroots intermediaries may often serve the needs of content creators, demonstrating how audiences become part of the logic of the marketplace and challenging what 'grassroots' means, as such activities often coexist or even coincide with corporate agendas. They are not, however, employed or regulated by content creators and also may act to counter corporate goals." Jenkins, Ford, and Green, *Spreadable Media*, 7.

22. Gregory Brothers [schmoyoho], "Bed Intruder Song!!!"

23. Dave MacDowell, *Hide Your Husbands!*, 2013, acrylic on canvas, 18 × 24," DirtyPilot, https://dirtypilot.com/products/dave-macdowell-hide-your-husbands-painting.

24. RobotKristen14, "They're climbing your districts They're snatchin your tributes up, tryna reap em so y'all need to hid [*sic*] your kids, hide your wife and hide your husband cuz they're reapin errbody out there . . . ," February 18, 2014, comment on "Bed Intruder Song!!!," then titled "Auto-Tune the News: Bed Intruder Song!!! (Now on iTunes)."

25. The infamous double rainbow broadcast has also been autotuned by the Gregory Brothers. Yosemitebear62, "Yosemitebear Mountain Double Rainbow 1–8–10," January 8, 2010, YouTube, 3:29, https://www.youtube.com/watch?v=OQSNhk5ICTI.

26. A&E, "Best Cry Ever," posted April 16, 2010, by Dan Allen, YouTube video, 0:37, https://www.youtube.com/watch?v=ee925OTFBCA.

27. Jessi Slaughter, "Jessi Slaughter—Ya Dun Goofed," posted July 25, 2010, by MemeTownUSA, YouTube video, 2:00, https://www.youtube.com/watch?v=NEfY3kMnG4E&feature=emb_title.

28. B. Brown, "Thing Theory," 3.

29. B. Brown, 5.

30. "Google Taps into Search Patterns," *BBC News*, December 22, 2005, http://news.bbc.co.uk/2/hi/technology/4551936.stm.

31. Rob Sheffield, "How Nipplegate Created YouTube," *Rolling Stone*, February 11, 2020, https://www.rollingstone.com/culture/culture-features/youtube-origin-nipplegate-janet-jackson-justin-timberlake-949019/.

32. When I began this project, I wish I had anticipated the extent to which media would be lost, delisted, or completely transformed. I did not take screenshots of the main videos I discuss on YouTube and WorldStarHipHop as they appeared in 2010 and 2009. Other people's screenshots, nonetheless, served to illustrate the general web design that I gesture to. From what I recall, between 2010 and 2011, not much changed regarding YouTube's aesthetic design, which is why this example from 2011 mostly works here.

33. R. Benjamin, *Race after Technology*, Anti-Black Box section, approximately p. 67.

34. S. Browne, *Dark Matters*, 18.

35. McKittrick and Woods, *Black Geographies*, 7.

36. Steve Doyle, "Huntsville Housing Authority's Lincoln Park Public Housing Site in Line for Facelift," *Advance Local* (blog), January 23, 2012, http://blog.al.com/breaking/2012/01/huntsville_housing_authoritys_2.html.

37. Steve Doyle, "Huntsville Housing Authority Pushes Redevelopment of Sparkman Homes, Lincoln Park Public Housing Sites to Back Burner," *Advance Local* (blog), updated July 1, 2013, http://blog.al.com/breaking/2013/07/huntsville_housing_authority_p.html.

38. See Loftus, "Hide Your Kids." I find it notable that Kevin Antoine Dodson later revealed that he had opened the kitchen window to release the smoke produced from cooking steak that evening. This action allowed the intruder to escape when he was later confronted in the apartment. I also understand this circumstance as stemming from a lack of ventilation, making the residence less secure.

39. "White men have said over and over—and we have believed it because it was repeated so often—that not only was there no such thing as a chaste Negro woman—but that a Negro woman could not be assaulted, that it was never against her will.—Jessie Daniel Ames (1936)." See J. Hall, "'Mind That Burns,'" 331. Treva B. Lindsey also discusses the importance of countering the historical inviolability of Black women in *Colored No More*, 12.

40. McGlotten, "Black Data," approximately para 41.

41. E. B. Brown, "Negotiating and Transforming," 119.

42. McKittrick, *Demonic Grounds*, xii.

43. Goodwin and Alim, "Whatever," 190.

44. While Black feminist scholar of visual culture Nicole R. Fleetwood considers iconicity to suggest "the ways in which singular images or [(trans)aesthetic] signs come to represent a whole host of historical occurrences and processes," I move to think about how one viral performance can come to represent a host of related performances. Fleetwood, *Troubling Vision*, 2.

45. E. P. Johnson, *Appropriating Blackness*, 68.

46. Yao, *Disaffected*, 6. Here, Kelly Dodson's antisociality functions as a kind of disaffection, a survival tactic that allows her to care for and control representations of her life beyond the trauma that had already been derisively recognized.

47. NPR Staff, "Antoine Dodson: Riding YouTube out of the 'Hood,'" *NPR*, August 23, 2010, http://www.npr.org/templates/story/story.php?storyId=129381037.

48. S. Browne, *Dark Matters*, 21.

49. See Diamond, *Performance and Cultural Politics*, 1. Performance is inter-referential, "embed[ding] features of previous performances," but appears as one performance.

50. Loftus, "Hide Your Kids."

51. S. Browne, *Dark Matters*, 9.

52. Campt, *Listening to Images*, 8.

53. Jones, *Theatrical Jazz*, 118.

54. Dodson, "Antoine Dodson NPR Interview."

55. Antoine Dodson, "Antoine Dodson on Judge Alex!," from *Judge Alex*, posted February 20, 2011, WorldStarHipHop, 11:12, https://worldstar.com/videos/wshhdhppJv6uZH1kfv17/antoine-dodson-on-judge-alex.

56. E. P. Johnson, "'Quare' Studies," 10 (italics in the original).

57. See Diamond, *Performance and Cultural Politics*, 5.

58. E. P. Johnson, "'Quare' Studies," 7.

59. H. Young, *Embodying Black Experience*, 8–9.

60. Spillers, "Mama's Baby," 67.

61. Petty, *Stealing the Show*, 6.

62. L3M0NP3PPA, Twitter, August 1, 2010, https://twitter.com/L3M0NP3PPA/status/20086767080?s=20. See #ghettowitness on Twitter.

63. J. L. Jackson, *Real Black*, 59–60.

64. Brock, *Distributed Blackness*, 146. Black digital studies scholar André Brock discusses the signifyin' practices of Black Twitter through inventive pseudonym display names alongside usernames that afford interactors "cultural specificity" and belonging while cueing their audiences in to Black culture. Here, the lemon pepper spice is a pseudonym, instead used as a username similar to display names, cueing audiences into the diverse finger-licking palate of Blackness.

65. KRON 4 News, "The Whistles Go . . . Whoo Whoo!," posted January 25, 2006, by LILOUTLAW209, YouTube, 2:21, https://www.youtube.com/watch?v=Nnzw_i4YmKk&feature=youtube_gdata_player.

66. WPMI, "Leprechaun in Mobile, Alabama."

67. KFORTV and K. Querry, "Oklahoma City Apartment Complex Catches Fire, 5 Units Damaged; Sweet Brown Explains," *KFOR*, April 8, 2012, https://kfor.com/news/okc-apartment-complex-catches-fire-5-units-damaged/.

68. News 5 Cleveland, "Charles Ramsey Interview."

69. *Unbreakable Kimmy Schmidt*, season 1, episode 12, "Kimmy Goes to Court," directed by Tina Fey and Robert Carlock, Netflix video, March 6, 2015. It is important to note here that the Gregory Brothers produced *The Unbreakable Kimmy Schmidt* theme song, which features a fictional Ghetto Witness named Walter Bankston.

70. Andy Carvin, "'Bed Intruder' Meme: A Perfect Storm of Race, Music, Comedy and Celebrity," *NPR*, August 5, 2010, http://www.npr.org/sections/alltechconsidered/2010/08/05/129005122/youtube-bed-intruder-meme.

71. J. L. Jackson, *Real Black*, 15.

72. Alsultany, "Arabs and Muslims," 162.

73. Larson, *Media and Minorities*, 82.

74. E. P. Johnson, *Appropriating Blackness*, 217.

75. E. P. Johnson, 83.

76. Black feminist and Black performance theorist Leticia Ridley discusses the tension between excess and abundance of Black performances. Where the white normative gaze views a Black performance as too much, a Black gaze might consider it as abundant with necessities. For me, the tension between the two concepts relies on a spectator's sensibilities, which determines the appropriateness of the Black performance. Convening (Black Performance Theory 2023: Choreographing in Black, Northwestern University, Chicago Campus, April 21–23, 2023), https://bpt202304.wixsite.com/choreographinblack.

77. Muñoz, "Disidentifications," 5.

78. McGlotten, "Black Data." We might also consider postcolonial theorist Edouard Glissant's notion of opacity as a strategy to protect "that which cannot be reduced." Glissant, *Poetics of Relation*, 191.

79. See Neal, *Looking for Leroy*, 4.

80. Neal, 62.

81. E. P. Johnson, *Appropriating Blackness*, 68.

82. The Gregory Brothers, "The Gregory Brothers (Creators of Antoine Dodson Bed Intruder) Interview On Monique," from *The Mo'Nique Show*, season 2, episode 63, aired February 2, 2011, posted March 25, 2011, by MJTheKingOfDance4, YouTube. URL delisted.

83. See Higginbotham, *Righteous Discontent*, 187–219. I refer to "conservative respectability politics" because the Black clubwomen at the turn of the nineteenth century, referenced when Black feminist historian Evelyn Brooks Higginbotham coined the term, used the politics of respectability as a strategy for defending their humanity against those who would denigrate them for their decorum in light of ideas around racialized gender and sexuality. The broader politics involve the respect of one's dignity, which can be understood conservatively or liberally.

84. Gentle, "Overnight Internet Sensation."

85. See Duggan, *Twilight of Equality*, 5. Neoliberalists, for instance, assign inequalities to "private" life and label them as "natural," and, as a result of the concept of the private (civil society, family, etc.) vs. the public (state, economy, etc.), those inequalities have nothing to do with the life of the state or economy and everything to do with personal responsibility.

86. Dodson, "Antoine Dodson NPR Interview."

87. Dodson, "Antoine Dodson NPR Interview."

88. Antoine Dodson, "'Bed Intruder Song' Exclusive Interview," interview by Shira Lazar, CBS, August 18, 2010, YouTube, 5:23, http://www.youtube.com/watch?v=og5znBpNEh8&feature=youtube_gdata_player.

89. Spade, "Keynote Address," 291.

90. Esparza, "Queering the Homeland," 150.

91. Esparza, 150.

92. Esparza, 154.

93. In expanding our notion of punishment under slavery to include sexual coercion, Angela Davis points out that this framing of Black women as aggressive and promiscuous was a projection of deviance originating with the sexual violence that enslavers inflicted on enslaved Africans. She writes, "The deviance of the slave master was transferred to the slave woman, whom he victimized. . . . The notion that female 'deviance' always has a sexual dimension persists in the contemporary era, and this intersection of criminality and sexuality continues to be racialized." A. Y. Davis, *Are Prisons Obsolete?*, 68.

94. Cooper, *Voice from the South*, 25.

95. Dodson, "Antoine Dodson NPR Interview."

96. Crenshaw, "Mapping the Margins," 1253.

97. Hine, "Rape and Inner Lives," 912–20.

98. Antoine Dodson, "'Bed Intruder Song' Exclusive Interview." Responding to interviewer Shira Lazar about making a difference, Dodson revealed that most of his fans were "victims of rape or molestation" who had reached out to him and

that he would console and comfort them. I am specific about US public housing, as other countries, such as Singapore, are very active and innovative in the infrastructure of their public housing; therefore, public housing should not be taken as a synonym for poorly maintained housing.

99. Carpenter, *Coloring Whiteness*, 211–12.

100. "Thingification," Duriel E. Harris, accessed September 2, 2014, http://www.thingification.org/. An earlier 1955 use of *thingification* by poet, Pan-African scholar, and postcolonial theorist Aimé Césaire is literally equated to colonization, which is more limiting than the ways Harris repurposes it through performance. See Césaire, *Discourse on Colonialism*, 42.

101. hooks, *Black Looks*, 128.

102. Moten, *In The Break*, 10–11.

103. A. Johnson, "(Mis)Appropriation," 161. Communication studies scholar Amber Johnson's intersectional examination of this incident was concerned with how Antoine Dodson began to use the unique defense of his sister for monetary gain and how social media users perceived that as "coonery." Johnson also explores the ways in which his behavior challenged normative gender roles.

104. See A. Y. Davis, *Women, Race and Class*, 19.

105. Spillers, "Mama's Baby," 80.

106. Spillers, 80.

107. M. M. Bailey, *Butch Queens*, 31, 36.

108. Muñoz, "Disidentifications," 4.

109. Muñoz, 1–34. "When used positively, [fierce] is said of a characteristic that is exceptionally good or of behavior that is well done; when used ironically, it expresses a negative judgment." M. M. Bailey, *Butch Queens*, 253. I use the exceptional quality encompassed by "fierce" positively here.

110. Wallace, *Black Macho*, 106–7.

111. Dodson, "Antoine Dodson NPR Interview."

Chapter 4. Suggestions

Epigraph: AwesomeAostin, comment on "Auto-Tune the News: Bed Intruder Song!!! (Now on iTunes)," since renamed "Bed Intruder Song!!!"

1. Simon Reynolds, "How Auto-Tune Revolutionized the Sound of Popular Music," *Pitchfork*, September 17, 2018, https://pitchfork.com/features/article/how-auto-tune-revolutionized-the-sound-of-popular-music/.

2. schmoyoho, "Bed Intruder Song!!!" The Gregory Brothers changed the title "Auto-Tune the News: Bed Intruder Song!!!" to "Bed Intruder Song!!! (Now on iTunes)," signaling the choice to brand the song and sell it. Today, long after its peak virality, it is known simply as "Bed Intruder Song!!!"

3. Noble, *Algorithms of Oppression*, 25. Media and African American studies scholar Safiya Umoja Noble differentiates the algorithms of today's Internet from those of the early Internet directories, where there was more human curation.

4. Williams-Forson, *Building Houses*, 166.

5. Kozinets, "I Want to Believe," 470. The term "netnography" was an anonymous reviewer's suggestion for this qualitative method informed by consumer research, conventions and approaches of cultural anthropology, and cultural studies.

6. The World Wide Web is a system of interlinked hypertext documents accessed through the Internet, not to be confused with the Internet itself, which is an infrastructure of interconnected networks.

7. For additional details on netnography, see Kozinets, "I Want to Believe"; "On Netnography"; and *Netnography*.

8. Kozinets, *Netnography*, 32–34. A *newbie* is a new member attempting to learn about an online community and reach out to establish social relationships; a *maker* constructs the online spaces in which communities are situated; an *interactor* is defined more narrowly than my use of the term implies, and it encompasses hybrid involvement by someone who is between online and in-person whereby their online interactions are in relationship to their consumption and involvement in an in-person space; and a *networker* becomes involved in communities for the explicit purpose of creating social ties and interactions with online community members.

9. Kozinets, 35.

10. I appreciate African studies scholar, anthropologist, and queer theorist Kwame Otu's insight into my use of *they* here and how it is important in how I navigate race, gender, and other ways to identify and be identified in these digital performances as I use netnography.

11. Here, I borrow language from performer and musical anthropologist Jonathan H. Shannon's description of Tarab—the process of reaching that special state of emotional rapture or enchantment, sadness or joy, experienced while listening to and performing good Arab music; it is "that feeling you get when you listen to music, and it just makes you want to say aah!" and describes the affectual labor that is a necessary aspect of a performance's going viral. Shannon, "Emotion, Performance, and Temporality," 72, 74.

12. The Gregory Brothers, "Info: A White 'Country and Soul, Folk and Roll' band," Facebook, January 7, 2010, http://www.facebook.com/gregorybrothers?v=info. They self-described as a country and soul, folk and roll band in 2010; however, this particular self-identification has likely changed.

13. Annoying Orange, "Annoying Orange—Kitchen Intruder (Bed Intruder Spoof) with AutoTune Remix!," November 23, 2010, YouTube, 2:11, https://www.youtube.com/watch?v=pezdRcVe04c&feature=kp.

14. Annoying Orange, "Kitchen Intruder."

15. Butler, "Imitation," 313 (italics in the original).

16. White, *Jim Crow to Jay-Z*, 99.

17. See Colbert, "Black Movements," 140. Black performance theorist Soyica Diggs Colbert's notion of "absent presence" informs me here. In her essay, Colbert describes a woman named Ryna (from novelist and Black feminist scholar Toni Morrison's *Song of Solomon*), who haunts walkers who pass by the area where she had lost her mind—Ryna's Gulch—flinging herself on the ground and crying without the rest of her corporeality present.

18. J. L. Jackson, *Thin Description*, 178.

19. blezard2011, comment on "Bed Intruder Song!!!," November 3, 2010.

20. jackred5, comment on "Bed Intruder Song!!!," December 5, 2010.

21. Zceed, comment on "Bed Intruder Song!!!," December 5, 2010.

22. The title change from "Bed Intruder Song!!! (Now on iTunes)" to "Antoine Dodson—They Rape'n Everybody Out Here (Auto Tune Edition)" shifts attention, once again, to Antoine, erasing the rape attempt on Kelly Dodson and the home invasion that sparked the conflict in the first place.

23. Thomas, "Frames," 119–35.

24. Thomas, 122.

25. McCune, "'Out' in the Club," 311.

26. Peter V. Milo, "'CNN of the Ghetto': WorldStarHipHop Becoming YouTube for Urban Violence," *CBS Atlanta*, March 29, 2012, https://web.archive.org/web/20120502141528/http://atlanta.cbslocal.com/2012/03/29/worldstarhiphop-website-becoming-youtube-for-urban-violence/.

27. Breakfast Club Power 105.1 FM, "Breakfast Club Classic—Lee 'Q' O'Denat Talks How WorldStarHipHop Was Created and More," January 24, 2017, YouTube, 15:47, https://www.youtube.com/watch?v=3Sbm5HVYQsk.

28. Mark Jacobson, "WorldStar, Baby!," *New York Magazine*, February 5, 2012, https://nymag.com/news/features/worldstar-2012-2/?curator=MusicREDEF.

29. David Zurawick, "Worldstarhiphop.com Makes a Name for Itself with Violent Viral Videos," *Baltimore Sun*, March 23, 2012, http://articles.baltimoresun.com/2012-03-23/entertainment/bs-ae-zontv-worldstar-20120323_1_shock-video-ski-mask-third-video.

30. Zurawick, "Worldstarhiphop.com."

31. Marc Kerschhagel, "Media Market: Media Consumption Trends among Black Men" (New York: Opportunity Agenda, 2011), 109. https://www.opensocietyfoundations.org/publications/opportunity-black-men-and-boys-public-opinion-media-depictions-and-media-consumption#publications_download.

32. "Statistics," YouTube, accessed June 4, 2014, http://www.youtube.com/yt/press/statistics.html. URL delisted; Zotero snapshot in the author's possession.

33. Hayley Tsukayama, "In Online Video, Minorities Find an Audience," *Washington Post,* April 20, 2012, https://www.washingtonpost.com/business/economy/in-online-video-minorities-find-an-audience/2012/04/20/gIQAdhliWT_story.html.

34. Tsukayama, "Online Video."

35. Currency refers to popularity as much as it nods toward fiscal capital—with users able to generate income based on channel subscriptions and views.

36. The Gregory Brothers rebranded the series *Songify the News*.

37. "Antoine Dodson / Bed Intruder," added July 30, 2010, created by Chris Watson, Know Your Meme, http://knowyourmeme.com/memes/antoine-dodson-bed-intruder.

38. Nigel D, "The Fruits of Antoine Dodson's Labor," *Uproxx*, December 12, 2010, http://smokingsection.uproxx.com/TSS/2010/09/the-fruits-of-antoine-dodsons-labor. URL delisted; Zotero snapshot in the author's possession. The source is also archived in the Wayback Machine, an initiative of the Internet Archive.

39. Antoine Dodson and the Gregory Brothers, "Antoine and the Gregory Brothers Meet the Press," posted March 24, 2011, by antoinedodson24, YouTube. URL delisted.

40. Antoine Dodson, "Antoine Dodson," Facebook page, August 14, 2010. URL delisted.

41. E. P. Johnson, *Appropriating Blackness*, 5.

42. schmoyoho [The Gregory Brothers], "Michael Gregory Performs Tupac/Twista," April 30, 2007, YouTube, 4:33, https://www.youtube.com/watch?v=fE1j06-qeTk.

43. "The history moves from public rapes, beatings, and lynchings to the gladiatorial arenas of basketball and boxing. . . . White men have been the stagers and consumers of the historical spectacles I have mentioned, but in one way or another, Black people have been looking, too, forging a traumatized collective historical memory which is reinvoked, I believe, at contemporary sites." E. P. Johnson, *Appropriating Blackness*, 44.

44. The sales of the songs are reported according to Antoine Dodson's Web Redemption episode on *Tosh.0*, season 3, episode 1. See Antoine Dodson, "Tosh.0—January 11, 2011—Antoine Dodson," January 10, 2011, YouTube, 21:00, https://www.youtube.com/watch?v=nzxxSnPeAS8.

45. "Gold and Platinum: The Gregory Brothers and Antoine Dodson," Recording Industry Association of America, April 10, 2014, https://www.riaa.com/gold-platinum/?tab_active=default-award&se=antoine+dodson#search_section.

46. Dodson, "Tosh.0—January 11, 2011."

47. Antoine Dodson, "'Bed Intruder Song' Exclusive Interview," interviewed by Shira Lazar, posted August 18, 2010, by CBS, YouTube, 5:23, http://www.youtube.com/watch?v=og5znBpNEh8&feature=youtube_gdata_player.

48. schmoyoho, "Bed Intruder Song!!!"

49. For more about trap music as well as its differentiation from trap in electronic dance music, see Miles Raymer, "Who Owns Trap? Does Music Born of Dirty South Drug Wars Have Any Place in Squeaky-Clean Dance Clubs?" *Chicago Reader*, November 20, 2012, http://www.chicagoreader.com/chicago/trap-rap-edm-flosstradamus-uz-jeffrees-lex-luger/Content?oid=7975249.

50. "SpottieOttieDopaliscious," featuring Sleepy Brown, CD audio, track 12 on OutKast, *Aquemini*, LaFace, 1998.

51. Bradley, *Chronicling Stankonia*, 82.

52. This description also appears in Moten's chapter "Visible Music" in *In The Break*, 200.

53. The Gregory Brothers, "The Gregory Brothers (Creators of Antoine Dodson Bed Intruder) Interview on Monique," from *The Mo'Nique Show*, season 2, episode 63, aired February 2, 2011, posted March 25, 2011, by MJTheKingOfDance4, YouTube. URL delisted.

54. MaNgAnlmE, comment on "Bed Intruder Song!!!," January 26, 2011.

55. airstrike141, comment on "Bed Intruder Song!!!," February 27, 2011.

56. Eliot Van Buskirk, "Gregory Brothers of 'Bed Intruder' Fame Discuss TV Pilot, Antoine Dodson," *Wired*, August 13, 2010, http://www.wired.com/2010/08/gregory-brothers-bed-intruder-antoine-dodson-autotune/.

57. I borrow "miscasting" from performance studies scholar and theater historian Joseph Roach, who, in *Cities of the Dead: Circum-Atlantic Performance* (1), studies how cultures of the past or the voices of the dead are (re)imagined, (re)presented, and embodied by the performance of their descendants in the present. These revisions create new identities and performances that evoke theatrical expressions "such as casting and miscasting, script and improvisation, memory and imagination."

58. "Antoine Dodson—They Rape'n Everybody Out Here [Auto Tune Edition]," August 1, 2010, submitted by louisdaprince, WorldStarHipHop, 2:08, http://www.worldstarhiphop.com/videos/video.php?v=wshhYiib0xKG1Tu8tpG1.

59. D. Roberts, *Killing the Black Body*, 11.

60. "They Rape'n Everybody."

61. Manning, *Race in Motion*, 10.

62. Manning, xvi.

63. Laplap9370, comment on "Bed Intruder Song!!!," January 5, 2011.

64. Irockgame1, comment on January 23, 2011.

65. baradona10, comment on May 8, 2011.

66. Collins, *Black Feminist Thought*, 147.

67. See "Toddler Removed from Home after Viral Swearing Video," *NPR*, January 14, 2014, http://www.npr.org/2014/01/14/262404302/toddler-removed-from-home-after-viral-swearing-video. A case that reflects this criminalization of Black boys involved a Facebook post of a Black baby boy being abusively cursed at by an adult and responding by cursing back at that adult. Omaha police found the video and reposted it on their union's website with the words "The thug cycle continues," which suggests a direct correlation between an abusive social moment in this Black boy's childhood and anticipated thug behavior in his adulthood.

68. Stallings, *Dirty South Manifesto*, 189.

69. Hughey and Daniels, "Racist Comments," 336.

70. jcords400z, comment on "Bed Intruder Song!!!," November 3, 2010.

71. McBride, "Can the Queen Speak?," 371.

72. Ross, *Sissy Insurgencies*, x.

73. Riggs, "Black Macho Revisited," 390.

74. "They Rape'n Everybody."

75. E. P. Johnson, *Appropriating Blackness*, 69.

76. While Antoine Dodson did reveal that he was gay later in 2010, I am attempting to treat his sexuality in this section as unknowable, challenging the popular anticipation of his sexuality simply based on his perceived femininity. I am offering a capacity for his sexuality to be fluid and unmoored to visual and sonic cues, let alone a lifetime desire. My disloyalty to the fixity of sexuality is useful in considering the reality that Dodson has identified as straight since 2013. This, however, falls beyond the scope of my project. Pat Ammons, "YouTube Sensation Antoine Dodson Confirms: He's Leaving the Gay Life, Wants a Wife," AL.com, May 3, 2013, https://www.al.com/breaking/2013/05/youtube_sensation_antoine_dods_1.html.

77. Dodson, "Exclusive Interview." Shira Lazar of CBS News asks Dodson if he "realize[d] how people would react to [his] reaction and the way [he was] answering

the questions." He tells Lazar that he "really didn't care" because he was "so angry" and "didn't want [what happened] to get swept under the rug," so he just "put it out there like it was."

78. See Kelley, *Race Rebels*, 210–13. Marxist surrealist feminist Robin Kelley uses the ways that "nigga" is employed on the West Coast to understand ghettocentricity.

79. Kelley, 213.

80. "They Rape'n Everybody."

81. Jonathan Green, "jigaboo," *Green's Dictionary of Slang*, New Oxford American Dictionary, 2011, http://www.oxfordreference.com/view/10.1093/acref/9780199829941.001.0001/acref-9780199829941-e-25614?rskey=TNunH3&result=2.

82. A. Everett, "Revolution Will Be Digitized," 133.

83. J. L. Jackson, *Thin Description*, 177.

84. Franck, "When I Enter," 240–45.

85. See Haraway, "Cyborg Manifesto," 149–81; Nelson, "Future Texts," 1–15; Nakamura and Chow-White, "Race and Digital Technology," 1–2; and Maragh-Lloyd, *Black Networked Resistance*, 126–27.

86. McGlotten, *Virtual Intimacies*, 122.

87. Nakamura and Chow-White, "Race and Digital Technology," 17.

88. Topos Partnership, *Literature Review: Media Representations and Impact on the Lives of Black Men and Boys* (New York: Opportunity Agenda, 2011), 13–14.

89. Topos Partnership, 43.

90. US Department of Justice Civil Rights Division, *Investigation*, 74.

91. Civil Rights Division, 62.

92. Walcott, *Long Emancipation*, 2.

93. S. Hall, "What Is This 'Black'?," 113 (italics in the original).

94. Quashie, *Sovereignty of Quiet*, 3.

95. Keeling, "Passing for Human," 246–47.

96. KFOR Oklahoma's News 4, "Sweet Brown on Apartment Fire."

97. Tompkins, *Racial Indigestion*, 90–91.

98. Tompkins, 91.

99. Parody Factory, "Sweet Brown—Ain't Nobody."

100. Maultsby, "Africanisms," 201.

101. Maultsby, 201.

102. Photo stills taken from Parody Factory, "Sweet Brown—Ain't Nobody."

103. Keeling, "Passing for Human," 248.

104. Keeling, 242.

105. MadXMaverick, comment on "Sweet Brown—Ain't Nobody," May 24, 2012.

106. mynameissparkle1, comment on "Sweet Brown—Ain't Nobody," August 4, 2012.

107. suparboysean, *The Justice League*, Reddit, May 11, 2013, https://www.reddit.com/r/funny/comments/1e4zjf/the_justice_league/.

108. News 5 Cleveland, "Charles Ramsey Interview"; and schmoyoho, "Dead Giveaway!," May 7, 2013, YouTube, 1:28, https://www.youtube.com/watch?v=nZcRU00p5P4&t=5s. Ramsey of Cleveland was responsible for the 2013

rescue of three kidnapped girls—Amanda Berry, Georgina "Gina" DeJesus, and Michelle Knight—who had gone missing more than a decade before. In a WEWS News Channel 5 interview, Ramsey is asked, "What was the reaction on the girls' faces?" Dismissing the question and instead analyzing the fact that Berry had run into his arms, he remarks, "Bro, I knew som'n was wrong when a little pretty white girl ran into a Black man's arms. Something is wrooooong here . . ." Someone starts laughing in the background. The newscaster, attempting to end the interview at this point says, "Charles." Ramsey continues, "Deead giveaway." Trying again to end the interview, the newscaster replies, "Charles, thank you very much." Ramsey insists, "Deeeeeeeeaaaaad giveaway!" The newscaster continues, "Thank you very much for your time." Ramsey concludes, "Either she homeless or she got problems, that's the only reason why she run to a Black man." Smiling, the newscaster replies, "Charles, thank—" patting Ramsey once on the chest, "—thank you for being there, man." Ramsey was memeified and further popularized by the Gregory Brothers before appearing in *The Justice League*. He was also referenced on the comment wall of "Bed Intruder Song!!!" For example, YouTube interactor MoizAudio (May 7, 2013) commented "CHARLES RAMSEY!!!," receiving fifty-six likes; billytan888 (May 7, 2013) commented, "I was watching Charles Ramsey . . . now I am here."

109. RealCharlesRamsey, "I Am Charles Ramsey, the Scary-Looking Black Dude Who Helped Rescue Three Kidnapped Women from That Freak Ariel Castro in Cleveland One Year Ago . . . AMA," Reddit, May 14, 2014, https://www.reddit.com/r/IAmA/comments/25ghyz/i_am_charles_ramsey_the_scarylooking_black_dude/.

110. Gene Demby, "Are We Laughing with Charles Ramsey?," *NPR*, May 7, 2013, sec. Code Switch, https://www.npr.org/sections/codeswitch/2013/05/07/181982154/are-we-laughing-with-charles-ramsey.

111. Ralston, "Intersectional Approach," 285. There are some insightful episodes on this in the HBO series *I May Destroy You* (2020), specifically "That Was Fun" and ". . . It Just Came Up."

112. Ipwnatcardgamesinc, comment on "Bed Intruder Song!!!," December 24, 2010. For example, they commented, "THE RAPIST HAS BEEN FOUNDED! ITS THIS GUY!" Having received forty-one likes the same morning they made the comment, they were not the only one who suspected this.

113. Jenner Furst and Julia Willoughby Nason, *Fyre Fraud*, Hulu video, 2019, https://www.hulu.com/movie/fyre-fraud-e47078f3-1c0e-49a8-9da9-c571a7a20fec.

114. schmoyoho, "It's Corn—Songify This Ft. Tariq and Recess Therapy," August 28, 2022, YouTube, 2:56, https://www.youtube.com/watch?v=_caMQpiwiaU.

115. *Unbreakable Kimmy Schmidt*, season 1, episode 12, "Kimmy Goes to Court!," directed by Tina Fey and Robert Carlock, Netflix video, March 6, 2015. As mentioned in a previous note, the Gregory Brothers also autotuned this fictional Ghetto Witness, Walter Bankston, for the series' theme song. I quote from a later episode in the season where Bankston is giving advice to protagonist Titus Andromedon regarding his seeking of the spotlight. I read this as a critique of the currency that Bankston received from capitalizing on the trope of the Ghetto Witness.

116. A. Johnson, "(Mis)Appropriation," 158.

117. J. L. Jackson, "On Ethnographic Sincerity," S285.

118. Andy Carvin, "'Bed Intruder' Meme: A Perfect Storm of Race, Music, Comedy and Celebrity," *NPR*, August 5, 2010, http://www.npr.org/blogs/alltech considered/2010/08/05/129005122/YouTube-bed-intruder-meme?print=1.

119. I think here of the biopic of Bojangles where, in the opening scene, he tap-dances while smiling at the audience. Yet what they cannot see is his expression of fatigue and exhaustion as he turns his back to them only to face them again, smiling. He seems to be exhausted not only by the act of smiling while tapdancing but also by the circumscription of his being by this role, which is steeped in unlivable pedestrian notions of anti-Blackness, where his presence is acceptable only in the form of an entertainer. See *Bojangles*, directed by Joseph Sargent (Beverly Hills: MGM Television, 2001), DVD.

120. McCune, "Queerness of Blackness," 173–76; and Bey, "Trans*-Ness," 275–95.

Coda

Epigraph: The Midnight Miracle, "Gladiator Circus World (Side B) | The Midnight Miracle Podcast," April 17, 2024, YouTube, 21:42, https://www.youtube.com/watch?v=10030-dboeQ.

1. Karen Hawkins, "Holder, Duncan Plan to Fight Chicago Teen Violence," *Seattle Times*, October 7, 2009, http://www.seattletimes.com/nation-world/holder-duncan-plan-to-fight-chicago-teen-violence/.

2. "Tragic: Teens Give a Chicago Student from a Rivarly [*sic*] Hi [*sic*] School a Deadly Beating with Huge Wooden Boards! *Warning* (Very Graphic) (R. I. P. Derrion Albert) (This Has to Stop)—World Star Uncut," posted September 27, 2009, by WorldStarHipHop, 2:26. URL delisted.

3. I am reminded of the moment in the novel *Erasure* when the protagonist Thelonious "Monk" Ellison, with all his awareness of how Black bodies in discourse are pigeonholed and consumed, says, "Egads, I'm on television." P. Everett, *Erasure*, 265.

4. Coates, *Between the World and Me*, 63.

5. Nas, "Open Letter to Young Warriors In Chicago," *GlobalGrind* (blog), September 28, 2009, https://globalgrind.com/206659/open-letter-to-young-warriors-in-chicago-2/.

6. Sanders, *Perfect Day*.

7. Chicago Tribune, "A Tale of 2 Neighborhoods," *RedEye*, October 6, 2009.

8. See Ewing, *Ghosts in the Schoolyard*, 84–89, 112. Chicago Housing Authority began the Plan for Transformation in 1999 to demolish, rehabilitate, and build new public housing throughout the city. Renaissance 2010, started in June of 2004, was a plan conceived between for-profit education companies, Richard M. Daley, and Arne Duncan to replace Chicago public schools with charter schools.

9. Annie Sweeney, Azam Ahmed, and Kristen Mack, "Fenger Kids Tell Why They Fight," *Chicago Tribune* (blog), October 6, 2009, https://www.chicagotribune.com/2009/10/06/fenger-kids-tell-why-they-fight-4/.

10. "Last Year, the Police Maced the Whole Hallway," *Salon*, October 19, 2009, https://www.salon.com/2009/10/19/chicago_fenger/.

11. Spencer McAvoy, "Lost in the Shuffle," *South Side Weekly* (blog), January 8, 2014, https://southsideweekly.com/lost-in-the-shuffle/.

12. Susan Cosier, "What a Gutted EPA Could Mean for Chicago's 'Toxic Doughnut,'" April 17, 2017, *National Resources Defense Council*, https://www.nrdc.org/stories/what-gutted-epa-could-mean-chicagos-toxic-doughnut.

13. "Black males, with an incarceration rate of 4,749 inmates per 100,000 US residents, were incarcerated at a rate more than six times higher than white males (708 inmates per 100,000 US residents) and 2.6 times higher than Hispanic males (1,822 inmates per 100,000 US residents)." "Prisoners at Yearend 2009—Advance Counts," Bureau of Justice Statistics, June 23, 2010, https://bjs.ojp.gov/press-release/prisoners-yearend-2009-advance-counts.

14. Davis, *Are Prisons Obsolete?*, 12.

15. Ransby, *Making All Black Lives Matter*, 201.

16. Associated Press, "Man with Deferred Sentence in Fatal Beating Faces Gun Charge," August 27, 2019, https://apnews.com/d98f8de8f1514c5fbffe043fdd5b2a3c.

17. Immortal Technique, "Immortal Technique Drops Gems about Fascism, War, Religion, and Teases New Music," posted August 31, 2023, by Amanda Seales TV, YouTube, 1:27:38, https://www.youtube.com/watch?v=e60VDg-nk0g&list=PLvOB01wtIyk2wVtkxujWr812898q5SF19&index=99.

18. Elizabeth Day, "#BlackLivesMatter: The Birth of a New Civil Rights Movement," *Guardian* (US edition), July 19, 2015, World News, http://www.theguardian.com/world/2015/jul/19/blacklivesmatter-birth-civil-rights-movement.

19. ReignofApril, Twitter, July 17, 2015, https://twitter.com/ReignOfApril/status/621996332631355392?lang=en.

20. Seale, "Foreword," 14.

21. *The Black Panther Black Community News Service*, June 20, 1967, vol. 1, no. 3. See Black Panther Party, "Complete Archive." By the third issue of the Black Panther Party's newspaper, graphic artist and minister of culture for the party, Emory Douglas, had created the first of many graphics of police as pigs, which has ever since become commonplace in US Black vernacular.

22. *Black Panther Black Community News Service*, June 20, 1967, 6.

23. *Black Panther Black Community News Service*, vol. 1, no. 1, April 25, 1967, https://ilbpp.org/volume-1-black-panther-newspaper-1966.

24. Wendell Rawls Jr., "F. B. I. Admits Planting a Rumor to Discredit Jean Seberg in 1970," *New York Times*, September 15, 1979. https://www.nytimes.com/1979/09/15/archives/fbi-admits-planting-a-rumor-to-discredit-jean-seberg-in-1970-former.html.

25. Carbado, "O. J. Simpson as a Racial Victim," 173.

26. See Browne-Marshall, *Race, Law, and American Society*, 184; and Fleetwood, *On Racial Icons*, 23–25.

27. Jason Parham, "TikTok and the Evolution of Digital Blackface," *Wired*, August 4, 2020, https://www.wired.com/story/tiktok-evolution-digital-blackface.

28. Lauren Michele Jackson, "We Need to Talk about Digital Blackface in GIFs," *Teen Vogue*, August 2, 2017, https://www.teenvogue.com/story/digital-blackface-reaction-gifs.

29. Parham, "TikTok and the Evolution."

30. Manning, "Katherine Dunham," 492.

31. Taylor Lorenz, "The Original Renegade," *New York Times*, February 13, 2020, https://www.nytimes.com/2020/02/13/style/the-original-renegade.html.

32. Boffone, *Renegades*.

33. Sian Cain, "Capitol Records Drops 'Offensive' AI Rapper FN Meka after Outcry over Racial Stereotyping," *Guardian* (US edition), August 24, 2022, Music, https://www.theguardian.com/music/2022/aug/24/major-record-label-drops-offensive-ai-rapper-after-outcry-over-racial-stereotyping.

34. Evan Minsker and Madison Bloom, "FN Meka Backer Walks Away from Project; Rapper Claims to Be Unpaid for Work as Meka's Voice," *Pitchfork*, August 25, 2022, https://pitchfork.com/news/fn-meka-backer-walks-away-from-project-rapper-claims-to-be-unpaid-for-work-as-mekas-voice/.

35. Enongo Lumumba-Kasongo, "(A)I, Rapper: Who Voices Hip-Hop's Future?," *Public Books* (blog), April 21, 2022, https://www.publicbooks.org/ai-rap-synthesis-tools-black-hip-hop/. I like the application of Black feminist game design (BFGD) as an ethos to address the issue of anti-Black and misogynoir bias embedded in large collections of data and the benefits to an interactor's safety when programmers curate the encounter with BFGD from the backend to the frontend of development.

36. Adam Schrader, "Arrest Warrants Issued for 3 Men in Montgomery, Ala., Riverfront Brawl," United Press International, https://www.upi.com/Top_News/US/2023/08/08/arrest-warrants-issued-three-men-montgomery-riverfront-brawl/8421691536204/.

37. Curtis Bunn, "Black Riverfront Worker Said He 'Hung On for Dear Life' during Montgomery Attack," *NBC News*, August 10, 2023, https://www.nbcnews.com/news/nbcblk/black-montgomery-riverfront-worker-describes-sparked-viral-brawl-rcna99238.

38. "Massive Brawl Breaks Out at Riverfront after Several White People Attack Black Man over Boat Dock Space!," posted August 6, 2023, by WorldStarHipHop, 4:22, https://worldstarhiphop.com/videos/wshh8pbBwnmN03M988QD/massive-brawl-breaks-out-at-riverfront-after-several-white-people-attack-black-man-over-boat-dock-space.

39. Jim Gilstrap and Blinky Williams sing "keeping your head above water" as we see yet another nickname for Aaren Hamilton-Rudolph: Michael Evans Phelps.

40. jamescharlesmorris, Instagram, August 8, 2023, https://www.instagram.com/p/CvsIMjWAxsx/.

41. Nicole Curtis, Deena Zaru, and Vera Drymon, "Dock Worker Assaulted in Alabama Brawl Speaks Out in 'GMA' Exclusive," *ABC7 New York*, September 25, 2023, https://abc7ny.com/alabama-dock-brawl-boat-fight-on/13828083/.

Bibliography

Abdurraqib, Hanif. *A Little Devil in America: Notes in Praise of Black Performance.* New York: Random House, 2021.

Adeyemi, Kemi. *Feels Right: Black Queer Women and the Politics of Partying in Chicago.* Durham, NC: Duke University Press, 2022.

Adeyemi, Kemi, Kareem Khubchandani, and Ramón H. Rivera-Servera. *Queer Nightlife.* Ann Arbor: University of Michigan Press, 2021.

Alexander, Michelle. *The New Jim Crow: Mass Incarceration in the Age of Colorblindness.* New York: The New Press, 2010.

Alsultany, Evelyn. "Arabs and Muslims in the Media after 9/11: Representational Strategies for a 'Postrace' Era." *American Quarterly* 65, no. 1 (2013): 161–69. https://doi.org/10.1353/aq.2013.0008.

Althusser, Louis. *On the Reproduction of Capitalism: Ideology and Ideological State Apparatuses.* Translated by G. M. Goshgarian. First published 1971 by New Left Books (London). London: Verso, 2014.

The American Anti-Slavery Society. *The Anti-Slavery Record, for 1837.* Vol. 3. New York: American Anti-Slavery Society, 1838.

Auslander, Philip. *Liveness.* 3rd edition. London and New York, NY: Routledge, 2022.

Bailey, Marlon M. *Butch Queens Up in Pumps: Gender, Performance, and Ballroom Culture in Detroit.* Ann Arbor: University of Michigan Press, 2013.

———. "The Queerness of Touch: Mutual Recognition and Deep Intimacy in *Moonlight.*" *QED: A Journal in GLBTQ Worldmaking* 9, no. 1 (2022): 59–65. https://doi.org/10.14321/qed.9.issue-1.0059.

Bailey, Marlon M., and L. H. Stallings. "Antiblack Racism and the Metalanguage of Sexuality." *Signs* 42, no. 3 (2017): 614–21.

Bailey, Moya. *Misogynoir Transformed: Black Women's Digital Resistance.* Reprint, New York: New York University Press, 2022.

Bailey, Moya, and Trudy. "On Misogynoir: Citation, Erasure, and Plagiarism." *Feminist Media Studies* 18, no. 4 (2018): 762–68. https://doi.org/10.1080/14680777.2018.1447395.

Baraka, Amiri. *Black Music: Essays by LeRoi Jones (Amiri Baraka)*. New York: Akashi Classics, 2010.

Barkley Brown, Elsa. "Negotiating and Transforming the Public Sphere: African American Political Life in the Transition from Slavery to Freedom." *Public Culture* 7, no. 1 (Fall 1994): 107–46.

Barthes, Roland. *Camera Lucida: Reflections on Photography*. Translated by Richard Howard. New York: Hill and Wang, 1982.

Batiste, Stephanie Leigh. *Darkening Mirrors: Imperial Representation in Depression-Era African American Performance*. Durham, NC: Duke University Press, 2012.

Benjamin, Ruha. *Race after Technology: Abolitionist Tools for the New Jim Code*, ebook, accessed through Apple Books. Medford, MA: Polity, 2019.

Benjamin, Walter. "The Work of Art in the Age of Mechanical Reproduction." In *Illuminations: Essays and Reflections*, 217–51. Edited by Hannah Arendt. Translated by Harry Zohn. New York: Schocken Books, 1968.

Bernstein, Robin. "Dances with Things: Material Culture and the Performance of Race." *Social Text* 27, no. 4 (Winter 2009): 67–94. https://doi.org/10.1215/01642472-2009-055.

——. *Racial Innocence: Performing American Childhood from Slavery to Civil Rights*. New York: New York University Press, 2011.

Bey, Marquis. "The Trans*-ness of Blackness, the Blackness of Trans*-ness." *Transgender Studies Quarterly* 4, no. 2 (May 2017): 275–95.

Black Panther Party. "A Complete Archive of the Black Panther Party's Newspapers from Beginning to End." Reddit, posted June 2, 2016, by bperki8. www.reddit.com/r/communism/comments/4m7axa/a_complete_archive_of_the_black_panther_partys/.

The Black Public Sphere Collective, ed. *The Black Public Sphere: A Public Culture Book*. Chicago: University of Chicago Press, 1995.

Blassingame, John W. *The Slave Community: Plantation Life in the Antebellum South*. 2nd ed. New York: Oxford University Press, 1979.

Boffone, Trevor. *Renegades: Digital Dance Cultures from Dubsmash to TikTok*. New York: Oxford University Press, 2021.

Bogle, Donald. *Toms, Coons, Mulattoes, Mammies, and Bucks: An Interpretive History of Blacks in American Films*. 4th ed. New York: Continuum, 2003.

Bradley, Regina N. *Chronicling Stankonia: The Rise of the Hip-Hop South*. Chapel Hill: University of North Carolina Press, 2021.

Brock, André, Jr. *Distributed Blackness: African American Cybercultures*. New York: New York University Press, 2020.

brown, adrienne maree. *Emergent Strategy: Shaping Change, Changing Worlds*, e-book, accessed through Apple Books. Chico, CA: AK Press, 2017.

Brown, Bill. "Thing Theory." *Critical Inquiry* 28, no. 1 (Autumn 2001): 1–22.

Browne, Ray B., and Pat Browne, eds. *The Guide to United States Popular Culture*. Madison, WI: Popular Press, 2001.

Browne, Simone. *Dark Matters: On the Surveillance of Blackness*. Durham, NC: Duke University Press, 2015.

Browne-Marshall, Gloria J. *Race, Law, and American Society, 1607 to Present*. New York: Routledge, 2007.

Butler, Judith. "Imitation and Gender Insubordination." In *The Lesbian and Gay Studies Reader*, edited by Henry Abelove, Michèle Aina Barale, and David M. Halperin, 307–20. New York: Routledge, 1993.

——. "Performative Acts and Gender Constitution: An Essay in Phenomenology and Feminist Theory." *Theatre Journal* 40, no. 4 (December 1988): 519–31. https://doi.org/10.2307/3207893.

——. *Undoing Gender*. New York: Routledge, 2004.

Campt, Tina M. *A Black Gaze: Artists Changing How We See*. Cambridge, MA: MIT Press, 2021.

——. *Listening to Images*, Reprint, Durham, NC: Duke University Press, 2017.

Carbado, Devon W. "The Construction of O. J. Simpson as a Racial Victim." In *Black Men On Race, Gender, and Sexuality: A Critical Reader*, edited by Devon W. Carbado, 159–93. New York: New York University Press, 1999.

Carpenter, Faedra Chatard. *Coloring Whiteness: Acts of Critique in Black Performance*. Illustrated ed. Ann Arbor: University of Michigan Press, 2014.

Césaire, Aimé. *Discourse on Colonialism*. Translated by Joan Pinkham. New York: Monthly Review Press, 2001.

Chang, Jeff. *Can't Stop Won't Stop: A History of the Hip-Hop Generation*. London: Macmillan, 2005.

Coates, Ta-Nehisi. *Between the World and Me*. New York: One World, 2015.

Cobb, Jasmine Nichole. *Picture Freedom: Remaking Black Visuality in the Early Nineteenth Century*. New York: New York University Press, 2015.

Cohen, Lizabeth. "Encountering Mass Culture at the Grassroots: The Experience of Chicago Workers in the 1920s." In *Consumer Society in American History: A Reader*, edited by Lawrence B. Glickman, 147–69. Ithaca, NY: Cornell University Press, 1999.

Colbert, Soyica Diggs. "Black Movements: Flying Africans in Spaceships." In *Black Performance Theory*. Edited by Thomas F. DeFrantz and Anita Gonzalez, 129–48. Durham, NC: Duke University Press, 2014.

Coleman, Catherine A. "Classic Campaigns - 'It's Gotta Be the Shoes': Nike, Mike and Mars and the 'Sneaker Killings.'" *Advertising and Society Review* 14, no. 2 (2013). https://doi.org/10.1353/asr.2013.0016.

Collins, Patricia Hill. *Black Feminist Thought: Knowledge, Consciousness, and the Politics of Empowerment*. 2nd ed. London: Routledge, 2002.

Committee for the Abolition of the Slave-Trade. *Remarks on the Advertisement of the Committee for the Abolition of the Slave-Trade, Inserted in the Public Papers*. London: T. Spilsbury and Son, for T. and J. Egerton, 1790.

Connor, Steven. "Edison's Teeth: Touching Hearing." In *Hearing Cultures: Essays on Sound, Listening and Modernity*, edited by Veit Erlmann, 153–72. Oxford: Bloomsbury Academic, 2004.

Conquergood, Dwight. "Performance Studies: Interventions and Radical Research." *Drama Review* 46, no. 2 (June 2002): 145–56.

Cooper, Anna Julia. *A Voice from the South*. Xenia, OH: Aldine Printing House, 1892. http://docsouth.unc.edu/church/cooper/cooper.html.

Craft, Renee Alexander. "Afrofuturism and the 2018 Wakanda Diaspora Carnival." In Perkins, Richards, Craft, and DeFrantz, *Routledge Companion to African American Theatre and Performance*, 385–94.

Crawley, Ashon T. *Blackpentecostal Breath: The Aesthetics of Possibility*. New York: Fordham University Press, 2017.

Crenshaw, Kimberlé. "Mapping the Margins: Intersectionality, Identity Politics, and Violence against Women of Color." *Stanford Law Review* 43, no. 6 (1991): 1241–99. https://doi.org/10.2307/1229039.

Davis, Adrienne D., and the BSE Collective, eds. *Black Sexual Economies: Race and Sex in a Culture of Capital*. Urbana: University of Illinois Press, 2019.

Davis, Angela Y. *Are Prisons Obsolete?* New York: Seven Stories Press, 2003.

———. *Women, Race and Class*. New York: Random House, 1981.

Deeble, T. Plan of ship used for trafficking enslaved Africans, n.d. Bristol Archives. https://archives.bristol.gov.uk/records/PicBox/5/Doc/56a.

DeFrantz, Thomas F., and Anita Gonzalez, eds. *Black Performance Theory*. Durham, NC: Duke University Press, 2014.

Diamond, Elin, ed. Introduction to *Performance and Cultural Politics*, 1–11. New York: Routledge, 1996.

Dick, Philip K. *Minority Report*. New York: Pantheon Books, 2002, Apple Books.

Diekmann, O., J. A. P. Heesterbeek, and J. A. J. Metz. "On the Definition and the Computation of the Basic Reproduction Ratio R_0 in Models for Infectious Diseases in Heterogeneous Populations." *Journal of Mathematical Biology* 28, no. 4 (1990): 365–82.

Douglass, Frederick. *Narrative of the Life of Frederick Douglass, An American Slave*. New York: Penguin, 1986. First published in 1845 by Anti-slavery Office (Boston).

Drootin, Anna. "'Community Guidelines': The Legal Implications of Workplace Conditions for Internet Content Moderators." *Fordham Law Review* 90, no. 3 (2021): 1197–1244.

Duggan, Lisa. *The Twilight of Equality? Neoliberalism, Cultural Politics, and the Attack on Democracy*. Boston: Beacon Press, 2003.

Eglash, Ron. *African Fractals: Modern Computing and Indigenous Design*. New Brunswick, NJ: Rutgers University Press, 1999.

Eidsheim, Nina Sun. *The Race of Sound: Listening, Timbre, and Vocality in African American Music*. Illustrated ed. Durham, NC: Duke University Press, 2019.

Esparza, René. "Queering the Homeland: Chicanidad, Racialized Homophobia, and the Political Economy of Homopatriarchy." *Feminist Formations* 29, no. 2 (2017): 147–76. https://doi.org/10.1353/ff.2017.0020.

Estes, Steve. *I Am a Man! Race, Manhood, and the Civil Rights Movement*. Chapel Hill: University of North Carolina Press, 2005.

Evans, Chris, and Göran Rydén. *Baltic Iron in the Atlantic World in the Eighteenth Century*. Leiden: Brill, 2007.

Everett, Anna. "The Revolution Will Be Digitized: Afrocentricity and the Digital Public Sphere." *Social Text* 71, vol. 20, no. 2 (Summer 2002): 125–46.

Everett, Percival. *Erasure: A Novel.* New York: Hyperion, 2001.

Ewing, Eve L. *Ghosts in the Schoolyard: Racism and School Closings on Chicago's South Side.* Chicago: University of Chicago Press, 2018.

Fairchild, Charles. "Deterritorializing Radio: Deregulation and the Continuing Triumph of the Corporatist Perspective in the USA." *Media, Culture and Society* 21, no. 4 (July 1999): 549–61. https://doi.org/10.1177/016344399021004006.

Fairclough, Norman. *Media Discourse.* London: Edward Arnold, 1995.

Fanon, Frantz. *Black Skin, White Masks.* Translated by Charles Lam Markmann. London: Pluto Press, 1986.

Fedo, Michael. *The Lynchings in Duluth.* St. Paul: Minnesota Historical Society Press, 2000.

Felton-Dansky, Miriam. "Viral Performance: Contagious Hoaxes in the Digital Public Sphere." *Theater* 42, no. 2 (2012): 119–37.

———. *Viral Performance: Contagious Theaters from Modernism to the Digital Age.* Evanston, IL: Northwestern University Press, 2018.

Fine, Gary Alan, and Patricia A. Turner. *Whispers on the Color Line: Rumor and Race in America.* Berkeley: University of California Press, 2004.

Finley, Cheryl. "Committed to Memory: The Slave-Ship Icon in the Black-Atlantic Imagination." *Chicago Art Journal* 9 (Spring 1999): 2–21.

Fleetwood, Nicole R. *On Racial Icons: Blackness and the Public Imagination.* New Brunswick, NJ: Rutgers University Press, 2015.

———. *Troubling Vision: Performance, Visuality, and Blackness.* Chicago: University of Chicago Press, 2011.

Fleming, Julius B., Jr. *Black Patience: Performance, Civil Rights, and the Unfinished Project of Emancipation.* New York: New York University Press, 2022.

Foster, Laura A. *Reinventing Hoodia: Peoples, Plants, and Patents in South Africa.* Seattle: University of Washington Press, 2017.

Foucault, Michel. *The Foucault Reader.* Edited by Paul Rabinow. New York: Pantheon Books, 1984.

Foy, Jessica H. "The Home Set to Music." In *The Arts and the American Home, 1890–1930*, edited by Jessica H. Foy and Karal Ann Marling, 62–84. Knoxville: University of Tennessee Press, 1994.

Franck, Karen A. "When I Enter Virtual Reality, What Body Will I Leave Behind?" In *Cyber Reader: Critical Writings for the Digital Era*, edited by Neil Spiller, 240–45. London: Phaidon Press, 2002.

Fraser, Nancy. "Rethinking the Public Sphere: A Contribution to the Critique of Actually Existing Democracy." In *The Phantom Public Sphere*, edited by Bruce Robbins, 1–32. Minneapolis: University of Minnesota Press, 1993.

Gary, Lawrence E. "Drinking, Homicide, and the Black Male." *Journal of Black Studies* 17, no. 1 (September 1986): 15–31.

Gates, Henry Louis, Jr. *The Signifying Monkey: A Theory of African-American Literary Criticism.* New York: Oxford University Press, 1988.

Gaunt, Kyra D. "YouTube, Twerking and You: Context Collapse and the Handheld Co-presence of Black Girls and Miley Cyrus." *Journal of Popular Music Studies* 27, no. 3 (2015): 244–73. https://doi.org/10.1111/jpms.12130.

Genovese, Eugene D. "Rebelliousness and Docility in the Negro Slave: A Critique of the Elkins Thesis." *Civil War History* 13, no. 4 (1967): 293–314.

Gilroy, Paul. *The Black Atlantic: Modernity and Double Consciousness.* New York: Verso, 1993.

Glissant, Edouard. *Poetics of Relation.* Translated by Betsy Wing. Ann Arbor: University of Michigan Press, 1997.

Goodwin, Marjorie Harness, and H. Samy Alim. "'Whatever (Neck Roll, Eye Roll, Teeth Suck)': The Situated Coproduction of Social Categories and Identities through Stancetaking and Transmodal Stylization." *Journal of Linguistic Anthropology* 20, no. 1 (June 2010): 179–94.

Gordon, Avery F. *Ghostly Matters: Haunting and the Sociological Imagination.* Minneapolis: University of Minnesota Press, 2008.

Gray, Herman. "Black Masculinity and Visual Culture." *Callaloo* 18, no. 2 (1995): 401–5.

Gregory Brothers [schmoyoho]. "Bed Intruder Song!!!" July 31, 2010. YouTube video, 1:15. https://www.youtube.com/watch?v=hMtZfW2z9dw.

Gumbs, Alexis Pauline. *Dub: Finding Ceremony.* Durham, NC: Duke University Press, 2020.

Guterl, Matthew Pratt. *Seeing Race in Modern America.* Chapel Hill: University of North Carolina Press, 2013.

Habermas, Jürgen. *The Structural Transformation of the Public Sphere: An Inquiry into a Category of Bourgeois Society.* Translated by Thomas Burger with the assistance of Frederick Lawrence. Cambridge, MA: MIT Press, 1989.

Haley, Sarah. *No Mercy Here: Gender, Punishment, and the Making of Jim Crow Modernity.* Reprint, Chapel Hill: University of North Carolina Press, 2019.

Hall, Jacquelyn Dowd. "'The Mind That Burns in Each Body': Women, Rape, and Racial Violence." In *Powers of Desire: The Politics of Sexuality*, edited by Ann Barr Snitow, Christine Stansell, and Sharon Thompson, 328–49. New York: Monthly Review Press, 1983.

Hall, Stuart. "Notes on Deconstructing 'the Popular.'" In *Cultural Resistance Reader*, edited by Stephen Duncombe, 185–92. New York: Verso, 2002.

———. "What Is This 'Black' in Black Popular Culture?" *Social Justice* 20, no. 1/2 (1993): 104–14.

Haraway, Donna. "A Cyborg Manifesto: Science, Technology, and Socialist-Feminism in the Late Twentieth Century." In *Simians, Cyborgs, and Women: The Reinvention of Nature*, 149–81. New York: Routledge, 1991.

Hartman, Saidiya V. *Scenes of Subjection: Terror, Slavery, and Self-Making in Nineteenth-Century America.* Revised and updated edition with new preface by the author. New York: W. W. Norton, 2022.

Higginbotham, Evelyn Brooks. "African-American Women's History and the Metalanguage of Race." *Signs* 17, no. 2 (Winter 1992): 251–74.

——. *Righteous Discontent: The Women's Movement in the Black Baptist Church, 1880–1920*. Cambridge, MA: Harvard University Press, 1994.

Hine, Darlene Clark. "Rape and the Inner Lives of Black Women in the Middle West: Preliminary Thoughts on a Culture of Dissemblance." *Signs* 14, no. 4 (Summer 1989): 912–20.

Hine, Darlene Clark, and Earnestine Jenkins, eds. *A Question of Manhood: A Reader in U.S. Black Men's History and Masculinity*. Vol. 2 of *The 19th Century: From Emancipation to Jim Crow*. Bloomington: Indiana University Press, 2001.

Holland, Sharon Patricia. *The Erotic Life of Racism*. Durham, NC: Duke University Press, 2012.

hooks, bell. *Black Looks: Race and Representation*. Boston: South End Press, 1992.

——. *Yearning: Race, Gender, and Cultural Politics*. Boston: South End Press, 1999.

Hoover, Secretary of Commerce, v. Intercity Radio Co., Inc., 286 F. 1003, United States Court of Appeals, District of Columbia Circuit, 1923.

Hughey, Matthew W., and Jessie Daniels. "Racist Comments at Online News Sites: A Methodological Dilemma for Discourse Analysis." *Media, Culture and Society* 35, no. 3 (April 2013): 332–47.

Hull, Gloria T., Patricia Bell Scott, and Barbara Smith, eds. *All the Women Are White, All the Blacks Are Men, but Some of Us Are Brave: Black Women's Studies*. New York: Feminist Press, 1982.

Issacharoff, Michael. *Discourse as Performance*. Stanford: Stanford University Press, 1989.

Jackson, John L., Jr. "On Ethnographic Sincerity." *Current Anthropology* 51, no. S2 (2010): S279–87.

——. *Real Black: Adventures in Racial Sincerity*. Chicago: University of Chicago Press, 2005.

——. *Thin Description: Ethnography and the African Hebrew Israelites of Jerusalem*. Cambridge, MA: Harvard University Press, 2013.

Jackson, Ronald L., II. *Scripting the Black Masculine Body: Identity, Discourse, and Racial Politics in Popular Media*. Albany: State University of New York Press, 2006.

Jackson, Shannon. *Professing Performance: Theatre in the Academy from Philology to Performativity*. Cambridge: Cambridge University Press, 2004.

JanMohamed, Abdul R. "Sexuality on/of the Racial Border: Foucault, Wright, and the Articulation of 'Racialized Sexuality.'" In *Discourses of Sexuality: From Aristotle to AIDS*, edited by Domna C. Stanton, 94–116. Ann Arbor: University of Michigan Press, 1992.

Jenkins, Henry, Sam Ford, and Joshua Green. *Spreadable Media: Creating Value and Meaning in a Networked Culture*. New York: New York University Press, 2013.

Johnson, Amber. "Antoine Dodson and the (Mis)Appropriation of the Homo Coon: An Intersectional Approach to the Performative Possibilities of Social Media." *Critical Studies in Media Communication* 30, no. 2 (2013): 152–70.

Johnson, E. Patrick. *Appropriating Blackness: Performance and the Politics of Authenticity*. Durham, NC: Duke University Press, 2003.

——. "Black Performance Studies: Genealogies, Politics, Futures." In *The Sage Handbook of Performance Studies*, edited by D. Soyini Madison and Judith Hamera, 446–64. Thousand Oaks, CA: SAGE, 2006.

——. "'Quare' Studies, or (Almost) Everything I Know about Queer Studies I Learned from My Grandmother." *Text and Performance Quarterly* 21, no. 1 (2001): 1–25.

Johnson, Javon. *Killing Poetry: Blackness and the Making of Slam and Spoken Word Communities*. New Brunswick, NJ: Rutgers University Press, 2017.

Jones, Joni L. "'Sista Docta': Performance as Critique of the Academy." *The Drama Review* 41, no. 2 (Summer 1997): 51–67.

Jones, Omi Osun Joni L. *Theatrical Jazz: Performance, Àṣẹ, and the Power of the Present Moment*. Columbus: Ohio State University Press, 2015.

Keeling, Kara. "Passing for Human: *Bamboozled* and Digital Humanism." *Women and Performance: A Journal of Feminist Theory* 15, no. 1 (2005): 237–50.

——. *The Witch's Flight: The Cinematic, the Black Femme, and the Image of Common Sense*. Illustrated ed. Durham, NC: Duke University Press, 2007.

Kelley, Robin D. G. "Burning Symbols: The Work of Art in the Age of Tyrannical (Re)Production." In *Hank Willis Thomas: Pitch Blackness*, by Hank Willis Thomas, 102–9. New York: Aperture, 2008.

——. *Freedom Dreams: The Black Radical Imagination*. First electronic edition. Boston: Beacon Press, 2002.

——. *Race Rebels: Culture, Politics, and the Black Working Class*. New York: Free Press, 1996.

Kendall, Lori. "'White and Nerdy': Computers, Race, and the Nerd Stereotype." *Journal of Popular Culture* 44, no. 3 (June 2011): 505–24.

KFOR Oklahoma's News 4. "Sweet Brown on Apartment Fire: 'Ain't Nobody Got Time for That!'" April 11, 2012. YouTube video, 0:41. https://www.youtube.com/watch?v=ydmPh4MXT3g.

Kim, Kwang Chung, ed. *Koreans in the Hood: Conflict with African Americans*. Baltimore: Johns Hopkins University Press, 1999.

Kimbwandende Kia Bunseki Fu-Kiau. *African Cosmology of the Bântu-Kôngo: Tying the Spiritual Knot; Principles of Life and Living*. 2nd ed. Brooklyn, NY: Athelia Henrietta Press, 2001.

King, Tiffany Lethabo. "Black 'Feminisms' and Pessimism: Abolishing Moynihan's Negro Family." *Theory and Event* 21, no. 1 (January 2018): 68–87.

——. *The Black Shoals: Offshore Formations of Black and Native Studies*, Illustrated edition. Durham, NC: Duke University Press, 2019.

Kozinets, Robert V. "I Want To Believe": A Netnography of The X-Philes' Subculture of Consumption." *Advances in Consumer Research* 27, no. 1 (1997): 470–75.

——. *Netnography: Doing Ethnographic Research Online*. Thousand Oaks, CA: SAGE, 2009.

——. "On Netnography: Initial Reflections on Consumer Research Investigations of Cyberculture." *Advances in Consumer Research* 25, no. 1 (1998): 366–71.

LaRoche, Cheryl Janifer. *Free Black Communities and the Underground Railroad: The Geography of Resistance*. Urbana: University of Illinois Press, 2014.

Larson, Stephanie Greco. *Media and Minorities: The Politics of Race in News and Entertainment*. Lanham, MD: Rowman and Littlefield, 2006.

Lee, Spike, dir. *Do the Right Thing*. 1989; Los Angeles: Universal Pictures Home Entertainment, 2010. Blu-ray Disc, 1080p HD.

Lee, Spike, and Lisa Jones. *Do the Right Thing: A Spike Lee Joint*. New York: Fireside, 1989.

Lhamon, W. T., Jr. "Optic Black: Naturalizing the Refusal to Fit." In *Black Cultural Traffic: Crossroads in Global Performance and Popular Culture*, edited by Harry J. Elam, Jr., and Kennell Jackson, 111–40. Ann Arbor: University of Michigan Press, 2005.

Lindsey, Treva B. *America, Goddam: Violence, Black Women, and the Struggle for Justice*. Oakland: University of California Press, 2022.

———. "The #BlackFeministFiyah Re-Up: An Introduction." *Black Scholar* 46, no. 2 (2016): 1–4. https://doi.org/10.1080/00064246.2016.1147931.

———. *Colored No More: Reinventing Black Womanhood in Washington, D.C.* Urbana: University of Illinois Press, 2017.

———. "Post-Ferguson: A 'Herstorical' Approach to Black Violability." *Feminist Studies* 41, no. 1 (2015): 232–37. https://doi.org/10.15767/feministstudies.41.1.232.

Lipsitz, George. *The Possessive Investment In Whiteness: How White People Profit from Identity Politics*. Philadelphia: Temple University Press, 1998.

Lorde, Audre. "The Uses of The Erotic: The Erotic as Power." In *The Lesbian and Gay Studies Reader*, edited by Henry Abelove, Michèle Aina Barale, and David M. Halperin, 339–343. New York: Routledge, 1993.

Lubiano, Wahneema. "But Compared to What? Reading Realism, Representation, and Essentialism in *School Daze, Do the Right Thing*, and the Spike Lee Discourse." In "Black Film Issue." Special issue, *Black American Literature Forum* 25, no. 2 (Summer 1991): 253–82.

Madison, D. Soyini. "Performance Ethnography." In *Critical Ethnography: Method, Ethics, and Performance*, 149–80. Thousand Oaks, CA: SAGE, 2005.

———. "Staging Fieldwork/Performing Human Rights." In *The SAGE Handbook of Performance Studies*, edited by D. Soyini Madison and Judith Hamera, 397–418. Thousand Oaks, CA: SAGE, 2006.

Majors, Richard, and Janet Mancini Billson. *Cool Pose: The Dilemmas of Black Manhood in America*. Reprint, New York: Touchstone, 1993.

Manning, Susan. "Modern Dance, Negro Dance, and Katherine Dunham." *Textual Practice* 15, no. 3 (2001): 487–505.

———. *Modern Dance, Negro Dance: Race in Motion*. Minneapolis: University of Minnesota Press, 2004.

Manring, Maurice M. *Slave in a Box: The Strange Career of Aunt Jemima*. Charlottesville: University of Virginia Press, 1998.

Mapp, Edward. *Blacks in American Films: Today and Yesterday*. Metuchen, NJ: Scarecrow Press, 1972.

Maragh-Lloyd, Raven. *Black Networked Resistance: Strategic Rearticulations in the Digital Age*. Oakland: University of California Press, 2024.

Marks, Laura U. *The Skin of the Film: Intercultural Cinema, Embodiment, and the Senses*. Durham, NC: Duke University Press, 2000.

Maultsby, Portia K. "Africanisms in African-American Music." In *Africanisms in American Culture*, edited by Joseph E. Holloway, 185–210. Bloomington: Indiana University Press, 1990.

McBride, Dwight A. "Can the Queen Speak? Racial Essentialism, Sexuality and the Problem of Authority." In "Emerging Male Writers, Part II." Special issue, *Callaloo* 21, no. 2 (Spring 1998): 363–79.

——. "Straight Black Studies: On African American Studies, James Baldwin, and Black Queer Studies." In *Black Queer Studies: A Critical Anthology*, edited by E. Patrick Johnson and Mae G. Henderson, 68–89. Durham, NC: Duke University Press, 2005.

——. *Why I Hate Abercrombie and Fitch: Essays on Race and Sexuality*. New York: New York University Press, 2005.

McCall, Hugh. *The History of Georgia: Containing Brief Sketches of the Most Remarkable Events, Up to the Present Day*. Savannah: Seymour and Williams, 1811.

McCune, Jeffrey Q., Jr. "'Out' in the Club: The Down Low, Hip-Hop, and the Architexture of Black Masculinity." *Text and Performance Quarterly* 28, no. 3 (2008): 298–314.

——. "The Queerness of Blackness." *QED: A Journal in GLBTQ Worldmaking* 2, no. 2 (2015): 173–76.

McGinnis, Carol. *Michigan Genealogy: Sources and Resources*. 2nd ed. Baltimore: Genealogical Publishing, 2005.

McGlotten, Shaka. "Black Data." In "Traversing Technologies," edited by Patrick Keilty and Leslie Regan Shade. Special issue, *Scholar and Feminist Online*, no. 13.3–14.1 (2016). http://sfonline.barnard.edu/traversing-technologies/shaka-mcglotten-black-data/.

——. *Virtual Intimacies: Media, Affect, and Queer Sociality*. Albany: State University of New York Press, 2014.

McKittrick, Katherine. *Demonic Grounds: Black Women and the Cartographies of Struggle*.. Minneapolis: University of Minnesota Press, 2006.

McKittrick, Katherine, and Clyde Woods, eds. *Black Geographies and the Politics of Place*. Cambridge, MA: South End Press, 2007.

McMillan, Uri. "Introduction: Performing Objects." In *Embodied Avatars: Genealogies of Black Feminist Art and Performance*, 1–22. New York: New York University Press, 2015.

Mitchell, Koritha. *Living with Lynching: African American Lynching Plays, Performance, and Citizenship, 1890–1930*. Urbana: University of Illinois Press, 2011.

Mitchell, W. J. T. "The Violence of Public Art: *Do the Right Thing*." *Critical Inquiry* 16, no. 4 (Summer 1990): 880–99.

Moore, Darnell L., and Hashim Khalil Pipkin. "Are *All* the Blacks Still Men? Collective Struggle and Black Male Feminism." In *Are All the Women Still White? Rethinking Race, Expanding Feminisms*, edited by Janell Hobson, 29–36. Albany: State University of New York Press, 2016.

Moraga, Cherríe, and Gloria Anzaldúa, eds. *This Bridge Called My Back: Writings by Radical Women of Color*. 4th ed. Albany: State University of New York Press, 2015.

Morrison, Matthew D. "The Sound(s) of Subjection: Constructing American Popular Music and Racial Identity through Blacksound." *Women and Performance: A Journal of Feminist Theory* 27, no. 1 (2017): 13–24. https://doi.org/10.1080/0740770X.2017.1282120.

Moten, Fred. *In the Break: The Aesthetics of the Black Radical Tradition*. Minneapolis: University of Minnesota Press, 2003.

Mullins, Paul R. *Race and Affluence: An Archaeology of African America and Consumer Culture*. New York: Springer Science and Business Media, 2006.

Muñoz, José Esteban. "Introduction: Performing Disidentifications." In *Disidentifications: Queers of Color and the Performance of Politics*, 1–34. Minneapolis: University of Minnesota Press, 1999.

Nahon, Karine, and Jeff Hemsley. *Going Viral*, e-book, accessed through Apple Books. Malden, MA: Polity Press, 2013.

Nakamura, Lisa. *Digitizing Race: Visual Cultures of the Internet*. Minneapolis: University of Minnesota Press, 2007.

Nakamura, Lisa, and Peter A. Chow-White, eds. "Introduction—Race and Digital Technology: Code, the Color Line, and the Information Society." In *Race after the Internet*. New York: Routledge, 2012.

Neal, Mark Anthony. *Looking for Leroy: Illegible Black Masculinities*. New York: New York University Press, 2013.

———. *New Black Man*. New York: Routledge, 2006.

Negrón-Gonzales, Genevieve. "Undocumented Youth Activism as Counter-Spectacle." *Aztlán* 40, no. 1 (Spring 2015): 87–112.

Nelson, Alondra. "Introduction: Future Texts." *Social Text* 20, no. 2 (Summer 2002): 1–15.

News 5 Cleveland. "Charles Ramsey Interview, Rescuer of Amanda Berry, Gina DeJesus and Michelle Knight in Cleveland." May 6, 2013. YouTube video, 2:54. https://www.youtube.com/watch?v=axCn04iXkBg.

Noble, Safiya Umoja. *Algorithms of Oppression: How Search Engines Reinforce Racism*. Illustrated ed. New York: New York University Press, 2018.

Omi, Michael, and Howard Winant. *Racial Formation in the United States*. 3rd edition. New York and London: Routledge, 2014.

Ore, Ersula J. *Lynching: Violence, Rhetoric, and American Identity*. Jackson: University Press of Mississippi, 2019.

Owerko, Lyle. *The Boombox Project: The Machines, the Music, and the Urban Underground*. With a foreword by Spike Lee. New York: Harry N. Abrams, 2010.

Pabst, Naomi. "Blackness/Mixedness: Contestations over Crossing Signs." *Cultural Critique*, no. 54 (Spring 2003): 178–212.

Parker, Andrew, and Eve Kosofsky Sedgwick, eds. "Introduction: Performativity and Performance." In *Performativity and Performance*, 1–18. New York: Routledge, 1995.

The Parody Factory, "Sweet Brown – Ain't Nobody Got Time for That (Autotune Remix)." April 14, 2012. YouTube video, 1:56. https://www.youtube.com/watch?v=bFEoMO0pc7k.

Patton, Cindy. *Sex and Germs: The Politics of AIDS*. Montreal: Black Rose Books, 1986.

Peña, Vincent. "From Protest to Movement: A Longitudinal Content Analysis of ESPN's Colin Kaepernick Coverage." *International Journal of Sport and Society* 12, no. 1 (2021): 191–204.

Peoples, Gabriel A. "The Forgotten Kelly Dodson: Viral Performance and the Interplay of Excess and Erasure." *Women and Performance: A Journal of Feminist Theory* 30, no. 2 (2020): 170–94. https://doi.org/10.1080/0740770X.2020.1869412.

——. "Play (Loudly): The Racialized Erotics of Sound in Spike Lee's *Do the Right Thing*." In "Black Performance." Special issue, *Frontiers: A Journal of Women Studies* 42, no. 1 (2021): 109–40.

Perkins, Kathy A., Sandra L. Richards, Renée Alexander Craft, and Thomas F. DeFrantz, eds. *The Routledge Companion to African American Theatre and Performance*. London: Routledge, 2018.

Petty, Miriam J. *Stealing the Show: African American Performers and Audiences in 1930s Hollywood*. First Edition. Oakland: University of California Press, 2016.

Phelan, Peggy. "Performance, Live Culture and Things of the Heart." *Journal of Visual Culture* 2, no. 3 (December 2003): 291–302.

——. *Unmarked: The Politics of Performance*. London: Routledge, 1993.

Posey, Sandra Mizumoto. "The Body Art of Brotherhood." In *African American Fraternities and Sororities: The Legacy and the Vision*, edited by Tamara L. Brown, Gregory S. Parks, and Clarenda M. Phillips, 269–94. Lexington: University Press of Kentucky, 2005.

Powell, Elliot H. "The Ghosts Got You: Exploring the Queer (After) Lives of Sample-Based Hip Hop." In *The Oxford Handbook of Hip Hop Music*, edited by Justin D. Burton and Jason Lee Oakes. New York: Oxford University Press, 2018. https://www.oxfordhandbooks.com/view/10.1093/oxfordhb/9780190281090.001.0001/oxfordhb-9780190281090-e-29.

Primo, Leslie. "Visual Arts 1: Representations of Blacks." In *The Oxford Companion to Black British History*, edited by David Dabydeen, John Gilmore, and Cecily Jones. Oxford: Oxford University Press, 2007.

Quashie, Kevin. *The Sovereignty of Quiet: Beyond Resistance in Black Culture*. New Brunswick, NJ; London: Rutgers University Press, 2012.

Raiford, Leigh. "Restaging Revolution: Black Power, *Vibe* Magazine, and Photographic Memory." In *The Civil Rights Movement in American Memory*, eds. Renee Christine Romano and Leigh Raiford, 220–50. Athens: University of Georgia Press, 2006.

Ralston, Kevin M. "An Intersectional Approach to Understanding Stigma Associated with Male Sexual Assault Victimization." *Sociology Compass* 6, no. 4 (April 2012): 283–92.

Ransby, Barbara. *Making All Black Lives Matter: Reimagining Freedom in the Twenty-First Century*. Oakland: University of California Press, 2018.

Rice, Anne P., ed. *Witnessing Lynching: American Writers Respond*. New Brunswick, NJ: Rutgers University Press, 2003.

Riggs, Marlon T. "Black Macho Revisited: Reflections of a Snap! Queen." *Black American Literature Forum* 25, no. 2 (1991): 389–94. https://doi.org/10.2307/3041695.

Rivera-Servera, Ramón H. *Performing Queer Latinidad: Dance, Sexuality, Politics*. Ann Arbor: University of Michigan Press, 2012.

Roach, Joseph. *Cities of the Dead: Circum-Atlantic Performance*. New York: Columbia University Press, 1996.

Roberts, Dorothy. *Killing the Black Body: Race, Reproduction, and the Meaning of Liberty*. Pantheon Books, 1997.

Roberts, John W. *From Trickster to Badman: The Black Folk Hero in Slavery and Freedom*. Philadelphia: University of Pennsylvania Press, 1990.

Rodgers, Tara. "'What, for Me, Constitutes Life in a Sound?': Electronic Sounds as Lively and Differentiated Individuals." In "Sound Clash: Listening to American Studies," edited by Kara Keeling and Josh Kun. Special issue, *American Quarterly* 63, no. 3 (September 2011): 509–30. https://doi.org/10.1353/aq.2011.0046.

Rodriguez, Yelaine. "Afro-Latinx at NYU: How Multiple Facets of Black *Latinidad* Are Claiming Space within Visual Culture," *Latin American and Latinx Visual Culture* 3, no. 2 (April 2021): 50–59. https://doi.org/10.1525/lavc.2021.3.2.50.

Ross, Marlon B. *Sissy Insurgencies: A Racial Anatomy of Unfit Manliness*. Durham, NC: Duke University Press, 2022.

Rothenberg, Paula S. *Race, Class, and Gender in the United States: An Integrated Study*. 6th ed. New York: Worth, 2004.

Rothstein, Richard. Historian Says Don't "Sanitize" How Our Government Created Ghettos. Interview by Terry Gross. *Fresh Air*, May 14, 2015. http://www.npr.org/2015/05/14/406699264/historian-says-dont-sanitize-how-our-government-created-the-ghettos.

Ryan, Patrick S. "The ITU and the Internet's *Titanic* Moment." *Stanford Technology Law Review* 8 (2012): 1–36.

Sanders, Derrick. *Perfect Day (A Short Film)*. Soothsower Productions, 2013. YouTube video, 16:49. https://www.youtube.com/watch?v=sjuNaM6bRLk.

Schechner, Richard. *Between Theater and Anthropology*. With foreword by Victor Turner. Philadelphia: University of Pennsylvania Press, 1985.

——. *Performance Studies: An Introduction*. 3rd ed. Media edited by Sara Brady. London: Routledge, 2013.

Schrøder, Kim Christian. "Media Discourse Analysis: Researching Cultural Meanings from Inception to Reception." *Textual Cultures* 2, no. 2 (2007): 77–99.

Scott, Darieck. *Extravagant Abjection: Blackness, Power, and Sexuality in the African American Literary Imagination*. New York: New York University Press, 2010.

Scott, James C. *Domination and the Arts of Resistance: Hidden Transcripts*. New Haven, CT: Yale University Press, 1990.

Seale, Bobby. "Foreword." In *Black Panther: The Revolutionary Art of Emory Douglas*, edited by Sam Durant, Illustrated edition. New York: Rizzoli, 2014.

Shabazz, Rashad. *Spatializing Blackness: Architectures of Confinement and Black Masculinity in Chicago*. Urbana: University of Illinois Press, 2015.

Shakur, Assata. *Assata: An Autobiography*. With forewords by Angela Davis and Lennox S. Hinds. Chicago: Lawrence Hill Books, 2001.

Shannon, Jonathan H. "Emotion, Performance, and Temporality in Arab Music: Reflections on *Tarab*." *Cultural Anthropology* 18, no. 1 (February 2003): 72–98. https://doi.org/10.1525/can.2003.18.1.72.

Sharma, Sanjay. "Black Twitter? Racial Hashtags, Networks and Contagion." *New Formations* 2012, no. 78 (2012): 46–64.

Sharpe, Christina. *Monstrous Intimacies: Making Post-Slavery Subjects*. Durham, NC: Duke University Press, 2010.

Shifman, Limor. "An Anatomy of a YouTube Meme." *New Media and Society* 14, no. 2 (2011): 187–203. https://doi.org/10.1177/1461444811412160.

Sirmans, M. Eugene. "The Legal Status of the Slave in South Carolina, 1670–1740." *Journal of Southern History* 28, no. 4 (November 1962): 462–73.

Smalls, Shanté Paradigm. *Hip Hop Heresies: Queer Aesthetics in New York City*. New York: New York University Press, 2022.

Smith, Andrea. "Heteropatriarchy and the Three Pillars of White Supremacy: Rethinking Women of Color Organizing." In *Are All the Women Still White? Rethinking Race, Expanding Feminisms*. Edited by Janell Hobson, 61–71. Albany: State University of New York Press, 2016.

Spade, Dean. "Keynote Address: Trans Law Reform Strategies, Co-optation, and the Potential for Transformative Change." *Women's Rights Law Reporter* 30, no. 2 (Winter 2009): 288–314.

Spillers, Hortense J. *Black, White, and in Color: Essays on American Literature and Culture*. Chicago: University of Chicago Press, 2003.

——. "Mama's Baby, Papa's Maybe: An American Grammar Book." *Diacritics* 17, no. 2 (Summer 1987): 65–81. https://doi.org/10.2307/464747.

Staddon, Patsy. *Women and Alcohol: Social Perspectives*. Bristol, UK: Policy Press, 2015.

Stallings, L. H. *A Dirty South Manifesto: Sexual Resistance and Imagination in the New South*. Oakland: University of California Press, 2019.

——. *Funk the Erotic: Transaesthetics and Black Sexual Cultures*. Urbana: University of Illinois Press, 2015.

Taylor, Diana. *The Archive and the Repertoire: Performing Cultural Memory in the Americas*. Durham, NC: Duke University Press, 2003.

Teal, Kimberley Hannon. "Beyond the Cotton Club: The Persistence of Duke Ellington's Jungle Style." *Jazz Perspectives* 6, no. 1–2 (2012): 123–49. https://doi.org/10.1080/17494060.2012.721292.

Thomas, Hank Willis. "Frames." *Qui Parle* 13, no. 2 (Spring/Summer 2003): 119–35.

——. *Pitch Blackness*. With contributions by René de Guzman and Robin D. G. Kelley. New York: Aperture, 2008.

Tompkins, Kyla Wazana. *Racial Indigestion: Eating Bodies in the 19th Century*. New York: New York University Press, 2012.

"Tragic: Teens Give a Chicago Student from a Rivalry [*sic*] Hi [*sic*] School a Deadly Beating with Huge Wooden Boards! *Warning* (Very Graphic) (R.I.P. Derrion

Albert) (This Has to Stop) – World Star Uncut." 2009. Digital video, hyperlink delisted.

Turner, Patricia A. *I Heard It through the Grapevine: Rumor in African-American Culture*. Berkeley: University of California Press, 1993.

Turner, Victor. *From Ritual to Theatre: The Human Seriousness of Play*. New York: Performing Arts Journal, 1982.

United States Department of Justice Civil Rights Division. *Investigation of the Ferguson Police Department*. Washington, DC: United States Department of Justice, March 4, 2015. http://www.justice.gov/sites/default/files/opa/press-releases/attachments/2015/03/04/ferguson_police_department_report.pdf.

Van Deburg, William L. *Slavery and Race in American Popular Culture*. Madison: University of Wisconsin Press, 1984.

Vidal-Ortiz, Salvador, Brandon Andrew Robinson, and Cristina Khan. *Race and Sexuality*. Cambridge, UK: Polity Press, 2018.

Wade, Ashleigh Greene. "'New Genres of Being Human': World Making through Viral Blackness." *Black Scholar* 47, no. 3 (July 3, 2017): 33–44. https://doi.org/10.1080/00064246.2017.1330108.

WAFF 48 News. "Woman Wakes Up to Find Intruder in Her Bed." July 29, 2010. YouTube video, 2:01. https://www.youtube.com/watch?v=uzKtPezPsqE.

Walcott, Rinaldo. *The Long Emancipation: Moving toward Black Freedom*. Durham, NC: Duke University Press, 2021.

Wallace, Maurice O. *Constructing the Black Masculine: Identity and Ideality in African American Men's Literature and Culture, 1775–1995*. Durham, NC: Duke University Press, 2002.

Wallace, Michele. *Black Macho and the Myth of the Superwoman*. Reprint, London: Verso, 2015.

White, Miles. *From Jim Crow to Jay-Z: Race, Rap, and the Performance of Masculinity*. Urbana: University of Illinois Press, 2011.

Williams, James S. "The Lost Boys of Baltimore: Beauty and Desire in the Hood." *Film Quarterly* 62, no. 2 (Winter 2008): 58–63. https://doi.org/10.1525/fq.2008.62.2.58.

Williams-Forson, Psyche A. *Building Houses out of Chicken Legs: Black Women, Food, and Power*. Chapel Hill: University of North Carolina Press, 2006.

Wolff, Kristina. "Strategic Essentialism." In *The Blackwell Encyclopedia of Sociology*, edited by George Ritzer, 2007. https://doi.org/10.1002/9781405165518.wbeoss268.

Woods, Clyde. *Development Arrested: The Blues and Plantation Power in the Mississippi Delta*. New York: Verso, 1998.

Yao, Xine. *Disaffected: The Cultural Politics of Unfeeling in Nineteenth-Century America*. Durham, NC: Duke University Press, 2021.

Young, Harvey. "The Black Body as Souvenir in American Lynching." *Theatre Journal* 57, no. 4 (2005): 639–57.

———. *Embodying Black Experience: Stillness, Critical Memory, and the Black Body*. Ann Arbor: University of Michigan Press, 2010.

Young, Hershini Bhana. "Twenty-First-Century Post-humans: The Rise of the See-J." In *Black Performance Theory*, edited by Thomas F. DeFrantz and Anita Gonzalez, 45–62. Durham, NC: Duke University Press, 2014.

Young, Vershawn Ashanti. *Your Average Nigga: Performing Race, Literacy, and Masculinity*. Detroit: Wayne State University Press, 2007.

Zien, Katherine. "Sidelong Glances: Black Divas in Transit, 1945–1955." In Perkins, Richards, Craft, and DeFrantz, *Routledge Companion to African American Theatre and Performance*, 364–70.

Index

GABRIEL A. PEOPLES is an assistant professor of gender studies at Indiana University.

The University of Illinois Press
is a founding member of the
Association of University Presses.

Composed in 10.5/13 Mercury Text G1
with Avenir LT Std display
by Kirsten Dennison
at the University of Illinois Press

University of Illinois Press
1325 South Oak Street
Champaign, IL 61820-6903
www.press.uillinois.edu